P9-BYM-832

An Introduction to Modern Japanese

by
Osamu Mizutani
Nobuko Mizutani

The Japan Times

ISBN4-7890-0058-3

First edition: September 1977
36th printing: November 1989

Library of Congress Catalog Card Number: 78-300022

Jacket design by Koji Detake
Illustrations by Koji Detake and Atsushi Kayada

Published by The Japan Times, Ltd.
5-4, Shibaura 4-chome, Minato-ku, Tokyo 108, Japan

Phototype set and printed by Seikosha Printing Co., Ltd.

Printed in Japan

ACKNOWLEDGEMENTS

In presenting this book for publication, we wish to express our sincere gratitude to the many people who have made it possible.

First, we are deeply indebted, indirectly but immeasurably, to the colleagues and many students we have had at International Christian University and at Inter-University Center for Japanese Language Studies in Tokyo. They provided us with opportunities to think seriously about what Japanese is and how it should be taught as a foreign language.

In the actual preparation of this book, Ruth Stevens and Janet Ashby gave us valuable assistance by contributing useful suggestions and checking the English.

We also wish to thank the editorial staff of the Japan Times' Publications Department for their understanding and patience in the preparation of this book.

Osamu and Nobuko Mizutani

CONTENTS

QUIZZES

INTRODUCTION

THE PURPOSE OF THIS BOOK

This book is intended for those who want to learn modern Japanese. It is designed to give a foundation in Japanese sufficient to handle everyday, practical conversations as well as discussions concerning his own interest or occupation. After studying this book thoroughly and carefully, you should be able to read all of the *hiragana* and *katakana*, recognize about 450 basic words in *kanji*, and have a good knowledge of basic grammar.

The Japanese introduced in this book is up-to-date and standard; it is the language actually used by educated people and acceptable to Japanese everywhere regardless of age, sex, or occupation. Also, it covers different levels of conversation from rather polite and formal ones to more intimate ones between friends or family members.

This book consists of 30 lessons in 5 units. Each lesson consists of the following:

- Dialogue (accompanied by English and romanized equivalents)
- Explanation
- Drills
- Reading Comprehension
- Aural Comprehension
- Pronunciation Practice
- Writing Practice (in Lessons 13 through 29)

The Dialogue is a short conversation in modern, standard Japanese. The Explanation gives all necessary information about the Dialogue. The Drills reinforce this knowledge; the Reading and Aural Comprehensions provide a chance to both apply and check one's mastery of the material. The Pronunciation and Writing Practices are basic exercises.

Each lesson is integrated so that the student will acquire an all-around language ability—to be able to understand both written and spoken Japanese, to speak, and to write in *hiragana*.

This book can be used for both classroom and independent study. The instructions for the drills are designed so that if an experienced instructor is not available a Japanese friend or acquaintance can serve as a drill partner. In either case, with or without an instructor, you can profit greatly by using the tapes which accompany this book.

Grammatical explanations and meanings are given in English. The drill instructions are given in English in the first part of the book, in both English and Japanese in the middle section, and only in Japanese in the last six lessons.

HOW TO USE THIS BOOK

Dialogues

The dialogues in this book are based on actual conversations heard in the offices, homes, and streets of Tokyo. Although those conversations may be more complex, the conversations introduced here are portions taken from the natural flow of everyday conversation. To make the dialogues "come alive," they should be practiced with a teacher or some other partner, memorizing whenever possible. (It is not necessary to memorize the dialogue before going on to the drills; an equally effective method is to return to it for memorization after completing the lesson.)

As for the orthography of the dialogue, those words that are usually written in *kanji* (Chinese characters) are written in *kanji* with the reading *hiragana* beneath them. By introducing the *kanji* for vocabulary items as they appear, you will not have to later learn the characters for words you already have a spoken command of. The characters in the early lessons are those most commonly used; later lessons include more difficult ones. (*Kanji* are only taught for recognition in this textbook.)

The dialogue in each lesson is written in *hiragana* on the assumption that the student has spent sufficient time on the sections entitled

THE JAPANESE SOUND SYSTEM AND ITS ROMANIZATION and HIRAGANA AND KATAKANA and can therefore read *hiragana* before beginning Lesson 1.

The translations of the dialogues are not exact line-by-line equivalents but rather an attempt to put the Japanese into natural English; they are meant to provide the meaning of the conversation as a whole.

A romanized version of the dialogue is also provided. This text serves two purposes: to aid the reading of the *hiragana* text and to show which part of the sentence should be spoken with more stress. The part with ▲ on top should be spoken with a higher pitch. For example,

▲*Doko-ni arimasu-ka.* (Where is it?) should be pronounced as

Doko-ni

arimasu-ka.

The context determines which part is emphasized. In the following sentence, emphasis shifts from *Doko-ni* to a different phrase.

Ja, ▲*ginkoo-wa doko-ni arimasu-ka.* (Where is the bank, then?)

Explanations

Most language textbooks have separate sections for vocabulary, grammar, and other explanations. This book, however, has a single section in each lesson which combines explanation of vocabulary, grammar, and usage. In the classroom situation with a traditional textbook, the instructor reads each sentence, explains the grammar and gives the meaning; in this sense the "Explanation" section in this book takes the place of an instructor. Most questions that may rise about the dialogue should be answered in this section. Additional comments at the end of this section has been made as brief as possible.

In Lessons 1 through 24, each sentence in the Explanation is accompanied by its romanized equivalent. It is recommended that you cover the romanized portion and try to read the sentence in Japanese, using the romanization as a check. Newly introduced words are accompanied by marks which indicate the accent.

In the earlier lessons almost every sentence in the Dialogue is explained, but as the student's knowledge increases, self-explanatory sentences are omitted. Further, example sentences are given illustrating meaning and usage; these are accompanied by English translation. These should be read aloud for reading practice.

Drills

The drills in this book are divided into two types—structure drills and usage drills.

The structure drills are designed for practice in proper sentence structure. Their purpose is to train the student so that he can make grammatically correct sentences. Sometimes you will be required to practice saying sentences that differ slightly from those that occur in actual conversation. For example, English native speakers will answer the question "Did you go there yesterday?" in various ways such as "Yes," "Sure," "Yes, yesterday afternoon," and so on; they do not always say "Yes, I went there yesterday." But a student of English has to learn the basic sentence "Yes, I went there yesterday" before he is able to give these other answers. The same is true in learning Japanese.

The usage drills illustrate the way the basic sentence patterns learned in the structure drills occur in natural conversation. They are written as natural exchanges of conversation. As the lessons progress, the drills change from simple question-and-answer exchanges to conversations of several lines. The shorter conversations should be memorized to give the student the freedom to act them out, pointing to objects as he speaks about them and bowing in situations where a Japanese person would bow. For these exercises you will need a partner; this partner should be a native speaker but he does not have to be a professional teacher.

Living conversation in any language is not something that ends with one or two exchanges. This book is designed to introduce longer, naturally-flowing conversations.

An effective method to review using this book is to concentrate on the drills, particularly the usage drills.

Pronunciation Practices

The exercises in each section entitled "Pronunciation Practice" is designed so that the student can shift naturally from the sound system of English to that of Japanese. A good method of studying this section is to do all three parts, A, B, and C, for a few minutes at the beginning of each study period.

Part A consists of groups of meaningless syllables. These exercises are designed for practice in keeping each syllable approximately the same length and in avoiding stress on any particular syllable. In Lessons 1 through 12, where the pronunciation exercises are romanized, the individual syllables are separated by hyphens. This is to remind you to pronounce each syllable distinctly and of equal length. The exercises in part B are made up of individual words and phrases. Here careful attention should be paid to not only the length of each syllable but also to the accent. Part C has practice sentences. Here attention should be paid to the marks indicating intonation. Only when the student can pronounce entire sentences correctly has he really completed the pronunciation exercises.

Reading Comprehension

This section consists of a short passage using vocabulary and grammar introduced in the lesson. If you cannot read or understand some part of it, it is best to review the lesson.

This passage is not a dialogue but an ordinary text; it may be taken from a diary, a letter, an essay or an expository article.

It also differs from the rest of the lesson in that it is written without spaces between the words, the way Japanese is usually written. Practice in reading this type of passage will help prepare you for more advanced stages where you will probably have to read this type of writing all the time.

Writing Practices

Exercises in writing *hiragana* are given in Lessons 13 through 29, starting with single *hiragana* and advancing to words, phrases, and sentences in *hiragana*.

There are no exercises in writing *kanji* or *katakana*; in this book these two are introduced for recognition only.

Aural Comprehension

Here you are asked to listen to a taped conversation and then answer the questions found in the textbook. These conversations are a departure from the usual "textbook" conversation in that they more closely resemble actual conversation. Each conversation is a short exchange utilizing the vocabulary and grammatical patterns learned in the lesson, spoken at a natural speed and with various emotions. You should not try to catch each word in isolation but to understand the meaning of the conversation as a whole.

Since the primary aim of this section is to drill the student in comprehension, the answers can be given in English, although Japanese is preferred. (In the first twelve lessons the questions are given in English; in Lessons 13 through 18 in both Japanese and English; from Lesson 19 on all questions are in Japanese.)

The answers to the questions can be found at the back of the book.

Quizzes

The thirty lessons in this book are divided into five units, with a quiz to check your progress at the end of each unit. If there are any questions which you cannot answer, it is recommended that you review the unit. The answers to these questions are at the back of the book.

THE JAPANESE SOUND SYSTEM AND ITS ROMANIZATION

Japanese is usually written in a combination of *kanji* and *hiragana* with foreign loan words and certain other words written in *katakana*. Ideally the student should begin by reading Japanese as it is commonly written, but romanization can be effectively used as an aid until the *hiragana* are completely mastered.

Of the several systems for romanizing Japanese, the *Kunreishiki* system ("Official System") can be considered the most systematic, but the Hepburn system is easier to use for the native speaker of English who is learning Japanese; it is easier to switch from the sound system of English to that of Japanese with this system. In addition most Japanese-English dictionaries use the Hepburn system. Therefore this book employs a slightly modified version of the Hepburn system.

The following description of the sounds used in Japanese includes, 1) *hiragana* for a Japanese sound, 2) the romanized equivalent, and 3) a description of its pronunciation.

Vowels

あ (*a*) is roughly equivalent to the "a" in "father," but the mouth is not opened as wide.

い (*i*) is similar to the vowel in "eat," but is short and slightly strained.

う (*u*) is similar to the vowel in "look" except that the lips are spread rather than rounded.

え (*e*) is like the vowel in "egg" but the mouth is not opened as wide.

お (*o*) is similar to the first part of the "o" in "go" with less lip-rounding. Be careful not to pronounce the Japanese *o* as you would an English diphthong, as in "home."

Consonant plus vowel sounds

か (*ka*), き (*ki*), く (*ku*), け (*ke*), こ (*ko*)

These are the combination of the consonant sound "k" with the five vowels, *a*, *i*, *u*, *e*, and *o*. When pronouncing them remember:

* The force with which they are pronounced is not as strong as in English. This is true of most Japanese consonants so that the Japanese sounds seem lighter than their English equivalents.
* The "k" in *ki* is pronounced slightly forward in the mouth because of influence from the "i."
* The vowels in *ki* and *ku* often become "whispered syllable." In Japanese "i" and "u" often sound as if they are being whispered when they occur between the voiceless consonants "k," "t," "p," "s (or sh)," and "h (or f)."

  Examples: ***shita, kusuri*** (The underlined vowels are voiceless.)

が (*ga*), ぎ (*gi*), ぐ (*gu*), げ (*ge*), ご (*go*)

The first sound in these syllables is similar to the "g" in "go" when it occurs at the beginning of a word. When used within a word or as a particle, it is close to the "ng" sound of "king."

さ (*sa*), す (*su*), せ (*se*), そ (*so*)

The consonant in these syllables is similar to that in "son." The initial sound in し (*shi*) differs, being close to the consonant in the word "she" with less lip-rounding. The initial sounds in *sa*, *shi*, *su*, *se*, and *so* have less aspiration than do their closest English equivalents; that is, the corresponding English sounds are followed by a stronger puff of breath than in the Japanese sounds.

ざ (*za*), ず (*zu*), ぜ (*ze*), ぞ (*zo*)

The sound at the beginning of these syllables is like the "z" in "zone." However, when *za* or *zu* comes at the beginning of a word, a sound like "d" precedes the initial sound, producing a sound like the end of "roads." じ (*ji*) also has a "d" sound at the beginning, making it sound like the "j" in "jump" rather than the "s" in "television."

た (*ta*), て (*te*), と (*to*)

These syllables begin with a sound like the "t" in "time." In making the Japanese sound, the tip of the tongue touches both the back of the teeth and the gum behind the teeth. (The English "t" is pronounced further back in the mouth.) ち(*chi*) is similar to the first part of "cheese" but without any lip-rounding. つ(*tsu*) The initial sound here is like that of "ts" in "it's." *Chi* and *tsu* become often voiceless. Remember that in the Japanese *ta*, *chi*, *tsu*, *te*, and *to* the pressure is not as strong as that for the corresponding English consonants.

だ (*da*), で (*de*), ど (*do*)

The position of the tongue is the same in the initial sounds of these syllables as it is for the Japanese "t" described above. It is similar to the "d" in "dime."

There is no distinction made between ぢ and じ, and between づ and ず in modern Japanese.

な (*na*), に (*ni*), ぬ (*nu*), ね (*ne*), の (*no*)

The initial sound in these syllables is similar to that in "note." However, the "n" sound in the syllable *ni* is pronounced slightly further back in the mouth because of influence from the "i."

は (*ha*), へ (*he*), ほ (*ho*)

Though transcribed with an "h," the initial sound here is much weaker than that of the English "h" in words like "hat" and "home." ひ (*hi*) The "h" before an "i" is pronounced by raising the tongue close to the hard palate and producing friction, somewhat similar to the German "ch" as in "ich." ふ (*fu*) This consonant differs from the English "h" or the "f" of "fox." It is made by bringing both lips together as if blowing hot soup and producing friction. The lips are not rounded, and the teeth do not come in contact with the lips.

ば (*ba*), び (*bi*), ぶ (*bu*), べ (*be*), ぼ (*bo*)

This consonant is similar to that in "boy."

ぱ (*pa*), ぴ (*pi*), ぷ (*pu*), ぺ (*pe*), ぽ (*po*)

This consonant is like the "p" in "pie," but is not as strongly aspirated.

ま (*ma*), み (*mi*), む (*mu*), め (*me*), も (*mo*)

The initial sound here is like that in "my" but with less force behind it.

や (*ya*), ゆ (*yu*), よ (*yo*)

The consonant in these syllables is like the first sound in "yes."

The sounds *yi* and *ye* do not exist in standard Japanese.

ら (*ra*), り (*ri*), る (*ru*), れ (*re*), ろ (*ro*)

The Japanese "r" is made by flicking the tip of the tongue against the gum behind the upper teeth. (There are variations in the pronunciation of this sound but the one described here is the standard pronunciation.)

わ (*wa*)

When pronouncing *wa* in Japanese, the lips are more relaxed than in English; sometimes it sounds very similar to *a*.

The sounds *wi*, *wu*, *we*, and *wo* do not exist in standard Japanese.

Sounds with -ya, -yu, and -yo

For the following syllables a sound like the "y" in "yes" is pronounced after the initial consonant and before moving into the vowel sound.

きゃ (*kya*), きゅ (*kyu*), きょ (*kyo*)
ぎゃ (*gya*), ぎゅ (*gyu*), ぎょ (*gyo*)
しゃ (*sha*), しゅ (*shu*), しょ (*sho*)

Here the initial consonant is the "sh" in "she."

じゃ (*ja*), じゅ (*ju*), じょ (*jo*)

The first sound in "jump" followed by *a*, *u*, and *o* forms these syllables.

ちゃ (*cha*), ちゅ (*chu*), ちょ (*cho*)

The first sound in these syllables is similar to the first sound in "cheese."

にゃ (*nya*), にゅ (*nyu*), にょ (*nyo*)
ひゃ (*hya*), ひゅ (*hyu*), ひょ (*hyo*)
びゃ (*bya*), びゅ (*byu*), びょ (*byo*)
ぴゃ (*pya*), ぴゅ (*pyu*), ぴょ (*pyo*)
みゃ (*mya*), みゅ (*myu*), みょ (*myo*)
りゃ (*rya*), りゅ (*ryu*), りょ (*ryo*)

Syllabic consonants

ん (*n*)

The sound represented in *hiragana* by ん is not always the same sound. It always is pronounced through the nose with the length of a full syllable; but according to its location *n* will have one of the following sounds:

1) before *m*, *p*, or *b* —it is pronounced "m" as in "my."
2) before *n*, *t*, *d*, or *z* —it is pronounced "n" as in "night."
3) before *k*, *g*, or *ng*, and at the end of a word —it is pronounced like the "ng" in "king."
4) before vowels or sounds other than those mentioned above —it is pronounced by emitting air through the nose without the tongue touching either the roof of the mouth or the gums.

In the Hepburn system of romanization, *n* is represented by *m* before *m*, *p*, and *b*. Although this is close to the actual pronunciation, for consistency this sound is represented by *n* (for example, *shinbun*) in the romanization used in this book.

っ (*p*, *t*, *s*, *k*)

The sound that is represented by small っ between two syllables in Japanese is written with double consonants in romanization. The first of the two consonants in the romanized transcription is given the length of a full syllable.

Example: やっぱり (*yappari*); もって (*motte*)
しっかり (*shikkari*); まっすぐ (*massugu*)

HIRAGANA AND KATAKANA

(Katakana in 〔　〕)

あ〔ア〕(*a*)	い〔イ〕(*i*)	う〔ウ〕(*u*)	え〔エ〕(*e*)	お〔オ〕(*o*)
か〔カ〕(*ka*)	き〔キ〕(*ki*)	く〔ク〕(*ku*)	け〔ケ〕(*ke*)	こ〔コ〕(*ko*)
さ〔サ〕(*sa*)	し〔シ〕(*shi*)	す〔ス〕(*su*)	せ〔セ〕(*se*)	そ〔ソ〕(*so*)
た〔タ〕(*ta*)	ち〔チ〕(*chi*)	つ〔ツ〕(*tsu*)	て〔テ〕(*te*)	と〔ト〕(*to*)
な〔ナ〕(*na*)	に〔ニ〕(*ni*)	ぬ〔ヌ〕(*nu*)	ね〔ネ〕(*ne*)	の〔ノ〕(*no*)
は〔ハ〕(*ha*)	ひ〔ヒ〕(*hi*)	ふ〔フ〕(*fu*)	へ〔ヘ〕(*he*)	ほ〔ホ〕(*ho*)
ま〔マ〕(*ma*)	み〔ミ〕(*mi*)	む〔ム〕(*mu*)	め〔メ〕(*me*)	も〔モ〕(*mo*)
や〔ヤ〕(*ya*)		ゆ〔ユ〕(*yu*)		よ〔ヨ〕(*yo*)
ら〔ラ〕(*ra*)	り〔リ〕(*ri*)	る〔ル〕(*ru*)	れ〔レ〕(*re*)	ろ〔ロ〕(*ro*)
わ〔ワ〕(*wa*)				を*〔ヲ〕(*o*)

が〔ガ〕(*ga*)	ぎ〔ギ〕(*gi*)	ぐ〔グ〕(*gu*)	げ〔ゲ〕(*ge*)	ご〔ゴ〕(*go*)
ざ〔ザ〕(*za*)	じ〔ジ〕(*ji*)	ず〔ズ〕(*zu*)	ぜ〔ゼ〕(*ze*)	ぞ〔ゾ〕(*zo*)
だ〔ダ〕(*da*)	(ぢ)**〔ヂ〕(*ji*)	(づ)***〔ヅ〕(*zu*)	で〔デ〕(*de*)	ど〔ド〕(*do*)
ば〔バ〕(*ba*)	び〔ビ〕(*bi*)	ぶ〔ブ〕(*bu*)	べ〔ベ〕(*be*)	ぼ〔ボ〕(*bo*)
ぱ〔パ〕(*pa*)	ぴ〔ピ〕(*pi*)	ぷ〔プ〕(*pu*)	ぺ〔ペ〕(*pe*)	ぽ〔ポ〕(*po*)

きゃ〔キャ〕(*kya*)	きゅ〔キュ〕(*kyu*)	きょ〔キョ〕(*kyo*)
しゃ〔シャ〕(*sha*)	しゅ〔シュ〕(*shu*)	しょ〔ショ〕(*sho*)
ちゃ〔チャ〕(*cha*)	ちゅ〔チュ〕(*chu*)	ちょ〔チョ〕(*cho*)
にゃ〔ニャ〕(*nya*)	にゅ〔ニュ〕(*nyu*)	にょ〔ニョ〕(*nyo*)
ひゃ〔ヒャ〕(*hya*)	ひゅ〔ヒュ〕(*hyu*)	ひょ〔ヒョ〕(*hyo*)
みゃ〔ミャ〕(*mya*)	みゅ〔ミュ〕(*myu*)	みょ〔ミョ〕(*myo*)
りゃ〔リャ〕(*rya*)	りゅ〔リュ〕(*ryu*)	りょ〔リョ〕(*ryo*)
ぎゃ〔ギャ〕(*gya*)	ぎゅ〔ギュ〕(*gyu*)	ぎょ〔ギョ〕(*gyo*)

じゃ〔ジャ〕(*ja*)　じゅ〔ジュ〕(*ju*)　じょ〔ジョ〕(*jo*)
びゃ〔ビャ〕(*bya*)　びゅ〔ビュ〕(*byu*)　びょ〔ビョ〕(*byo*)
ぴゃ〔ピャ〕(*pya*)　ぴゅ〔ピュ〕(*pyu*)　ぴょ〔ピョ〕(*pyo*)
ん〔ン〕(*n*)

っ〔ッ〕(p, t, s, k)

* This を is used to show the particle *o*. See "The use of *hiragana* for particles."
** The "*ji*" sound is usually written with じ.
*** The "*zu*" sound is usually written with ず.

The use of *hiragana* for two successive vowels

When two of the same vowel occur in succession, the method of transcription in *hiragana* is different from that in romanization.

"aa" ex. ***Aa*** (Oh!) ああ ; *o**kaa**san* (mother) おかあさん
" ii " ex. ***ii*** (good) いい ; *sabi**shii*** (lonely) さびしい
"uu" ex. ***suu*** (to smoke) すう ; *is**shuu**kan* (a week) いっしゅうかん
"ee" ex. ***ee**ga* (movie) えいが ; *sen**see*** (teacher) せんせい
(with a few exceptions where it is written ええ)
"oo" ex. *o**too**san* (father) おとうさん; *tabe**yoo*** (I'll eat) たべよう
(with a few exceptions where it is written おお)

The use of *hiragana* for particles

The particles in Japanese are written in the following *hiragana*:

は (*wa*) わたしは がくせいです。 *Watashi-**wa** gakusee-desu.*
(I am a student.)

へ (*e*) がっこうへ いきました。 *Gakkoo-**e** ikimashita.*
(I went to school.)

を (*o*) ほんを よみました。 *Hon-**o** yomimashita.*
(I read a book.)

Katakana

Katakana as well as *kanji* are accompanied by *hiragana* equivalents in this book so that you need not memorize the *katakana* before beginning Lesson 1. However, you will probably be able to read almost all of the *katakana* by the time you finish the book. In Lessons 28 through 30 there is a section to check your mastery of the *katakana*; if you cannot read some of them, their romanization can be found on the right-hand side of the page.

ENGLISH SYLLABLES AND JAPANESE SYLLABLES

In Japanese the syllable plays a different role from that in English. The relatively equal length that each syllable receives is an important feature of Japanese. Each *hiragana* symbol, including ん and the small っ, is given a beat of approximately the same length. The only exception to this rule is a syllable like きゃ and しゅ, where the combination of the two *hiragana* has one beat. Care should be taken that no syllable is any longer or shorter than any other one. When two vowels occur together the second vowel does not change; it does not become weak as in a diphthong in English.

The fact that each sound unit has a whole beat distinguishes the Japanese sound system from that of English where some syllables are lengthened and some shortened. A true understanding of this concept is essential for the student who wishes to fully master Japanese pronunciation. Part A in the "Pronunciation Practice" section of each lesson is designed for practice in this feature of the Japanese sound system.

ACCENT

Accent in Japanese is a pitch accent in contrast to the stress accent in English. Each word in Japanese has a set accent, that is, certain syllables have a high pitch and others have a low pitch. We say that syllables within a word are either high or low, but this is a matter of *relative* rather than absolute pitch.

The accent patterns shown in this book are those of standard Tokyo Japanese, which has relatively simple accent patterns. The following accent patterns occur in Tokyo speech.

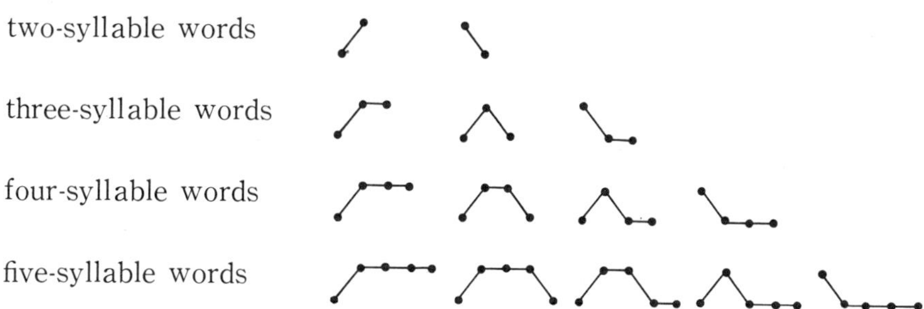

The first two syllables of a word are always different in pitch. Therefore, accent patterns like and do not occur in standard Japanese.

In this book the mark ⌜ is used to show where the pitch rises within a word and the mark ⌝ to show where the pitch falls. For example, the marks on the following words indicate the corresponding accent patterns.

ni⌜hongo (Japanese)

ni⌜hongo-de (in Japanese)

ni⌜hongo-de⌝su (it's Japanese)

to⌜sho⌝kan (library)

to⌜sho⌝kan-e (to the library)

to⌜sho⌝kan-desu (it's a library)

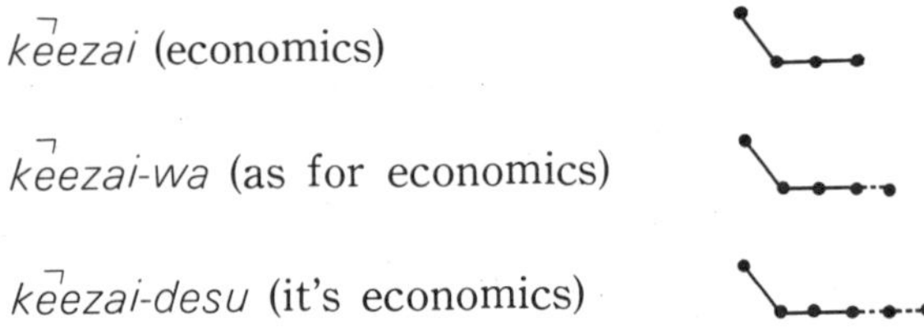

(If the mark falls on the last syllable of a word, the pitch is high to the end of that word and falls with the following particle or *desu*.)

ichinichi (a day)

ichinichi-ni (in a day)

ichinichi-desu (it's a day)

The words connected with hyphens are pronounced as one unit.

*　　*　　*　　*　　*

The use of *hiragana* to show the reading of *kanji* and *katakana*

In this book the small *hiragana* which show the reading of the *kanji* and *katakana* appear below the word (ex. 東京 (とうきょう)). *Hiragana* used this way are called *furigana* and are usually given above the word (or on the right side of the word when written vertically), but in this book the *furigana* are underneath so that the student will concentrate on reading the word itself before looking at the *furigana*. This method also makes it easier for the student to practice reading by covering these *furigana* readings with a piece of paper.

An Introduction to Modern Japanese

第一課(だいいっか)　何時(なんじ)ですか

Dialogue

I．(On a plane from New York to Tokyo)

Passenger：　いま　何時(なんじ)ですか。 1

Stewardess：六時(ろくじ)です。 2

P：　東京(とうきょう)は　いま　何時(なんじ)ですか。 3

S：　八時(はちじ)です。 4

P：　午後(ごご)　八時(はちじ)ですか。 5

S：　ええ、そうです。東京(とうきょう)は　いま　よるです。 6

II．(On the street)

A：　すみません、何時(なんじ)ですか。 7

B：　二時(にじ)です。 8

A：　ありがとうございます。 9

B：　どういたしまして。 10

Dialogue

Lesson 1

WHAT TIME IS IT?

I.

Passenger: What time is it now?

Stewardess: It's six o'clock.

P: What time is it now in Tokyo?

S: It's eight o'clock.

P: Eight P.M.?

S: Yes, that's right. It's night in Tokyo now.

II.

A: Excuse me, what time is it?

B: Two o'clock.

A: Thank you.

B: You're welcome.

Dai-ikka

NANJI-DESU-KA

I.

P: *Ima nanji-desu-ka.*

S: *Rokuji-desu.*

P: *Tookyoo-wa ima nanji-desu-ka.*

S: *Hachiji-desu.*

P: *Gogo hachiji-desu-ka.*

S: *Ee, soo-desu. Tookyoo-wa ima yoru-desu.*

II.

A: *Sumimasen, nanji-desu-ka.*

B: *Niji-desu.*

A: *Arigatoo-gozaimasu.*

B: *Doo-itashimashite.*

Explanation

(In this lesson you will learn how to ask and tell time and how to express thanks.)

いま　何時(なんじ)ですか。 **line 1**

Ima nanji-desu-ka.

ima	now
nanji	what time
-desu	be; it is, they are, etc.
-desu-ka	is it, are they, etc.

This is the most common expression used for asking the time. *Ima* can be left out as it is in line 7 of the dialogue.

The *nan* of *nanji* means 'what' and *ji* means 'o'clock.' *Nan* can be used to form various compounds such as *nanban* (what number), *nannin* (how many people), *nanmai* (how many sheets), etc.

Desu roughly corresponds to the English verb 'to be' and can mean 'it is,' 'we are,' 'they are,' etc. depending on context. *Tookyoo-desu* means 'It's Tokyo,' as if in answer to a question like 'What's the name of this city?'

Ka added at the end of a sentence makes it into a question. The word order does not change as it does in English. If you add *-ka* to *Tookyoo-desu*, it forms the question, *Tookyoo-desu-ka*, 'Is it Tokyo?' (See Note on Intonation)

六時(ろくじ)です。 **line 2**

Rokuji-desu.

rokuji	six o'clock

Roku (six) and *ji* (o'clock) combine to mean 'six o'clock.' The hours of the day are read in the following way:

1—*ichiji*	2—*niji*	3—*sanji*	4—*yoji*
5—*goji*	6—*rokuji*	7—*shichiji*	8—*hachiji*
9—*kuji*	10—*juuji*	11—*juuichiji*	12—*juuniji*

By replacing *ji* with other "counters" you can form various compounds, for example, *ichimai* (one sheet), *nimai* (two sheets), *sannin* (three people), *yoban* or *yonban* (number 4). (4 is sometimes read *shi*, especially when it is used alone.)

東京(とうきょう)は　何時(なんじ)ですか。 **line 3**

Tookyoo-wa nanji-desu-ka.

Tookyoo	Tokyo
Tookyoo-wa	as for Tokyo

Wa follows the topic that the speaker wants to talk about. Here, the topic that the speaker wishes to emphasize is 'Tokyo,' so he starts his sentence with *Tookyoo-wa*. To find out what time it is in New York he would say *Nyuuyooku-wa nanji-desu-ka*.

午後(ごご)　八時(はちじ)ですか。 **line 5**

Gogo hachiji-desu-ka.

gogo hachiji	eight P.M.

Gogo means P.M., and *gozen* means A.M.

ex. *gozen juuji* (10 A.M.); *gogo sanji* (3 P.M.)
gozen ichiji (1 A.M.); *gogo juuniji* (12 P.M.)

ええ、そうです。　東京(とうきょう)は　いま　よるです。 **line 6**

Ee, soo-desu. Tookyoo-wa ima yoru-desu.

ee	yes
soo-desu	it is so; that's right
yoru	night; evening

Ee is used to show agreement. *Soo-desu* means 'It's (exactly) as you say.'

The structure of the sentence *Tookyoo-wa ima yoru-desu* is identical to that in line 3, except that this sentence is a statement rather than a question.

すみません。 **line 7**

Sumimasen.

Sumimasen.	I'm sorry. Excuse me.

Sumimasen is used to express either apology or gratitude. Here it is used to apologize for troubling someone.

ありがとうございます。 **line 9**

Arigatoo-gozaimasu.

Arigatoo-gozaimasu. Thank you very much (polite).

This is the most common expression of thanks. In familiar speech *gozaimasu* is dropped.

どういたしまして。 **line 10**

Doo-itashimashite.

Doo-itashimashite. You're welcome.

This literally means 'How can it be?' but usually means 'Not at all,' and is the most common response to *Arigatoo-gozaimasu.*

Note **Intonation of *-desu-ka***

The last *-ka* can be higher than *-desu.*

Be careful not to rise continually like

Na nji de su ka.

Only *-ka* rises:

Na nji desu ka.

Drills

I. . . . *ji-desu*

("Structure Drills," as used in this book, are basic drills in grammatical structure; they should be practiced over and over with the tape or with a teacher until the patterns can be reproduced without hesitation.)

Structure Drill 1 Practice saying the following numbers aloud.

ichi, ni, san, shi, go, roku, shichi, hachi, ku, juu, juuichi, juuni.

Structure Drill 2 Practice the hours of the day.

ichiji, niji, sanji, yoji, goji, rokuji, shichiji, hachiji, kuji, juuji, juuichiji, juuniji.

Structure Drill 3 Practice the following sentences:

Ichiji-desu.	*Niji-desu.*	*Sanji-desu.*	*Yoji-desu.*
Goji-desu.	*Rokuji-desu.*	*Shichiji-desu.*	*Hachiji-desu.*
Kuji-desu.	*Juuji-desu.*	*Juuichiji-desu.*	*Juuniji-desu.*

Structure Drill 4 Practice saying the following sentences:

Ima ichiji-desu.	*Ima niji-desu.*	*Ima sanji-desu.*
Ima yoji-desu.	*Ima goji-desu.*	*Ima rokuji-desu.*
Ima shichiji-desu.	*Ima hachiji-desu.*	*Ima kuji-desu.*
Ima juuji-desu.	*Ima juuichiji-desu.*	*Ima juuniji-desu.*

Structure Drill 5 Add *gozen* and then *gogo* to the sentences above.

ex. *Ima ichiji-desu.*—*Ima gozen ichiji-desu.*
Ima gogo ichiji-desu.

("Usage Drills" are for practice in actual usage. Practice saying the dialogues with your teacher or with a fellow student taking the roles of A and B in turns.)

Usage Drill 1 Look at the pictures and practice the following conversation.

ex.

A: *Ima nanji-desu-ka.*
B: *Niji-desu.*

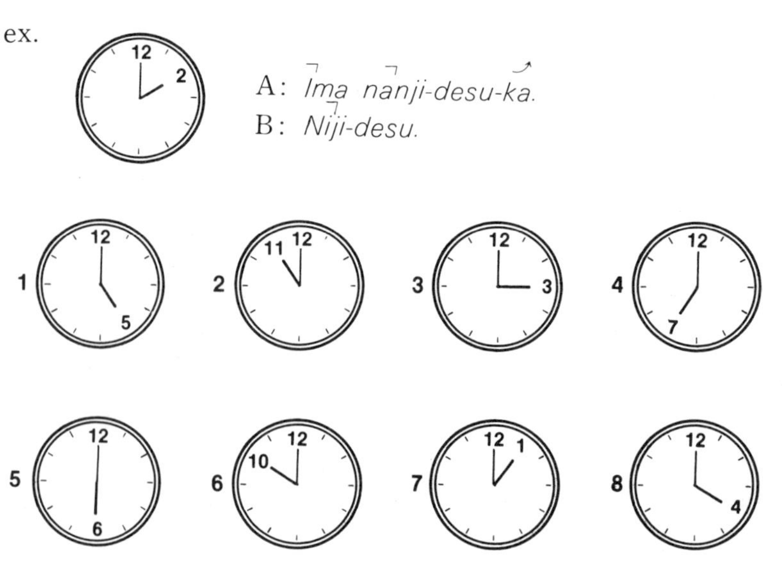

Usage Drill 2 This time add *-han*, 'half past,' and practice the following conversation. Then change the underlined part by substituting the times given below.

ex. 1:30 A: *Ima nanji-desu-ka.*
B: *Ichiji-han-desu.*

1. 2:30 2. 4:30 3. 5:30 4. 10:30
5. 7:30 6. 9:30 7. 12:30 8. 11:30

II. *sumimasen...... arigatoo-gozaimasu*

Structure Drill Practice saying the following aloud.

sumimasen, arigatoo-gozaimasu, doo-itashimashite

Usage Drill Practice the following conversation changing the underlined part.

ex. *ichiji* A: *Sumimasen nanji-desu-ka.*
B: *Ichiji-desu.*
A: *Arigatoo-gozaimasu.*
B: *Doo-itashimashite.*

1. *ichiji-han* 2. *sanji* 3. *goji-han* 4. *hachiji*
5. *kuji-han* 6. *juuji* 7. *juuji-han* 8. *juuniji*

III. *... wa..... desu*

Structure Drill Substitute the underlined word with the cue words given below.

ex. *ichiji→Tookyoo-wa ima ichiji-desu.*

1. *shichiji* 2. *gozen niji* 3. *yoru* 4. *hachiji-han*
5. *gogo rokuji* 6. *ichiji-han* 7. *juuniji-han* 8. *asa* (morning)

Usage Drill Practice the following conversation, changing the underlined word.

ex. *hachiji* A: *Tookyoo-wa ima nanji-desu-ka.*
B: *Hachiji-desu.*
A: *Gozen hachiji-desu-ka.*
B: *Ee, soo-desu. Tookyoo-wa ima asa-desu.*

1. *kuji* 2. *rokuji-han* 3. *shichiji*
4. *kuji-han* 5. *goji-han* 6. *hachiji-han*

IV. Numbers up to 100

1. Practice the numbers from 13 to 20.

13—juusan *14—juushi* *15—juugo* *16—juuroku*
17—juushichi *18—juuhachi* *19—juuku* *20—nijuu*

2. Practice the multiples of ten.

10—juu *20—nijuu* *30—sanjuu* *40—yonjuu, shijuu*
50—gojuu *60—rokujuu* *70—shichijuu, nanajuu*
80—hachijuu *90—kyuujuu* *100—hyaku*

3. Practice the numbers from 21 to 100.

nijuuichi, nijuuni, nijuusan, nijuushi, nijuugo, nijuuroku, nijuushichi, nijuuhachi, nijuuku, sanjuu; sanjuuichi, sanjuuni, sanjuusan, sanjuushi, sanjuugo, sanjuuroku, sanjuushichi, sanjuuhachi, sanjuuku, yonjuu (shijuu); yonjuuichi............ gojuu;...... rokujuu;...... shichijuu;...... hachijuu;........... kyuujuu;...... kyuujuuku, hyaku.

Pronunciation Practice

Practice saying the following aloud, paying careful attention to the accent of each word or combination of syllables. Pronounce each syllable clearly.

A. 1. *a -i -a -u* 2. *o -i -i -e* 3. *e -i -u -o*
4. *ma -i -ma -u* 5. *mo -i -mi -e* 6. *me -i -mu -o*
7. *pa -i -pa -u* 8. *po -i -pi -e* 9. *pe -i -pu -o*
10. *ba -i -ba -u* 11. *bo -i -bi -e* 12. *be -i -bu -o*

B. 1. *gakusee* (student) 2. *shitsumon* (question)
3. *setsumee* (explanation) 4. *Tookyoo* 5. *Yokohama* (place name)
6. *Kawasaki* (place name) 7. *Yamamoto* (personal name)
8. *Kawakami* (personal name)

C. Add *-desu-ka* to the words in B and say first with a falling and then with a rising intonation.

ex. *Gakusee-desu-ka.* ↗

Gakusee-desu-ka. ↘

To show intonation in the pronunciation practices, the mark ↗ is used for a rising intonation and ↘ for a falling one. In the drill sections, only the rising intonation is marked. In this case, a falling intonation is implied in sentences without an intonation mark.

Reading Comprehension

Please read the following passage. If you cannot read or understand some part of it, review the lesson.

This is not a dialogue but an ordinary text. And it also differs from the rest of the lesson in that it is written with no spaces between the words. Japanese is usually written in this way, and practice in reading this passage will help prepare you for more advanced stages where you will have to read this sort of writing all the time.

東京(とうきょう)はいま午後八時(ごごはちじ)です。よるです。ニューヨーク(にゅーよーく)*はいま午前六時(ごぜんろくじ)です。あさです。

(*When two of the same vowel occur in succession, it is transcribed in *katakana* with a "—.")

Aural Comprehension

Listen to the conversations on the tape and answer the following questions. The answers may be given either in Japanese or in English. Check your answers with those at the end of the book.

It isn't necessary to understand the conversation completely, but try to get accustomed to the sound and the rythm of the language.

Question: What time is it in each of the conversations?

(A)

(B)

(C)

第二課(だいにか)　いくらですか

Dialogue

I. (Buying a bag)

A：　これは　いくらですか。 1

B：　五千円(ごせんえん)です。

A：　これも　五千円(ごせんえん)ですか。 3

B：　いいえ。それは　七千円(ななせんえん)です。

A：　あれは　いくらですか。 5

B：　どれですか。

A：　あの　かばんです。 7

B：　あの　あかい　かばんですか。

A：　そうです。 9

B：　あれは　八千円(はっせんえん)です。

II. (Buying socks)

A：　この　くつしたは　ナイロン(ないろん)ですか。 11

B：　ちがいます。もめんです。

A：　いくらですか。 13

B：　千円(せんえん)です。

A：　これを　ください。 15

B：　はい、ありがとうございます。

III. (On the street)

A：　あれは　なんですか。 17

B：　どれですか。

A：　あの　しろい　たてものです。 19

B：　ああ、あれは　病院(びょういん)です。

Dialogue

Lesson 2	Dai--nika
HOW MUCH IS IT?	***IKURA-DESU-KA***
I.	I.
A: How much is this?	*A: Kore-wa ikura-desu-ka.*
B: It's five thousand yen.	*B: Gosen-en-desu.*
A: Is this five thousand yen, too?	*A: Kore-mo gosen-en-desu-ka.*
B: No, that's seven thousand yen.	*B: Iie. Sore-wa nanasen-en-desu.*
A: How much is that over there?	*A: Are-wa ikura-desu-ka.*
B: Which one?	*B: Dore-desu-ka.*
A: That bag.	*A: Ano kaban-desu.*
B: That red bag?	*B: Ano akai kaban-desu-ka.*
A: Yes.	*A: Soo-desu.*
B: That's eight thousand yen.	*B: Are-wa hassen-en-desu.*
II.	II.
A: Are these socks nylon?	*A: Kono kutsushita-wa nairon-desu-ka.*
B: No, they're cotton.	*B: Chigaimasu. Momen-desu.*
A: How much are they?	*A: Ikura-desu-ka.*
B: One thousand yen.	*B: Sen-en-desu.*
A: I'll take them.	*A: Kore-o kudasai.*
B: Thank you very much.	*B: Hai, arigatoo-gozaimasu.*
III.	III.
A: What's that?	*A: Are-wa nan-desu-ka.*
B: Which one?	*B: Dore-desu-ka.*
A: That white building.	*A: Ano shiroi tatemono-desu.*
B: Oh, that's a hospital.	*B: Aa, are-wa byooin-desu.*

Explanation

(In this lesson you will learn several demonstrative words used to point to or refer to things, and how to ask and give prices.)

これは　いくらですか。 **line 1**

Kore-wa ikura-desu-ka.

kore	this
ikura	how much

Kore refers to a thing or things close to the speaker. *Ikura* is used in asking prices.

line 2

五千円(ごせんえん)です。
Gosen-en-desu.

gosen-en	5,000 yen

Sen stands for 'thousand.' Multiples of a thousand are read as follows.

1,000	*sen* or *issen*	2,000	*nisen*
3,000	*sanzen*	4,000	*yonsen*
5,000	*gosen*	6,000	*rokusen*
7,000	*nanasen*	8,000	*hassen*
9,000	*kyuusen*		

(See Note on Pronunciation of the sound「ん」.)

line 3

これも　五千円(ごせんえん)ですか。
Kore-mo gosen-en-desu-ka.

. . . . . *mo*	. . . . , too

In this sentence *-mo* replaces *-wa* to add the meaning 'too' or 'also.' In the sentence *Tookyoo-mo sanji-desu, mo* replaces *wa* and the meaning is 'It's three o'clock in Tokyo, too.'

line 4

いいえ。それは　七千円(ななせんえん)です。
Iie. Sore-wa nanasen-en-desu.

iie	no
sore	that

In line 3, speaker A is talking about a bag that is close to him, and therefore uses *kore.* In line 4 speaker B, the shopkeeper, refers to the same bag, which is close to A, as *sore.*

Sore refers to a thing or things close to the person addressed. It might be translated as 'the thing near you.'

line 5

あれは　いくらですか。
Are-wa ikura-desu-ka.

are	that over there

Are refers to a thing or things far from both the speaker and the person addressed.

line 6

どれですか。
Dore-desu-ka.

dore　　which one(s)

Dore can be used to ask 'which one' or 'which ones' of a group of three or more things are indicated.

あの　かばんです。 **line 7**

Ano kaban-desu.

ano　　that (those) over there

kaban　　bag ; satchel

While *kore, sore, are,* and *dore* are pronouns that refer to things (*kore* stands alone to mean 'this thing'), *kono, sono, ano,* and *dono* are never used alone, but precede nouns.

ex. *kono kaban*　　(this bag ; these bags)

sono hon　　(that book ; those books)

ano tokee　　(that clock (watch) over there ; those clocks (watches) over there)

dono hon　　(which book(s))

あの　あかい　かばんですか。 **line 8**

Ano akai kaban-desu-ka.

akai　　red

Akai is an adjective used to modify nouns.

ex. *akai hon*　　(a red book ; red books)

kono akai hon　　(this red book ; these red books)

そうです。 **line 9**

Soo-desu.

We had the expression *Ee, soo-desu* in Lesson 1. *Ee* is frequently omitted.

あれは　八千円(はっせんえん)です。 **line 10**

Are-wa hassen-en-desu.

hassen-en　　8,000 yen

この　くつしたは　ナイロン(ないろん)ですか。 **line 11**

Kono kutsushita-wa nairon-desu-ka.

kutsushita　　socks ; stockings

nairon　　nylon

ちがいます。もめんです。 **line 12**

Chigaimasu. Momen-desu.

Chigaimasu. No.
momen cotton

Chigaimasu literally means 'That's wrong.' This phrase is very often used to mean 'No, it isn't' in daily conversation. *Iie* is often left out.

いくらですか。 **line 13**

Ikura-desu-ka.

Kore-wa is understood and left out.

千円(せんえん)です。 **line 14**

Sen-en-desu.

sen-en 1,000 yen

Here also, *sore-wa* is left out.

これを　ください。 **line 15**

Kore-o kudasai.

... o kudasai please give me....

The phrase *...o kudasai* is the most common expression for 'I'll take...'

はい、ありがとうございます。 **line 16**

Hai, arigatoo-gozaimasu.

Hai is sometimes used to express agreement as is *Ee,* and sometimes in the sense that 'Certainly,' 'With pleasure,' or 'I understand' is used in English. (In showing agreement both *Hai* and *Ee* are used; however, *Hai* is more formal.)

あれは　なんですか。 **line 17**

Are-wa nan-desu-ka.

nan-desu-ka what is it? (cf. Lesson 1)

あの　しろい　たてものです。 **line 19**

Ano shiroi tatemono-desu.

shiroi white
tatemono building

ああ、あれは　病院(びょういん)です。 **line 20**

Aa, are-wa byooin-desu.

aa,	oh,
byooin	hospital

Note Pronunciation of the sound 「ん」

When 「ん」 occurs between vowels it is pronounced somewhat differently from the sound [n] in English. Practice pronouncing this sound in a word like *gosen-en* by trying to keep the tip of your tongue from touching the roof of your mouth. If it is not pronounced in this way, but like the [n] in English, you may find yourself saying something that sounds like *gosennen,* 'five thousand years' instead of 'five thousand yen.'

Drills

I. *kore, sore*

Structure Drill Answer the questions following the example:

ex. *Kore-wa kaban-desu-ka.*
→*Hai, sore-wa kaban-desu.*

1. *Kore-wa kutsushita-desu-ka.*
2. *Kore-wa hon*(book)*-desu-ka.*
3. *Kore-wa kaban-desu-ka.*
4. *Kore-wa pen* (pen)*-desu-ka.*
5. *Kore-wa tokee* (watch)*-desu-ka.*
6. *Kore-wa enpitsu* (pencil)*-desu-ka.*

Usuge Drill 1

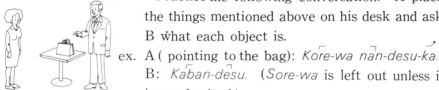

Practice the following conversation. A places the things mentioned above on his desk and asks B what each object is.

ex. A (pointing to the bag): *Kore-wa nan-desu-ka.*
B: *Kaban-desu.* (*Sore-wa* is left out unless it is emphasized.)

Usage Drill 2

Practice the following conversation. A steps away from the desk on which the things are placed, and asks B what each object is. (B stands by the desk.)

ex. A (pointing to the bag): *Sore-wa nan-desu-ka.*
B: *Kaban-desu.* (*Kore-wa* is left out unless it is emphasized.)

II. *are*

Structure Drill Answer the questions following the example:

ex. *Are-wa kaban-desu-ka.*
→*Hai, are-wa kaban-desu.*

1. *Are-wa hon-desu-ka.*
2. *Are-wa tokee-desu-ka.*
3. *Are-wa kutsushita-desu-ka.*
4. *Are-wa mado* (window)-*desu-ka.*
5. *Are-wa tsukue* (desk)-*desu-ka.*
6. *Are-wa isu* (chair)-*desu-ka.*

Usage Drill Practice the following conversation. Both A and B stand away from the objects that they talk about.

ex. A (pointing to a bag): *Are-wa nan-desu-ka.*
B: *Kaban-desu.* (*Are-wa* is left out unless it is emphasized.)

III. *kono, sono, ano, dono*

Structure Drill Change the given sentences as shown in the example.

ex. *Kaban-desu.*
→*Kono kaban-desu.* *Sono kaban-desu.*
Ano kaban-desu. *Dono kaban-desu-ka.*

1. *Hon-desu.*
2. *Tsukue-desu.*
3. *Isu-desu.*
4. *Enpitsu-desu.*
5. *Tokee-desu.*
6. *Mado-desu.*
7. *Tatemono-desu.*
8. *Byooin-desu.*

Usage Drill 1 Practice the following conversation, substituting a new word each time.

ex. *kaban*
A: *Kore-wa ikura-desu-ka.*
B: *Dore-desu-ka.*
A: *Kono kaban-desu.*
B: *Sore-wa gosen-en-desu.*

1. *hon*
2. *tsukue*
3. *tokee*
4. *isu*
5. *kasa* (umbrella)
6. *jibiki* (dictionary)

Usage Drill 2 Practice the following conversation, substituting a new word each time. This time substitute adjective +noun expressions.

ex. *kaban, akai* A: *Ano kaban-wa ikura-desu-ka.*
B: *Dono kaban-desu-ka.*
A: *Ano akai kaban-desu.*
B: *Are-wa rokusen-en-desu.*

1. *kaban, shiroi* 2. *tokee, shiroi* 3. *tokee, akai*
4. *kasa, akai* 5. *kasa, kuroi* (black) 6. *kaban, aoi* (blue)

IV. ...*mo,* ...*wa*

Structure Drill Change the sentences, as in the example, replacing *-wa* with *-mo.*

ex. *Kono tsukue-wa gosen-en-desu.*
→*Kono tsukue-mo gosen-en-desu.*

1. *Kono kaban-wa yonsen-en-desu.*
2. *Kono isu-wa sanzen-en-desu.*
3. *Sono tokee-wa nisen-en-desu.*
4. *Sono hon-wa sen-en-desu.*
5. *Ano kasa-wa nairon-desu.*
6. *Kono tatemono-wa byooin-desu.*

Usage Drill Practice the following conversation, substituting two words as shown in the example.

ex. *gosen-en, rokusen-en* A: *Kono kaban-wa gosen-en-desu-ka.*
B: *Ee, soo-desu.*
A: *Ano kaban-mo gosen-en-desu-ka.*
B: *Chigaimasu. Are-wa rokusen-en-desu.*

1. *nanasen-en, hassen-en* 2. *yonsen-en, gosen-en*
3. *nairon, momen* 4. *nisen-en, sanzen-en*
5. *hassen-en, kyuusen-en* 6. *sanzen-en, rokusen-en*

V. Numbers 100—1,000

1. Learn how to say the multiples of a hundred from 100 to 900.
100—hyaku; 200—nihyaku; 300—sanbyaku; 400—yonhyaku; 500—gohyaku; 600—roppyaku; 700—nanahyaku; 800—happyaku, 900—kyuuhyaku

2. Learn how to say the multiples of hundred from 1100 to 9900.
1100—sen hyaku; 1200—sen nihyaku; 1300—sen sanbyaku...
(You merely have to add multiples of a hundred to multiples of a thousand.)

Structure Drill Read the following numbers:

1. 1,200 2. 1,800 3. 2,300
4. 3,700 5. 4,100 6. 5,900

Usage Drill Prepare several price tags and practice asking and giving prices.

ex. 8,400 A: *Ikura-desu-ka.*
B: *Hassen yonhyaku-en-desu.*

Pronunciation Practice

Practice saying the following, paying careful attention to the accent.

A. 1. *a -i -a -u* 2. *o -i -i -e* 3. *e -i -u -o*
4. *na -i -na -u* 5. *no -i -ni -e* 6. *ne -i -nu -o*
7. *ta -i -ta -u* 8. *to -i -chi -e* 9. *te -i -tsu -o*
10. *da -i -da -u* 11. *do -i -ji -e* 12. *de -i -zu -o*

B. 1. *byooin* 2. *kyooshitsu* (classroom)
3. *Shinjuku* (place name) 4. *Shinagawa* (place name)
5. *Nakamura* (personal name) 6. *Saitoo* (personal name)
7. *soodan* (consultation) 8. *yakusoku* (engagement)

C. Add *-desu-ka* to the words in B and say first with a rising and then with a falling intonation.

ex. *Byooin-desu-ka.*↗
Byooin-desu-ka.↘

Reading Comprehension

Read the following passage.

I．この時計(とけい)は八千円(はっせんえん)です。あのあかい時計(とけい)も八千円(はっせんえん)です。

II．あのしろいたてものは病院(びょういん)です。

Aural Comprehension

Listen to the conversations on the tape and answer the following questions.

(A) 1. How much does the woman pay for the umbrella?
    2. What color is it?

(B) How much does the man pay for the clock?

(C) 1. How much does the woman pay for the socks?
    2. Are they made of nylon or cotton?

第三課(だいさんか)　どこに　ありますか

Dialogue

I.　(On the street)

A：　あそこに　喫茶店(きっさてん)が　ありますね。 1

B：　ええ。

A：　その　となりに　しろい　たてものが　ありますね。あれは　なんですか。 3

B：　郵便局(ゆうびんきょく)です。 5

A：　ホテル(ほてる)は　どこに　ありますか。

B：　あの　銀行(ぎんこう)の　そばに　あります。 7

II.　(In the hotel)

A：　あそこに　男(おとこ)の人(ひと)が　いますね。

B：　どこに　いますか。 9

A：　エレベーター(えれべーたー)の　まえに　います。

B：　ああ、そうですね。 11

A：　あの人(ひと)は　だれですか。

B：　田中(たなか)さんです。 13

A：　女(おんな)の人(ひと)も　いますね。

B：　ええ。田中(たなか)さんの　おくさんです。 15

A：　中村(なかむら)さんたちは　どこに　いますか。

B：　食堂(しょくどう)の　なかに　います。 17

A：　食堂(しょくどう)は　どこですか。

B：　ロビー(ろびー)の　うえです。 19

Dialogue

Lesson 3 **WHERE IS IT?**	*Dai-sanka* ***DOKO-NI ARIMASU-KA***
I.	I.
A: There's a coffee shop over there.	*A: Asoko-ni kissaten-ga arimasu-ne.*
B: Oh, yes.	*B: Ee.*
A: There's a white building next to it. What's that?	*A: Sono tonari-ni shiroi tatemono-ga arimasu-ne. Are-wa nan-desu-ka.*
B: It's a post office.	*B: Yuubinkyoku-desu.*
A: Where is the hotel?	*A: Hoteru-wa doko-ni arimasu-ka.*
B: It's near that bank.	*B: Ano ginkoo-no soba-ni arimasu.*
II.	II.
A: There's a man over there.	*A: Asoko-ni otoko-no-hito-ga imasu-ne.*
B: Where?	*B: Doko-ni imasu-ka.*
A: In front of the elevator.	*A: Erebeetaa-no mae-ni imasu.*
B: Oh, yes, there is.	*B: Aa, soo-desu-ne.*
A: Who is he?	*A: Ano-hito-wa dare-desu-ka.*
B: He's Mr. Tanaka.	*B: Tanaka-san-desu.*
A: There's a woman, too.	*A: Onna-no-hito-mo imasu-ne.*
B: Yes. She's Mrs. Tanaka.	*B: Ee. Tanaka-san-no okusan-desu.*
A: Where are Mr. Nakamura and the others?	*A: Nakamura-san-tachi-wa doko-ni imasu-ka.*
B: They're in the dining room.	*B: Shokudoo-no naka-ni imasu.*
A: Where's the dining room?	*A: Shokudoo-wa doko-desu-ka.*
B: It's above the lobby.	*B: Robii-no ue-desu.*

Explanation

(In this lesson you will learn how to express the existence of both animate and inanimate objects. Pay careful attention to the use of different verbs depending on whether the object is animate or inanimate.)

あそこに　喫茶店(きっさてん)が　ありますね。 **line 1**

Asoko-ni kissaten-ga arimasu-ne.

asoko — over there

kissaten — coffee shop
...ga arimasu — there is (are)....
... ne — (isn't there?)

Asoko is used to refer to a place which is not close to either the speaker or the person addressed. *Koko* means 'this place' (close to the speaker), *soko* 'that place' (close to the person addressed), and *doko* 'which place.' (See Note 1.)

Ni indicates location. X-*ga* Y-*ni arimasu* is the basic pattern expressing existence of an inanimate object (or objects) in a certain place.

ex. *Asoko-ni kaban-ga arimasu.* (There is a bag over there.)
Tookyoo-ni chikatetsu-ga arimasu-ka. (Are there subways in Tokyo?)

Ne is used at the end of a sentence. Usually it is used, as in this sentence, to either solicit agreement from the hearer or to make sure that he is following the flow of the conversation. It roughly corresponds to English tag questions (isn't it?, aren't you?, etc.). It is usually pronounced with a rising pitch. (See Note 2.)

ex. *Ima sanji-desu-ne.* (It's three o'clock now, isn't it?)

その　となりに　しろい　たてものが　ありますね。 **line 3**
Sono tonari-ni shiroi tatemono-ga arimasu-ne.

sono tonari-ni — next to that

Tonari by itself means 'next door.' '*... no tonari-ni*' forms an expression of relative location.

ex. *Ginkoo-no tonari-ni yuubinkyoku-ga arimasu.* (There is a post office next to the bank.)

郵便局(ゆうびんきょく)です。 **line 5**
Yuubinkyoku-desu.

yuubinkyoku — post office

ホテル(ほてる)は　どこに　ありますか。 **line 6**
Hoteru-wa doko-ni arimasu-ka.

hoteru — hotel
doko — which place; where

'*.... wa doko-ni arimasu-ka*' is a very common expression to ask the location of an inanimate object.

ex. A: *Tokee-wa doko-ni arimasu-ka.* (Where is the watch?)
B: *Koko-ni arimasu.* (It's here.)

あの　銀行(ぎんこう)の　そばに　あります。 **line 7**

Ano ginkoo-no soba-ni arimasu.

ginkoo	bank
... no soba-ni	near...; close to...

あそこに　男(おとこ)の人(ひと)が　いますね。 **line 8**

Asoko-ni otoko-no-hito-ga imasu-ne.

otoko-no-hito	man
...ga imasu	there is (are) ...

Otoko-no means 'male' while *onna-no* means 'female'; *hito* means a person. *Otoko-no-ko* (literally, 'male child') means 'boy,' and *onna-no-ko* means 'girl.'

Imasu is used to express the existence of animate entities while *arimasu* is used for inanimate things.

ex. *Asoko-ni onna-no-ko-ga imasu.* (There is a girl over there.)

エレベーター(えれべーたー)の　まえに　います。 **line 10**

Erebeetaa-no mae-ni imasu.

erebeetaa	elevator
...no mae-ni	in front of....

ああ、そうですね。 **line 11**

Aa, soo-desu-ne.

Ne here is used to show that the speaker agrees with what the other person has said. When used for this purpose, it is usually pronounced with a falling intonation. (See Note 2.)

あの人(ひと)は　だれですか。 **line 12**

Ano-hito-wa dare-desu-ka.

ano-hito	he; she
dare	who

Ano-hito, meaning 'that person' can be used for both males and females.

田中(たなか)さんです。 **line 13**

Tanaka-san-desu.

Tanaka-san	Mr. Tanaka

San is an honorific suffix used after a personal name, having the meaning that Mr., Mrs., Miss, and Ms. do in English. *San* differs, however, from English terms of respect in that it can be used after a fiirst name as well as a last name. A person named Yoshio Nakamura can be called Nakamura-*san* or Yoshio-*san.* Another difference is that it can never be used after one's own name. In English, one may call himself Mr. Johnson or Mrs. Johnson, but in Japanese one never calls oneself Tanaka-*san* or Yoshio-*san.*

女の人も　いますね。 **line 14**

Onna-no-hito-mo imasu-ne.

onna-no-hito woman

In this sentence *mo* replaces *-ga* to add the meaning 'too' or 'also.' (*Mo* replaces *-wa,* too. cf. Lesson 2)

ex. *Koko-ni tsukue-ga arimasu. Isu-mo arimasu.* (Here's a desk. Here's a chair, too.)

ええ。田中さんの　おくさんです。 **line 15**

Ee. Tanaka-san-no okusan-desu.

. . . no of . . .

okusan wife (polite)

Tanaka-san-no okusan literally means 'Mr. Tanaka's wife.' Remember that both a man named Tanaka and his wife can be called Tanaka-*san*, since *-san* does not distinguish between Mr., Mrs., and Miss. Here Mrs. Tanaka is called *Tanaka-san-no okusan* to indicate her relationship to Mr. Tanaka.

中村さんたちは　どこに　いますか。 **line 16**

Nakamura-san-tachi-wa doko-ni imasu-ka.

Nakamura-san-tachi Nakamura-san and the others; the Nakamuras

Tachi is a pluralizing suffix used with nouns indicating people. *Otoko-no-hito-tachi* means 'men' and *okusan-tachi* means 'wives.'

However, you should keep in mind that it is possible for a Japanese noun to be plural without the use of any suffix. Therefore, *otoko-no-hito* can either mean 'a man' or 'men,' and *okusan* can mean either 'wife' or 'wives,' depending on the context.

食堂(しょくどう)の　なかに　います。 **line 17**

Shokudoo-no naka-ni imasu.

shokudoo	dining hall ; restaurant
...no naka-ni	in...; inside...

食堂(しょくどう)は　どこですか。 **line 18**

Shokudoo-wa doko-desu-ka.

Desu can take the place of *...ni arimasu* or *...ni imasu.*

ex. A: *Ginkoo-wa doko-desu-ka.* (Where is the bank ?)
B: *Kissaten-no tonari-desu.* (It's next to the coffee shop.)

ロビーの　うえです。 **line 19**

Robii-no ue-desu.

robii	lobby
...no ue	above...; over...; on...

Ue-desu stands for *ue-ni arimasu,* just as *Doko-desu-ka* stands for *Doko-ni arimasu-ka.*

Note 1 *Kosoado* words

We have learned three sets of demonstrative words starting with *ko-, so-, a-,* and *do-.* These are sometimes called *kosoado* words.

ko-	*kore* (this one)	*kono* (this)	*koko* (here)
so-	*sore* (that one)	*sono* (that)	*soko* (there)
a-	*are* (that one over there)	*ano* (that over there)	*asoko* (over there)
do-	*dore* (which one, which ones)	*dono* (which of three or more)	*doko* (where)

There are a few other sets which will come up later in this book.

Note 2 Intonation of *-ne*

Ne varies in pitch in the same way that *-ka* can be pronounced either higher or lower than the main part of the sentence.

```
                              ne.
  soko-ni   to-ga  ma
A         hi     i   su

  soko-ni   to-ga  ma
A         hi     i   su
                              ne.
```

The height in pitch corresponds to the degree of eagerness with which the speaker seeks to solicit agreement. (The higher the pitch, the more excited the speaker.)

Drills

I. ... *ga arimasu*

Structure Drill Replace the cue word in the example with each word below.

ex. *kissaten*→*Asoko-ni kissaten-ga arimasu.*

1. *ginkoo* 2. *yuubinkyoku* 3. *shokudoo*
4. *shiroi tatemono* 5. *akai kaban* 6. *gakkoo* (school)

Usage Drill Practice the following conversation, substituting the underlined word.

ex. *hon* A: *Asoko-ni nani-ga arimasu-ka.*
B: *Hon-ga arimasu.*

1. *mado* 2. *akai kaban* 3. *tsukue*
4. *isu* 5. *yuubinkyoku* 6. *ginkoo*

II. ... *ga imasu*

Structure Drill Replace the cue word in the example with each word below.

ex. *otoko-no hito*→*Asoko-ni otoko-no-hito-ga imasu.*

1. *onna-no-hito* 2. *Tanaka-san* 3. *Nakamura-san*
4. *Tanaka-san-no okusan* 5. *gakusee* (student) 6. *otoko-no-hito*

Usage Drill 1 Practice the following conversation, substituting the underlined word.

ex. *otoko-no-hito* A: *Asoko-ni otoko-no-hito-ga imasu-ne.*
B: *Ee, soo-desu-ne.*
A: *Are-wa dare-desu-ka.*
B: *Tanaka-san-desu.*

1. *onna-no-hito* 2. *gakusee* 3. *otoko-no-hito*

Usage Drill 2 Practice Usage Drill 1 again, this time using names of people you know in place of *Tanaka-san.*

III. *. . . no*

Structure Drill Replace the cue word in the example with each word below.

ex. *hon→Tanaka-san-no hon-desu.*

1. *tokee* 2. *kasa* 3. *tsukue*
4. *enpitsu* 5. *okusan* 6. *goshujin* (husband)

Usage Drill A picks up things and asks B who they belong to.

ex. A: *Kore-wa dare-no hon-desu-ka.*

B: ...(real name)-*san-no hon-desu.*

IV. *Doko-ni arimasu (imasu)-ka*

Structure Drill Replace the cue word in the example with each word below.

A. ex. *tonari→Byooin-no tonari-ni arimasu.*

1. *soba* 2. *mae* 3. *naka* 4. *ue* 5. *ushiro* (back)

B. ex. *tonari→Tanaka-san-no tonari-ni imasu.*

1. *soba* 2. *mae* 3. *ushiro* 4. *yoko* (side)

Usage Drill 1 Practice the following conversation, substituting the underlined phrase with each phrase below.

ex. *ginkoo-no tonari*

A: *Sumimasen.*

B: *Hai. Nan-desu-ka.*

A: *Kissaten-wa doko-ni arimasu-ka.*

B: *Ano <u>ginkoo-no tonari</u>-ni arimasu.*

A: *Arigatoo-gozaimasu.*

B: *Doo-itashimashite.*

1. *byooin-no mae* 2. *gakkoo-no mae* 3. *yuubinkyoku-no soba*
4. *hoteru-no naka* 5. *shokudoo-no ue* 6. *ginkoo-no ushiro*

Usage Drill 2 Practice the following conversation, substituting the underlined word.

ex. *soba* A: *Asoko-ni onna-no-hito-ga imasu-ne.*
B: *Doko-ni imasu-ka.*
A: *Tanaka-san-no soba-ni imasu.*
B: *Aa, soo-desu-ne.*
A: *Ano-hito-wa dare-desu-ka.*
B: *Tanaka-san-no okusan-desu.*

1. *mae* 2. *ushiro* 3. *tonari* 4. *yoko*

V. *Nani-ga arimasu-ka*

Structure Drill Replace the phrase in the example with each phrase below.

ex. *mado-no soba→Mado-no soba-ni nani-ga arimasu-ka.*

1. *tsukue-no ue*
2. *Tanaka-san-no ushiro*
3. *isu-no soba*
4. *kaban-no naka*
5. *to* (door)*-no soba*
6. *tsukue-no shita* (under)

Usage Drill A asks B what object exists in different locations throughout the room.

ex. A: *Mado-no soba-ni nani-ga arimasu-ka.*
B: *Tsukue-ga arimasu.*

VI. *...no tonari-ni, ...no mae-ni*

Usage Drill A asks B the questions, looking at the picture. (Answers are given below.)

ex. A: *Ginkoo-wa doko-ni arimasu-ka.*
B: *Yuubinkyoku-no tonari-ni arimasu.*
or; *Byooin-no mae-ni arimasu.*

Questions:
1. *Gakkoo-wa doko-ni arimasu-ka.*
2. *Kissaten-wa doko-ni arimasu-ka.*
3. *Byooin-wa doko-ni arimasu-ka.*
4. *Shokudoo-wa doko-ni arimasu-ka.*
5. *Yuubinkyoku-wa doko-ni arimasu-ka.*

Byooin 病院	Shokudoo 食堂	Kissaten 喫茶店
Ginkoo 銀行	Yuubinkyoku 郵便局	Gakkoo 学校

(Answers—1. *Yuubinkyoku-no tonari-ni arimasu.* or: *Kissaten-no mae-ni arimasu.* 2. *Shokudoo-no tonari-ni arimasu.* or: *Gakkoo-no mae-ni arimasu.* 3. *Shokudoo-no tonari-ni arimasu.* or: *Ginkoo-no mae-ni arimasu.* 4. *Byooin* (or *Kissaten*)*-no tonari-ni arimasu.* or: *Yuubinkyoku-no mae-ni arimasu.* 5. *Ginkoo* (or *Gakkoo*)*-no tonari-ni arimasu.* or: *Shokudoo-no mae-ni arimasu.*)

VII. *...no soba-ni, ...no ue-ni, ...no naka-ni*

Usage Drill A asks B the questions, looking at the picture. (Answers are given below.)

Questions (a) 1. *Tsukue-wa doko-ni arimasu-ka.*

2. *Isu-wa doko-ni arimasu-ka.*

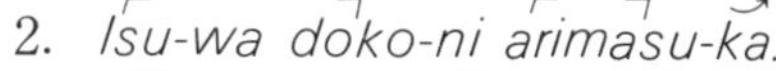

3. *Enpitsu-wa doko-ni arimasu-ka.*

4. *Hon-wa doko-ni arimasu-ka.*

(b) 1. *Kaban-no naka-ni nani*(what)*-ga arimasu ka.*

2. *Mado-no soba-ni nani-ga arimasu-ka.*

3. *Isu-no ue-ni nani-ga arimasu-ka.*

(Answers—(a) 1. *Mado-no soba-ni arimasu.* 2. *Tsukue-no soba-ni arimasu.* 3. *Tsukue-no ue-ni arimasu.* 4. *Kaban-no naka-ni arimasu.* (b) 1. *Hon-ga arimasu.* 2. *Tsukue-ga arimasu.* 3. *Kaban-ga arimasu.*)

Pronunciation Practice

Practice saying the following, paying careful attention to the accent.

A. 1. *a -i -a -u* 2. *o -i -i -e* 3. *e -i -u -o*
4. *ra -i -ra -u* 5. *ro -i -ri -e* 6. *re -i -ru -o*
7. *sa -i -sa -u* 8. *so -i -shi -e* 9. *se -i -su -o*
10. *za -i -za -u* 11. *zo -i -ji -e* 12. *ze -i -zu -o*

B. 1. *tatemono* 2. *toshokan* (library)
3. *goshujin* 4. *Yamakawa* (personal name)
5. *Kurokawa* (personal name) 6. *Akasaka* (place name)
7. *Aoyama* (place name) 8. *Nagasaki* (place name)

C. Add *-desu-ne* to the words in B and practice saying the sentences with a rising and then a falling intonation.

ex. *Tatemono-desu-ne.*↗
Tatemono-desu-ne.↘

Reading Comprehension

Read the following passage.

銀行(ぎんこう)のまえにしろいたてものがあります。病院(びょういん)です。病院(びょういん)のとなりは喫茶店(きっさてん)です。

喫茶店(きっさてん)のなかに人(ひと)がたくさん(1)います。田中(たなか)さんもいます。田中(たなか)さんのおくさんもいます。田中(たなか)さんたちのそばにあかいテーブル(てーぶる)(2)があります。テーブル(てーぶる)のうえにコーヒー(こーひー)(3)があります。

(1) many (2) table (3) coffee

Aural Comprehension

Listen to the conversations on the tape and answer the following questions.

(A) 1. What is the woman looking for?
2. Where is it located?

(B) 1. Where is the man in question standing?
2. Who is he?

(C) 1. What is the man looking for?
2. Where is it located?
3. What color is the post office?

Japanese Currency

Paper money

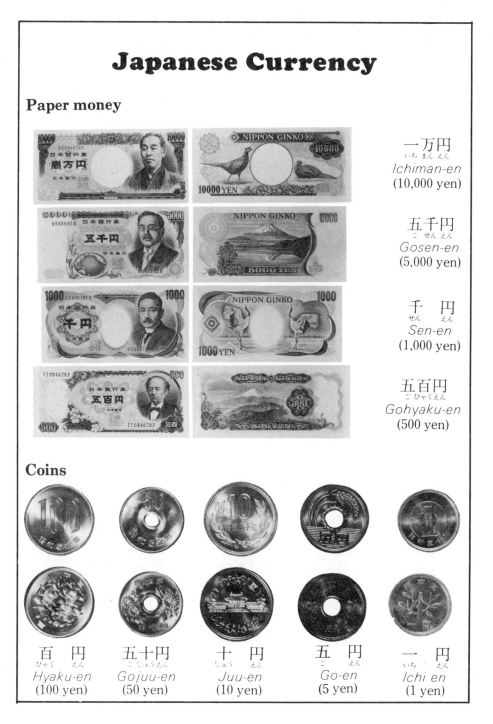

一万円
いちまんえん
Ichiman-en
(10,000 yen)

五千円
ごせんえん
Gosen-en
(5,000 yen)

千　円
せん　えん
Sen-en
(1,000 yen)

五百円
ごひゃくえん
Gohyaku-en
(500 yen)

Coins

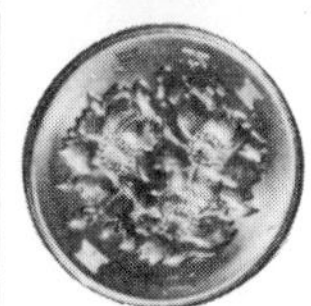

百　円
ひゃく　えん
Hyaku-en
(100 yen)

五十円
ごじゅうえん
Gojuu-en
(50 yen)

十　円
じゅう　えん
Juu-en
(10 yen)

五　円
ご　えん
Go-en
(5 yen)

一　円
いち　えん
Ichi en
(1 yen)

第四課(だいよんか)　何時(なんじ)に　おきますか

Dialogue

(Yamashita and Suzuki, two acquaintances, meet on the street and talk while walking to the station.)

山下(やました)：　おはようございます。

鈴木(すずき)：　おはようございます。きょうは　いい　天気(てんき)ですね。

山下(やました)：　そうですね。

鈴木(すずき)：　山下(やました)さんは　あさ　何時(なんじ)に　おきますか。

山下(やました)：　七時(しちじ)に　おきます。

鈴木(すずき)：　はやいですね。わたしは　八時(はちじ)ごろ　おきます。よるは　何時(なんじ)ごろ　ねますか。

山下(やました)：　十一時(じゅういちじ)ごろ　ねます。

鈴木(すずき)：　会社(かいしゃ)は　何時(なんじ)に　はじまりますか。

山下(やました)：　九時(くじ)に　はじまります。

鈴木(すずき)：　何時(なんじ)ごろ　おわりますか。

山下(やました)：　六時(ろくじ)ごろです。

鈴木(すずき)：　その　あと　すぐ　うちへ　かえりますか。

山下(やました)：　いいえ。たいてい　喫茶店(きっさてん)で　コーヒー(こーひー)を　のみます。ときどき　映画(えいが)を　みます。

鈴木(すずき)：　今晩(こんばん)は　なにを　しますか。

山下(やました)：　まだ　わかりません。

鈴木(すずき)：　毎日(まいにち)　会社(かいしゃ)へ　いきますか。

山下(やました)：　ええ。

鈴木(すずき)：　土曜日(どようび)にも　いきますか。

山下(やました)：　いいえ、いきません。土曜日(どようび)は　やすみです。
鈴木(すずき)：　あ、もう　駅(えき)ですね。　ここで　失礼(しつれい)します。
山下(やました)：　さようなら。

Dialogue

Lesson 4

WHAT TIME DO YOU GET UP?

Yamashita: Good morning.
Suzuki: Good morning. Today's a fine day, isn't it?
Y: Yes, isn't it?
S: What time do you get up in the morning, Mr. Yamashita?
Y: At seven.
S: That's early. I get up around eight. What time do you go to bed?
Y: About eleven.

S: What time does your office start?
Y: At nine.
S: What time does it close?
Y: About six.
S: Do you go home immediately after that?
Y: No. I usually have a cup of coffee at a coffee shop. Sometimes I go to the movies.
S: What will you do this evening?
Y: I don't know yet.

S: Do you go to the office every day?
Y: Yes, I do.

Dai-yonka

NANJI-NI OKIMASU-KA

Yamashita: Ohayoo-gozaimasu.
Suzuki: Ohayoo-gozaimasu. Kyoo-wa ii tenki-desu-ne.
Y: Soo-desu-ne.
S: Yamashita-san-wa asa nanji-ni okimasu-ka.
Y: Shichiji-ni okimasu.
S: Hayai-desu-ne. Watashi-wa hachiji-goro okimasu. Yoru-wa nanji-goro nemasu-ka.
Y: Juuichiji-goro nemasu.

S: Kaisha-wa nanji-ni hajimari-masu-ka.
Y: Kuji-ni hajimarimasu.
S: Nanji-goro owarimasu-ka.
Y: Rokuji-goro-desu.
S: Sono ato sugu uchi-e kaeri-masu-ka.
Y: Iie. Taitee kissaten-de koohii-o nomimasu. Tokidoki eega-o mimasu.
S: Konban-wa nani-o shimasu-ka.
Y: Mada wakarimasen.

S: Mainichi kaisha-e ikimasu-ka.
Y: Ee.

S: On Saturdays, too?
Y: No. Saturdays are holidays.

S: Oh, we're at the station now. Please excuse me.
Y: Good-bye.

S: Doyoobi-nimo ikimasu-ka.
Y: Iie, ikimasen. Doyoobi-wa yasumi-desu.

S: A, moo eki-desu-ne. Koko-de shitsuree-shimasu.
Y: Sayoonara.

Explanation

(In this lesson you will learn several verbs, objects of verbs, particles indicating time and place, and the names of the days of the week.)

おはようございます。 **line 1**

Ohayoo-gozaimasu.

Ohayoo-gozaimasu. Good morning.

Memorize the following greetings.

Konnichiwa. Good afternoon; Good day; Hello

Konbanwa. Good evening.

Oyasumi-nasai. Good night.

きょうは いい 天気(てんき)ですね。 **line 2**

Kyoo-wa ii tenki-desu-ne.

kyoo today

ii good; fine

tenki weather

Ii (o)tenki-desu-ne is a very common form of greeting. When the weather is bad, one says, *Iyana (o-)tenki-desu-ne.* (*o-* is a polite prefix)

山下(やました)さんは あさ 何時(なんじ)に おきますか。 **line 3**

Yamashita-san-wa asa nanji-ni okimasu-ka.

asa morning

nanji-ni at what time

okimasu-ka do you get up? (dictionary form *okiru*)

Personal pronouns are used far less often in Japanese than in European languages. When addressing someone, it is more common to use his first or last name where you would use the second person pronoun 'you' in English.

To find the verb *okimasu* in the dictionary you must look it up under its dictionary form *okiru*. *Masu* is called a "formal affirmative ending" and verbs in this form are more polite than verbs in the dictionary form. *Okimasu* can mean 'I get up,' 'you get up,' 'he gets up,' etc. as can *okiru*.

Ni indicates the time of action, and corresponds to the English prepositions 'at,' 'in,' 'on,' etc.

ex. *gogo-ni*	(in the afternoon)
doyoobi-ni	(on Saturday)

七時(しちじ)に　おきます。 **line 5**

Shichiji-ni okimasu.

Watashi-wa is left out, but is understood.

はやいですね。わたしは　八時(はちじ)ごろ　おきます。 **line 6**

Hayai-desu-ne. Watashi-wa hachiji-goro okimasu.

hayai	early
watashi	I
hachiji-goro	about eight o'clook

Before *hayai-desu-ne, Anata* (you)*-wa*, or *Yamashita-san-wa* is left out because it is understood. However, *Watashi-wa* is mentioned in the second sentence to make the meaning clear.

Goro is used to show approximate time.

ex. *gogo goji-goro*	(about five in the afternoon)
doyoobi-goro	(around Saturday)

よるは　何時(なんじ)ごろ　ねますか。 **lines 6-7**

Yoru-wa nanji-goro nemasu-ka.

nemasu	you go to bed (dict. *neru*)

会社(かいしゃ)は　何時(なんじ)に　はじまりますか。 **line 9**

Kaisha-wa nanji-ni hajimarimasu-ka.

kaisha	company ; here, your company
hajimarimasu	it starts (dict. *hajimaru*)

何時ごろ　おわりますか。 **line 11**

Nanji-goro owarimasu-ka.

owarimasu	it closes (dict. *owaru*)

その　あと　すぐ　うちへ　かえりますか。 **line 13**

Sono ato sugu uchi-e kaerimasu-ka.

sono ato	after that
sugu	immediately ; soon
uchi	(your) home
uchi-e	to your home
kaerimasu	you return (dict. *kaeru*)

E is a particle indicating direction.

ex. *Ginkoo-e ikimasu.* (I go to the bank.)
Doko-e ikimasu-ka. (Where are you going?)

いいえ。たいてい　喫茶店で　コーヒーを　のみます。 **line 14**

Iie. Taitee kissaten-de koohii-o nomimasu.

taitee	usually ; generally
kissaten-de	at a coffee shop
koohii	coffee
. . . o nomimasu	I drink. . . (dict. *nomu*)

O is a particle which indicates that the noun preceding it is the direct object of the verb following it.

ex. *Hon-o yomimasu.* (I read a book.)

De is used to indicate the place where an action is performed.

ex. *Uchi-de shinbun-o yomimasu.* (I read a newspaper at home.)
Kaisha-de shigoto-o shimasu. (I work at the office.)

ときどき　映画を　みます。 **line 15**

Tokidoki eega-o mimasu.

tokidoki	sometimes
eega	movies
. . . o mimasu	I see . . . ; I watch . . . (dict. *miru*)

今晩(こんばん)は　なにを　しますか。 **line 16**

Konban-wa nani-o shimasu-ka.

konban	this evening; tonight
nani	what
. . . o shimasu	you do . . . (dict. *suru*)

The *-masu* form can be used for future as well as present tense.

ex. *Ashita ginkoo-e ikimasu.* (I'll go to the bank tomorrow.)

まだ　わかりません。 **line 17**

Mada wakarimasen.

mada	(not) yet; still
wakarimasen	I don't know; I don't understand (dict. *wakaru*)

The ending *-masen* is the negative equivalent of the *-masu* form. (See Note 1.)

ex. *Kyoo-wa kaisha-e ikimasen.* (I won't go to the office today.)

毎日(まいにち)　会社(かいしゃ)へ　いきますか。 **line 18**

Mainichi kaisha-e ikimasu-ka.

mainichi	every day
ikimasu	you go (dict. *iku*)

土曜日(どようび)にも　いきますか。 **line 20**

Doyoobi-nimo ikimasu-ka.

doyoobi	Saturday
doyoobi-nimo	on Saturday, too

Mo is added after the particles *-ni, -e,* and *-de.* (See Note 2.) See Note 3 for the names of the days of the week.

いいえ、いきません。土曜日(どようび)は　やすみです。 **line 21**

Iie, ikimasen. Doyoobi-wa yasumi-desu.

ikimasen	I do not go (dict. *iku*)
yasumi	holiday

あ、もう　駅(えき)ですね。ここで　失礼(しつれい)します。 **line 22**

A, moo eki-desu-ne. Koko-de shitsuree-shimasu.

a. . . .	oh, . . .
moo	already

eki station

shitsuree-shimasu excuse me

Shitsuree-shimasu, which literally means 'I'm going to be rude,' is a polite expression used to excuse oneself. It is sometimes used, as in this sentence, as a polite way to say 'Good-bye.'

さようなら。 **line 23**

Sayoonara.

Sayoonara. Good-bye.

Note 1 *-masu, -masen*

For purposes of conjugation, all Japanese verbs can be divided into two groups, with only two exceptions, *suru* and *kuru.*

Group 1 Verbs (*-u* verbs)

Verbs in Group 1 end with *-u* in their dictionary form. The *-masu* form of these verbs is formed by replacing the final *-u* with *-imasu.*

iku (to go) *ikimasu*

nomu (to drink) *nomimasu*

hajimaru (to start) *hajimarimasu*

owaru (to end) *owarimasu*

wakaru (to understand) *wakarimasu*

Group 2 Verbs (*-ru* verbs)

Verbs in this group end in *-ru,* preceded by *-e,* or *-i* in their dictionary form. The *-masu* form of these verbs is formed by replacing the final *-ru* with *-masu.*

okiru (to get up) *okimasu*

neru (to go to bed) *nemasu*

miru (to see) *mimasu*

The verb *kaeru* (to go home) is one of the few exceptions: it ends with *-eru* but belongs to Group 1.

The two irregular verbs are:

suru (to do) *shimasu*

kuru (to come) *kimasu*

Note 2 Particles *-e, -ni, -de* **and** *-mo*

Mo is added after *-e, -ni,* and *-de.*

ex. *Kyoo-wa kaisha-**e** ikimasu. Ginkoo-**emo** ikimasu.* (I will go to the office today. I will go to the bank, too.)

*Mainichi juuji-**ni** koohii-o nomimasu. Sanji-**nimo** nomimasu.* (I drink coffee at ten every day. I drink it at three, too.)

*Uchi-**de** terebi-o mimasu. Kaisha-**demo** mimasu.* (I watch TV at home. I watch it at the office, too.)

Mo is not added after *-wa* (Lesson 2), *-ga* (Lesson 3), or *-o* (Lesson 5).

Note 3 The names of **the days of the week** are as follows: (*-bi* at the end of each word is optional.)

日曜日	*nichiyoobi*	Sunday
月曜日	*getsuyoobi*	Monday
火曜日	*kayoobi*	Tuesday
水曜日	*suiyoobi*	Wednesday
木曜日	*mokuyoobi*	Thursday
金曜日	*kin'yoobi*	Friday
土曜日	*doyoobi*	Saturday

Drills

I. *-masu, -masen*

Structure Drill Answer the following questions first in the affirmative and then in the negative form.

ex. *Okimasu-ka.* → *Hai, okimasu.*
→ *Iie, okimasen.*

1. *Nemasu-ka.*
2. *Ikimasu-ka.*
3. *Kaerimasu-ka.*
4. *Owarimasu-ka.*
5. *Nomimasu-ka.*
6. *Shimasu-ka.*
7. *Mimasu-ka.*
8. *Hajimarimasu-ka.*

II. Particles *-ni, -e, -o, -de*

Structure Drill

(-ni) A. Complete the following expressions by adding *hajimarimasu.*

ex. *shichiji-ni* →*Shichiji-ni hajimarimasu.*

1. *hachiji-ni* 2. *kuji-ni* 3. *doyoobi-ni*
4. *rokuji-ni* 5. *ichiji-ni* 6. *nichiyoobi-ni*

B. This time complete the expressions by adding *owarimasu.*

ex. *shichiji-ni* →*Shichiji-ni owarimasu.*

1. *rokuji-ni* 2. *getsuyoobi-ni* 3. *sanji-ni*
4. *kayoobi-ni* 5. *gogo goji-ni* 6. *gozen juuji-ni*

(-e) Add *ikimasu.*

ex. *kaisha-e* →*Kaisha-e ikimasu.*

1. *ginkoo-e* 2. *byooin-e* 3. *yuubinkyoku-e*
4. *kissaten-e* 5. *eki-e* 6. *gakkoo* (school) *-e*

(-o) Put *-o* between the given words.

ex. *koohii, nomimasu* →*Koohii-o nomimasu.*

1. *eega, mimasu* 2. *terebi* (TV), *mimasu*
3. *hon, yomimasu* (I read) 4. *mizu* (water), *nomimasu*
5. *shigoto* (work), *shimasu*

(-de) Put *uchi-de* in front of each given expression.

ex. *koohii-o nomimasu* →*Uchi-de koohii-o nomimasu.*

1. *terebi-o mimasu* 2. *hon-o yomimasu*
3. *ocha* (tea) *-o nomimasu* 4. *shigoto-o shimasu*

III. *Taitee . . . masu*

Structure Drill Practice making sentences. You can make any variety of sentences by combining the words shown in braces below.

ex. *Taitee shichiji-ni okimasu.*
Taitee hachiji-ni kaerimasu. etc.

Say them aloud.

A)

Taitee	*shichiji-ni*	*okimasu.*
Mainichi	*hachiji-ni*	*kaerimasu.*
Kyoo-wa	*kuji-ni*	*nemasu.*
Konban-wa	*juuji-ni*	*koohii-o nomimasu.*

B) {*Watashi-wa* / *Yamashita san-wa* / *Ano-hito wa* / *Watashi-tachi* (We) *-wa* / *Yamashita-san-no okusan-wa*} {*uchi-de* / *kaisha-de* / *gakkoo-de* / *koko-de* / *kissaten-de*} {*koohii-o nomimasu.* / *shigoto-o shimasu.* / *terebi-o mimasu.* / *hon-o yomimasu.*}

IV. *-masu, -masen ; -ni, -e, -o, -de*

Usage Drill Practice the following conversations, substituting the underlined part with the cue words given below.

A) ex. *kaisha*

A: *Mainichi kaisha-e ikimasu-ka.*
B: *Ee, ikimasu.*
A: *Doyoobi-nimo ikimasu-ka.*
B: *Iie, ikimasen. Doyoobi-wa yasumi-desu.*

1. *gakkoo* 2. *ginkoo* 3. *byooin* 4. *toshokan* (library)

B) ex. *terebi-o mimasu*

A: *Nanji-goro uchi-e kaerimasu-ka.*
B: *Hachiji-goro kaerimasu.*
A: *Yoru-wa nani-o shimasu-ka.*
B: *Taitee terebi-o mimasu.*

1. *koohii-o nomimasu* 2. *sugu nemasu*
3. *shigoto-o shimasu* 4. *hon-o yomimasu*
5. *benkyoo* (study) *-o shimasu*

C) ex. *getsuyoobi*

A: *Toshokan-e ikimasu-ka.*
B: *Ee, tokidoki ikimasu.*
A: *Doyoobi-ni ikimasu ka.*
B: *Iie, ikimasen. Taitee getsuyoobi-ni ikimasu.*

1. *kayoobi* 2. *suiyoobi* 3. *mokuyoobi*
4. *kin'yoobi* 5. *nichiyoobi*

D) Carry out the following conversation using the names of you and your instructor (or fellow student) and the actual times you go to sleep and get up.

A: *... san-wa nanji-ni okimasu-ka.*
B: *... ji-ni okimasu.*
A: *Hayai-desu-ne.** *Watashi-wa ... ji-ni okimasu. Yoru-wa nanji-goro nemasu-ka.*
B: *... ji-goro nemasu.*

(* If A feels B gets up late, he says *Osoi-desu-ne.*)

Pronunciation Practice

Practice saying the following, paying careful attention to the accent.

A.

1. *a -i -a -u*	2. *o -i -i -e*	3. *e -i -u -o*
4. *ka -i -ka -u*	5. *ko -i -ki -e*	6. *ke -i -ku -o*
7. *ga -i -ga -u*	8. *go -i -gi -e*	9. *ge -i -gu -o*
10. *ha -i -ha -u*	11. *ho -i -hi -e*	12. *he -i -fu -o*

B.

1. *doyoobi*
2. *kayoobi*
3. *toshokan*
4. *otenki*
5. *Yamashita*
6. *Mizutani* (personal name)
7. *Shimazaki* (personal name)
8. *Harajuku* (place name)

C. Add *-desu-ne* to the words in B and say the sentences first with a rising and then a falling intonation.

ex. *Doyoobi-desu-ne.* ↗
Doyoobi-desu-ne. ↘

Reading Comprehension

Read the following passage.

わたしは毎日八時に学校へいきます。学校は八時半にはじまります。三時ごろおわります。そのあとたいていすぐうちへかえります。ときどき図書館へいきます。

よるはうちで勉強をします。すこし(1)テレビをみます。土曜日には勉強*しません。たいてい雑誌(2)をよみます。

(1) a little (2) magazine

*Here, *-o* after *benkyoo* is left out. Some nouns can be used without *-o* when followed by *shimasu* (dict. *suru*).

Aural Comprehension

Listen to the conversations on the tape and answer the following questions.

(A) 1. What time of the day is it?
2. What time does Mr. Yoshida go to bed?
3. What does he do at night?

(B) 1. Where is the woman going?
2. What time is it?

(C) 1. What day of the week is it?
2. What are the man and woman going to do tomorrow?
3. When and where will they meet?

第五課（だいごか）　なにを　しましたか

Dialogue

(Two acquaintances talking on a Monday morning)

吉田（よしだ）：　きのうは　よく　ふりましたねえ。

佐藤（さとう）：　そうですね。一日（いちにち）じゅう　ふりましたねえ。

吉田（よしだ）：　どこかへ　でかけましたか。

佐藤（さとう）：　いいえ、どこへも　いきませんでした。吉田（よしだ）さんは　でかけましたか。

吉田（よしだ）：　いいえ、うちで　本（ほん）を　よみました。

佐藤（さとう）：　どんな　本（ほん）ですか。

吉田（よしだ）：　小説（しょうせつ）です。夏目漱石（なつめそうせき）の「こころ」です。

佐藤（さとう）：　ああ、あれは　いいですね。わたしは　高校（こうこう）の　とき　よみました。

吉田（よしだ）：　そうですか。

佐藤（さとう）：　高校（こうこう）の　ときは　よく　小説（しょうせつ）を　よみました。一週間（いっしゅうかん）に　五（ご）さつぐらい　よみました。

吉田（よしだ）：　映画（えいが）も　みましたか。

佐藤（さとう）：　ええ、よく　みました。三日（みっか）に　一度（いちど）ぐらい　みました。

吉田（よしだ）：　スポーツ（すぽーつ）は　やりませんでしたか。

佐藤（さとう）：　しましたよ。野球（やきゅう）と　水泳（すいえい）を　しました。

吉田（よしだ）：　いろいろな　ことを　しましたね。

佐藤（さとう）：　ええ。でも　勉強（べんきょう）は　あまり　しませんでした。

Dialogue

Lesson 5 **WHAT DID YOU DO?**	*Dai-goka* ***NANI-O SHIMASHITA-KA***
Yoshida: It rained a lot yesterday, didn't it?	*Yoshida: Kinoo-wa yoku furimashita-nee.*
Sato: Yes, didn't it? It rained the whole day.	*Sato: Soo-desu-ne. Ichinichi-juu furimashita-nee.*
Y: Did you go out?	*Y: Dokoka-e dekakemashita-ka.*
S: No, I didn't. Did you, Mr. Yoshida?	*S: Iie, doko-emo ikimasen-deshita. Yoshida-san-wa dekakemashita-ka.*
Y: No, I read a book at home.	*Y: Iie, uchi-de hon-o yomimashita.*
S: What type of book did you read?	*S: Donna hon-desu-ka.*
Y: A novel, *Kokoro,* by Soseki Natsume.	*Y: Shoosetsu-desu. Natsume Sooseki-no 'Kokoro' -desu.*
S: Oh, that's a good book. I read it when I was in high school.	*S: Aa, are-wa ii-desu-ne. Watashi-wa kookoo-no toki yomimashita.*
Y: Did you?	*Y: Soo-desu-ka.*
S: I used to read many novels when I was in high school. I read about five a week.	*S: Kookoo-no toki-wa yoku shoosetsu-o yomimashita. Isshuukan-ni gosatsu-gurai yomimashita.*
Y: Did you watch movies, too?	*Y: Eega-mo mimashita-ka.*
S: Yes, very often. I watched them about once every three days.	*S: Ee, yoku mimashita. Mikka-ni ichido-gurai mimashita.*
Y: Didn't you do any sports?	*Y: Supootsu-wa yarimasen-deshita-ka.*
S: Yes, I did. I played baseball and swam.	*S: Shimashita-yo. Yakyuu-to suiee-o shimashita.*
Y: You were quite active, weren't you?	*Y: Iroirona koto-o shimashita-ne.*

S: Well, yes, but I didn't do much studying.

S: Ee. Demo benkyoo-wa amari shimasen-deshita.

Explanation

(In this lesson you will learn *-mashita*, the past form of *-masu*. You will also learn how to count books and how to say the days of the month.)

きのうは　よく　ふりましたねえ。 **line 1**

Kinoo-wa yoku furimashita-nee.

kinoo	yesterday
yoku	a lot
furimashita	it rained(dict. *furu*)
. . . . nee	didn't it?; isn't it true?

Furimashita describes what happened in the past while *furimasu* refers to what happens in the present or what will happen in the future.

Actually *furu* means 'to fall,' and *furimashita* can mean 'it snowed' as well as 'it rained.'

Nee at the end of a sentence, pronounced with a falling intonation, expresses a strong feeling.

ex. *Takai-desu-nee.* (How expensive!)

一日(いちにち)じゅう　ふりましたねえ。 **line 2**

Ichinichi-juu furimashita-nee.

ichinichi-juu	all day long

Ichinichi means 'one day.' *Juu* is added to nouns referring to time or place to form compounds meaning 'all through (something).' For example, *ichinen-juu* means 'all the year round,' and *sekai-juu* means 'all over the world.'

どこかへ　でかけましたか。 **line 3**

Dokoka-e dekakemashita-ka.

dokoka-e	to some place; somewhere; anywhere
dekakemashita-ka	did you go out? (dict. *dekakeru*)

Notice how the meaning changes when *-ka* is added to the following interrogative nouns.

nani (what) *nani**ka*** (something, anything)
doko (where) *doko**ka*** (somewhere, anywhere)
dare (who) *dare**ka*** (someone, anyone)

Note that particles *-ga* and *-o* are usually omitted after words consisting of an interrogative noun plus *-ka.*

ex. *Dareka kimashita-ka.* (Did anyone come?) (*-ga* omitted)
Nanika nomimashita-ka. (Did you drink anything?) (*-o* omitted)
Asoko-ni dareka imasu-ne. (There's someone over there.) (*-ga* omitted.)

いいえ、どこへも　いきませんでした。 **line 4**

lie, doko-emo ikimasen-deshita.

doko-emo (not) to any place
ikimasen-deshita (I) did not go (dict. *iku*)

The interrogative nouns *doko, dare,* and *nani* used with *-mo* and the negative form of a verb mean 'not any.' *Doko-emo ikimasen* means 'I do not go anywhere.'

Deshita is added to *-masen* and changes the verb into the past tense. The negative of *furimashita* is *furimasen-deshita.*

ex. *Kinoo-wa ichinichi-juu nani-mo shimasen-deshita.* (I didn't do anything all day yesterday.)

いいえ、うちで　本(ほん)を　よみました。 **line 6**

lie, uchi-de hon-o yomimashita.

hon book
yomimashita I read (past) (dict. *yomu*)

どんな　本(ほん)ですか。 **line 7**

Donna hon-desu-ka.

donna what kind of

The *-nna* ending is added to *ko, so* and *a,* as well as *do.*

ex. A: *Yoku furimasu-ne.* (It really rains a lot.)
B: *Ee, konna hi-wa iya-desu-ne.* (Yes. This kind of day is awful, isn't it?)

小説です。夏目漱石の　「こころ」です。 **line 8**

Shoosetsu-desu. Natsume Sooseki-no `Kokoro'-desu.

shoosetsu	novel
Natsume Sooseki	name of a famous novelist (1867-1916)
. . . no	written by . . .

ああ、あれは　いいですね。　わたしは　高校の　とき　よみました。 **lines 9-10**

Aa, are-wa ii-desu-ne. Watashi-wa kookoo-no toki yomimashita.

kookoo	high school
. . . no toki	at the time of . . .

Notice that *are* is used instead of *sore.* When both the listener and the speaker share the knowledge of the subject matter, it is referred to as *are,* while it is referred to as *sore* when the listener is hearing about it for the first time.

ex. A: *Natsume Sooseki-no `Kokoro'-o yomimashita.* (I read ***Kokoro*** by Natsume Soseki.)

B: *Sore-wa donna shoosetsu-desu-ka.* (What kind of novel is it?)

一週間に　五さつぐらい　よみました。 **line 13**

Isshuukan-ni gosatsu-gurai yomimashita.

isshuukan	a week
isshuukan-ni	in a week
gosatsu-gurai	about five volumes; about five books

Ni in *isshuukan-ni* indicates the span of time.

ex. *Ichinichi-ni rokujikan benkyoo-shimasu.* (I study six hours a day.)

Satsu is the counter for books, magazines, notebooks and other units of bound objects. Articles in this category are counted in the following way:

1 --*issatsu*	2 --*nisatsu*	3 --*sansatsu*
4 --*yonsatsu*	5 --*gosatsu*	6 --*rokusatsu*
7 --*nanasatsu*	8 --*hassatsu*	9 --*kyuusatsu*

10 --*jissatsu*. . . . . Above ten, they are counted using the same set of numbers we learned for giving prices.

Gurai denotes approximate extent.

ex. *Kono tokee-wa hassen-en-gurai-deshita.* (This watch was about 8,000 yen.)

映画(えいが)も　みましたか。 **line 14**

Eega-mo mimashita-ka.

mimashita-ka — did you see? (dict. *miru*)

Mimashita or *mimasu* (dictionary form *miru*) usually follows a noun plus *-o*, as in *Tokidoki eega-o mimasu* (Lesson 4). Here *-o* is replaced by *-mo*. (*Mo* replaces *-wa* and *-ga*, too. See Lessons 2 and 3.)

ex. *Shinbun-o yomimashita. Zasshi-mo yomimashita.* (I read a newspaper. I read a magazine, too.)

三日(みっか)に　一度(いちど)ぐらい　みました。 **lines 15-16**

Mikka-ni ichido-gurai mimashita.

mikka — three days

ichido — once

Once you have learned how to tell the day of the month in Japanese, you will also know how to describe any given span of days. For example, *mikka* means ‘the third’ and can also mean ‘three days.’ The single exception to this is *tsuitachi* which can only be used to mean ‘the first (day) of the month.’ (See Drill VI.)

Do is the counter for number of times something occurs or something is done. It is added to the same set of numbers you learned for giving prices.

1 --*ichido*; 2 --*nido*; 3 --*sando*; 4 --*yodo*; 5 --*godo*; etc.

スポーツ(すぽーつ)は　やりませんでしたか。 **line 17**

Supootsu-wa yarimasen-deshita-ka.

supootsu — sports

yarimasen-deshita-ka — didn’t you do? (dict. *yaru*)

Yaru is similar to *suru* in meaning, but somewhat more colloquial.

しましたよ。野球(やきゅう)と　水泳(すいえい)を　しました。 **line 18**

Shimashita-yo. Yakyuu-to suiee-o shimashita.

yakyuu — baseball

. . . to . . . — . . . and . . .

suiee — swimming

Yo at the end of a sentence emphasizes the speaker's assertion. *Shimashita-yo* means 'Oh, yes, I did!' or 'I surely did.'

The particle *-to* is used only between nouns or pronouns.

いろいろな　ことを　しましたね。 **line 19**

Iroirona koto-o shimashita-ne.

iroirona	various
iroirona koto	various activities (*lit.* various things)

ええ。でも　勉強(べんきょう)は　あまり　しませんでした。 **line 20**

Ee. Demo benkyoo-wa amari shimasen-deshita.

demo	but
benkyoo	studying
amari	(not) much

Shimasu (dict. *suru*) usually follows a noun plus *-o*, as in *benkyoo-o shimasu*. Here, *-wa* is used instead of *-o* to emphasize the contrast between studying and the other activities Sato was engaged in.

Drills

I. *-mashita, -masen-deshita*

Structure Drill 1 Memorize the following table by practicing aloud.

furu (to rain)

furimasu *furimashita* *furimasen* *furimasen-deshita*

aru (to be)

arimasu *arimashita* *arimasen* *arimasen-deshita*

iku (to go)

ikimasu *ikimashita* *ikimasen* *ikimasen-deshita*

yomu (to read)

yomimasu *yomimashita* *yomimasen* *yomimasen-deshita*

kaeru (to go back)

kaerimasu *kaerimashita* *kaerimasen* *kaerimasen-deshita*

miru (to see)

mimasu *mimashita* *mimasen* *mimasen-deshita*

dekakeru (to go out)

dekakemasu *dekakemashita* *dekakemasen* *dekakemasen-deshita iru* (to be)

imasu *imashita* *imasen* *imasen-deshita*

suru (to do)

shimasu *shimashita* *shimasen* *shimasen-deshita*

kuru (to come)

kimasu *kimashita* *kimasen* *kimasen-deshita*

Structure Drill 2 Answer the following questions as shown in the example.

ex. *Kinoo-wa uchi-ni imashita-ka.* →*Hai, imashita.*
→*Iie, imasen-deshita.*

1. *Kinoo-wa eega-o mimashita-ka.*
2. *Kinoo-wa toshokan-e ikimashita-ka.*
3. *Tsukue-no ue-ni kaban-ga arimashita-ka.*
4. *Kookoo-no toki yoku benkyoo-o shimashita-ka.*
5. *Kinoo-wa sugu kaerimashita-ka.*
6. *Asa Suzuki-san-ga kimashita-ka.*
7. *Kinoo-no asa shinbun* (newspaper) *-o yomimashita-ka.*
8. *Kookoo-no toki iroirona supootsu-o yarimashita-ka.*

Usage Drill Practice the following conversation, changing the underlined words.

ex. *shoosetsu-o yomimasu*

A: *Kyoo-wa nani-o shimasu-ka.*
B: <u>*Shoosetsu-o yomimasu.*</u>
A: *Kinoo-wa nani-o shimashita-ka.*
B: *Kinoo-mo* <u>*shoosetsu-o yomimashita.*</u>

1. *eega-o mimasu*
2. *benkyoo-o shimasu*
3. *kaisha-e ikimasu*
4. *supootsu-o yarimasu*
5. *toshokan-e ikimasu*

II. *-o* replaced by *-wa* and *-mo*

Structure Drill Answer the following questions as shown in the example.

ex. *Eega-o mimashita-ka.* →*Ee, eega-mo mimashita.*
→*Iie, eega-wa mimasen-deshita.*

1. *Hon-o yomimashita-ka.* 2. *Benkyoo-o shimashita-ka.*
3. *Koohii-o nomimashita-ka.* 4. *Yakyuu-o shimashita-ka.*
5. *Terebi-o mimashita-ka.*

Usage Drill Practice the following conversation, changing the underlined words.

ex. *mimashita, terebi, eega*

A: *Nanika mimashita-ka.*
B: *Ee, terebi-o mimashita.*
A: *Eega-mo mimashita-ka.*
B: *Eega-wa mimasen-deshita.*

1. *yomimashita, shinbun, hon* 2. *shimashita, supootsu, benkyoo*
3. *nomimashita, koohii, ocha* 4. *shimashita, suiee, yakyuu*
5. *mimashita, eega, terebi*

III. *dokoka, nanika, dareka*

Structure Drill 1 Answer the questions as shown in the example.

ex. *Nanika arimashita-ka.* →*Iie, nanimo arimasen-deshita.*
Nanika nomimashita-ka.
→*Iie, nanimo nomimasen-deshita.*

1. *Dareka imashita-ka.* 2. *Nanika mimashita-ka.*
3. *Nanika kimashita-ka.* 4. *Nanika shimashita-ka.*
5. *Dareka ikimashita-ka.* 6. *Nanika arimashita-ka.*

Structure Drill 2 Answer the questions as in the example.

ex. *Dokoka-e ikimashita-ka.*
→*Iie, doko-emo ikimasen-deshita.*
Dokoka-ni arimashita-ka.
→*Iie, doko-nimo arimasen-deshita.*

1. *Dokoka-e dekakemashita-ka.* 2. *Dokoka-ni arimashita-ka.*
3. *Dokoka-de mimashita-ka.* 4. *Dokoka-ni imashita-ka.*
5. *Dokoka-de koohii-o nomimashita-ka.*

IV. *-gurai*

Structure Drill 1 Change the following sentences using *-gurai,* as shown in the example.

ex. *Isshuukan-ni gosatsu yomimashita.*
→*Isshuukan-ni gosatsu-gurai yomimashita.*

1. *Ichinichi-ni nisatsu yomimashita.*
2. *Isshuukan-ni sansatsu kaimashita* (I bought).
3. *Isshuukan-ni nido ikimashita.*
4. *Mikka-ni ichido eega-o mimashita.*
5. *Ichinen* (one year) *-ni sando dekakemashita.*
6. *Ichinichi-ni gojikan benkyoo-o shimashita.*

Structure Drill 2 Make questions that would elicit the responses given in Structure Drill 1.

ex. *Dono-gurai yomimashita-ka.* (How much did you read?)
→*Isshuukan-ni gosatsu-gurai yomimashita.*

V. *yoku* and *amari*

Structure Drill Answer the following questions in the negative, using *amari.*

ex. *Kookoo-no toki yoku benkyoo-o shimashita-ka.*
→*Iie, amari shimasen-deshita.*

1. *Kookoo-no toki yoku supootsu-o yarimashita-ka.*
2. *Doyoobi-ni yoku benkyoo-o shimashita-ka.*
3. *Gakusee-no toki yoku shoosetsu-o yomimashita-ka.*
4. *Kinoo-wa yoku nemashita-ka.* (Did you get a lot of sleep yesterday?)
5. *Nichiyoobi-ni yoku dekakemasu-ka.*
(Do you often go out on Sundays?)

VI. Days of the month

The days of the month are as follows. Practice saying them.

1st --*tsuitachi* 2nd --*futsuka* 3rd --*mikka* 4th --*yokka*
5th --*itsuka* 6th --*muika* 7th --*nanoka* 8th --*yooka*
9th --*kokonoka* 10th --*tooka* 11th --*juuichinichi*...

Above the 10th, they are said using the same set of numbers for giving prices plus *-nichi*. Exceptions are : 14th --*juuyokka*, 24th --*nijuuyokka*, and 20th --*hatsuka*.

Pronunciation Practice

Practice saying the following aloud, pausing slightly after each comma.

A: 1. *a -i -a -u, a -u -a -i* 2. *wa -i -wa -u, -wa -u -wa -i*
3. *a -i -a -u, a -u -a -i* 4. *ya -i -ya -u, -ya -u -ya -i*
5. *o -i -u -o, u -o -o -i* 6. *yo -i -yu -o, -yu -o -yo -i*

B: 1. *ginkoo, toshokan*
2. *Tookyoo, Nagasaki* (place name)
3. *Shinjuku, Harajuku* (place name)
4. *Yamamoto, Yamashita*
5. *ten'in* (clerk), *go-shujin* (master)

C: Add *-desu-ka* to each of the words in B to form questions. Use a rising intonation.

ex. *Ginkoo-desu-ka. Toshokan-desu-ka.*
(Is it a bank or a library?)

Reading Comprehension

Read the following passage.

きのうは一日(いちにち)じゅう雨(あめ)(1)がふりました。どこへもいきませんでした。うちで二(に)時間(じかん)ぐらい勉強(べんきょう)しました。そのあとテレビ(てれび)をみました。いろいろな番組(ばんぐみ)(2)をみました。夕方(ゆうがた)(3)山下(やました)さんと吉川(よしかわ)さんがきました。

(1) rain (2) program (3) in the evening

Aural Comprehension

Listen to the conversations on the tape and answer the following questions.

(A) 1. What did the woman do yesterday?
　　2. Was the movie a good one?

(B) 1. Has the man finished reading the newspaper?
　　2. Is he going to read the magazine?

(C) 1. What did the woman buy at the department store?
　　2. How often does she go to department stores?
　　3. How often does the man go to department stores?

第六課(だいろっか)　どうでしたか

Dialogue

I. (Two acquaintances talking)

A：　先週(せんしゅう)の　パーティー(ぱーてぃー)は　どうでしたか。 1

B：　にぎやかな　パーティー(ぱーてぃー)でした。

A：　会場(かいじょう)は　どこでしたか。 3

B：　新宿(しんじゅく)の　ホテル(ほてる)でした。ひろくて　きれいでした。

A：　そうですか。 5

B：　いろいろな　人(ひと)に　あいましたよ。

A：　吉田(よしだ)さんも　きましたか。 7

B：　きませんでした。

A：　ざんねんでしたね。川上(かわかみ)さんは…？ 9

B：　川上(かわかみ)さんは　きました。

A：　元気(げんき)でしたか。 11

B：　元気(げんき)でしたが、はやく　かえりました。

A：　じゃ、あまり　話(はなし)を　しませんでしたね。 13

B：　ええ、時間(じかん)が　たりませんでした。

II. (Yamamoto and Kobayashi, two acquaintances, meet.)

山本(やまもと)：　このごろは　どうですか。いそがしいですか。 15

小林(こばやし)：　きのうは　ひまでしたが、きょうは　いそがしいです。
　山本(やまもと)さんは…？ 17

山本(やまもと)：　今週(こんしゅう)は　あまり　いそがしく　ありません。先週(せんしゅう)は　たいへんでしたが。 19

Dialogue

Lesson 6

HOW WAS IT?

I.

A: How was the party last week?

B: It was quite lively.

A: Where did you meet?

B: At a hotel in Shinjuku. It was spacious and beautiful.

A: Is that right?

B: I met lots of people.

A: Did Mr. Yoshida come?

B: No, he didn't.

A: That's too bad. And Mr. Kawakami?

B: He showed up.

A: Did he seem well?

B: Yes, he did, but he left early.

A: Then you didn't talk with him much, did you?

B: No, there wasn't enough time.

Dai-rokka

DOO-DESHITA-KA

I.

A: Senshuu-no paatii-wa ▲doo-deshita-ka.

B: ▲Nigiyakana paatii-deshita.

A: Kaijoo-wa ▲doko-deshita-ka.

B: ▲Shinjuku-no hoteru-deshita. ▲Hirokute ▲kiree-deshita.

A: Soo-desu-ka.

B: ▲Iroirona hito-ni aimashita-yo.

A: ▲Yoshida-san-mo kimashita-ka.

B: Kimasen-deshita.

A: Zannen-deshita-ne. Kawakami-san-wa . . . ?

B: ▲Kawakami-san-wa kimashita.

A: Genki-deshita-ka.

B: Genki-deshita-ga, ▲hayaku kaerimashita.

A: Ja, amari hanashi-o ▲shimasen-deshita-ne.

B: Ee, ▲jikan-ga tarimasen-deshita.

II.

Yamamoto: How are you these days? Busy?

Kobayashi: I wasn't busy at all yesterday, but I'm busy today. How about you, Mr. Yamamoto?

Y: I'm not very busy this week. It was tough last week, though.

II.

Y: Kono-goro-wa ▲doo-desu-ka. Isogashii-desu-ka.

K: ▲Kinoo-wa hima-deshita-ga, ▲kyoo-wa isogashii-desu. Yamamoto-san-wa . . . ?

Y: Konshuu-wa amari ▲isogashiku arimasen. ▲Senshuu-wa taihen-deshita-ga.

Explanation

(In this lesson you will learn the past form of *-desu,* and another set of adjectives different from those you have learned so far.)

先週(せんしゅう)の パーティー(ぱーてぃー)は どうでしたか。 **line 1**

Senshuu-no paatii-wa doo-deshita-ka.

senshuu	last week
paatii	party
doo-deshita-ka	how was it?

Some people pronounce *paatii* as *paatee.*

Doo belongs to another set of *kosoado* words:

koo (this way); *soo* (that way);

aa (that way); *doo* (what way, how).

Soo-desu, which is used as an answer meaning 'That's right,' literally means 'It's that way.'

Deshita is used as the past form of *-desu.*

ex. *Kinoo-wa ii otenki-deshita.* (It was fine yesterday.)

にぎやかな パーティー(ぱーてぃー)でした。 **line 2**

Nigiyakana paatii-deshita.

nigiyakana	lively

Nigiyakana is an adjective, but is different from such adjectives as *akai* and *shiroi* which end with *-i.* This new type of adjectives end with *-na* when they come before nouns, and can be called '*-na* adjectives,' while *akai, shiroi,* etc. can be called '*-i* adjectives.'

会場(かいじょう)は どこでしたか。 **line 3**

Kaijoo-wa doko-deshita-ka.

kaijoo	place of meeting

新宿(しんじゅく)の ホテル(ほてる)でした。 **line 4**

Shinjuku-no hoteru-deshita.

Shinjuku	name of a place in Tokyo

ひろくて きれいでした。 **line 4**

Hirokute kiree-deshita.

hirokute	it's spacious and . . .
kiree-deshita	it was beautiful

When an *-i* adjective is followed by another adjective or by a verb, its ending changes from *-i* to *-kute*; thus *hiroi* becomes *hirokute*, and *akai* becomes *akakute*.

ex. (*-i* adj.+*-i* adj.) *shirokute ookii tatemono* (a big, white building)

(*-i* adj.+ *-na* adj.) *Akakute kiree-deshita.* (It was red and beautiful.)

(*-i* adj. + verb) *Isogashikute tsukaremashita.* (I'm busy and tired.)

When *-na* adjectives are followed by *-desu* or *-deshita,* the ending *-na* disappears; *kireena* becomes *kiree-desu* or *kiree-deshita.*

ex. *Kireena kaijoo-deshita.* (Where we met was a beautiful place.)

Kaijoo-wa kiree-deshita. (The place where we met was beautiful.)

When a *-na* adjective is followed by another adjective or by a verb, its ending changes from *-na* to *-de.*

ex. (*-na* adj. + *-i* adj.) *kiree de yasui* (pretty and inexpensive)

(*-na* adj. + *-na* adj.) *shizuka-de kireena* (quiet and beautiful)

(*-na* adj. + verb) *Genki-de yoku benkyoo-o shimasu.* (He's healthy and he studies hard.)

いろいろな　人(ひと)に　あいましたよ。 **line 6**

Iroirona hito-ni aimashita-yo.

iroirona various (*-na* adjective)

...ni aimashita I met ... (dict. *au*)

The verb *au,* 'to meet' is preceded by the particle *-ni.*

きませんでした。 **line 8**

Kimasen-deshita.

kimasen-deshita he didn't come (dict. *kuru*)

ざんねんでしたね。 **line 9**

Zannen-deshita-ne.

zannen-deshita it was too bad

You could start this sentence by saying *Sore-wa.* *Zannen* is a *-na* adjective.

元気でしたか。 **line 11**

Genki-deshita-ka.

genki-deshita-ka was he well?

Genki is a *-na* adjective.

ex. *O-genki-desu-ka.* (How are you? I hope you're fine.)
(*O-* is added to show politeness.)
Genkina otoko-no-ko-desu. (He's a vigorous boy.)

元気でしたが、はやく かえりました。 **line 12**

Genki-deshita-ga, hayaku kaerimashita.

... ga ... but
hayaku early; quickly

Both *demo,* introduced in Lesson 5, and *ga* mean 'but,' however *ga* sounds somewhat more formal, and softer.

Hayaku is derived from *hayai.* This form ending in *-ku* is used as an adverb modifying other adjectives or verbs. A similar adverb is *osoku* (late), derived from the adjective *osoi.*

ex. *Watashi-wa mainichi osoku nemasu.* (I go to bed late every day.)

じゃ、あまり 話を しませんでしたね。 **line 13**

Ja, amari hanashi-o shimasen-deshita-ne.

ja then; in that case
hanashi talk

ええ、時間が たりませんでした。 **line 14**

Ee, jikan-ga tarimasen-deshita.

jikan time
... ga tarimasen-deshita ... wasn't enough (dict. *tariru*)

See Note for the use of *Ee.*

このごろは どうですか。いそがしいですか。 **line 15**

Kono-goro-wa doo-desu-ka. Isogashii-desu-ka.

kono-goro these days; nowadays
isogashii-desu-ka are you busy?

Doo-desu-ka is commonly used to ask someone how things are going. *Ikaga-desu-ka*, which sounds more polite, is also used.

ex. *Okusan-wa kono-goro doo-desu-ka.* (How's your wife these days?)

O-shigoto-wa ikaga-desu-ka. (How's your work going?)

きのうは　ひまでしたが、きょうは　いそがしいです。 **line 16**

Kinoo-wa hima-deshita-ga, kyoo-wa isogashii-desu.

hima-deshita — I had some free time; I wasn't busy

Hima-deshita is the past form of *hima-desu.*

今週(こんしゅう)は　あまり　いそがしく　ありません。先週(せんしゅう)は　たいへんでしたが。 **lines 18–19**

Konshuu-wa amari isogashiku arimasen. Senshuu-wa taihen-deshita-ga.

konshuu — this week

isogashiku arimasen — I'm not busy. (dict. *isogashii*)

taihen — tough; hard (*-na* adj.)

The form, an *-i* adjective plus *-desu* (ex. *isogashii-desu*), is changed into the negative by adding *arimasen* or *-wa arimasen* after its *-ku* form.

ex. *Akai-desu.* (It's red.) *Akaku (-wa) arimasen.* (It's not red.)

Ookii-desu. (It's big.) *Ookiku (-wa) arimasen.* (It's not big.)

A *-na* adjective plus *-desu* is changed into the negative form by replacing *-desu* with *-ja arimasen.*

ex. *Kiree-desu.* (It's beautiful.) *Kiree-ja arimasen.* (It's not beautiful.)

Notice that the last sentence ends with ... *ga,* giving the impression that the sentence is not completed. The last two sentences can be reversed in order and made into the single sentence, *Senshuu-wa taihen-deshita-ga, konshuu-wa amari isogashiku arimasen.* However, the first way sounds more conversational, and actually not completing a sentence is often preferred because it seems softer.

Note Use of *Ee* in answering negative questions

Ee (or *Hai*) is used to show agreement and *Iie* to show disagreement whether the question asked is in the affirmative or in the negative. This contrasts with English, where 'No' is usually used to show agreement to a question in the negative form.

Question in the affirmative:
- A: *Hanashi-o shimashita-ka.* (Did you talk with him?)
- B: ***Iie,*** *shimasen-deshita.* (**No,** I didn't.)

Question in the negative:
- A: *Hanashi-o shimasen-deshita-ka.* (Didn't you talk with him?)
- B: ***Ee,*** *shimasen-deshita.* (**No,** I didn't.)

Drills

I. *-deshita*

Structure Drill Answer the questions as shown in the example.

ex. *Doyoobi-deshita-ka. Nichiyoobi-deshita-ka.* (Was it Saturday or Sunday?)
→*Nichiyoobi-deshita.* (It was Sunday.)

1. *Konshuu-deshita-ka. Senshuu-deshita-ka.*
2. *Yamashita-san-deshita-ka. Yoshida-san-deshita-ka.*
3. *Gakusee-deshita-ka. Sensee* (teacher) *-deshita-ka.*
4. *Gosen-en-deshita-ka. Rokusen-en-deshita-ka.*
5. *Tooka-deshita-ka. Kokonoka-deshita-ka.*
6. *Nisatsu-deshita-ka. Sansatsu-deshita-ka.*

II. *-na* adjectives

Structure Drill Change the sentence structure as shown in the example.

ex. *Paatii-wa nigiyaka-deshita.*
→*Nigiyakana paatii-deshita.*

1. *Shigoto-wa taihen-deshita.*
2. *Kaijoo-wa kiree-deshita.*
3. *Shokudoo-wa kiree-deshita.*
4. *Kaisha-wa hima-deshita.*
5. *Kodomo* (child) *-wa genki-deshita.*
6. *Hoteru-wa shizuka* (quiet) *-deshita.*

Usage Drill Practice the following conversation changing the underlined words.

ex. *hima* A: *Kyoo-wa doo-desu-ka. Hima-desu-ka.*
B: *Ee, hima-desu.*

A: *Kinoo-wa doo-deshita-ka.*
B: *Kinoo-mo hima-deshita. Kono-goro-wa mainichi hima-desu.*

1. *taihen* 2. *genki* 3. *shizuka* 4. *nigiyaka*

III. *. . . ni aimashita*

Structure Drill Substitute each given word in the example sentence.

ex. *Yoshida-san*→*Yoshida-san-ni aimashita.*

1. *Yamamoto-san* 2. *Kawakami-san* 3. *Kawakami-san-no okusan*
4. *Satoo-san-no goshujin* 5. *iroirona hito*

I+II+III

Usage Drill Practice the following conversation changing the underlined words.

ex. *Yamamoto-san*
A: *Senshuu Yamamoto-san-ni aimashita.*
B: *Soo-desu-ka.* (a little surprised) *Genki-deshita-ka.*
A: *Ee, genki-deshita-yo.*
B: *Nanika hanashi-o shimashita-ka.*
A: *Ee, kissaten-de iroirona hanashi-o shimashita.*
B: *Soo-desu-ka.* (happy about the news)

1. *Yoshida-san* 2. *Tanaka-san* 3. *Satoo-san-no okusan*
4. *kookoo-no toki-no tomodachi* (friend in my high school days)

IV. *-kute*

Structure Drill Combine two sentences as shown in the example.

ex. *hiroi-desu, kiree-desu*
→*Hirokute kiree-desu.*

1. *shiroi-desu, kiree-desu*
2. *hiroi-desu, shizuka-desu*
3. *isogashii-desu, taihen-desu*
4. *akai-desu, kiree-desu*
5. *hayai-desu, yasui* (cheap) *-desu*
6. *atarashii* (new, fresh) *-desu, kiree-desu*

Usage Drill Practice the following conversation changing the underlined words.

ex. *kissaten, yasui* A: *Sumimasen. Kono hen* (neighborhood) *-ni ii kissaten-wa arimasen-ka.*

B: *Arimasu. Eki-no mae-ni yasukute kireena kissaten-ga arimasu-yo.*

A: *Soo-desu-ka. Arigatoo-gozaimasu.*

B: *Doo-itashimashite.*

1. *mise*(store), *yasui* 2. *shokudoo, hiroi* 3. *kissaten, atarashii*
4. *nikuya*(butcher's), *yasui* 5. *sakanaya*(fishmonger's), *yasui*

V. *Iie, amari . . . masen-deshita*

Usage Drill Practice the following conversation, changing the underlined parts.

ex. *hanashi-o, shimashita*

A: *Iroirona hanashi-o shimashita-ka.*

B: *Iie, amari shimasen-deshita.*

A: *Dooshite-desu-ka.* (Why not?)

B: *Jikan-ga tarimasen-deshita.*

A: *Zannen-deshita-ne.*

1. *mono* (things) *-o, mimashita*
2. *mono-o, kaimashita* (you bought)
3. *tokoro* (place) *-e, ikimashita*
4. *mono-o, tabemashita* (you ate)
5. *hito-ni, aimashita*
6. *koto-o, hanashimashita* (you talked about)

VI. Telling time

In Lesson 1 you learned how to say '. . . o'clock.' Now practice the minutes.

1 --ippun 2 --nifun 3 --sanpun 4 --yonpun 5 --gofun 6 --roppun
7 --nanafun 8 --happun 9 --kyuufun 10 --jippun 11 --juuippun
12 --juunifun 13 --juusanpun 14 --juuyonpun 15 --juugofun

16 --juuroppun *17 --juunanafun* *18 --juuhappun, juuhachifun*
19 --juukyuufun *20 --nijippun* ... (goes on regularly) ...
30 --sanjippun ..... *40 --yonjippun* ..... *50 --gojippun* .....
60 --rokujippun

In telling time, ... *sugi* means 'after,' and ... *mae* means 'before'; however, *-sugi* is often omitted in conversation. There is no Japanese word corresponding to 'a quarter' as a unit of time.

ex. 1 : 15 *ichiji juugofun (-sugi)*
6 : 30 *rokuji sanjippun (-sugi), rokuji-han*
8 : 47 *hachiji yonjuunanafun (-sugi),*
or *kuji juusanpun-mae*

Read the following:

9 : 04, 11 : 57, 2 : 19, 4 : 31, 12 : 10, 3 : 01, 1 : 48

VII. Memorize the names of the months.

ichigatsu (January), *nigatsu* (February), *sangatsu* (March), *shigatsu* (April), *gogatsu* (May), *rokugatsu* (June), *shichigatsu* (July), *hachigatsu* (August), *kugatsu* (September), *juugatsu* (October), *juuichigatsu* (November), *juunigatsu* (December)

Pronunciation Practice

Practice saying the following aloud, pausing slightly after each comma.

A: 1. *a -i -a -u, a -u -a -i* 2. *e -i -o -o, o -i -e -e*
3. *da -i -da -u, da -u -da -i* 4. *de -i -do -o, do -i -de -e*
5. *ra -i -ra -u, ra -u -ra -i* 6. *re -i -ro -o, ro -i -re -e*

B: 1. *ichi-en* (1 yen), *nana-en* (7 yen) 2. *sannen* (3 years), *ichinen* (1 year)
3. *gakkoo, apaato* (apartment) 4. *shippai* (failure), *shitsuree*
5. *Kawakami, Nishimoto* (personal name)
6. *Shinagawa* (place name), *Akasaka* (place name)

C: Add *-desu-ka* to each of the words in B to form questions. Use a rising intonation.

ex. *Ichi-en-desu-ka. Nana-en-desu-ka.*

Reading Comprehension

Read the following passage.

先週(せんしゅう)の金曜日(きんようび)に松本(まつもと)さんのあたらしいうちで、パーティー(ぱーてぃー)をしました。大(おお)きくて(1)りっぱな(2)うちでした。おくさんもきれいな人(ひと)でした。高校(こうこう)のときのともだちがたくさんきました。いろいろなことをはなしました。森(もり)さんもきました。にぎやかでした。でも小林(こばやし)さんは病気(びょうき)で(3)きませんでした。

(1) big and (2) fine (3) was sick and

Aural Comprehension

Listen to the conversations on the tape and answer the following questions.

(A) 1. Is the man's new apartment quiet?
2. Who lives next door?
3. Do they stay up late at night?
4. What do they do at night?

(B) 1. Where did the woman meet Yoshiko?
2. Did she talk a lot with Yoshiko?

(C) 1. Is Mr. Sato's business thriving now?
2. Does he like having a lot of free time?

Quiz (Lesson 1 — Lesson 6)

I. Say "it's a —" in Japanese.

II. Read the following.

1. 1,500 yen 2. 800 yen 3. 7,200 yen 4. May 1
5. Jan. 3 6. 9 : 30 7. 10 : 20 8. 3 : 15
9. 7 : 30 P.M. 10. 11 : 55 A.M.

III. Fill in the blanks with appropriate question words.

1. Q : *Ano otoko-no-hito-wa _______-desu-ka.*
   A : *Tanaka-san-desu.*
2. Q : *Ano tatemono-wa _______-desu-ka.*
   A : *Ginkoo-desu.*
3. Q : *Tanaka-san-no okusan-wa_____-ni imasu-ka.*
   A : *Mado-no soba-ni imasu.*
4. Q : *Kinoo-wa _______-ka-e ikimashita-ka.*
   A : *Iie, doko-emo ikimasen-deshita.*

5. Q: *Kono-goro-wa* _____*-desu-ka.*
A: *Genki-desu-ga, isogashii-desu.*
6. Q: *Ima* ________*-desu-ka.*
A: *Goji yonjippun-desu.*
7. Q: *Kono isu-wa* ________*-desu-ka.*
A: *Hassen-en-desu.*
8. Q: *Mainichi* ________ *-goro okimasu-ka.*
A: *Shichiji-goro-desu.*

IV. Fill in the blanks with verbs from below.

1. *Tsukue-no ue-ni hon-ga* ______________.
2. *Kissaten-de ocha-o* ______________.
3. *Asoko-ni Tanaka-san-ga* ______________.
4. *Kinoo-wa yoku* ______________.
5. *Kinoo-no asa ginkoo-e* ______________.
6. *Kinoo-wa ichinichi-juu uchi-ni* ______________.
7. *Nichiyoobi-ni eega-o* ______________.
8. *Kinoo-wa shoosetsu-o* ______________.
9. *Paatii-de iroirona hito-ni* ______________.

Verbs: *mimashita; nomimashita; imasu; arimasu; furimashita; shimasu; yomimashita; ikimashita; imashita; kimashita; aimashita*
(There are two too many listed.)

V. Match.

1. *Kinoo-wa ichinichi-juu* — a. *okimashita*
2. *Kyoo-wa asa hayaku* — b. *daremo imasen*
3. *Jikan-ga* — c. *uchi-ni imashita*
4. *Mainichi issatsu* — d. *tarimasen-deshita*
5. *Shokudoo-no naka-niwa* — e. *hon-o yomimasu*

1 ____; 2 ____; 3 ____; 4 ____; 5 ____

VI. Express in Japanese.

1. What time is it now?
2. How much is this?
3. Is this 5,000 yen, too?
4. Is this a window or a door?
5. The hotel was spacious and beautiful.
6. That white building over there is a hospital.
7. I wasn't busy last week.
8. I get up at 6 : 30 every morning (*maiasa*).
9. What type of book did you read?
10. Didn't you do any sports?

第七課(だいななか)　ちょっと　まってください

Dialogue

(Michiko Saito visits Miss Yamaguchi, her teacher.)

(At a fruit shop)

みちこ：　おねがいします。

店(みせ)の人(ひと)：　はい。なにを　さしあげましょう。

みちこ：　その　りんごを　いつつ　つつんでください。

店(みせ)の人(ひと)：　はい。リボン(りぼん)を　つけましょうか。

みちこ：　ええ、つけてください。

(At Miss Yamaguchi's)

みちこ：　ごめんください。山口先生(やまぐちせんせい)の　おたくは　こちらでしょうか。

山口(やまぐち)：　はい、そうです。ああ、斎藤(さいとう)さん、どうぞ　あがってください。

みちこ：　おじゃまします。

みちこ：　これ、つまらない　ものですが、どうぞ。

山口(やまぐち)：　どうも　すみません。ちょっと　まってください。お茶(ちゃ)を　いれますから。

みちこ：　どうぞ　おかまいなく。すぐ　失礼(しつれい)しますから。

みちこ：　この　参考書(さんこうしょ)、ありがとうございました。

山口(やまぐち)：　どういたしまして。やくに　たちましたか。

みちこ：　ええ、たいへん　たすかりました。

山口(やまぐち)：　また　いつでも　つかってください。

みちこ：　ありがとうございます。....おじゃましました。

山口(やまぐち)：　また　きてください。

Dialogue

Lesson 7	*Dai-nanaka*
WAIT A MINUTE, PLEASE	***CHOTTO MATTE-KUDASAI***
Michiko: Excuse me.	*Michiko: Onegai-shimasu.*
Shopkeeper: Yes? What can I do for you?	*Mise-no hito: Hai. ▲Nani-o sashi-agemashoo.*
M: I'd like to have five of those apples wrapped up.	*M: Sono ringo-o ▲itsutsu tsutsu-nde-kudasai.*
Shop: Certainly. Shall I put a rib-bon on the package?	*Mise: Hai. ▲Ribon-o tsukemashoo-ka.*
M: Yes, please.	*M: Ee, tsukete-kudasai.*
M: Excuse me. Is this where Miss Yamaguchi lives?	*M: Gomen-kudasai. ▲Yamaguchi-sensee-no otaku-wa kochira-deshoo-ka.*
Yamaguchi: Yes, that's right. Oh, it's you, Miss Saito. Please come in.	*Y: Hai, soo-desu. Aa, Saitoo-san, ▲doozo agatte-kudasai.*
M: Thank you.	*M: Ojama-shimasu.*
M: Here's a little something for you.	*M: Kore, ▲tsumaranai mono-desu-ga, doozo.*
Y: Thank you. Wait a minute, please. I'll make some tea.	*Y: Doomo ▲sumimasen. ▲Chotto matte-kudasai. ▲Ocha-o irema-su-kara.*
M: Please don't bother. Il'l be leaving soon.	*M: Doozo ▲okamai-naku. ▲Sugu shitsuree-shimasu-kara. . . .*
M: Thank you very much for this reference book that you lent me.	*M: ▲Kono sankoosho, arigatoo-gozaimashita.*
Y: You're welcome. Did it help?	*Y: Doo-itashimashite. ▲Yaku-ni ta-chimashita-ka.*
M: Yes, a great deal. Thank you very much.	*M: Ee, ▲taihen tasukarimashita.*

Y: Please feel free to borrow it any time.	Y: *Mata itsudemo tsukatte-kudasai.*
M: Thank you....I'll be going now.	M: *Arigatoo-gozaimasu. ....Ojama-shimashita.*
Y: Come again, will you?	: *Mata kite-kudasai.*

Explanation

(In this lesson you will learn how to express requests and how to offer help.)

おねがいします。 **line 1**
Onegai-shimasu.

onegai request

This expression, which literally means 'I request you to do something,' can be used to catch a store clerk's attention, as it is used in the dialogue. More generally, it is used to ask favors of others.

はい。なにを さしあげましょう。 **line 2**
Hai. Nani-o sashiagemashoo.

sashiagemashoo shall I give you? (humble) (dict. *sashiageru*)

Sashiagemasu is used when one gives something to a superior, while the verb *ageru* is used when giving something to one's equal or inferior.

The *-mashoo* ending corresponds to 'I will' or 'let us.' Although this sentence does not end in *-ka*, the interrogative pronoun *Nani* shows that it is a question.

ex. *Doko-e ikimashoo (-ka).* (Where shall we go?)
Kooen-e ikimashoo. (Let's go to the park.)

その りんごを いつつ つつんでください。 **line 3**
Sono ringo-o itsutsu tsutsunde-kudasai.

ringo apple
itsutsu five pieces
...o tsutsunde-kudasai please wrap ... up (dict. *tsutsumu*)

The *-te (-de)* form of the verb plus *kudasai* is used to make a request. Here *tsutsunde* is derived from the verb *tsutsumu.* See Note to learn how to make the *-te* form of verbs.

Single units of most objects are counted in the following way:

1 --hitotsu; 2 --futatsu, 3 --mittsu; 4 --yottsu, 5 --itsutsu
6 --muttsu; 7 --nanatsu; 8 --yattsu; 9 --kokonotsu; 10 --too

This series goes only up to 10. To count above 10, simply use the same set of numbers learned for quoting prices.

Notice the position of the number in a sentence.

ex. *Isu-o futatsu kaimashita.* (I bought two chairs.)
Ringo-o mittsu kudasai. (Give me three apples.)

はい。リボン(りぼん)を　つけましょうか。 **line 4**

Hai. Ribon-o tsukemashoo-ka.

ribon	ribbon
... o tsukemashoo-ka	shall I put ... on? (dict. *tsukeru* attach)

ごめんください。山口先生(やまぐちせんせい)の　おたくは　こちらでしょうか。 **lines 6-7**

Gomen-kudasai. Yamaguchi-sensee-no otaku-wa kochira-deshoo-ka.

Gomen-kudasai.	Excuse me.
Yamaguchi-sensee	Prof. (Mr., Miss, Mrs.) Yamaguchi
... no otaku	...'s house; ...'s residence (polite)
... wa kochira-deshoo-ka	is this ...?

Gomen-kudasai is used when entering someone else's house or room; it compares to English greeting 'Hello.' It is also used in place of *Sayoonara,* 'Good-bye.'

Sensee means 'teacher' and is used to show respect to doctors, lawyers, statesmen, and certain specialists as well as teachers and professors. It may be added to the last name or used alone.

Kochira belongs to another set of *kosoado* words:

kochira (this way); *sochira* (that way); *achira* (that way over there); *dochira* (which way)

In certain contexts the words in this set refer to direction; at other times they are used as polite synonyms for *koko soko asoko doko* or *kore sore are dore.*

ex. *(=doko) Otaku-wa dochira-desu-ka.* (Where do you live? *lit.* Where is your residence?)

(=dore, kore) A: *Dochira-o sashiagemashoo.* (Which one would you like?)

B: *Kochira-o kudasai.* (Please give me this one.)

Deshoo is a more indirect and therefore more polite form of *-desu.* If *-desu* is translated as 'it is' in English, then *-deshoo* can be translated as 'it would be' or 'it probably is.'

ex. A: *Dochira-ga ii-deshoo-ne.* (Which one would be better?)

B: *Kochira-ga ii-deshoo.* (This one might be better.)

はい、そうです。ああ、斎藤(さいとう)さん、どうぞ　あがってください。 **lines 8-9**

Hai, soo-desu. Aa, Saitoo-san, doozo agatte-kudasai.

doozo — please

agatte-kudasai — come up, please (dict. *agaru*)

Miss Yamaguchi, Michiko's teacher, calls Michiko *Saitoo-san.* It is common for a Japanese teacher to call students by their last names.

Agatte-kudasai is used to invite a visitor to 'step up' into a Japanese-style house. Otherwise, *haitte-kudasai* (please enter) is used. The addition of *doozo* makes the welcome more hearty.

おじゃまします。 **line 10**

Ojama-shimasu.

ojama — interruption

Ojama-shimasu literally means 'I'm going to get in your way,' and it is used as a polite greeting when entering someone's home. When leaving another's home, say '*Ojama-shimashita,*' which literally means 'I have been in your way,' as used in line 19 of the dialogue.

これ、つまらない　ものですが、どうぞ。 **line 11**

Kore, tsumaranai mono-desu-ga, doozo.

tsumaranai mono — very little thing

This is one of the most common expressions used when offering a gift. After *doozo* a phrase meaning 'take this' or 'please accept this' may be omitted.

Wa showing the subject matter is sometimes left out in somewhat informal conversation.

どうも　すみません。 **line 12**

Doomo sumimasen.

doomo indeed; very much

This can be used to express thanks as well as apology.

ちょっと　まってください。お茶(ちゃ)を　いれますから。 **lines 12-13**

Chotto matte-kudasai. Ocha-o iremasu-kara.

chotto (or *chotto*)	a little
matte-kudasai	please wait (dict. *matsu*)
ocha	tea (usu. with *o-*)
ocha-o iremasu	I'll make some tea (dict. *ireru* put in)
. . . kara	because . . . ; so

Kara is used to give the reason, which can be rather emotional or psychological so that it is not always expressed in English.

ex. *Ocha-ga hairimashita-kara kite-kudasai.* (Tea is served. Please come and have some.)

Actually a phrase ending in *-kara* is often added to the main sentence, rather than preceding it, as in lines 13 and 14. This expression sounds less abrupt.

どうぞ　おかまいなく。すぐ　失礼(しつれい)しますから。 **line 14**

Doozo okamai-naku. Sugu shitsuree-shimasu-kara.

okamai-naku don't bother

Here *shitsuree-shimasu* means 'I'm going to leave.'

この　参考書(さんこうしょ)、ありがとうございました。 **line 15**

Kono sankoosho, arigatoo-gozaimashita.

sankoosho reference book

Both *arigatoo-gozaimasu* and *arigatoo-gozaimashita* mean 'thank you,' but the latter implies the completion of an action, and might be translated as 'You have been kind, thank you.'

Kono . . . . , arigatoo-gozaimashita is used when returning something you borrowed or used.

ex. *Kono kasa, arigatoo-gozaimashita.* (Thank you for lending me this umbrella.)

やくに　たちましたか。 **line 16**

Yaku-ni tachimashita-ka.

yaku-ni tachimashita-ka did it help you? (dict. *tatsu*)

Yaku by itself means 'use,' and *yaku-ni tatsu* means 'to help' or 'to be of use.'

ええ、たいへん　たすかりました。 **line 17**

Ee, taihen tasukarimashita.

taihen	very much
tasukarimashita	I was helped; it was a help to me (dict. *tasukaru*)

Taihen here is used as an adverb, and the meaning is different from that of *taihenna* as in *taihenna shigoto* introduced in Lesson 6.

ex. A: *O-yaku-ni tachimashita-ka.* (Did it help you?)

B: *Ee, taihen yaku-ni tachimashita.* (Yes, a great deal.)

また　いつでも　つかってください。 **line 18**

Mata itsudemo tsukatte-kudasai.

mata	again
itsudemo (or *itsudemo*)	any time
tsukatte-kudasai	please use it (dict. *tsukau*)

Itsudemo is derived from *itsu* which means 'when?' Here are some other interrogative words with *-demo* meaning 'any . . .'

dokodemo (anywhere); *daredemo* (anybody); *ikurademo* (any amount of); *ikutsudemo* (any number of); *doredemo* (any one of them); *nandemo* (anything) (*nani* changes into *nan* when preceding *-demo*.)

また　きてください。 **line 20**

Mata kite-kudasai.

kite-kudasai	please come (dict. *kuru*)

Note The *-te* form of verbs

A: Group 1 verbs (*-u* verbs)

Change the dictionary form of the verb as shown in the chart.

(change *-u* to *-tte*) *ka**u*** (to buy) —*ka**tte***
(change *-tsu* to *-tte*) *ma**tsu*** (to wait) —*ma**tte***
(change *-ru* to *-tte*) *aga**ru*** (to go up) —*aga**tte***
(change *-su* to *-shite*) *hana**su*** (to talk) —*hana**shite***
(change *-ku* to *ite*) *ki**ku*** (to listen) —*ki**ite***
(change *-gu* to *-ide*) *iso**gu*** (to hurry) —*iso**ide***
(change *-bu* to *-nde*) *yo**bu*** (to call) —*yo**nde***
(change *-mu* to *-nde*) *yo**mu*** (to read) —*yo**nde***
(change *-nu* to *-nde*) *shi**nu*** (to die) —*shi**nde***
exception: ***iku*** (to go) —***itte***

B: Group 2 verbs (*-ru* verbs)
Change the final *-ru* to *-te*
examples: *mi**ru*** (to see) —*mi**te***; *oki**ru*** (to get up) —*oki**te***
*tabe**ru*** (to eat) —*tabe**te***; *tsuke**ru*** (to attach) —*tsuke**te***

C: Irregular verbs
suru (to do) —***shite***; ***kuru*** (to come) —***kite***

Drills

I. *-te*

Structure Drill Memorize the verb forms by reading them aloud.

tsukau (use)	*tsukaimasu*	*tsukatte-kudasai*
matsu (wait)	*machimasu*	*matte-kudasai*
agaru (go up)	*agarimasu*	*agatte-kudasai*
hanasu (talk)	*hanashimasu*	*hanashite-kudasai*
kiku (listen)	*kikimasu*	*kiite-kudasai*
tsutsumu (wrap)	*tsutsumimasu*	*tsutsunde-kudasai*
ireru (put in)	*iremasu*	*irete-kudasai*
tsukeru (attach)	*tsukemasu*	*tsukete-kudasai*
suru (do)	*shimasu*	*shite-kudasai*
kuru (come)	*kimasu*	*kite-kudasai*

II. *-te* and *-mashoo*

Structure Drill Memorize the verb forms by reading them aloud.

kau (buy)	*kaimashoo*	*katte-kudasai*
au (meet)	*aimashoo*	*atte-kudasai*
kaeru (go home)	*kaerimashoo*	*kaette-kudasai*
yomu (read)	*yomimashoo*	*yonde-kudasai*
nomu (drink)	*nomimashoo*	*nonde-kudasai*
iku (go)	*ikimashoo*	*itte-kudasai*
miru (see)	*mimashoo*	*mite-kudasai*
taberu (eat)	*tabemashoo*	*tabete-kudasai*
okiru (get up)	*okimashoo*	*okite-kudasai*
iru (be)	*imashoo*	*ite-kudasai*

I., II. Structure Drill Answer the questions as shown in the example.

ex. *Machimashoo-ka.* →*Ee, matte-kudasai.*

1. *Hanashimashoo-ka.*
2. *Kikimashoo-ka.*
3. *Yomimashoo-ka.*
4. *Mimashoo-ka.*
5. *Ikimashoo-ka.*
6. *Kaimashoo-ka.*

Usage Drill 1 Answer the questions as shown in the example.

ex. A: *Ribon-o tsukemashoo-ka.*
B: *Ee, sumimasen-ga, tsukete-kudasai.*

1. *Kono ringo-o tsutsumimashoo-ka.*
2. *Ocha-o iremashoo-ka.*
3. *Ashita* (tomorrow) *mata kimashoo-ka.*
4. *Ashita-no asa goji-ni okimashoo-ka.*
5. *Kippu* (ticket) *-o kaimashoo-ka.*
6. *Terebi-o tsukemashoo-ka.* (Shall I turn the TV on?)

Usage Drill 2 Practice the following conversation changing the underlined words.

ex. *miru, terebi-o tsukeru*
A: *Jikan-ga arimasu-ka.*
B: *Ee, chotto arimasu.*
A: *Nanika mimashoo-ka.*

B: *Soo-desu-ne. Soo shimashoo.* (Let's do that)
A: *Ja, sumimasen-ga, terebi-o tsukete-kudasai.*
B: *Hai.*

1. *kiku, rajio* (radio) *-o tsukeru* 2. *nomu, ocha-o ireru*
3. *miru, kippu-o kau* 4. *nomu, koohii-o ireru*

III. *-demo*

Structure Drill Substitute the underlined word with each of the cue words below.

ex. *dore* → *Doredemo ii-desu.* (Any of them will do.)

1. *doko* 2. *itsu* 3. *ikutsu* 4. *dare*
5. *nani (nan)* 6. *dochira* 7. *ikura*

Usage Drill Practice the following conversation changing the underlined words.

ex. *dokoka (-e) iku* A: *Dokoka-e ikimashoo-ka.*
B: *Ee, ikimashoo.*
A: *Doko-ga ii-deshoo.*
B: *Dokodemo ii-desu.*

1. *dokoka (-e) dekakeru* 2. *doreka, kau*
3. *dareka (-ni), kiku* (ask) 4. *dokoka (-de), matsu*
5. *dochiraka, miru* 6. *nanika, taberu*

IV. Visiting

Structure Drill Practice the following expressions until you have memorized them completely.

1. Visitor: *Gomen-kudasai.*
Host(ess): *A, ... san, doozo agatte-kudasai.*
V: *Ojama-shimasu.*
2. H: *Chotto matte-kudasai. Ocha-o iremasu-kara.*
V: *Doozo okamai-naku. Sugu shitsuree-shimasu-kara.*
3. V: *Kore, tsumaranai mono-desu-ga.*
H: *Doomo sumimasen.*
4. V: *Doomo ojama-shimashita.*
H: *Iie, mata kite-kudasai.*

Usage Drill Act out the conversation in Structure Drill with your teacher or with a fellow student. (3. may be omitted during the initial practice.)

V. Shopping

Usage Drill Practice the following conversation changing the underlined parts.

ex. *ringo-o itsutsu*

A: *Onegai-shimasu.*
B: *Hai, nani-o sashiagemashoo.*
A: *Ringo-o itsutsu kudasai.*
B: *Hai. Tsutsumimashoo-ka.*
A: *Ee, tsutsunde-kudasai.*

1. *mikan* (tangerine) *-o nanatsu*
2. *ringo-o yattsu*
3. *meron* (melon) *-o hitotsu*
4. *nooto* (notebooks) *-o gosatsu*
5. *ringo-o mittsu*
6. *mikan-o juuni*

Pronunciation Practice

Practice saying the following aloud, pausing slightly after each comma.

A. 1. *a -u -a -i, a -i -a -u*
2. *o -i -e -e, e -i -o -o*
3. *ha -u -ha -i, ha -i -ha -u*
4. *ho -i -he -e, he -i -ho -o*
5. *ka -u -ka -i, ka -i -ka -u*
6. *ko -i -ke -e, ke -i -ko -o*

B. 1. *Saitoo, Yamashita*
2. *asahan* (breakfast), *kudamono* (fruit)
3. *kooen* (park), *tatemono*
4. *Yamamoto, Yamazaki* (personal name)
5. *Kawakami, Kawaguchi* (personal name)
6. *agatte, tsutsunde*

C. Add *-desu-ka* to the words in B and say the sentences with a rising intonation.

ex. *Saitoo-desu-ka. Yamashita-desu-ka.*

Reading Comprehension

Read the following passage.

I. きのう山口先生のおたくへいきました。えきのそばでりんごをいつつかいました。店の人はりんごをつつみました。そして(1)きれいなリボンをつけました。

II. 先月(2)この参考書をかいました。三千円でした。たいへんやくにたちますから毎日つかいます。

(1) and (2) last month

Aural Comprehension

Listen to the conversations on the tape and answer the following questions.

(A) 1. What does the man buy?
2. How much does he pay for it?
3. What else does the shopkeeper suggest that he buy?

(B) 1. Is Mr. Yamamoto at home?
2. Does Miss Tanaka go into his house to wait for him?

(C) 1. Who brings tea?
2. Did the visitor bring a gift?

第八課（だいはっか）　はじめまして

Dialogue

I. (At Kawakami's home. He introduces Johnson to Tanaka.)

川上（かわかみ）：　田中（たなか）さん、こちらは　ジョンソン（じょんそん）さんです。

ジョンソン（じょんそん）：　はじめまして。

田中（たなか）：　どうぞ　よろしく。ジョンソン（じょんそん）さんは　学生（がくせい）ですか。

ジョンソン（じょんそん）：　ええ。専門（せんもん）は　経済（けいざい）ですが、いまは　日本語（にほんご）を　勉強（べんきょう）しています。

川上（かわかみ）：　ちょっと　失礼（しつれい）します。客（きゃく）が　まっていますので。

田中（たなか）：　どうぞ。

ジョンソン（じょんそん）：　田中（たなか）さんは　どんな　お仕事（しごと）ですか。

田中（たなか）：　貿易会社（ぼうえきがいしゃ）に　つとめています。名刺（めいし）を　どうぞ。

ジョンソン（じょんそん）：　ありがとうございます。ああ、会社（かいしゃ）は　銀座（ぎんざ）ですね。

田中（たなか）：　ええ。こんど　あそびに　きてください。

ジョンソン（じょんそん）：　はい。でも　おいそがしいでしょう。

田中（たなか）：　そうですね。……じゃ、電話（でんわ）を　してください。ここに　電話番号（でんわばんごう）が　ありますから。

II. (At the station)

山下（やました）：　ジョンソン（じょんそん）さん、もう　切符（きっぷ）を　かいましたか。

ジョンソン（じょんそん）：　まだです。どこで　うっていますか。

山下（やました）：　あそこの　機械（きかい）で　かってください。こまかい　お金（かね）を　もっていますか。

ジョンソン（じょんそん）：　ええ、たくさん　もっています。あ、みちこさんは　どこですか。

山下（やました）：　あそこで　電話（でんわ）を　かけています。

Dialogue

Lesson 8 / *Dai-hakka*

HOW DO YOU DO? / *HAJIMEMASHITE*

I. Kawakami: Mr. Tanaka, this is Mr. Johnson.

Johnson: How do you do?

Tanaka: Glad to meet you, Mr. Johnson. Are you a student?

J: Yes. My field of study is economics, but I'm studying Japanese now.

K: Excuse me a moment. I have a visitor waiting for me.

T: Please go ahead.

J: What sort of work do you do, Mr. Tanaka?

T: I work for a trading company. Here's my name card.

J: Thank you. Oh, your company is in Ginza.

T: Yes. Drop in sometime to see me.

J: But you must be busy.

T: Well, call me (before you show up). Here's the phone number.

II. Yamashita: Have you bought a ticket?

Johnson: Not yet. Where can I buy one?

Y: At the (vending) machine over there. Do you have small change?

J: Yes, lots of. Where's Michiko?

I. *Kawakami: Tanaka-san, kochira-wa Jonson-san-desu.*

Jonson: Hajimemashite.

Tanaka: Doozo yoroshiku. Jonson-san-wa gakusee-desu-ka.

J: Ee. Senmon-wa keezai-desu-ga, ima-wa nihongo-o benkyoo-shite-imasu.

K: Chotto shitsuree-shimasu. Kyaku-ga matte-imasu-node.

T: Doozo.

J: Tanaka-san-wa donna o-shigoto-desu-ka.

T: Booeki-gaisha-ni tsutomete-imasu. Meeshi-o doozo.

J: Arigatoo-gozaimasu. Aa, kaisha-wa Ginza-desu-ne.

T: Ee. Kondo asobi-ni kite-kudasai.

J: Hai. Demo o-isogashii-deshoo.

T: Soo-desu-ne.... Ja, denwa-o shite-kudasai. Koko-ni denwa-bangoo-ga arimasu-kara.

II. *Yamashita: Jonson-san, moo kippu-o kaimashita-ka.*

Jonson: Mada-desu. Doko-de utte-imasu-ka.

Y: Asoko-no kikai-de katte-kudasai. Komakai o-kane-o motte-imasu-ka.

J: Ee, takusan motte-imasu. ... ...A, Michiko-san-wa doko-desu-ka.

Y: She's making a telephone call over there. — *Y: Asoko-de denwa-o kakete-imasu.*

Explanation

(In this lesson you will learn how to describe action in progress and how to introduce people.)

田中さん、こちらは　ジョンソンさんです。 **line 1**

Tanaka-san, kochira-wa Jonson-san-desu.

This is the most common pattern used for introducing people. *Kochira*, which you learned as the polite synonym for *koko* in Lesson 7, is used here as the polite synonym for *kono-hito*, 'this person.'

はじめまして。 **line 2**

Hajimemashite.

This expression, which literally means 'I am meeting you for the first time,' corresponds to 'How do you do?' or 'Glad to meet you' in English.

どうぞ　よろしく。 **line 3**

Doozo yoroshiku.

This literally means 'Please be good to me' and is used as a common expression corresponding to 'I'm glad to meet you,' or 'How do you do?' It is similar to *Hajimemashite*, which sounds a little more formal. Sometimes the two expressions are used together as *Hajimemashite. Doozo yoroshiku.*

ええ。専門は　経済ですが、いまは　日本語を　勉強しています。 **lines 4-5**

Ee. Senmon-wa keezai-desu-ga, ima-wa nihongo-o benkyoo-shite-imasu.

senmon	field of study; major
keezai	economics (=*keezaigaku*)
nihongo	the Japanese language
. . .o benkyoo-shite-imasu	I'm studying . . . . .

Go means 'language' and is used in compounds with the name of a country to mean the language of that country.

ex. *eego* —(English) (*ee* stands for *Eekoku*, 'England.')
furansugo —(French); *doitsugo* —(German)
chuugokugo —(Chinese); *roshiago* —(Russian)

The *-te* form plus *imasu*, as in *benkyoo-shite-imasu*, shows that the action is now in progress. (Hereafter we call it the *-te-imasu* form.)

ex. A: *Ima nani-o shite-imasu-ka.* (What are you doing now?)
B: *Koohii-o nonde-imasu.* (I'm drinking some coffee.)

ちょっと 失礼(しつれい)します。 客(きゃく)が まっていますので。 **line 6**

Chotto shitsuree-shimasu. Kyaku-ga matte-imasu-node.

kyaku	visitor
matte-imasu	is waiting (dict. *matsu*)
. . . node	because . . . . .

Node indicates reason. As compared with *-kara*, which is similar in function, *-node* sounds more reserved and polite.

田中(たなか)さんは どんな お仕事(しごと)ですか。 **line 8**

Tanaka-san-wa donna o-shigoto-desu-ka.

o-shigoto work (polite)

'*o*' in '*oshigoto*' is used to show respect; it is called the honorific prefix.

Taken literally this sentence means 'What kind of work is Mr. Tanaka?' The actual meaning is 'What kind of work do you do, Mr. Tanaka?' The use of *o-* plus noun plus *-desu* makes this a politer expression than referring to the action by using a verb—in this case, saying '*donna shigoto-o shite-imasu-ka.*'

Some nouns take the polite prefix *go-* rather than *o-*.

ex. *Go-benkyoo-desu-ka.* (Are you studying?)

A verb minus its *-masu* ending can also be used as follows:

ex. *O-dekake-desu-ka.* (Are you going out?) (*Dekake* is derived from *dekakemasu.*)

貿易会社(ぼうえきがいしゃ)に つとめています。 **line 9**

Booeki-gaisha-ni tsutomete-imasu.

booeki-gaisha trading company
. . . ni tsutomete-imasu I'm working for . . . (dict. *tsutomeru*)

See the Note on pronunciation for the accent of compounds such as *booeki-gaisha*.

名刺(めいし)を どうぞ。 **line 9**

Meeshi-o doozo.

meeshi name card; calling card

After *doozo*, a phrase meaning 'please take' is left out as explained in Lesson 7.

Japanese often exchange name cards when they meet each other for the first time.

ああ、会社(かいしゃ)は 銀座(ぎんざ)ですね。 **lines 10-11**

Aa, kaisha-wa Ginza-desu-ne.

Ginza name of one of Tokyo's most famous shopping and business districts

Ginza-desu stands for *Ginza-ni arimasu.* (cf. Lesson 3)

ええ。こんど あそびに きてください。 **line 12**

Ee. Kondo asobi-ni kite-kudasai.

kondo sometime in the future (*lit.* next time)
asobi-ni to see me (dict. *asobu*)

Asobi is a noun derived from the verb *asobu*, just as *o-dekake* comes from the verb *dekakeru*. *Ni* as used here, shows the purpose of an action.

ex. *Eega-o mi-ni ikimashoo-ka.* (Shall we go see a movie?)
Sankoosho-o kai-ni hon'ya-e ikimashita.
(I went to a bookstore to buy a reference book.)

The verb *asobu* means 'to play, to have a good time': *asobi-ni iku* or *asobi-ni kuru* is often used to mean 'to visit a person.'

はい。でも おいそがしいでしょう。 **line 13**

Hai. Demo o-isogashii-deshoo.

The honorific prefix *o-* is used with adjectives in the following way.

ex. *Kyoo-wa o-hima-desu-ka.* (Do you have free time today?)
O-wakai-desu-ne. (You're young.) or (You look young.)

そうですね。…じゃ、電話(でんわ)を　してください。ここに　電話番号(でんわばんごう)が　ありますから。
Soo-desu-ne. . . . Ja, denwa-o shite-kudasai. Koko-ni denwa-bangoo-ga arimasu-kara. **lines 14-15**

denwa-o shite-kudasai	please call me
denwa-bangoo	telephone number

Soo-desu-ne here is used as a kind of interjection, similar to the English 'Well, let me see.'

Both *denwa-o suru* and *denwa-o kakeru* (line 22) are used to mean 'to call on the telephone.'

The use of *kara* at the end of a sentence, as in *denwa-bangoo-ga arimasu-kara*, is explained in Lesson 7.

ジョンソン(じよんそん)さん、もう　切符(きっぷ)を　かいましたか。 **line 16**
Jonson-san, moo kippu-o kaimashita-ka.

moo	already; yet
kippu	ticket
. . . o kaimashita-ka	have you bought . . .? (dict. *kau*)

まだです。どこで　うっていますか。 **line 17**
Mada-desu. Doko-de utte-imasu-ka.

mada-desu	not yet
(. . . o)utte-imasu-ka	are they selling (. . .)? (dict. *uru*)

あそこの　機械(きかい)で　かってください。 **line 18**
Asoko-no kikai-de katte-kudasai.

kikai	machine
kikai-de	by the machine
(. . .o)katte-kudasai	please buy (. . .) (dict. *kau*)

De used here indicates the means by which or with which an action is performed.

ex. *Pen-de kaite-kudasai.* (Please write with a pen.) (dict. *kaku*)
Denwa-de hanashimashita. (We talked on the phone.)

(*De* in line 17 and line 22 is used to indicate the place where an action is performed. cf. Lesson 4)

こまかい　お金を　もっていますか。 **lines 18-19**

Komakai o-kane-o motte-imasu-ka.

komakai	small
o-kane	money (usu. with *o-*)
. . . o motte-imasu-ka	do you have . . . ? (dict. *motsu*)

In words like *o-kane, o-tera* (temple, Lesson 10), and *o-kashi* (cake, Lesson 10), the honorific prefix *o-* is used to make the speech more polite rather than to indicate respect for a particular person. Women use words with this kind of *o-* more often than men do.

The *-te-imasu* form sometimes indicates a state or condition, rather than action in progress. *Motte* is derived from *motsu*, 'to hold,' and *motte-imasu* means that someone is 'in a state of possessing something.' The following examples show this use of the *-te-imasu* form.

ex. *Moo kekkon-shite-imasu.* (I'm married.) (dict. *kekkon-suru*, 'to marry')
Atarashii fuku-o kite-imasu. (She's wearing new clothes) (dict. *kiru*, 'to wear')

ええ、たくさん　もっています。 **line 20**

Ee, takusan motte-imasu.

takusan	plenty ; many

あそこで　電話を　かけています。 **line 22**

Asoko-de denwa-o kakete-imasu.

denwa-o kakete-imasu	she's making a phone call (dict. *kakeru*)

Note **Pronunciation of compounds**

When two or more words are combined into one word, the original accent of each word is lost and the compound has a distinct accent pattern. (cf. Lessons 17 and 18, pronunciation practice)

ex. *denwa* + *bangoo* → *denwa-bangoo*
booeki + *kaisha* → *booeki-gaisha* (In compounds the [k] sound often changes to a [g] (nasalized) sound.)

Notice that the pitch does not fluctuate up and down within a compound word but goes up only once.

Drills

I. . . . *te-imasu*

Structure Drill 1 Practice the following table, reading aloud.

tsutomeru (work)	*tsutomemasu*	*tsutomete-imasu*
asobu (play)	*asobimasu*	*asonde-imasu*
uru (sell)	*urimasu*	*utte-imasu*
kau (buy)	*kaimasu*	*katte-imasu*
motsu (have)	*mochimasu*	*motte-imasu*
(*denwa-o*) *kakeru* (call)	*kakemasu*	*kakete-imasu*

Structure Drill 2 Change the *-masu* form into the *-te-imasu* form.

ex. *booeki-gaisha-ni tsutomemasu*
→ *Booeki-gaisha-ni tsutomete-imasu.*

1. *terebi-o mimasu*
2. *kippu-o kaimasu*
3. *denwa-o kakemasu*
4. *shinbun-o yomimasu*
5. *kooen-de asobimasu*
6. *shigoto-o shimasu*

Usage Drill Look at the pictures and describe what each person is doing.

ex. *Ichiban* (No. 1); *Terebi-o mite-imasu.*

Then practice asking and answering questions about what each person in the picture is doing.

ex. A: *Ichiban-no hito-wa nani-o shite-imasu-ka.*

B: *Terebi-o mite-imasu.*

II. ... *de* ... *te-imasu*

Structure Drill Practice making sentences choosing phrases from the braces.

Watashi-wa { *uchi-de* / *gakkoo-de* / *eki-de* / *toshokan-de* / *koko-de* } { *matte-imasu.* / *shigoto-o shite-imasu.* / *denwa-o kakete-imasu.* }

III. ... *ni tsutomete-imasu*

Structure Drill Change the following as shown in the example.

ex. *kaisha* → *Kaisha-ni tsutomete-imasu.*

1. *ginkoo* 2. *toshokan* 3. *yuubinkyoku*
4. *byooin* 5. *gakkoo* 6. *yakusho* (government office)

Usage Drill Practice the following conversation changing the underlined parts.

ex. *booeki-gaisha, toshokan*

A: *...san, ima doko-ni tsutomete-imasu-ka.*

B: *Booeki-gaisha-ni tsutomete-imasu.*

A: *O-isogashii-desu-ka.*

B: *Ee, taihen-desu. ...san wa?*

A: *Watashi-wa toshokan-ni tsutomete-imasu.*

B: *Sore-wa ii-desu-ne.*

1. *ginkoo, gakkoo* 2. *yuubinkyoku, toshokan*
3. *byooin, ginkoo* 4. *shokudoo, yakusho*
5. *yakusho, daigaku* (college)

IV. Telephone calls

Usage Drill Practice the following conversations alone until you memorize them, then practice them with a partner.

A) Having someone called to the phone:

A: *Moshi-moshi* (Hello), *. . . san-no otaku-desu-ka.*

B: *Hai, ... desu.*

A: *Kochira-wa . . . . desu. Sumimasen-ga, ... san-o onegai-shimasu.* (I'd like to talk to . . . . san)

B: *Hai, chotto matte-kudasai.*

B) When the person you want to talk to is out:

A: *Sumimasen-ga. . . . . san-o onegai-shimasu.*

B: *. . . . san-wa sakki* (a while ago) *dekakemashita.*

A: *Nanji-goro o-kaeri-deshoo-ka.* (When will he be back?)

B: *Saa* (Well), *wakarimasen-ga . . . .*

A: *Soo-desu-ka. Ja, mata ato-de* (later) *kakemasu. Shitsuree-shimashita.*

V. Meeting people

Usage Drill Practice the following expressions until you memorize them, then carry out the conversation with partners. Remember that when introduced you should make a slight bow.

1. A: *. . . . san, kochira-wa . . . . san-desu.*
   B: *Hajimemashite.*
   C: *Doozo yoroshiku.*
2. C: *. . . san-wa gakusee-desu-ka.*
   B: *Ee, . .*. . o benkyoo-shite-imasu.*
3. B: *. . . . san-wa o-shigoto-desu-ka.*
   C: *Ee, .**. . ni tsutomete-imasu.*

* Use one of these words —*nihongo, keezai, seeji* (politics), *kagaku* (science), *igaku* (medical science), *bungaku* (literature), *rekishi* (history)

** Use one of these words —*kaisha, ginkoo, byooin, toshokan, yakusho, daigaku, kookoo*

VI. Phone numbers

Phone numbers are read in the following way, either with or without counter *-ban*. *No* is said where a hyphen occurs in the number.

123-4567 —*ichi-ni-san-no yon-go-roku-nana*

03-281-1659 —*ree* (or *zero*)*-san-no ni-hachi-ichi-no ichi-roku-go-kyuu*

For the number '2' is sometimes read *futa*; '4' is usually read *yon*, and '9' *kyuu* rather than *ku*; for '7' *nana* is preferred to *shichi*. This prevents difficulty in comprehension.

Practice saying the following numbers.

294-5418; 721-3864; 03-337-2950; 457-1106

Pronunciation Practice

Practice saying the following aloud, pausing slightly after each comma.

A. 1. *o -i -i -e, i -e -o -i* 2. *e -i -u -o, u -o -e -e*
3. *to -i-chi-e, chi-e-to-i* 4. *te -i-tsu-o, tsu-o-te-e*
5. *do-i -ji -e, ji -e-do -i* 6. *de-i -zu -o, zu -o-de-e*

B. 1. *taitee, mochiron* (of course)
2. *wareware* (we), *minasan* (all of you)
3. *kono-goro, hajimete* (for the first time)
4. *tetsudoo* (railway), *hikooki* (airplane)
5. *Matsumoto, Matsumura* (personal name)

C. Add *-desu-ka* to the words in B, and ask each question with a rising intonation.

ex. *Taitee-desu-ka. Mochiron-desu-ka.*

Reading Comprehension

Read the following passage.

(Johnson introduces himself to a group of Japanese students.)

ジョンソン(じょんそん)です。どうぞよろしく。去年(きょねん)(1)の九月(くがつ)に日本(にほん)(2)へきました。専門(せんもん)は経済(けいざい)ですが。いまは日本語(にほんご)を勉強(べんきょう)しています。中野(なかの)(3)にすんでいます(4)。駅(えき)のそばですから、しずかじゃありません。へや[5]もひろくありませんが、どうぞあそびにきてください。まっています。

(1) last year (2) Japan (3) place name (4) I live; dict. *sumu* (5) room

Aural Comprehension

Listen to the conversations on the tape and answer the following questions.

(A) 1. What kind of work does Mr. Yoshida do?

2. Does Mrs. Sato think a library is a nice place to work?

3. Does Mr. Yoshida sound as if he enjoys his work?

(B) 1. Was Sato disappointed when he was told Masao would be home late?

2. When is he going to call again?

(C) 1. How long has it been since Matsumoto and Imai last met?

2. Are they going to part now or are they going to go somewhere to talk?

3. If they are going somewhere, where is it?

第九課(だいきゅうか)　おそいと　おもいました

Dialogue

(Johnson arrives at the station hurriedly.)

ジョンソン：　おそく　なって　すみません。
山下(やました)：　いいえ。まだ　だれも　きません。
ジョンソン：　そうですか。もう　おそいと　おもいました。
山下(やました)：　鈴木(すずき)さんは　きません。けさ　電話(でんわ)が　ありました。
ジョンソン：　だめですか。
山下(やました)：　ええ。ざんねんだと　いっていました。
ジョンソン：　松本(まつもと)さんは　くるでしょうか。
山下(やました)：　ええ、松本(まつもと)さんは　くると　おもいますよ。
ジョンソン：　じゃ、もう　すこし　まちましょうか。

ジョンソン：　このあいだ　田中(たなか)さんと　いう　人(ひと)に　あいました。山下(やました)さんを　しっていると　いっていましたよ。
山下(やました)：　田中(たなか)さん？　どんな　人(ひと)ですか。
ジョンソン：　せいが　たかくて　やせている　人(ひと)です。貿易会社(ぼうえきがいしゃ)に　つとめていると　いっていました。
山下(やました)：　ああ、わかりました。大学(だいがく)の　先輩(せんぱい)です。
ジョンソン：あ、あれは　松本(まつもと)さんじゃ　ありませんか。
山下(やました)：　どこですか。
ジョンソン：　あそこです。売店(ばいてん)で　なにか　かっている　人(ひと)です。
山下(やました)：　松本(まつもと)さんじゃ　ないと　おもいますよ。松本(まつもと)さんは　めがねを　かけていませんから。

Dialogue Lesson 9 — *Dai-kyuuka*

I THOUGHT I WAS LATE — *OSOI-TO OMOIMASHITA*

Johnson: I'm sorry I'm late.	*Jonson: Osoku natte ▲sumimasen.*
Yamashita: That's all right. Nobody's here yet.	*Yamashita: Iie. Mada ▲daremo kimasen.*
J: Is that right? I thought I was late.	*J: Soo-desu-ka. Moo ▲osoi-to omoimashita.*
Y: Mr. Suzuki is not coming. He called me this morning.	*Y: Suzuki-san-wa ▲kimasen. Kesa ▲denwa-ga arimashita.*
J: Oh, he can't come?	*J: Dame-desu-ka.*
Y: No. He said he was sorry.	*Y: Ee. ▲Zannen-da-to itte-imashita.*
J: I wonder if Mr. Matsumoto's coming.	*J: ▲Matsumoto-san-wa kuru-deshoo-ka.*
Y: I think he is.	*Y: Ee, Matsumoto-san-wa ▲kuru-to omoimasu-yo.*
J: Then let's wait awhile, shall we?	*J: Ja, ▲moo sukoshi machimashoo-ka.*
J: I met a man named Tanaka the other day. He said he knows you, Mr. Yamashita.	*J: Kono-aida ▲Tanaka-san-to yuu hito-ni aimashita. Yamashita-san-o ▲shitte-iru-to itte-imashita-yo.*
Y: Mr. Tanaka? What does he look like?	*Y: Tanaka-san? ▲Donna hito-desu-ka.*
J: Tall and thin. He said he is working for a trading company.	*J: ▲See-ga takakute ▲yasete-iru hito-desu. ▲Booeki-gaisha-ni tsutome-te-iru-to itte-imashita.*
Y: Oh, I know. He was ahead of me in college.	*Y: Aa, wakarimashita. ▲Daigaku-no senpai-desu.*
J: Oh, isn't that Mr. Matsumoto?	*J: A, are-wa ▲Matsumoto-san-ja arimasen-ka.*
Y: Where?	*Y: Doko-desu-ka.*
J: There. The person buying something at the stand.	*J: Asoko-desu. ▲Baiten-de nanika katte-iru hito-desu.*
Y: I don't think that's Mr. Matsumoto. He doesn't wear glasses.	*Y: Matsumoto-san-ja ▲nai-to omoimasu-yo. Matsumoto-san-wa ▲megane-o kakete-imasen-kara.*

Explanation

(In this lesson you will learn expressions corresponding to 'He said ....,' and 'I thought ....' in English.)

おそく　なって　すみません。 **line 1**

Osoku natte sumimasen.

osoku	late (dict. *osoi*)
osoku natte	I have become late and ...(dict. *naru*)

When an *-i* adjective comes before a verb, it ends in its *-ku* form.

ex. *Hayaku kimashita.* (I came early.)

Kao-ga akaku narimashita. (My face turned red.)

The *-te* form of a verb is often used to indicate the reason for what follows, especially for an apology or complaint.

ex. *Osoku natte shitsuree-shimashita.* (I'm sorry I'm late.)

Okane-ga tarinakute dame-deshita. (I couldn't because I didn't have enough money.)

いいえ。まだ　だれも　きません。 **line 2**

Iie. Mada daremo kimasen.

daremo ...masen	not anybody ...

Here *kimasen* corresponds to 'hasn't come' in English. The present negative form of a verb can mean either 'isn't ... ing' or 'hasn't ...' depending on the context.

そうですか。もう　おそいと　おもいました。 **line 3**

Soo-desu-ka. Moo osoi-to omoimashita.

... to omoimashita	I thought that ... (dict. *omou*)

When the quoted portion of the sentence ends in an *-i* adjective, Japanese usually do not add *-desu* before *... to omoimasu* or *...to iimashita.* (See Note 1)

ex. A: *Kono hon-wa ii-desu-ne.* (This book is good, isn't it?)

B: *Ee, Kawakami-san-mo ii-to iimashita.* (Yes. Mr. Kawakami also said it was good.)

Note in the following examples that the verb at the end of the sentence carries the tense and that the adjective needn't be changed to the past as it does in English.

ex. *Moo osoi-to omoimashita.* (I thought I was late.)
Takai-to iimashita. (He said it was expensive.)

鈴木さんは　きません。けさ　電話が　ありました。 **line 4**
Suzuki-san-wa kimasen. Kesa denwa-ga arimashita.

kesa this morning

Here *kimasen* means 'he's not coming.'

だめですか。 **line 5**
Dame-desu-ka.

dame-desu no good; he can't make it

This sentence is in question form, but the speaker is actually half speaking to himself. In this type of statement, the *-ka* at the end of the sentence falls in pitch.

ええ。ざんねんだと　いっていました。 **line 6**
Ee. Zannen-da-to itte-imashita.

zannen-da (the plain form of *zannen-desu*)
... to itte-imashita he was saying ... (dict. *yuu*)

Da is the plain form of *-desu*, and is used both after nouns and *-na* adjectives. (See Note 1)

ex. *Gakusee-da-to omoimasu.* (I think he's a student.)

松本さんは　くるでしょうか。 **line 7**
Matsumoto-san-wa kuru-deshoo-ka.

kuru-deshoo-ka I wonder if he will come

Deshoo follows the plain form of verbs.

ex. *Ashita-wa ame-ga furu-deshoo-ne.* (I think it will rain tomorrow.)

じゃ、もう　すこし　まちましょうか。 **line 9**
Ja, moo sukoshi machimashoo-ka.

moo more
moo sukoshi a little more

Note that *moo* which means 'already' is pronounced *moo*, while this *moo* which means 'more' is pronounced *moo*.

ex. *Moo ichido itte-kudasai.* (Please say it once more.)

このあいだ 田中(たなか)さんと いう 人(ひと)に あいました。 **lines 10-11**

Kono-aida Tanaka-san-to yuu hito-ni aimashita.

kono-aida the other day

. . . to yuu hito a person who calls himself . . .(dict. *yuu*)

Tanaka-san-to yuu modifies *hito*. A verb used in a modifying phrase takes the plain form.

ex. *Asoko-de denwa-o kakete-iru hito-wa Miraa-san-desu.*

(The person who is making a telephone call over there is Miss Miller.)

The *hiragana* transcription of the verb *yuu* is いう, not ゆう.

山下(やました)さんを しっていると いっていましたよ。 **line 11**

Yamashita-san-o shitte-iru-to itte-imashita-yo.

shitte-iru he knows (dict. *shiru*)

The closest equivalent of the English 'know' is *shitte-iru*. To ask 'Do you know . . . ?' you must say *Shitte-imasu-ka*, never *Shirimasu-ka*. However, the negative form *shirimasen* is more common than *shitte-imasen*.

せいが たかくて やせている 人(ひと)です。 **line 13**

See-ga takakute yasete-iru hito-desu.

see stature

see-ga takakute tall and . . . (dict. *takai*)

yasete -iru thin (dict. *yaseru*)

'. . . . *te-iru*' is sometimes used to describe a state of persons or things. The verb *yaseru* means 'to become thin,' and *yasete-iru* means 'to be thin.' The antonym of *yaseru* is *futoru*.

貿易会社(ぼうえきがいしゃ)に つとめていると いっていました。 **lines 13-14**

Booeki-gaisha-ni tsutomete-iru-to itte-imashita.

Remember what Mr. Tanaka told Johnson in Lesson 8. He said, "*Booeki-gaisha-ni tsutomete-imasu.*" (See Note 1.)

ああ、わかりました。大学(だいがく)の 先輩(せんぱい)です。 **line 15**

Aa, wakarimashita. Daigaku-no senpai-desu.

wakarimashita I understand (*lit.* I have understood) (dict. *wakaru*)

daigaku college ; university
senpai one's senior (opp. *koohai*)

あ、あれは　松本(まつもと)さんじゃ　ありませんか。 **line 16**

A, are-wa Matsumoto-san-ja arimasen-ka.

. . . ja arimasen-ka isn't that . . . ?

'. . . *ja arimasen*' is the negative form of *-desu*. (See Lesson 6 for the negative form of *-na* adjectives.)

ex. *Watashi-wa moo gakusee-ja arimasen.* (I'm no longer a student.)

Attention must be paid to the difference between . . . . *ja arimasen*, 'is not . . . .' and . . . .*ga arimasen*, ". . . . does not exist.'

ex. *Watashi-no hon-ja arimasen.* (This is not my book.)
Watashi-no hon-ga arimasen. (My book is missing.)

あそこです。売店(ばいてん)で　なにか　かっている　人(ひと)です。 **lines 18-19**

Asoko-desu. Baiten-de nanika katte-iru hito-desu.

baiten a stand

松本(まつもと)さんじゃ　ないと　おもいますよ。 **line 20**

Matsumoto-san-ja nai-to omoimasu-yo.

'. . . *ja nai* ' is the plain form of '. . . *ja arimasen.*' See Note 2

松本(まつもと)さんは　めがねを　かけていませんから。 **lines 20-21**

Matsumoto-san-wa megane-o kakete-imasen-kara.

megane glasses
megane-o kakete wearing glasses (dict. *kakeru*)

Note 1 The plain form in quotation: affirmative

	-masu form	**plain form (I think that)**	
verbs	*mimasu ;*	*miru*	*-to omoimasu*
	kimasu ;	*kuru*	*-to omoimasu*
-desu	*gakusee-desu ;*	*gakusee-da-to omoimasu*	
	nigiyaka-desu ;	*nigiyaka-da-to omoimasu*	
***-i* adj.**	*takai-desu ;*	*takai*	*-to omoimasu*

Note 2 **The plain form in quotation: negative**

	-masen	**plain form (I think that)**
verbs	*mimasen*;	*minai -to omoimasu*
	kimasen;	*konai -to omoimasu*
-desu	*gakusee-ja arimasen*;	*gakusee-ja nai-to omoimasu*
	nigiyaka-ja arimasen;	*nigiyaka-ja nai-to omoimasu*
***-i* adj.**	*takaku arimasen*;	*takaku nai -to omoimasu*

The plain negative forms of verbs are made in the following way.

A: Group 1 (*-u* verbs)

Replace the final vowel by *-anai*.

ex. *ik**u*** —*ik**anai***; *hanas**u*** —*hanas**anai***; *yom**u*** —*yom**anai***

For *-u* verbs ending in a vowel + *-u*, replace the final vowel by *-wanai*.

ex. *a**u***—*a**wanai***; *omo**u***—*omo**wanai***

For *-u* verbs ending in *-tsu*, replace the *-tsu* by *-tanai*.

ex. *mo**tsu***—*mo**tanai***; *ta**tsu***—*ta**tanai***

B: Group 2 (*-ru* verbs)

Replace the final *-ru* by *-nai*.

ex. *tabe**ru*** —*tabe**nai***; *mi**ru*** —*mi**nai***; *tsutome**ru*** —*tsutome**nai***

Exceptions: ***kuru* —*konai*; *suru* —*shinai*; *yuu* —*iwanai***

The plain negative form of the verb *aru* is *nai*.

To make the plain negative form of *-i* adjectives, *nai* is added after the *-ku* form.

ex. *taka**i*** —*takaku arimasen* —*taka**ku nai***

*isogashi**i***—*isogashiku arimasen* —*isogashi**ku nai***

Exception: ii —*yoku arimasen* —***yoku nai***

Drills

I. The plain form

Structure Drill Memorize the following tables by saying each word aloud.

A) **verb**

ikimasu	*ikimasen*	*iku*	*ikanai*
kikimasu	*kikimasen*	*kiku*	*kikanai*
asobimasu	*asobimasen*	*asobu*	*asobanai*
machimasu	*machimasen*	*matsu*	*matanai*
hanashimasu	*hanashimasen*	*hanasu*	*hanasanai*
iimasu	*iimasen*	*yuu*	*iwanai*
dekakemasu	*dekakemasen*	*dekakeru*	*dekakenai*
tarimasu	*tarimasen*	*tariru*	*tarinai*
kimasu	*kimasen*	*kuru*	*konai*
shimasu	*shimasen*	*suru*	*shinai*

B) *-da*

watashi-desu	*watashi-ja arimasen*	*watashi-da*	*watashi-ja nai*
soo-desu	*soo-ja arimasen*	*soo-da*	*soo-ja nai*
genki-desu	*genki-ja arimasen*	*genki-da*	*genki-ja nai*
nigiyaka-desu	*nigiyaka-ja arimasen*	*nigiyaka-da*	*nigiyaka-ja nai*

C) *-i* adj,

osoi-desu	*osoku arimasen*	*osoi*	*osoku nai*
takai-desu	*takaku arimasen*	*takai*	*takaku nai*
ii-desu	*yoku arimasen*	*ii*	*yoku nai*

II. The plain form plus *-to omoimasu*

Structure Drill

A) **verb** Practice changing the verb form and using it in a sentence ending with *-to omoimasu.*

ex. *osoku narimasu* →*Osoku naru-to omoimasu.*

1. *asobi-ni dekakemasu* 2. *yasete-imasu* 3. *osoku kimasu*
4. *Yamashita-san-o shitte-imasu* 5. *iroirona supootsu-o yarimasu*
6. *nihongo-o hanashimasu*

B) **verb, negative** Practice changing each verb to its negative plain form and using it in a sentence ending in *-to omoimasu.*

ex. *kyoo-wa kimasen* → *Kyoo-wa konai-to omoimasu.*

1. *eega-o mimasen* 2. *amari benkyoo-shimasen*
3. *watashi-o shirimasen* 4. *nihongo-o hanashimasen*
5. *amari yaku-ni tachimasen* 6. *sonna hito-wa imasen*

C) ***-da*** Practice changing *-desu* to its plain form and using it in a sentence ending in *-to omoimasu.*

ex. *ano-hito-wa Yamashita-san-desu.*

→ *Ano-hito-wa Yamashita-san-da-to omoimasu.*

1. *kyoo-wa doyoobi-desu* 2. *ano tatemono-wa byooin-desu*
3. *asoko-wa nigiyaka-desu* 4. *kore-wa watashi-no hon-desu*
5. *kono shigoto-wa taihen-desu*
6. *ano-hito-wa Yamashita-san-no okusan-desu*

D) ***-ja nai*** Practice changing *-ja arimasen* to *-ja nai,* its plain form, and use it in a sentence ending in *-to omoimasu.*

ex. *ano-hito-wa Matsumoto-san-ja arimasen*
→ *Ano-hito-wa Matsumoto-san-ja nai-to omoimasu.*

1. *watashi-no megane-ja arimasen* 2. *ashita-wa hima-ja arimasen*
3. *amari kiree-ja arimasen* 4. *amari kiree-na tokoro-ja arimasen*
5. *ima-no shigoto-wa taihen-ja arimasen*
6. *amari ii jibiki* (dictionary)*-ja arimasen*

E) ***-ku nai*** Practice changing *-ku arimasen* to *-ku nai,* its plain form, and use it in a sentence ending in *-to omoimasu.*

ex. *see-wa takaku arimasen*
→ *See-wa takaku nai-to omoimasu.*

1. *ashita-wa isogashiku arimasen* 2. *mada osoku arimasen*
3. *see-wa hikuku arimasen* (not short) 4. *amari takaku arimasen*
5. *moo hayaku arimasen* 6. *kono jibiki-wa yoku arimasen*

Usage Drill Practice the following conversations changing the underlined words.

A) ex. *shinbun-o yomu*

A: *Ano-hito-wa dare-desu-ka.*
B: *Dono-hito-desu-ka.*
A: *Asoko-de shinbun-o yonde-iru hito-desu.*
B: *Aa, ano-hito-wa Yamashita-san-da-to omoimasu.*

1. *terebi-o miru*
2. *dareka-o matsu*
3. *koohii-o nomu*
4. *bentoo* (box lunch)*-o taberu*
5. *denwa-o kakeru*
6. *zasshi* (magazine)*-o kau*

B) ex. *kuru*

A: *Yamashita-san-wa kuru-deshoo-ka.*
B: *Ee, kuru-to omoimasu. Sakki* (a while ago) *denwa-ga arimashita-kara.*
A: *Kuru-to itte-imashita-ka.*
B: *Ee, soo itte-imashita.*

1. *iku*
2. *dekakeru*
3. *konai*
4. *kau*
5. *kawanai*
6. *ikanai*

C) This time, practice the conversation with your teacher or a fellow student using real names and facts.

A: *Kono-aida . . . .san-to yuu hito-ni aimashita.*
B: *Soo-desu-ka.*
A: *. . . .san-o shitte-iru-to itte-imashita-yo.*
B: *Donna hito-desu-ka.*
A: *See-ga takakute* yasete-iru** hito-desu.*
B: *Ikutsu-gurai* (about how old)*-desu-ka.*
A: *Yoku wakarimasen-ga, sanjuu-gurai***-deshoo.*
B: *Aa, wakarimashita. Daigaku-no toki-no tomodachi-desu.*

* *opp. hikukute*; ** *opp. futotte-iru*; *** Change according to situation.

Pronunciation Practice

Practice saying the following aloud, pausing slightly after each comma.

A. 1. *i -e -o -i, o -i -i -e* 2. *u -o -e -e, e -i -u -o*
3. *shi -e -so -i, so -i -shi -e* 4. *su -o -se -e, se -i -su -o*
5. *ji -e -zo -i, zo -i -ji -e* 6. *zu -o -ze -e, ze -i -zu -o*

B. (personal names)
1. *Tanaka* 2. *Suzuki* 3. *Itoo*
4. *Maeda* 5. *Yoshida* 6. *Mishima*

C. Add *-san-desu-ka* and *-sensee-desu-ka* to the words in B, and say the question with a rising intonation.
ex. *Tanaka-san-desu-ka*. *Tanaka-sensee-de su-ka.*

Reading Comprehension

Read the following.

このあいだ、用(よう)があって(1)川上(かわかみ)さんのうちへいきました。川上(かわかみ)さんはいませんでした。おくさんが「すぐかえるとおもいます」といいましたので、あがって(2)まちました。三十分(さんじっぷん)ぐらいまちましたが、川上(かわかみ)さんがかえらないので、川上(かわかみ)さんのうちをでました(3)。よる、電話(でんわ)で川上(かわかみ)さんと(4)はなしました。

(1) having some business (2) I went up and (3) I left (4) with Mr. Kawakami

Aural Comprehension

Listen to the conversations on the tape and answer the following questions.

(A) 1. Whose name does the woman want to know?
2. What kind of work does Mr. Ishida do?
3. How old is he?

(B) 1. How long have the man and woman been waiting for the train?
2. Did both of them hear the announcement about the delay?
3. Does the woman seem to be angry?

(C) 1. What's Mr. Yamada's problem?
2. Why can't he find a job?

第十課(だいじっか)　京都(きょうと)で　とった　写真(しゃしん)

Dialogue

山下(やました)：　このあいだ　京都(きょうと)で　とった　写真(しゃしん)が　できましたよ。

ジョンソン(じょんそん)：　ずいぶん　はやく　できましたね。みせてください。

山下(やました)：　ちょっと　まってください。この　なかに　あったと　おもいますが。

ジョンソン(じょんそん)：　べつの　ところじゃ　ありませんか。

山下(やました)：　いいえ、たしかに　この　なかだったと　おもいます。…あ、ありました。

ジョンソン(じょんそん)：　これは　三十三間堂(さんじゅうさんげんどう)ですね。

山下(やました)：　ええ。おべんとうを　たべた　ところですね。こちらは　清水寺(きよみずでら)です。

ジョンソン(じょんそん)：　お寺(てら)の　そばの　ちゃみせに　はいりましたね。

山下(やました)：　ええ。あそこで　たべた　おかしは　おいしかったですね。

ジョンソン(じょんそん)：　となりに　すわった　おばあさんと　いろいろ　話(はなし)を　しましたね。

山下(やました)：　ええ、そうでしたね。

ジョンソン(じょんそん)：　あの人(ひと)の　ことばは　よく　わかりませんでした。ぼくの　ならった　ことばと　ちがいますから。

山下(やました)：　ぼくも　よく　わかりませんでしたよ。

ジョンソン(じょんそん)：　平安神宮(へいあんじんぐう)の　写真(しゃしん)は　ありませんか。

山下(やました)：　平安神宮(へいあんじんぐう)では　とらなかったと　おもいます。

ジョンソン(じょんそん)：　ああ、そうそう。もう　くらく　なっていましたね。

Dialogue Lesson 10

THE PICTURES I TOOK IN KYOTO

Yamashita: The pictures I took in Kyoto the other day came out.

Johnson: They were developed very quickly, weren't they? May I have a look at them?

Y: Just a moment. I think they are in this, but......

J: Aren't they somewhere else?

Y: No, I'm sure they were here.... Here they are.

J: This is Sanjusangendo. isn't it?

Y: Yes, that's where we had lunch. This one shows Kiyomizu Temple.

J: We entered a little tea house near that temple, didn't we?

Y: Yes. The cakes we had there were delicious.

We talked a lot with that old woman who sat next to us.

Y: Yes.

J: I couldn't understand what she said very well. She used a different language from what I learned.

Y: I didn't understand her too well, either.

J: Don't you have some pictures of Heian Shrine?

Y: I don't think I took pictures there.

J: Oh, that's right. It was already dark by then.

Dai-jikka

KYOOTO-DE TOTTA SHASHIN

Yamashita: Kono-aida Kyooto-de totta shashin-ga dekimashita-yo.

Jonson: Zuibun hayaku dekimashita-ne. Misete-kudasai.

Y: Chotto matte-kudasai. Kono naka-ni atta-to omoimasu-ga.

J: Betsu-no tokoro-ja arimasen-ka.

Y: Iie, tashika-ni kono naka-datta-to omoimasu. ...A, arimashita.

J: Kore-wa Sanjuusangendoo-desu-ne.

Y: Ee. O-bentoo-o tabeta tokoro-desu. Kochira-wa Kiyomizudera-desu.

J: O-tera-no soba-no chamise-ni hairimashita-ne.

Y: Ee. Asoko-de tabeta o-kashi-wa oishikatta-desu-ne.

J: Tonari-ni suwatta obaasan-to iroiro hanashi-o shimashita-ne.

Y: Ee, soo-deshita-ne.

J: Ano-hito-no kotoba-wa yoku wakarimasen-deshita. Boku-no naratta kotoba-to chigaimasu-kara.

Y: Boku-mo yoku wakarimasen-deshita-yo.

J: Heean-jinguu-no shashin-wa arimasen-ka.

Y: Heean-jinguu-dewa toranakatta-to omoimasu.

J: Aa, soo-soo. Moo kuraku natte-imashita-ne.

Explanation

(In this lesson you will learn the affirmative and negative of plain past forms.)

このあいだ　京都で　とった　写真が　できましたよ。 **line 1**

Kono-aida Kyooto-de totta shashin-ga dekimashita-yo.

Kyooto	place name; capital of Japan, 794—1868
(*...o*)*totta*	I took (...) (dict. *toru*)
shashin	photograph
...ga dekimashita	...came out (dict. *dekiru*)

Totta is the past form of *toru*, 'to take.' The formation of the plain past form is quite simple; change the last part of the *-te* form to *-ta*. You might also call it the *-ta* form.

All modifiers come *before* the nouns or pronouns they modify. A modifying phrase can be quite long as in the following example.

ex. *Kono-aida Kawakami-san-ga Kyooto-de totta shashin-desu.* (These are the photographs that Mr. Kawakami took in Kyoto the other day.)

ずいぶん　はやく　できましたね。みせてください。 **lines 2-3**

Zuibun hayaku dekimashita-ne. Misete-kudasai.

zuibun	very
(*...o*)*misete-kudasai*	please show (...) to me (dict. *miseru*)

Zuibun is similar in meaning to *taihen* (adv.), and a little more emotional than *taihen.*

この　なかに　あったと　おもいますが。 **lines 4-5**

Kono naka-ni atta-to omoimasu-ga.

(*...ga*) *atta*	(...) existed (dict. *aru*)

べつの　ところじゃ　ありませんか。 **line 6**

Betsu-no tokoro-ja arimasen-ka.

betsu-no	other
tokoro	place

This actually means 'I think they are somewhere else.' Therefore Yamashita answers "*Iie*" in line 7 to indicate that he disagrees. (See Note on the use of *Ee* in answering negative questions, Lesson 6.)

いいえ、たしかに　この　なかだったと　おもいます。 **line 7**

Iie, tashika-ni kono naka-datta-to omoimasu.

tashika-ni surely; certainly

kono naka-datta they were in this

Tashika is a *-na* adjective; when *-na* adjectives take the *-ni* ending, they are used as adverbs.

ex. *Taihen kiree-ni dekimashita.* (They came out very beautifully.)

Tonari-no heya-ga shizuka-ni narimashita. (The next room became quiet.)

Datta is the past form of *-da*, the plain form of *-desu*.

ex. *Gakusee-datta Yamashita-san-ga ima-wa sensee-desu.* (Mr. Yamashita, who was a student then, is now a teacher.)

Paatee-wa nigiyaka-datta-to minna-ga itte-imasu. (Everyone says the party was lively.)

あ、ありました。 **line 8**

A, arimashita.

This expression is used to mean 'Here it is!' when you find something you've been looking for.

これは　三十三間堂(さんじゅうさんげんどう)ですね。 **line 9**

Kore-wa Sanjuusangendoo-desu-ne.

Sanjuusangendoo name of a temple

ええ。おべんとうを　たべた　ところですね。こちらは　清水寺(きよみずでら)です。

Ee. O-bentoo-o tabeta tokoro-desu-ne. Kochira-wa Kiyomizudera-desu.

lines 10-11

o-bentoo box lunch

...o tabeta tokoro the place where we ate... (dict. *taberu*)

Kiyomizudera name of a temple

A word corresponding to the English 'where' in phrases like 'the place where we had lunch' is not necessary in Japanese; the modifying phrase comes directly before the noun or pronoun.

ex. *Kono uchi-wa Natsume Sooseki-ga sunde-ita uchi-desu.* (This is the house where Natsume Soseki lived.)

お寺(てら)の　そばの　ちゃみせに　はいりましたね。 **line 12**

O-tera-no soba-no chamise-ni hairimashita-ne.

o-tera	temple
chamise	little tea house
. . .ni hairimashita	we entered . . . (dict. *hairu*)

Tera becomes *-dera* in a compound like *Kiyomizudera.*

Be careful not to say *chamise-o hairu*; *hairu* is preceded by *-ni.*

ええ。あそこで　たべた　おかしは　おいしかったですね。 **lines 13-14**

Ee. Asoko-de tabeta o-kashi-wa oishikatta-desu-ne.

o-kashi	sweet; candies; cakes
oishikatta	tasted good (dict. *oishii*)

The past form of *-i* adjectives is formed by replacing the last *-i* by *-katta*; in polite speech, *-desu* is added.

となりに　すわった　おばあさんと　いろいろ　話(はなし)を　しましたね。**lines 15-16**

Tonari-ni suwatta obaasan-to iroiro hanashi-o shimashita-ne.

tonari-ni	next to us
(*. . .ga*) *suwatta*	(. . .) sat (dict. *suwaru*)
obaasan	old woman
obaasan-to	with an old woman
iroiro	variously

To in *obaasan-to* means 'together.'

ex. *Kodomo-no toki Michiko-san-to yoku asobimashita.*

(I used to play a lot with Michiko when I was a child.)

あの人(ひと)の　ことばは　よく　わかりませんでした。　ぼくの　ならった

Ano-hito-no kotoba-wa yoku wakarimasen-deshita. Boku-no naratta

ことばと　ちがいますから。 **lines 18-19**

kotoba-to chigaimasu-kara.

kotoba	language; words
yoku	well
boku	I (male, familiar)

boku-no naratta... ...I learned (dict. *narau*)

...to chigaimasu it is different from ...(dict. *chigau*)

Boku is often used by males in informal speech, to mean 'I.'

In a modifying clause *-ga*, indicating the performer of an action, often becomes *-no* as in *boku-no naratta kotoba.*

ex. *Senshuu Tanaka-san-no totta shashin-wa kore-desu.* (This is the photograph that Mr. Tanaka took last week.)

Chigau takes *-to*.

ex. *Eego-wa nihongo-to zuibun chigaimasu.* (English is quite different from Japanese.)

(Because Yamashita is from Tokyo and familiar only with Tokyo speech, it is not unusual that he has trouble understanding the old woman who speaks in the Kyoto dialect.)

平安神宮(へいあんじんぐう)の 写真(しゃしん)は ありませんか。 **line 21**

Heean-jinguu-no shashin-wa arimasen-ka.

Heean-jinguu name of a shrine

平安神宮(へいあんじんぐう)では とらなかったと おもいます。 **line 22**

Heean-jinguu-dewa toranakatta-to omoimasu.

(... o)toranakatta I didn't take (...) (dict. *toru*)

The past form of a plain negative verbs is formed by changing the last *-nai* sound to *-nakatta*.

ex. *Matsumoto-san-wa kinoo konakatta-to omoimasu.* (I don't think Mr. Matsumoto came yesterday.)

ああ、そうそう。もう くらく なって いましたね。 **lines 23-24**

Aa, soo-soo. Moo kuraku natte-imashita-ne.

aa, soo-soo oh, yes, now I remember

kuraku natte-imashita it had become dark (dict. *kurai*)

The antonym of *kurai* is *akarui*.

ex. *Kono-goro-wa asa goji-goro-kara akaruku narimasu.* (Nowadays it begins to get light from about five in the morning.)

Drills

I. Plain past

Structure Drill 1 Memorize the following tables. Practice by saying each word aloud. (＊irregular)

A) **verbs**

toru	*totta*	*toranai*	*toranakatta*
hairu	*haitta*	*hairanai*	*hairanakatta*
wakaru	*wakatta*	*wakaranai*	*wakaranakatta*
matsu	*matta*	*matanai*	*matanakatta*
omou	*omotta*	*omowanai*	*omowanakatta*
aru	*atta*	*(nai*	*nakatta)*
yomu	*yonda*	*yomanai*	*yomanakatta*
iru	*ita*	*inai*	*inakatta*
dekiru	*dekita*	*dekinai*	*dekinakatta*
miseru	*miseta*	*misenai*	*misenakatta*
kuru	*kita*	*konai*	*konakatta*
suru	*shita*	*shinai*	*shinakatta*

B) **adjectives**

hayai	*hayakatta*	*hayaku nai*	*hayaku nakatta*
kurai	*kurakatta*	*kuraku nai*	*kuraku nakatta*
oishii	*oishikatta*	*oishiku nai*	*oishiku nakatta*
ii	*yokatta*＊	*yoku*＊ *nai*	*yoku*＊ *nakatta*

C) ***-da***

gakusee-da *gakusee-datta* *gakusee-ja nai*
gakusee-ja nakatta
tashika-da *tashika-datta* *tashika-ja nai*
tashika-ja nakatta
soo-da *soo-datta* *soo-ja nai* *soo-ja nakatta*

Structure Drill 2 Practice changing the following into plain forms.

a) ex. *wakarimasen* —*wakaranai*
wakarimashita —*wakatta*
wakarimasen-deshita —*wakaranakatta*

1. *machimashita* 2. *tabemasen* 3. *tabete-imashita*
4. *misemasen-deshita* 5. *hairimashita* 6. *torimasen-deshita*
7. *shashin-ga dekimasen-deshita* 8. *obaasan-ga kimashita*

b) ex. *gakusee-desu* —*gakusee-da*
gakusee-deshita —*gakusee-datta*
gakusee-ja arimasen-deshita —*gakusee-ja nakatta*

1. *Yamashita-san-deshita* 2. *soo-ja arimasen-deshita*
3. *hima-deshita* 4. *shizuka-ja arimasen-deshita*
5. *tashika-desu* 6. *kaban-no naka-deshita*
7. *mada gakusee-deshita* 8. *hima-ja arimasen-deshita*

Usage Drill 1 Practice the following conversation changing the underlined part.

ex. *o-hiru* (noon)*-goro*
A: *Rusu-ni* (while I was out) *dareka kimashita-ka.*
B: *Ee, Hayashi-san-ga kimashita.*
A: *Nanji-goro-deshita-ka.*
B: *O-hiru-goro-datta-to omoimasu.*

1. *yoji-goro* 2. *ichijikan-gurai mae* 3. *juuji chotto mae* (a little before 10) 4. *yuugata* (evening) 5. *yuuhan* (supper) *-no toki*

Usage Drill 2 Practice the following conversation changing the underlined phrase.

ex. *shashin-ga dekita*
A: *Kinoo ...to yuu hito-kara* (from) *denwa-ga arimashita.*
B: *Nanika itte-imashita-ka.*
A: *Ee, shashin-ga dekita-to itte-imashita.*
B: *Soo-desu-ka. Hoka-ni* (besides that) *nanika iimasen-deshita-ka.*
A: *Ee, iwanakatta-to omoimasu.*

1. *shigoto-ga owatta* (was finished)　　2. *tegami* (letter)*-ga kita*
3. *Kyooto-kara kaetta*　　4. *daigaku-ni haitta*
5. *okane-ga tarinakatta* (wasn't enough)
6. *kono-aida-wa shitsuree-shita* (was rude)

II. The plain form as a modifier

Structure Drill 1 Practice changing the following sentences into noun phrases.

A) ex. *Kyooto-de shashin-o torimashita*
→ *Kyooto-de totta shashin*

1. *chamise-de o-kashi-o tabemashita*
2. *otera-de butsuzoo* (Buddhist image)*-o mimashita*
3. *chamise-de obaasan-ni aimashita*
4. *kinoo Hayashi-san-ni shashin-o misemashita*
5. *kesa shinbun-o yomimashita*
6. *sakki kissaten-ni hairimashita*
7. *kono-aida obaasan-to hanashimashita*
8. *yuube* (last night) *eega-o mimashita*

B) ex. *watashi-ga shashin-o torimashita*
→ *watashi-no totta shashin*

1. *boku-ga eega-o mimashita*　2. *watashi-ga o-bentoo-o tabemashita*　3. *Kawakami-san-ga otera-e ikimashita*
4. *watashi-ga ojiisan* (old man)*-ni aimashita*
5. *watashi-tachi-ga shokudoo-ni hairimashita*
6. *mise-no hito-ga ringo-o tsutsumimashita*
7. *minna* (all of us)*-ga sakki ocha-o nomimashita*
8. *boku-ga nihongo-o naraimashita*

Structure Drill 2 Add *Kore-wa ....to chigaimasu* to the phrases you made in Structure Drill 1, A) and B).

ex. A) *Kyooto-de totta shashin*

→*Kore-wa Kyooto-de totta shashin-to chigaimasu.*

B) *watashi-no totta shashin*

→*Kore-wa watashi-no totta shashin-to chigaimasu.*

(When the thing discussed is a person say *Kono-hito-wa* instead of *Kore-wa.*)

Usage Drill Practice the following conversation changing the underlined words.

ex. *shashin, totta shashin*

A: *Doo shimashita-ka.* (What's the matter?)
B: *Shashin-ga arimasen.*
A: *Soo-desu-ka. Kore-ja arimasen-ka.*
B: *Iie, sore-wa watashi-no totta shashin-to chigaimasu.*
A: *Soo-desu-ka. ...A, arimashita. Isu-no ue-ni arimashita.*
B: *Doomo sumimasen.*

1. *megane, kakete-iru megane*
2. *jibiki, tsukatte-iru jibiki*
3. *saifu* (wallet), *katta saifu*
4. *tegami, moratta* (I received) *tegami*

Pronunciation Practice

Practice saying the following paying special attention to the accent.

A. 1. *za -i -za -u, za -u -za -i*
2. *za -i -zo -i, za -i -zo -u*
3. *ze -a -zo -a, ji -a -zu -a*
4. *ha -i -ha -u, ha -u -ha -i*
5. *-ha -i -ho -i, ha -i -ho -u*
6. *he -a -ho -a, hi -a -fu -a*

B. (personal names)

1. *Sakai*
2. *Mitsui*
3. *Tamura*
4. *Satoo*
5. *Sakuma*
6. *Mizuno*

C. Add *-san-desu-ka* and *-sensee-desu-ka* to the words in B, and say the resulting sentences with a rising intonation.

ex. *Sakai-san-desu-ka. Sakai-sensee-desu-ka.*

Reading Comprehension

Read the following.

このあいだ、みちこさんと映画(えいが)をみました。三十年(さんじゅうねん)まえにできた映画(えいが)でしたが、わたしはおもしろい[(1)]とおもいました。映画(えいが)のあと、喫茶店(きっさてん)にはいりました。はじめに[(2)]はいったみせは、せき[(3)]がありませんでした。つぎに[(4)]はいったみせは音楽(おんがく)[(5)]がうるさい[(6)]のですぐでました[(7)]。さいごに[(8)]はいったみせはしずかでした。わたしたちはそこでさっきみた映画(えいが)の話(はなし)をしました。

(1) interesting (2) first (3) seat (4) next (5) music (6) noisy (7) we left (8) last

Aural Comprehension

Listen to the conversations on the tape and answer the following questions.

(A) 1. Does the old woman come to this tea house very often?
2. What about the young man?
3. Is he going to order the cake the woman recommended?

(B) 1. Was Mr. Matsumoto there when Mr. Kawamura called yesterday?
2. What did Mr. Kawamura say?

(C) 1. Does the woman seem upset?
2. Where did she put the money?
3. Why did the man put the money in the bag?

Telephoning

Pay Phones

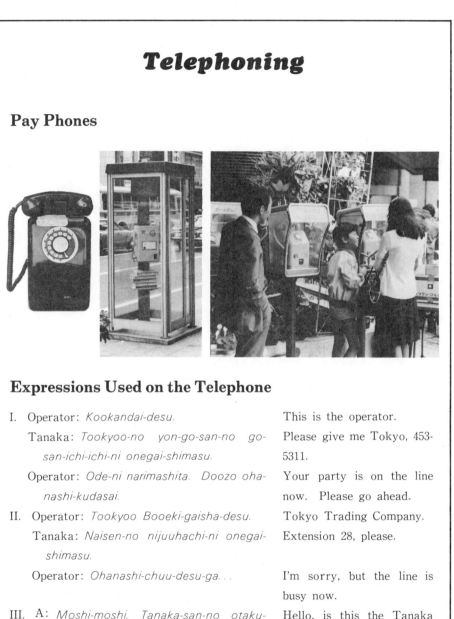

Expressions Used on the Telephone

I. Operator: *Kookandai-desu.*	This is the operator.
Tanaka: *Tookyoo-no yon-go-san-no go-san-ichi-ichi-ni onegai-shimasu.*	Please give me Tokyo, 453-5311.
Operator: *Ode-ni narimashita. Doozo ohanashi-kudasai.*	Your party is on the line now. Please go ahead.
II. Operator: *Tookyoo Booeki-gaisha-desu.*	Tokyo Trading Company.
Tanaka: *Naisen-no nijuuhachi-ni onegai-shimasu.*	Extension 28, please.
Operator: *Ohanashi-chuu-desu-ga...*	I'm sorry, but the line is busy now.
III. A: *Moshi-moshi, Tanaka-san-no otaku-desu-ka.*	Hello, is this the Tanaka residence?
B: *Chigaimasu.*	You have the wrong number.
A: *Shitsuree-shimashita.*	I'm sorry.

第十一課(だいじゅういっか)　やめた　ほうが　いいでしょう

Dialogue

(In Kamakura, a city of great historical interest 40 km south of Tokyo)

ジョンソン(じょんそん)：　この　大仏(だいぶつ)は　おおきくて　りっぱですね。

吉村(よしむら)：　ええ、りっぱですね。でも、奈良(なら)の　大仏(だいぶつ)は　もっと　おおきいですよ。たかさが　二倍(にばい)ぐらい　あるでしょう。

ジョンソン(じょんそん)：　どっちの　ほうが　ふるいですか。

吉村(よしむら)：　奈良(なら)の　大仏(だいぶつ)の　ほうが　ずっと　ふるいだろうと　おもいます。

ジョンソン(じょんそん)：　のどが　かわいたから、なにか　のみましょうか。

吉村(よしむら)：ええ。この　喫茶店(きっさてん)は　どうでしょう。

ジョンソン(じょんそん)：　そうですね。こんでいませんか。

吉村(よしむら)：　だいぶ　こんでいますね。

ジョンソン(じょんそん)：　じゃ、やめた　ほうが　いいですね。

吉村(よしむら)：　ええ。もっと　すいている　みせを　さがしましょう。

(At a coffee shop, after finishing their drinks)

吉村(よしむら)：　これから　どこかへ　いきますか。

ジョンソン(じょんそん)：　そうですね。わたしは　かまいませんが、吉村(よしむら)さんは　あまり　おそく　ならない　ほうが　いいでしょうね。

吉村(よしむら)：　ええ、その　ほうが　いいですね。

ジョンソン(じょんそん)：　じゃ、まっすぐ　かえりましょう。

Dialogue Lesson 11 — *Dai-juuikka*

WE'D BETTER NOT — *YAMETA HOO-GA II-DESHOO*

Johnson: This huge image of Buddha is really impressive.	*Jonson: Kono daibutsu-wa ookikute rippa-desu-ne.*
Yoshimura: Yes, it is, but the Great Statue of Nara is even bigger. It's probably about twice as tall.	*Yoshimura: Ee, rippa-desu-ne. Demo, Nara-no daibutsu-wa motto ookii-desu-yo. Takasa-ga nibai-gurai aru-deshoo.*
J: Which is older?	*J: Dotchi-no hoo-ga furui-desu-ka.*
Y: The one in Nara is much older, I think.	*Y: Nara-no daibutsu-no hoo-ga zutto furui-daroo-to omoimasu.*
J: I'm thirsty. Shall we have something to drink?	*J: Nodo-ga kawaita-kara, nanika nomimashoo-ka.*
Y: Yes. How about this coffee shop?	*Y: Ee. Kono kissaten-wa doo-deshoo.*
J: Well, but isn't it crowded?	*J: Soo-desu-ne. Konde-imasen-ka.*
Y: Yes, it's pretty crowded.	*Y: Daibu konde-imasu-ne.*
J: Then we'd better not go in.	*J: Ja, yameta hoo-ga ii-desu-ne.*
Y: Yes. Let's look for another place that's not as crowded.	*Y: Ee. Motto suite-iru mise-o sagashimashoo.*
Y: Shall we go elsewhere?	*Y: Kore-kara dokoka-e ikimasu-ka.*
J: Well, I don't mind, but you probably shouldn't be too late getting home.	*J: Soo-desu-ne. Watashi-wa kamaimasen-ga, Yoshimura-san-wa amari osoku naranai hoo-ga ii-deshoo-ne.*
Y: That's right.	*Y: Ee, sono hoo-ga ii-desu-ne.*
J: Then let's go back now.	*J: Ja, massugu kaerimashoo.*

Explanation

(In this lesson you will learn several ways to express comparison. The comparison in Japanese is expressed in various ways rather than in one fixed grammatical form.)

この 大仏(だいぶつ)は おおきくて りっぱですね。 **line 1**

Kono daibutsu-wa ookikute rippa-desu-ne.

daibutsu	a big image of Buddha
ookikute	big and . . . (dict. *ookii*)
rippa-desu	it is stately (*-na*)

でも、奈良(なら)の 大仏(だいぶつ)は もっと おおきいですよ。 **lines 2-3**

Demo, Nara-no daibutsu-wa motto ookii-desu-yo.

Nara	place name; city 35 km south of Kyoto, capital of Japan, 710-784
motto ookii	is bigger

In one kind of expression of comparison *motto* is placed before an adjective. The adjective does not undergo any change in form.

ex. *Nara-wa motto furui-desu.* (Nara is older.)
Motto rippa-na daibutsu-o mimashita. (I saw a more impressive image of Buddha.)

Instead of saying *Nara-no daibutsu-wa*, you can say *Nara-no-wa*, leaving out *daibutsu*. In the same way, nouns can be left out in the following examples.

ex. 1. A: *Kore-wa watashi-no kaban-desu. Are-wa dare-no-desu-ka.* (This is my bag. Whose is that over there?)
B: *Are-wa watashi-no-desu.* (That's mine.)
2. A: *Yamaguchi-san-no kasa-wa dotchi-desu-ka.* (Which one is Mr. Yamaguchi's umbrella?)
B: *Ano kuroi-no-desu.* (That black one.)

たかさが 二倍(にばい)ぐらい あるでしょう。 **line 3**

Takasa-ga nibai-gurai aru-deshoo.

takasa	height
nibai-gurai	about twice

Takasa is derived from the adjective *takai*. *Sa* makes a noun showing degree when it takes the place of the final syllable of *-i* and *-na* adjectives.

ex.	
takai (high)	*takasa* (height)
ookii (big)	*ookisa* (size)
omoi (heavy)	*omosa* (weight)

nagai (long) *nagasa* (length)

rippana (stately) *rippasa* (stateliness, grandeur)

Bai means 'times.'

ex. *sanbai* (3 times), *yonbai* (4 times), *gobai* (5 times) . . . .

(Continue using the same set of numbers you learned for quoting prices.)

どっちの ほうが ふるいですか。 **line 4**

Dotchi-no hoo-ga furui-desu-ka.

dotchi-no hoo-ga which one of the two

Dotchi is a more colloquial form of *dochira*. In the same way, *kochira*, *sochira*, and *achira* are pronounced respectively as *kotchi*, *sotchi*, and *atchi* in familiar speech.

'Which of A and B is the older' can be expressed in either of the following two ways: *A-to B-to dotchi-no hoo-ga furui-desu-ka* or *A-to B-dewa dotchi-no hoo-ga furui-desu-ka.* One way of answering is *A-no hoo-ga furui-desu.*

ex. *Tookyoo-to Kyooto-to* (or-*dewa*), *dotchi-no hoo-ga ookii-desu-ka.* (Which is bigger, Tokyo or Kyoto?)

Tookyoo-no hoo-ga ookii-desu. (Tokyo is bigger.)

To express 'A is bigger than B,' *-yori* is used.

ex. *Tookyoo-wa Kyooto-yori ookii-desu.* (Tokyo is bigger than Kyoto.)

奈良(なら)の 大仏(だいぶつ)の ほうが ずっと ふるいだろうと おもいます。 **lines 5-6**

Nara-no daibutsu-no hoo-ga zutto furui-daroo-to omoimasu.

zutto by far; much more

furui-daroo is probably older

Daroo is the plain form of *-deshoo*. It is used instead of *-deshoo* when followed by *-to omoimasu*.

ex. *Ano-hito-wa kyoo-wa konai-daroo-to omoimasu.* (I think he probably won't come today.)

のどが かわいたから、なにか のみましょうか。 **lines 7-8**

Nodo-ga kawaita-kara, nanika nomimashoo.

nodo throat

nodo-ga kawaita I'm thirsty (*lit.* my throat is dry.) (dict. *kawaku*)

(*o*) *nomimashoo* let's drink (...) (dict. *nomu*)

Nodo-ga kawaku means 'to become thirsty,' and the state of being thirsty is expressed by using the *-ta* form, i. e. *nodo-ga kawaita*, or *nodo-ga kawakimashita*.

Kara is preferable to *-node* when giving a reason and making a proposal.

ex. *Moo osoi (-desu)-kara kaerimashoo.* (Let's go home since it's already late.)

そうですね。こんでいませんか。 **line 10**

Soo-desu-ne. Konde-imasen-ka.

konde-imasen-ka isn't it crowded? (dict. *komu*)

Konde-iru is used to describe the state of a place just as *yasete-iru* is used to describe the way a person looks. The antonym of *konde-iru* is *suite-iru*, *komu* meaning 'to become crowded' and *suku* 'to become empty.'

だいぶ　こんでいますね。 **line 11**

Daibu konde-imasu-ne.

daibu quite; very

じゃ、やめた　ほうが　いいですね。 **line 12**

Ja, yameta hoo-ga ii-desu-ne.

yameta hoo-ga ii we had better give up; we had better not... (dict. *yameru*)

The *-ta* form plus *hoo-ga ii* roughly corresponds to 'had better' in English. *Yameru* means 'to stop doing something' or 'to give up the idea of doing something.'

ex. *Nanika nonda hoo-ga ii-desu-yo.* (You had better drink something; It might be better for you to drink something.)

ええ。もっと　すいている　みせを　さがしましょう。 **line 13**

Ee. Motto suite-iru mise-o sagashimashoo.

suite-iru uncrowded (dict. *suku*)

mise — shop ; store

...o sagashimashoo — let us look for ... (dict. *sagasu*)

これから　どこかへ　いきますか。 **line 14**

Kore-kara dokoka-e ikimasu-ka.

kore-kara — from now

わたしは　かまいませんが、吉村(よしむら)さんは　あまり　おそく　ならない

Watashi-wa kamaimasen-ga, Yoshimura-san-wa amari osoku naranai

ほうが　いいでしょうね。 **lines 15-17**

hoo-ga ii-deshoo-ne.

kamaimasen — I don't mind (dict. *kamau*)

osoku naranai hoo-ga ii — you had better not be late (dict. *naru*)

The negative form of *hoo-ga ii* is *-nai hoo-ga ii.*

ex. *Ikanai hoo-ga ii-desu-yo.* (I think you'd better not go.)

ええ、その　ほうが　いいですね。 **line 18**

Ee, sono hoo-ga ii-desu-ne.

sono hoo-ga ii — that way is better

じゃ、まっすぐ　かえりましょう。 **line 19**

Ja, massugu kaerimashoo.

massugu — directly

Note　Counters for people

Human beings are counted in the following way.

1 —*hitori*　　2 —*futari*　　3 —*sannin*
4 —*yonin*　　5 —*gonin*　　6 —*rokunin*
7 —*shichinin*　　8 —*hachinin*　　9 —*kunin*
10 —*juunin*

Above 10, *-nin* is added to the set of numbers used for giving prices.

Drills

I. . . .*daroo-to omoimasu*

Structure Drill 1 Change *-deshoo* to *-daroo-to omoimasu* in the following expressions.

A) ex. *ookii-deshoo* → *Ookii-daroo-to omoimasu.*

1. *isogashii-deshoo* 2. *takai-deshoo* 3. *ii-deshoo*
4. *furui-deshoo* 5. *samui* (cold)*-deshoo*
6. *omoshiroi* (interesting)*-deshoo*

B) ex. *daibutsu-deshoo* → *Daibutsu-daroo-to omoimasu.*

1. *nihongo-deshoo* 2. *hima-deshoo* 3. *taihen-deshoo*
4. *yuugata* (evening)*-deshoo* 5. *sangatsu mikka* (March 3rd) *-deshoo* 6. *benri* (convenient)*-deshoo*

C) ex. *nibai aru-deshoo* → *Nibai aru-daroo-to omoimasu.*

1. *suite-iru-deshoo* 2. *konde-iru-deshoo*
3. *sanbai aru-deshoo* 4. *raishuu* (next week) *kuru-deshoo*
5. *futotte-iru-deshoo* 6. *ashita furu-deshoo*

Structure Drill 2 Change the expressions in A), B), and C) into sentences ending in *nai-daroo-to omoimasu.*

A) ex. *ookii-deshoo* → *Ookiku nai-daroo-to omoimasu.*
B) ex. *daibutsu-deshoo* → *Daibutsu-ja nai-daroo-to omoimasu.*
C) ex. *nibai aru-deshoo* → *Nibai nai-daroo-to omoimasu.*
yasete-iru-deshoo → *Yasete-inai-daroo-to omoimasu.*

Usage Drill Practice the following conversation changing the underlined parts.

ex. *eega, omoshiroi, miru*

A: *Ano eega-wa omoshiroi-deshoo-ka.*
B: *Amari omoshiroku nai-daroo-to omoimasu.*
A: *Soo-desu-ka. Ja, minai hoo-ga ii-desu-ne.*
B: *Ee, minai hoo-ga ii-daroo-to omoimasu-yo.*

1. *jibiki,* *yaku-ni tatsu,* *kau*
2. *mise,* *suite-iru,* *hairu*
3. *hito,* *hima,* *denwa-o kakeru*
4. *kikai,* *benri,* *tsukau*
5. *hon,* *omoshiroi,* *yomu*

II. *motto. . .*

Structure Drill Change the following as shown in the example:

A) ex. *ookii* → *Kore-wa ookii-desu. Demo, are-wa motto ookii-desu.*

1. *takai* 2. *furui* 3. *muzukashii* (difficult) 4. *kiree*
5. *rippa* 6. *benri* 7. *chiisai* (small) 8. *ii*

B) ex. *hiroi* → *Koko-wa hiroi-desu. Demo, asoko-wa motto hiroi-desu.*
konde-iru → *Koko-wa konde-imasu. Demo, asoko-wa motto konde-imasu.*

1. *shizuka* 2. *konde-iru* 3. *nigiyaka*
4. *suite-iru* 5. *samui* 6. *atsui* (hot)

Usage Drill Practice the following conversation changing the underlined word.

ex. *mise*
A: *Kono mise-wa konde-imasu-ne.*
B: *Soo-desu-ne. Ano mise-wa doo-deshoo.*
A: *Asoko-wa motto konde-imasu-yo.*
B: *Ja, kyoo-wa yamemashoo-ka.*
A: *Ee, yameta hoo-ga ii-deshoo.*

1. *kissaten* 2. *chamise* 3. *shokudoo*
4. *eegakan* (movie theater)

III. *. . no hoo-ga. . .*

Structure Drill 1 Change the following as shown in the example.

ex. *kore, are, furui* → *Kore-to are-to, dotchi-no hoo-ga furui-deshoo.*

1. *kore, are, ii* 2. *Tookyoo, Yokohama, hiroi*
3. *kore, are, atarashii* (new) 4. *koko, soko, atsui*
5. *basu* (bus) *chikatetsu* (subway), *benri* 6. *koko, asoko, suite-iru*
7. *gozen, gogo, konde-iru* 8. *doyoo, nichiyoo, nigiyaka*

Usage Drill Practice the following conversation changing the underlined parts.

ex. *Kyooto, Nara, furui*

A: *Kyooto-mo Nara-mo* furui-desu-ne.*
*(both Kyoto and Nara)
B: *Ee, soo-desu-ne.*
A: *Dotchi-no hoo-ga furui-deshoo.*
B: *Nara no hoo-ga furui-daroo-to omoimasu.*
A: *Nara-no hoo-ga zutto furui-deshoo-ka.*
B: *Yoku wakarimasen-ga, soo-daroo-to omoimasu.*

1. *Kyooto, Tookyoo, nigiyaka* 2. *doyoobi, nichiyoobi, konde-iru*
3. *Tanaka-san, Yoshimura-san, see-ga takai*
4. *kono okashi, ano okashi, oishii*
5. *nihongo, chuugokugo, muzukashii*
6. *kono hon, ano hon, omoshiroi*

IV. {. . . *ta* / . . . *nai*} *hoo-ga ii*

Structure Drill Change the following as shown in the example.

ex. *taberu* → *Tabeta hoo-ga ii-deshoo.*
→ *Tabenai hoo-ga ii-deshoo.*

1. *miru* 2. *suru* 3. *kuru* 4. *iku*
5. *kau* 6. *uru* 7. *yuu* 8. *denwa-o kakeru*

Usage Drill Practice the following conversation changing the underlined parts.

ex. *Yamashita-san-no uchi-e iku*

A: *Yamashita-san-no uchi-e ikimashoo-ka.*

B: *Ee. Itsu* (when) *ikimashoo-ka.*

A: *Kyoo-wa doo-desu-ka.*

B: *Kyoo-wa ikanai hoo-ga ii-deshoo.*

A: *Ja, ashita ikimashoo-ka.*

B: *Ee, ashita itta hoo-ga ii-daroo-to omoimasu.*

1. *Yamashita-san-ni yuu* (tell him)
2. *kabu* (stock)*-o kau*
3. *kabu-o uru*
4. *denwa-o kakeru*
5. *shigoto-o hajimeru* (start)

Pronunciation Practice

A. Practice saying the following, pronouncing each syllable distinctly.

1. *o -a -u -i -e,* *u -o -i -e -a,* *a -i -u -e -o*
2. *ko-ka-ku-ki-ke,* *ku-ko-ki-ke-ka,* *ka-ki-ku-ke-ko*
3. *so-sa-su-shi-se,* *su-so-shi-se-sa,* *sa-shi-su-se-so*
4. *to-ta-tsu-chi-te,* *tsu-to-chi-te-ta,* *ta-chi-tsu-te-to*
5. *no-na-nu-ni-ne,* *nu-no-ni-ne-na,* *na-ni-nu-ne-no*
6. *ho-ha-fu-hi-he,* *fu-ho-hi-he-ha,* *ha-hi-fu-he-ho*
7. *mo-ma-mu-mi-me,* *mu-mo-mi-me- ma,* *ma-mi-mu-me-mo*
8. *yo-ya-yu-i-e,* *yu-yo-i-e-ya,* *ya-i-yu-e-yo*
9. *ro-ra-ru-ri-re,* *ru-ro-ri-re-ra,* *ra-ri-ru-re-ro*
10. *o-wa-u-i-e,* *u-o-i-e-wa,* *wa-i-u-e-o*

B. 1. *ikimashita* 2. *tabemashita* 3. *yomimashita*
4. *nomimashita* 5. *kakimashita* 6. *yarimashita*

C. Add *Ee* to the words in B and say each sentence with a falling intonation.

ex. *Ee, ikimashita.*

Reading Comprehension

Read the following.

東京は京都よりずっとにぎやかです。東京にすんでいる(1)人のかず(2)は京都の8倍ぐらいあるとおもいます。

東京には、役所(3)も会社も学校もたくさんあります。電車(4)もこんでいます。

京都には、ふるいお寺やふるいたてものがたくさんあります。やすみの日(5)には、それをみにいく人がたくさんいます。

わたしは東京のほうがすきです*が、山下さんは京都のほうがすきです。

(1) living (2) number (3) government office (4) train (5) holiday

(*I like Tokyo better.)

Aural Comprehension

Answer the following questions.

A) 1. Do the man and woman decide to go into the coffee shop?
2. If not, why?
3. Are they going to try to find another coffee shop or have they given up?

B) 1. Which one of the dresses does the woman decide to buy, the cheaper one or the more expensive one?
2. Was it easy for her to choose between the two?

Common Japanese Family Names

1.	林	*Hayashi*
2.	石川	*Ishikawa*
3.	伊藤	*Itoo*
4.	加藤	*Katoo*
5.	木村	*Kimura*
6.	小林	*Kobayashi*
7.	松本	*Matsumoto*
8.	中村	*Nakamura*
9.	中島	*Nakajima*
10.	小川	*Ogawa*

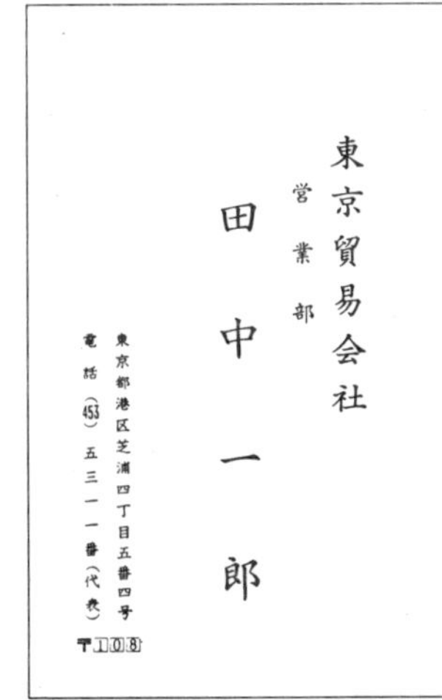

東京貿易会社
営業部
田中一郎
東京都港区芝浦四丁目五番四号
電話（453）五三一一番（代表）
〒108

A sample name card

A sample name plate

11.	斎藤	*Saitoo*
12.	佐藤	*Satoo*
13.	鈴木	*Suzuki*
14.	高橋	*Takahashi*
15.	田中	*Tanaka*
16.	渡辺	*Watanabe*
17.	山田	*Yamada*
18.	山口	*Yamaguchi*
19.	山本	*Yamamoto*
20.	吉田	*Yoshida*

第十二課(だいじゅうにか)　時間(じかん)が　なかったんです

Dialogue

(Before class begins)

学生(がくせい)A：　あのう、先生(せんせい)、予習(よしゅう)が　できませんでした。
先生(せんせい)：　どう　したんですか。
A：　時間(じかん)が　なかったんです。じつは　くにの　両親(りょうしん)が　きゅうに　たずねてきたので…
先生(せんせい)：　そうですか。それでは　しかたが　ありませんね。
A：　すみません。

先生(せんせい)：　ジョンソン(じょんそん)さんが　いませんね。
A：　ジョンソン(じょんそん)さんは　きょうは　こないかも　しれません。
先生(せんせい)：　どう　したんでしょう。
A：　きのう　あたまが　いたいと　いっていましたから。
先生(せんせい)：　かぜを　ひいたんでしょうか。
学生(がくせい)B：　かれは　このごろ　すこし　つかれているんです。アルバイト(あるばいと)が　たいへんなんでしょう。
先生(せんせい)：　そうですか。それは　こまりましたね。みなさんも　アルバイト(あるばいと)を　していますか。
B：　ええ、たいてい　しています。
A：　物価(ぶっか)が　たかいから、奨学金(しょうがっきん)では　たりないんです。
先生(せんせい)：　アルバイト(あるばいと)を　しながら　勉強(べんきょう)するのは　たいへんでしょうね。
A：　ええ、ほんとうに　たいへんなんです。

Dialogue

Lesson 12	*Dai-juunika*
I DIDN'T HAVE THE TIME	***JIKAN-GA NAKATTA-N-DESU***
Student A: Excuse me, I'm not prepared.	*Gakusee A: Anoo, sensee, yoshuu-ga dekimasen-deshita.*
Teacher: Why not?	*Sensee: Doo shita-n-desu-ka.*
S. A: I didn't have the time because my parents came up to see me all of sudden.	*A: Jikan-ga nakatta-n-desu. Jitsu-wa kuni-no ryooshin-ga kyuu-ni tazunete-kita-node....*
T: Is that right? Then you couldn't help it, could you?	*S: Soo-desu-ka. Sore-dewa shikata-ga arimasen-ne.*
S. A: I'm sorry.	*A: Sumimasen.*
T: Mr. Johnson isn't here yet, is he?	*S: Jonson-san-ga imasen-ne.*
S. A: He may not come today.	*A: Jonson-san-wa kyoo-wa konai-kamo shiremasen.*
T: I wonder what's the matter with him.	*S: Doo shita-n-deshoo.*
S. A: He said he had a headache yesterday.	*A: Kinoo atama-ga itai-to itte-imashita-kara.*
T: Has he caught a cold?	*S: Kaze-o hiita-n-deshoo-ka.*
Student B: He's been tired recently. He's overworking himself with his part-time job, I think.	*G.B.: Kare-wa kono-goro sukoshi tsukarete-iru-n-desu. Arubaito-ga taihenna-n-deshoo.*
T: Is that right? That's too bad. Are you students working part-time, too?	*S: Soo-desu-ka. Sore-wa komarimashita-ne. Minasan-mo arubaito-o shite-imasu-ka.*
S.B: Yes, most of us are.	*B: Ee, taitee shite-imasu.*
S.A: Since prices are so high, we can't get by on just our scholarships.	*A: Bukka-ga takai-kara, shoogakkin-dewa tarinai-n-desu.*
T: Studying while working part-time must be tough.	*S: Arubaito-o shinagara benkyoo-suru-no-wa taihen-deshoo-ne.*
S.A: Yes, it really is.	*A: Ee, hontoo-ni taihenna-n-desu.*

Explanation

(In this lesson you will learn an expression which combines the plain form and *-n-desu*, which is used when giving reason or to show emotional emphasis.)

あのう、先生(せんせい)、予習(よしゅう)が　できませんでした。 **line 1**

Anoo, sensee, yoshuu-ga dekimasen-deshita.

anoo	well···
yoshuu	preparation of lessons
····*ga dekimasen-deshita*	I couldn't do····(dict. *dekiru*)

Anoo is used before starting speech to show hesitation, diffidence, or politeness. You will hear it often in Japanese speech, but be careful not to overuse it or you may sound uneasy.

'····*ga dekiru*' means 'one can do something.'

ex.	*Tenisu-ga dekimasu.*	(I can play tennis.)
	Sore-wa dekimasen.	(That's impossible.)

Notice that the word *sensee* can be used alone to address a teacher. When there is only one teacher present, his or her name is usually not mentioned. (*Sensee* is used to show respect to doctors, lawyers, statesmen, and certain specialists as well as teachers and professors. cf. Lesson 7)

どう　したんですか。 **line 2**

Doo shita-n-desu-ka.

The plain form of a verb or adjective, in either its present or past form, plus *-no-desu* or *-n-desu* is used under the following circumstances:

(1) when emphatically giving reason or offering an explanation as shown in lines 3, 13, 14, and 18.

(2) when asking for an explanation with concern, as in lines 2, 10, and 12

(3) when displaying emotional emphasis as shown in line 21.

The use of *-n-desu* in line 3 falls into category (1) above. You might translate it as 'The reason is that I didn't have the time to.'

じつは　くにの　両親(りょうしん)が　きゅうに　たずねてきたので··· **lines 3-4**

Jitsu-wa kuni-no ryooshin-ga kyuu-ni tazunete-kita-node ···

jitsu-wa	in fact; the fact is
kuni	home country; home town

ryooshin parents
kyuu-ni suddenly
(・・・o)tazunete-kita they came to see me (dict. *tazuneru*)

Kuni as used here means one's home town or home country, but it can also mean 'country.'

ex. *Nihon-wa Chuugoku-no tonari-ni aru kuni-desu.*
(Japan is a country located next to China.)

Kuru, when it follows a verb in the *-te* form, adds the meaning that the action expressed by the verb is done 'towards the speaker.' For example, *tazunete-kuru* means 'someone comes to visit me.' *Iku*, when it follows a *-te* form verb, adds the meaning that the action is performed 'in a direction away from the speaker', i. e., *tazunete-iku* means that the speaker or the subject of the sentence goes to visit someone else.

それでは　しかたが　ありませんね。 **line 5**
Sore-dewa shikata-ga arimasen-ne.

sore-dewa in that case; then
shikata-ga arimasen it can't be helped (*lit.* there is no way to handle it.)

ジョンソンさんは　きょうは　こないかも　しれません。 **lines 8-9**
Jonson-san-wa kyoo-wa konai-kamo shiremasen.

konai-kamo shiremasen he may not come (dict. *kuru*)

'・・・・*kamo shirenai*' is used to denote uncertainty about the statement.

ex. *Ashita ame-ga furu-kamo shiremasen.* (It may rain tomorrow.)
Ano-hito-wa nihonjin-ja nai-kamo shiremasen. (She — or he — may not be a Japanese.)

きのう　あたまが　いたいと　いっていましたから。 **line 11**
Kinoo atama-ga itai-to itte-imashita-kara.

atama head
itai to have a pain
atama-ga itai he has a headache

'・・・・*ga itai*' means 'to have a pain in(at)・・・・' Here are some other expressions to learn: *ha-ga itai* (to have a toothache), *onaka-ga itai* (to have a stomachache), and *nodo-ga itai* (to have a sore throat).

かぜを　ひいたんでしょうか。 **line 12**

Kaze-o hiita-n-deshoo-ka.

kaze-o hiita	he has caught a cold (dict. *hiku*)

かれは　このごろ　すこし　つかれているんです。 **line 13**

Kare-wa kono-goro sukoshi tsukarete-iru-n-desu.

kare	he
kono-goro	these days; recently
sukoshi	a little
tsukarete-iru	is tired (dict. *tsukareru*)

Kare, 'he,' *kanojo*, 'she' and *karera*, 'they' are used mostly by young people. These words should not be used to refer to teachers, one's elders, or anyone deserving respect.

アルバイト(あるばいと)が　たいへんなんでしょう。 **line 14**

Arubaito-ga taihenna-n-deshoo.

arubaito	part-time job (from *Arbeit*, German)

Na adjectives end with *-na* when they are followed by *-no-desu* or *-n-desu.*

Da, the plain form of *-desu*, also changes into *-na* when followed by *-no-desu* or *-n-desu.*

ex. *Ima goji-na-n-desu.* (It's 5 o'clock now.)

それは　こまりましたね。 **line 15**

Sore-wa komarimashita-ne.

komarimashita	that's too bad (*lit.* I'm at a loss) (dict. *komaru*)

みなさんも　アルバイト(あるばいと)を　していますか。 **lines 15-16**

Minasan-mo arubaito-o shite-imasu-ka.

minasan	all of you; everybody

物価(ぶっか)が　たかいから、奨学金(しょうがっきん)では　たりないんです。 **line 18**

Bukka-ga takai-kara, shoogakkin-dewa tarinai-n-desu.

bukka	commodity prices
shoogakkin	scholarship
····*dewa tarinai*	····is not sufficient (dict. *tariru,* L 6)

Tariru is often used with *-de* when affirmative and with *-dewa* when negative.

ex. *Ichiman-en-de tarimasu-ka.* (Is 10,000 yen enough?)
Ichiman-en-de tarimasu. (10,000 yen is enough.)
Ichiman-en-dewa tarimasen (10,000 yen isn't enough.)

アルバイトを　しながら　勉強するのは　たいへんでしょうね。 **lines 19-20**

Arubaito-o shinagara benkyoo-suru-no-wa taihen-deshoo-ne.

····shinagara while doing····
benkyoo-suru-no to study; studying

Nagara is a suffix. The stem to which it is added is the same as that to which *-masu* is added. It shows that two actions take place at the same time.

ex. *Watashi-wa terebi-o minagara shokuji-o shimasu.* (I eat while I watch television.)
Koohii-o nominagara hanashimashita. (We talked over a cup of coffee.)

The *-no* in *benkyoo-suru-no-wa* is added to a verb to form a noun or phrase, which has a similar function to that of a gerund in English.

ex. *Asobu-no-wa omoshiroi-desu-ga, benkyoo-suru-no-wa muzukashii-desu.* (Playing is fun, but studying is difficult.)
Kyoo-wa iku-no-o yamemashita. (I decided on not going today.) (*lit.* I quit the idea of going today.)

ええ、ほんとうに　たいへんなんです。 **line 21**

Ee, hontoo-ni taihenna-n-desu.

hontoo-ni really; indeed

Note *-n-desu*

This form is often used to show the speaker's emotional emphasis. It expresses the speaker's concern, surprise, reprimand and other emotions. Which emotion is expressed must be judged by context and intonation. *Nani-o shite-imasu-ka* is a simple question whereas *Nani-o shite-iru-n-desu-ka* can be taken as an expression of the speaker's irritation, surprise, or concern.

Hon-o yonde-imasu is a simple statement, whereas *Hon-o yonde-iru -n-desu* can mean something like 'I'm reading a book. That's why I didn't hear you,' or 'I'm reading a book, so please don't worry about me,' or 'I'm reading, and not doing anything you should criticize me for, so please let me alone,' among other meanings.

It is also used, especially by women, to express gentleness and soften the statement.

Intonation has much to do with this expression. If *nani* or *yonde* in the above sentences are pronounced with a very hign pitch on the first syllable, the sentences imply reprimand or irritation.

Consequently, this form is more frequently used in familiar speech where one can express his feelings more freely.

Drills

I. . . . *n-desu*

Structure Drill Change into the *-n-desu* form.

A) ex. *atama-ga itai-desu→Atama-ga itai-n-desu.*

1. *nodo-ga itai-desu*
2. *onaka* (stomach)*-ga itai-desu*
3. *motto ookii-desu*
4. *ha* (tooth)*-ga itakatta-desu*
5. *okane-ga nakatta-desu*
6. *uchi-ga tooi* (far)*-desu*

B) ex. *benri-desu→Benrina-n-desu.*
benri-ja arimasen→Benri-ja nai-n-desu.

1. *sora* (sky) *-ga kiree-desu*
2. *mada gakusee-desu*
3. *moo gakusee-ja arimasen*
4. *amari kiree-ja arimasen*
5. *watashi-desu*
6. *onna-no-hito-desu*
7. *shizuka-ja arimasen*
8. *shigatsu* (April) *tsuitachi* (1st)*-desu*

C) ex. *genki-deshita→Genki-datta-n-desu.*

1. *byooki* (sick)*-deshita*
2. *dame-deshita*
3. *joozu* (skillful)*-deshita*
4. *yuubinkyoku-deshita*
5. *goman-en-deshita*
6. *sono sanbai-deshita*

D) ex. *kyoo ikimasu→Kyoo iku-n-desu.*

1. *ichinichi-juu uchi-ni imasu*
2. *ichido ikimashita*
3. *yoku shirimasen*
4. *yasete-imasu*
5. *ocha-o nomimashita*
6. *matte-imasu*
7. *mada kimasen*
8. *okane-ga tarimasen-deshita*

Usage Drill Practice the following conversation changing the underlined parts.

A) ex. *atama-ga itakatta-n-desu*

A: *Kinoo kimasen-deshita-ne. Doo shita-n-desu-ka.*

B: *Atama-ga itakatta-n-desu.*

A: *Soo-desu-ka. Kyoo-wa moo ii-n-desu-ka.*

(Are you all right today?)

B: *Ee, okagesama-de.* (Thank you. *lit.* Thanks to you and everything, I'm fine.)

1. *kaze-o hiita-n-desu*
2. *onaka-ga itakatta-n-desu*
3. *ha-ga itakatta-n-desu*
4. *byooki-datta-n-desu*
5. *taihen tsukareta-n-desu*
6. *nodo-ga itakatta-n-desu*

B) ex. *okane-ga tarinakatta-n-desu*

A: *Sankoosho-o kaimashita-ka.*

B: *Iie, mada-desu.*

A: *Kinoo kai-ni ikanakatta-n-desu-ka.*

B: *Iie, ikimashita.*

A: *Ja, dooshite*(why) *kawanakatta-n-desu-ka.*

B: *Okane-ga tarinakatta-n-desu.*

1. *mise-ga yasumi-datta*(was closed)*-n-desu*
2. *amari yoku nakatta-n-desu*
3. *ii mono-ga nakatta-n-desu*
4. *takai-node yameta-n-desu*

(After practicing the above conversation and its variations, replace the word *sankoosho* by *kaban, tsukue, rajio* and other words.)

II. ...*nagara*

Structure Drill Combine the two phrases as shown in the example.

ex. *tabako-o suu*(smoke), *hanasu*
→*Tabako-o suinagara hanashimasu.*

1. *taberu, hanasu*
2. *ocha-o nomu, hon-o yomu*
3. *shinbun-o yomu, shokuji-o suru*
4. *neru, tabako-o suu*
5. *tabako-o suu, shinbun-o yomu*
6. *rajio-o kiku, taberu*
7. *koohii-o nomu, hanasu*
8. *arubaito-o suru, benkyoo-o suru*

III. verb+*no-wa*

Structure Drill Change the following as shown in the example.

ex. *tabako-o suinagara hanashimasu*
→*Tabako-o suinagara hanasu-no-wa yoku nai-to omoimasu.*

Use the sentences given in II, nos. 1 through 5, above.

IV. ...*kamo shiremasen*

Structure Drill Change the following as shown in the example.

A) ex. *arubaito-o shimasu*→*Arubaito-o suru-kamo shiremasen.*
arubaito-wa shimasen→*Arubaito-wa shinai-kamo shiremasen.*

1. *asobu hima-wa arimasen*
2. *arubaito-o shite-imasu*
3. *jikan-wa tarimasen*
4. *kuni-no ryooshin-ga tazunete-kimasu*
5. *yoshuu-suru jikan-ga arimasen*
6. *shoogakkin-dewa tarimasen*

B) ex. *ano-hito-wa nihongo-ga joozu-desu* (He speaks Japanese well.)
→*Ano-hito-wa nihongo-ga joozu-kamo shiremasen.*
ano-hito-wa nihonjin-ja arimasen.
→*Ano-hito-wa nihonjin-ja nai-kamo shiremasen.*

1. *Michiko-san-wa genki-desu*
2. *asoko-wa shizuka-ja arimasen*
3. *arubaito-ga taihen-desu*
4. *tenisu-ga joozu-desu*
5. *ano futari-wa Yamashita-san-no ryooshin-ja arimasen*
6. *arubaito-o shinagara benkyoo-suru-no-wa taihen-desu*

V. Plain form in familiar speech

The plain form has been used, in this textbook, in phrases within sentences, but it is also used to end sentences in familiar speech, especially that of men. The following two conversations between a husband and wife are typical of the use of the familiar form by the husband and polite form by the wife that is used by most middle-aged couples. If you can find a partner, try them. It's fun.

Example 1. WIFE: *Kyoo-wa doko-e itta-n-desu-ka.*

HUSBAND: *Doko-emo ikanai-yo. Massugu kaisha-kara kaette-kita-n-da-yo.*

W: *Ja, dooshite konna-ni osoi-n-desu-ka.*

H: *Shigoto-ga takusan atta-n-da-yo. Shikata-ga nai-daroo.*

W: *Demo kodomo*(child)*-tachi-mo matte-ita-n-desu-yo.*

H: *Wakatta. Ashita-wa hayaku kaeru.*

Example 2. W: *Mata nenagara tabako-o sutte-imasu-ne.*

H: *Un* (yes). *Sukoshi-wa ii-daroo.*

W: *Dame-desu. Kaji*(fire)*-ni naru-kamo shiremasen.*

H: *Ja, ashita-kara yameru-yo.*

W: *Iie, ashita-kara-dewa dame-desu. Ima sugu yamete-kudasai.*

Pronunciation Practice

Practice saying the following, pronouncing each syllable distinctly.

A. 1. *o -a -u -i -e,* *u -o -i -e -a,* *a -i -u -e -o*

2. *go-ga-gu-gi-ge,* *gu-go-gi-ge-ga,* *ga-gi- gu-ge-go*

3. *zo-za-zu- ji-ze,* *zu-zo- ji-ze-za,* *za-ji-zu-ze-zo*

4. *do-da-zu- ji-de,* *zu-do- ji-de-da,* *da-ji-zu-de-do*

5. *bo-ba-bu-bi-be,* *bu-bo-bi-be-ba,* *ba-bi-bu-be-bo*

6. *po-pa-pu-pi-pe,* *pu-po-pi-pe-pa,* *pa-pi-pu-pe-po*

B. 1. *are-desu-ka* 2. *kore-desu-ka* 3. *sore-desu-ka*

4. *bai-desu-ka* 5. *san-desu-ka* 6. *betsu-desu-ka*

7. *hana*(nose)*-desu-ka* 8. *hima-desu-ka*

C. Add *anoo* to the phrases in B and say them with a rising intonation.

ex. *Anoo, are-desu-ka.*

Reading Comprehension

Read the following.

わたしの大学の学生は、たいていアルバイトをしています。このごろは物価がたかいので、おかねがたりないんです。経験(1)のない人はわからないかもしれませんが、アルバイトをしながら勉強するのは、ほんとうにたいへんです。十分(2)予習をする時間がないので、ざんねんだとおもいます。

(1) experience (2) sufficiently

Aural Comprehension

Listen to the conversations on the tape and answer the following questions.

(A) 1. Why was the student absent yesterday?
 2. Is he all right now?
 3. Is he prepared for today's lessons?

(B) 1. Has the maid been shopping today?
 2. Does the maid sound happy about having to go shopping again?

C, D) Compare conversations C and D. In which conversation does the husband seem to be hen-pecked?

Quiz

(Lesson 7—Lesson 12)

I. Look at the picture and answer the questions.

1. *Kono heya-ni hito-ga nannin imasu-ka.*
2. *Otoko-no-hito-wa suwatte-imasu-ka.*
3. *Otoko-no-hito-wa nani-o shite-imasu-ka.*
4. *Onna-no-hito-wa nani-o shite-imasu-ka.*
5. *Otoko-no-hito-to onna-no-hito-to, dotchi-no hoo-ga futotte-imasu-ka.*
6. *Kodomo-tachi-wa ben-kyoo-shite-imasu-ka, asonde-imasu-ka.*

II. Fill in the blanks.

1. *Ringo-o* __________(three)*kudasai.*
2. *Gakusee-ga* ____________(about 20) *kimashita.*
3. A: *Dore-o sashiagemashoo.*
   B: _____(any one of them) *ii-desu.*
4. *Kookoo-no toki*_____(what kind of) *supootsu-o yarimashita-ka.*
5. *Mata itsudemo*____________(please use it).

III. Answer the questions.

1. *Kinoo nanji-goro nemashita-ka.*
2. *Kyoo-wa ii otenki-desu-ka.*
3. *Yoru-wa taitee nani-o shimasu-ka.*
4. *Nanika tabenagara benkyoo-shimasu-ka.*

5. *Tabako-o suimasu-ka.*
6. *Anata-no tsukue-no ue-ni aru mono-o itte-kudasai.*
7. *Anata-no kuni-to Nihon-to dotchi-no hoo-ga ookii-desu-ka.*
8. *Ima okane-o ikura-gurai motte-imasu-ka.*
9. *Shigoto* (or *benkyoo*)*-wa omoshiroi-desu-ka.*
10. *Ashita ame-ga furu-to omoimasu-ka.*

IV. Match up the phrases on the left with the appropriate phrases on the right to make sentences.

1. *Moo osoi-kara*	a. *senpai-desu.*
2. *See-ga takakute*	b. *wakarimasen-deshita.*
3. *Kesa Matsumoto-san-kara*	c. *omoimashita.*
4. *Ano obaasan-no kotoba-wa*	d. *massugu kaetta hoo-ga ii-deshoo.*
5. *Aa, wakarimashita. Daigaku-no*	e. *yasete-iru hito-desu.*
6. *Watashi-wa kamaimasen-ga,*	f. *denwa-ga arimashita.*
7. *Moo osoi-to*	g. *anata-wa doo-desu-ka.*

1____; 2____; 3____; 4____; 5____; 6____; 7____

V. Express in Japanese.

1. Please don't bother.
2. Do you have small change?
3. Do you know the telephone number?
4. My parents came to see me last week.
5. Then it can't be helped, can it?
6. Michiko may not come today.
7. Let's drink something at that coffee shop.
8. This place is crowded. I think we'd better not go in.

VI. Read the following letter and see if you can understand it completely.

みちこさん

お手紙(てがみ)ありがとうございました。

返事(へんじ) (reply) がおそくなってすみません。

会社(かいしゃ)は毎日(まいにち)いそがしくてたいへんです。かぜをひいている人(ひと)がたくさんいます。わたしはおかげさまで病気(びょうき)になりませんが、このごろだいぶつかれました。けさはのどがいたくてこまりましたが、いまはだいじょうぶ (all right) です。

また手紙(てがみ)をください。

さようなら

第十三課(だいじゅうさんか)　書(か)こうと　おもっています

Dialogue

(Johnson and Matsumoto are fishing at the river.)

ジョンソン(じょんそん)：　どこが　いいでしょう。

松本(まつもと)：　そうですね。この　へんが　よさそうですね。

ジョンソン(じょんそん)：　山下(やました)さんが　来(こ)なくて　ざんねんですね。

松本(まつもと)：　ええ。きゅうに　用事(ようじ)が　できたと　いっていました。…ところで、ジョンソン(じょんそん)さんは　日本(にほん)に　ながく　いる　予定(よてい)ですか。

ジョンソン(じょんそん)：　来年(らいねん)の　三月(さんがつ)まで　いる　予定(よてい)です。その　あいだに　論文(ろんぶん)の　資料(しりょう)を　あつめようと　おもっています。

松本(まつもと)：　どんな　ことを　書(か)くんですか。

ジョンソン(じょんそん)：　日本(にほん)の　企業(きぎょう)の　雇用制度(こようせいど)に　ついて　書(か)こうと　おもっています。

松本(まつもと)：　そうですか。おもしろそうですね。…あ、ひいていますよ。

ジョンソン(じょんそん)：　そうですね。大(おお)きそうですね。

(The next day Matsumoto meets Yamashita.)

山下(やました)：　きのうの　つり　どうだった。

松本(まつもと)：　よかったよ。おもったより　たくさん　つれたよ。

山下(やました)：　天気(てんき)は　だいじょうぶだった？

松本(まつもと)：　うん、つっている　あいだは　だいじょうぶだったよ。かえろうと　した　とき　ふりだしたけど。

山下(やました)：　そう。ぼくも　いこうと　おもっていたんだけど、ざんねんだった。

松本：　来週か　さ来週　いっしょに　いこうよ。
山下：　うん、そう　しよう。 23

Dialogue

Lesson 13	*Dai-juusanka*
I THINK I'LL WRITE IT	***KAKOO-TO OMOTTE-IMASU***
Johnson: Where shall we fish?	*Jonson: Doko-ga ii-deshoo*
Matsumoto: Well, it looks good around here.	*Matsumoto: Soo-desu-ne. Kono hen-ga yosasoo-desu-ne.*
J: Too bad Yamashita couldn't come.	*J: Yamashita-san-ga konakute zan-nen-desu-ne.*
M: Yes. He said something urgent came up.... By the way, are you going to stay for long in Japan?	*M: Ee. Kyuu-ni yooji-ga dekita-to itte-imashita. ... Tokoro-de, Jonson-san-wa Nihon-ni nagaku iru yotee-desu-ka.*
J: I'm planning to stay until March of next year. I think I'll gather materials for my thesis during that time.	*J: Rainen-no sangatsu-made iru yotee-desu. Sono aida-ni ron-bun-no shiryoo-o atsumeyoo-to omotte-imasu.*
M: What are you going to write about?	*M: Donna koto-o kaku-n-desu-ka.*
J: On the employment system of Japansese enterprises.	*J: Nihon-no kigyoo-no koyoo-seedo-ni tsuite kakoo-to omotte-imasu.*
M: Sounds interesting. ...Oh, some-thing's biting.	*M: Soo-desu-ka. Omoshirosoo-desu-ne. ...A, hiite-imasu-yo.*
J: It is. It looks big.	*J: Soo-desu-ne. Ookisoo-desu-ne.*
Yamashita: How did you enjoy the fishing yesterday?	*Yamashita: Kinoo-no tsuri doo-datta.*
Matsumoto: Very much. We caught more fish than I expected.	*Matsumoto: Yokatta-yo. Omotta-yori takusan tsureta-yo.*
Y: Was the weather good?	*Y: Tenki-wa daijoobu-datta?*
M: It was while we were fishing. It started to rain when we started back, though.	*M: Un, tsutte-iru aida-wa daijoobu-datta-yo. Kaeroo-to shita toki furidashita-kedo.*

Y: Did it? I really wanted to go with you. Too bad I couldn't.
M: Let's go together next week or the week after next.
Y: Yes, let's.

Y: Soo. Boku-mo ikoo-to omotte-ita-n-da-kedo, zannen-datta.
M: Raishuu-ka saraishuu issho-ni ikoo-yo.
Y: Un, soo shiyoo.

Explanation

(In this lesson you will learn how to express your wish. You will also learn to express '...looking' in Japanese, for example, *omoshirosoo*, 'interesting looking.')

この　へんが　よさそうですね。 **line 2**

Kono hen-ga yosasoo-desu-ne.

kono hen around here; this neighborhood
yosasoo it looks good (dict. *ii* or *yoi*)

Add *-soo* to the base of an adjective or verb to derive an expression meaning 'looking as if,' or 'having the appearance of.' The base form for adjectives is the main part of the adjective without *-i* or *-na*; the base for verb + *soo* is the same as that base form to which *-masu* is attached. Thus *omoshiroi* becomes *omoshirosoo*, 'interesting looking': *genkina* becomes *genkisoo*, 'healthy looking.' *Ii* is an exception to the rules for this form; its *-soo* form is *yosasoo*. *Kuru* becomes *kisoo*, 'likely to come,' and *furu* becomes *furisoo*, 'likely to rain.' See Note 1.

ええ。きゅうに　用事(ようじ)が　できたと　いっていました。 **line 4**

Ee. Kyuu-ni yooji-ga dekita-to itte-imashita.

yooji something to do; business
yooji-ga dekiru something comes up

ところで、ジョンソン(じょんそん)さんは　日本(にほん)に　ながく　いる　予定(よてい)ですか。 **lines 5-6**

Tokoro-de, Jonson-san-wa Nihon-ni nagaku iru yotee-desu-ka.

tokoro-de by the way (expression used to change the subject)

Nihon	Japan
nagaku	for a long time (dict. *nagai*)
yotee	schedule; plan

Here it is possible to say ...*yotee-ga arimasu-ka*, too, but the most common expression is ...*yotee-desu-ka* as used here. *Yotee-ga aru* is usually used in the following way:

ex. *Kyoo-wa nanika yotee-ga arimasu-ka.* (Do you have any particular plans for today?)

来年(らいねん)の 三月(さんがつ)まで いる 予定(よてい)です。 **line 7**

Rainen-no sangatsu-made iru yotee-desu.

rainen	next year
sangatsu	March
...made	until...

Words related to *rainen* are: *kotoshi* (this year), *kyonen* (last year), *sarainen* (the year after next), *ototoshi* (the year before last). *Nen* stands for 'year.' The year 1976 is read *sen-kyuuhyaku-nanajuu-roku-nen.*

その あいだに 論文(ろんぶん)の 資料(しりょう)を あつめようと おもっています。 **lines 7-8**

Sono aida-ni ronbun-no shiryoo-o atsumeyoo-to omotte-imasu.

sono aida-ni	during that period
ronbun	thesis; essay; dissertation
shiryoo	material
atsumeyoo-to omotte-imasu	I'm thinking I'll collect (dict. *atsumeru*)

The verb form ending in *-yoo* (*-ru* verbs) or in *-oo* (*-u* verbs) is used to express one's intention. In polite speech, it is followed by *-to omoimasu.* This form might be called the plain volitional form.

ex. *Hon-o yomoo-to omoimasu.* (I think I'll read a book.)

See Note 2 for the formation of this form.

'*...to omotte-imasu*' indicates that the speaker has had the intention over a longer span of time, up to and including the moment he speaks.

どんな　ことを　書くんですか。 **line 9**

Donna koto-o kaku-n-desu-ka.

kaku write

This *-n-desu-ka* form was explained in Lesson 12. It is used here to show that the speaker is enthusiastic about hearing the explanation.

日本の　企業の　雇用制度に　ついて　書こうと　おもっています。**lines 10-11**

Nihon-no kigyoo-no koyoo-seedo-ni tsuite kakoo-to omotte-imasu.

kigyoo	enterprise
koyoo-seedo	employment system
...ni tsuite	on ... ; concerning ...
kakoo-to omotte-imasu	I think I'll write (dict. *kaku*)

おもしろそうですね。…　あ、ひいていますよ。 **lines 12-13**

Omoshirosoo-desu-ne.... A, hiite-imasu-yo.

omoshirosoo-desu	it looks interesting (dict. *omoshiroi*)
hiite-imasu	it's biting (*lit.* it's pulling) (dict. *hiku*)

大きそうですね。 **line 14**

Ookisoo-desu-ne.

ookisoo-desu it looks like it's big (dict. *ookii*)

(Lines 15—23 show familiar conversation between two men Yamashita and Matsumoto, good friends. All verbs and adjectives are in the plain form, and *-da* and *-datta* are used instead of *-desu* and *-deshita*.)

きのうの　つり　どうだった。 **line 15**

Kinoo-no tsuri doo-datta.

tsuri	fishing
doo-datta	how was it?

おもったより　たくさん　つれたよ。 **line 16**

Omotta-yori takusan tsureta-yo.

omotta-yori takusan	more than I expected
tsureta	we caught fish (*lit.* we could catch)

'*...yori*' means 'than.' (cf. Lesson 11)

ex. *Omotta-yori muzukashikatta.* (It was more difficult than I expected.)

天気(てんき)は　だいじょうぶだった？ **line 17**

Tenki-wa daijoobu-datta ?

daijoobu	all right

つっている　あいだは　だいじょうぶだったよ。かえろうと　した　とき ふりだしたけど。 **lines 18-19**

Tsutte-iru aida-wa daijoobu-datta-yo. Kaeroo-to shita toki furidashita-kedo.

tsutte-iru aida	while we were fishing (dict. *tsuru*)
kaeroo-to shita toki	when we were about to return (dict. *kaeru*)
furidashita	it started to rain (dict. *furidasu*)
...kedo	but ; though

Tsutte-iru aida here means 'while we *were* fishing,' because the tense is indicated by the main clause, here *daijoobu-datta*.

When *-to suru* is added to the plain volitional form, it means that the action is about to take place.

ex. *Dekakeyoo-to shita toki, ame-ga furidashimashita.* (When I was about to go out, it started to rain.)

Neyoo-to shita toki denwa-ga narimashita. (When I was about to go to bed, the telephone rang.)

Dasu is attached to the main part of verbs and adds the meaning that 'something starts.'

ex. *yomu—yomidasu; taberu—tabedasu*

The two sentences can be reversed in order and made into the single sentence, *Kaeroo-to shita toki furidashita-kedo, tsutte-iru aida-wa daijoobu-datta-yo,* but the first way is more natural and conversational. (See Lesson 7 for the similar structure ending in *-kara.*)

そう。ぼくもいこうとおもっていたんだけど、ざんねんだった。 **lines 20-21**

Soo. Boku-mo ikoo-to omotte-ita-n-da-kedo, zannen-datta.

soo	=*soo-desu-ka*
ikoo-to omotte-ita	I thought I would go (dict. *iku*)

来週か　さ来週　いっしょに　いこうよ。 **line 22**

Raishuu-ka saraishuu issho-ni ikoo-yo.

raishuu	next week
saraishuu	the week after next
...ka	...or
issho-ni	together; with you
ikoo-yo	let's go, shall we?

In familiar speech, the plain volitional form is used in place of the *-mashoo* form.

ex. *Ikimashoo* (Let's go–polite): *Ikoo (-yo)* (Let's go–plain)
Yomimashoo (Let's read–polite): *Yomoo (-yo)* (Let's read—plain)

うん、そう　しよう。 **line 23**

Un, soo shiyoo.

un	=*ee* (familiar, used mainly by men)
soo shiyoo	let's do that (dict. *suru*)

Note 1 *-soo*

All words with *-soo* are used as if they were *-na* adjectives; when they modify nouns they are followed by *-na*.

ex. *genki**soona** kodomo* (healthy-looking child)
*oishi**soona** okashi* (delicious-looking cakes)
*tenisu-ga deki**soona** gakusee* (student who seems to be able to play tennis)

Note 2 The plain volitional form (*-oo, -yoo* form)

-u verbs: the final ***-u*** is replaced by ***-oo***: (*-tsu* is replaced by *-too*)

*iku —ik**oo**; yom**u** —yom**oo**; a**u** —a**oo**; ma**tsu**—ma**too***

-ru verbs: the final ***-ru*** is replaced by ***-yoo***:

*mi**ru** —mi**yoo**; tabe**ru** —tabe**yoo**; yame**ru** —yame**yoo***

suru and ***kuru***: *suru—**shiyoo**; kuru—**koyoo***

Note 3 Some differences between men and women in familiar speech

In polite or formal speech, there is very little difference between men and women, but in familiar speech, there are some differences between the two.

	Men usually say	Women usually say
1. (vocabulary)	*boku*	*watashi* or *atashi*
	kimi	*anata*
	un	*ee*
2. (verb forms)	*ikoo-yo*	*ikimashoo-yo*
3. (sentence ending)	*ii-yo, ii-ne*	*ii-wayo, ii-wane*
	yokatta-yo, yokatta-ne	*yokatta-wayo, yokatta-wane*
	iku-yo, iku-ne	*iku-wayo, iku-wane*
	ikanai-yo, ikanai-ne	*ikanai-wayo, ikanai-wane*
	soo-da-yo, soo-da-ne	*soo-yo, soo-ne*
	soo-da, soo-datta	*soo-da-wa, soo-datta-wa*
	ashita-da-yo, ashita-da-ne	*ashita-yo, ashita-ne*

In the dialogue lines 15 through 23 are in informal male speech. Here is the same conversation as it would be spoken by women.

Y: *Kinoo-no tsuri doo-datta.*

M: *Yokatta-wayo. Omotta-yori takusan tsureta-wayo.*

Y: *Otenki-wa daijoobu-datta?*

M: *Ee, tsutte-iru aida-wa daijoobu-datta-wayo. Kaeroo-to shita toki furidashita-kedo.*

Y: *Soo. Watashi-mo ikoo-to omotte-ita-n-da-kedo, zannen-datta-wa.*

M: *Raishuu-ka saraishuu issho-ni ikimashoo-yo.*

Y: *Ee, soo shimashoo.*

Drills

I. ...*soo-desu*

Structure Drill Memorize the following table. Practice aloud.

omoshiroi-desu	*omoshirosoo-desu*	*omoshirosoona hon-desu*
ii-desu	*yosasoo-desu*	*yosasoona hon-desu*
takai-desu	*takasoo-desu*	*takasoona mise-desu*
genki-desu	*genkisoo-desu*	*genkisoona hito-desu*
hima-desu	*himasoo-desu*	*himasoona hito-desu*
sugu dekimasu	*sugu dekisoo-desu*	*sugu dekisoona shigoto-desu*
takusan tsuremasu	*takusan tsuresoo-desu*	*takusan tsuresoona tokoro-desu*
ame-ga furimasu	*ame-ga furisoo-desu*	*ame-ga furisoona sora-desu*
yaku-ni tachimasu	*yaku-ni tachisoo-desu*	*yaku-ni tachisoona jibiki-desu*

Usage Drill 1 Practice the following conversation changing the underlined parts:

A) ex. *hon, omoshiroi, yonda*

A: *Kono hon-wa omoshirosoo-desu-ne.*

B: *Ee, omoshiroi-desu-yo*

A: *Itsu yonda-n-desu-ka.*

B: *Kinoo yonda-n-desu. Omoshirokatta-desu-yo.*

1. *hon, muzukashii, yonda*
2. *okashi, oishii, tabeta*
3. *mise, yasui, haitta*
4. *eega, omoshiroi, mita*
5. *kikai, benri, tsukatta*
6. *jibiki, yaku-ni tatsu, hiita* (*jibiki-o hiku*=look up in a dictionary)

B) ex. *owaru*

A: *Anoo, itsu-goro* <u>*owarimasu*</u>*-ka.*

B: *Sugu* <u>*owarimasu.*</u>

A: *Jippun* (10 minutes)*-gurai-de* <u>*owaru*</u>*-deshoo-ka.*

B: *Ee,* <u>*owarisoo*</u>*-desu-yo.*

A: *Ja, koko-de matte-imasu.*

1. *kuru* 2. *kaette-kuru* 3. *dekiru*
4. *suku*

II. . . . *soona*

Structure Drill Change the following as shown in the example.

ex. *omoshiroi, hon* ⟶ *Omoshirosoona hon-desu-ga, jitsu-wa amari omoshiroku nai-n-desu.*

1. *muzukashii, hon* 2. *yasashii* (easy), *hon* 3. *ii, mise*
4. *genkina, kodomo* 5. *atarashii, sakana* (fish)
6. *oishii, niku* (meat) 7. *yaku-ni tatsu, kikai*
8. *tsureru, tokoro*

Usage Drill Practice the following conversation changing the underlined parts.

ex. *omoshiroi, hon*

A: <u>*Omoshirosoona hon*</u>*-desu-ne.*

B: *Ee,* <u>*omoshirosoona*</u>*-n-desu-ga, jitsu-wa soo-ja nai-n-desu.*

A: <u>*Omoshiroku nai*</u>*-n-desu-ka.*

B: *Ee, amari . . . .*

A: *Soo-desu-ka. Sore-wa zannen-desu-ne.*

1. *genkina, kodomo* 2. *oishii, niku* 3. *benrina, kikai*
4. *yasui, mise* 5. *tsureru, tokoro* 6. *yaku-ni tatsu, jibiki*

III. *...oo, ...yoo*

Structure Drill Practice the following table.

A)	*miru*	*mimasu*	*miyoo-to omoimasu*
	taberu	*tabemasu*	*tabeyoo-to omoimasu*
	kau	*kaimasu*	*kaoo-to omoimasu*
	kaku	*kakimasu*	*kakoo-to omoimasu*
	atsumeru	*atsumemasu*	*atsumeyoo -to omoimasu*
	kuru	*kimasu*	*koyoo-to omoimasu*
	suru	*shimasu*	*shiyoo-to omoimasu*

B)	*Nihon-ni imasu*	*Nihon-ni iyoo-to omoimasu*
	kare-ni aimasu	*kare-ni aoo-to omoimasu*
	denwa-o kakemasu	*denwa-o kakeyoo-to omoimasu*
	kaeru-no-o yamemasu	*kaeru-no-o yameyoo-to omoimasu* (I think I won't go home)

Usage Drill Practice the following conversation filling in the blanks with phrases from below.

A: *....san, ashita-wa nani-o suru yotee-desu-ka.*
B: ——(1)——*to omotte-imasu. ....san-wa?*
A: *Watashi-wa* ——(2)——*to omotte-imasu.*

Phrases to be used in ——— :

1. *eega-o miyoo* 2. *eega-o mi-ni ikoo* 3. *tomodachi-ni aoo*
4. *uchi-ni iyoo* 5. *hon-o yomoo* 6. *tegami-o kakoo*
7. *shigoto-o shiyoo* 8. *tsuri-ni ikoo* 9. *nomi-ni ikoo*
10. *kuni-e kaeroo* 11. *tomodachi-o tazuneyoo*
12. *uchi-de rekoodo* (records) *-o kikoo*

Use two different phrases to fill in the two blanks. If you use the same phrase in (2), change *Watashi-wa* into *Watashi-mo.*

IV. {*-oo* / *-yoo*} *-to shita toki*

Structure Drill Change the following as shown in the example.

ex. *koohii-o nomu* →*Koohii-o nomoo-to shita toki, tomodachi-ga tazunete-kimashita.*

1. *neru*
2. *dekakeru*
3. *tegami-o kaku*
4. *denwa-o kakeru*
5. *terebi-o miru*
6. *shigoto-o yameru*
7. *shokuji* (meal)*-o suru*
8. *yuuhan* (supper)*-o taberu*

Pronunciation Practice

Practice reading the following, paying special attention to the accent.

A. 1. あいうえお、あいうえお　2. かきくけこ、かきくけこ

3. さしすせそ、さしすせそ　4. たちつてと、たちつてと

5. なにぬねの、なにぬねの　6. はひふへほ、はひふへほ

7. まみむめも、まみむめも　8. やいゆえよ、やいゆえよ

9. らりるれろ、らりるれろ　10. わいうえお、わいうえお

B. 1. てがみですか、てがみ　2. ろんぶんですか、ろんぶん

3. すいえいですか、すいえい　4. がくせいですか、がくせい

5. おともだちですか、おともだち

6. まつもとさんですか、まつもとさん

C. Say the words and phrases in B with a rising intonation.

ex. てがみですか。てがみ。

Reading Comprehension

Read the following.

松本(まつもと)の日記(にっき)[(1)]

九月十五日(くがつじゅうごにち)。ジョンソン(じょんそん)さんといっしょにつりにいった。山下(やました)も来(く)る予定(よてい)だったが、きゅうに用事(ようじ)ができて、だめになった。さかなはおもったよりたくさんつれておもしろかった。

山下の日記

九月十五日。きゅうに用事ができて伊藤先生のおたくへいった。じつはつりにいく予定だったが、それはやめた。つりはどうだったのだろう。あした松本にきいてみよう。

(1) diary (2) I will ask and find out

Writing Practice

Practice writing the following *hiragana.*

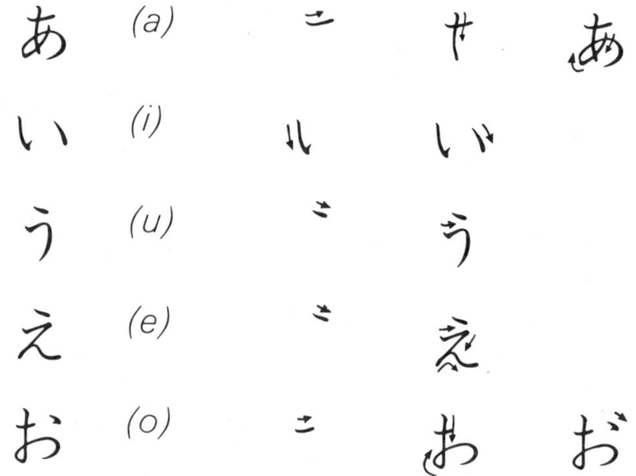

Aural Comprehension

Listen to the conversations on the tape and answer the following questions.

(A) 1. *Otoko-no-hito-wa dooshite osoku narimashita-ka.*
   2. *Yamada-san-wa denwa-de* (on the phone) *nan-to iimashita-ka.*
   3. *Yamada-san-wa donna hito-deshoo-ka.*

(B) 1. *Tsugi-no eega-ga hajimaru-made dono-gurai jikan-ga arimasu-ka.*
   2. *Eega-ga hajimaru-made futari* (the two people)*-wa nani-o shimasu-ka.*

(C) 1. *Futari-ga mita shokudoo-wa donna shokudoo-deshita-ka.*
   2. *Futari-wa dotchi-ni hairimashita-ka.*
   3. *Dooshite-desu-ka.*

Big Cities in Japan

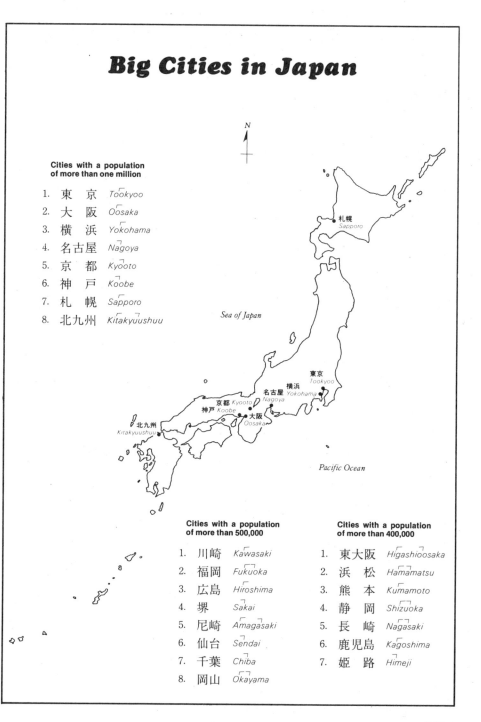

Cities with a population of more than one million

1. 東　京　*Tookyoo*
2. 大　阪　*Oosaka*
3. 横　浜　*Yokohama*
4. 名古屋　*Nagoya*
5. 京　都　*Kyooto*
6. 神　戸　*Koobe*
7. 札　幌　*Sapporo*
8. 北九州　*Kitakyuushuu*

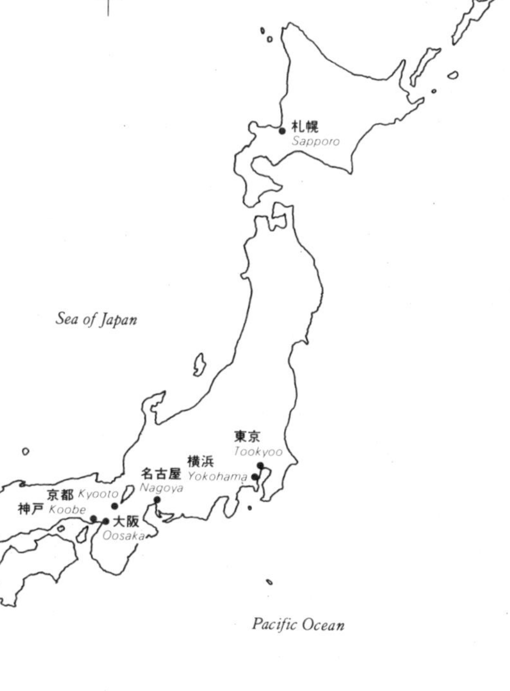

Cities with a population of more than 500,000

1. 川崎　*Kawasaki*
2. 福岡　*Fukuoka*
3. 広島　*Hiroshima*
4. 堺　*Sakai*
5. 尼崎　*Amagasaki*
6. 仙台　*Sendai*
7. 千葉　*Chiba*
8. 岡山　*Okayama*

Cities with a population of more than 400,000

1. 東大阪　*Higashioosaka*
2. 浜　松　*Hamamatsu*
3. 熊　本　*Kumamoto*
4. 静　岡　*Shizuoka*
5. 長　崎　*Nagasaki*
6. 鹿児島　*Kagoshima*
7. 姫　路　*Himeji*

第十四課(だいじゅうよんか)　かりても　いいですか

Dialogue

(In a library)

男子学生(だんしがくせい)：　これ、おねがいします。 1

図書館員(としょかんいん)：　これは　かしだしは　できません。ここで　読(よ)む-

のは　かまいませんが。 3

男子学生(だんしがくせい)：　そとへ　もちだしては　いけないんですね。

図書館員(としょかんいん)：　そうです。 5

男子学生(だんしがくせい)：　あの、こちらは　もちだしても　いいですか。

図書館員(としょかんいん)：　ええ、そちらは　かまいません。 7

男子学生(だんしがくせい)：　期間(きかん)は　何日(なんにち)ぐらいですか。

図書館員(としょかんいん)：　二週間以内(にしゅうかんいない)です。 9

(A girl student comes up to the librarian's desk after the boy has left.)

女子学生(じょしがくせい)：　(Showing the title of a book from her notes)

この　本(ほん)、ありますか。

図書館員(としょかんいん)：　ちょっと　まってください。しらべてみますから。 11

…わかりました。その　本(ほん)は　ほかの　人(ひと)が　かりだしてい-

ます。 13

女子学生(じょしがくせい)：　いつ　もどりますか。

図書館員(としょかんいん)：　一月十日(いちがつとおか)までに　もどる　はずですから、十一日(じゅういちにち)- 15

以後(いご)に　来(き)てください。

(Some time later, the boy and the girl meet.)

女子学生(じょしがくせい)：　高橋(たかはし)さん、本(ほん)、あった？ 17

男子学生(だんしがくせい)：　あったけど、かしだしは　できないって。

女子学生(じょしがくせい)：　そう。ざんねんね。 19

男子学生(だんしがくせい)：　いいよ。図書館(としょかん)へ　来(き)て　読(よ)めば　いいんだから。

女子学生(じょしがくせい)：　そうね。 21

男子学生(だんしがくせい)：　きみの　ほうは？

女子学生(じょしがくせい)：　ほかの　人(ひと)が　かりだしているの。十一日(じゅういちにち)まで 23
まってくださいって。

Dialogue

Lesson 14	*Dai-juuyonka*
MAY I BORROW IT?	***KARITE-MO II-DESU-KA***
Male student : I'd like to borrow this, please.	*Danshi-Gakusei: Kore, onegai-shimasu.*
Librarian : I'm afraid you can't borrow this book. You can read it here, though.	*Toshokan'in: Kore-wa kashida-shi-wa dekimasen. Koko-de yomu-no-wa kamaimasen-ga.*
M.S.: Oh, I can't take it out?	*D.G.: Soto-e mochidashite-wa ike-nai-n-desu-ne.*
L: No.	*T: Soo-desu.*
M.S.: Can I take out this one?	*D.G.: Ano, kochira-wa mochidashi-te-mo ii-desu-ka.*
L: Yes, that's all right.	*T: Ee, sochira-wa kamaimasen.*
M.S.: How many days can I keep it?	*D.G.: Kikan-wa nannichi-gurai- desu-ka.*
L: Not more than two weeks.	*T: Nishuukan-inai-desu.*
Female student : Do you have this book?	*Joshi-Gakusei: Kono hon, arimasu-ka.*
Librarian : Just a moment, please. I'll check. ... Someone has taken it out.	*Toshokan'in: Chotto matte-kudasai. Shirabete-mimasu-kara ....., Wakarimashita. Sono hon-wa hoka-no hito-ga karidashite-imasu.*
F.S.: When will it be returned?	*J.G.: Itsu modorimasu-ka.*

L:	It should be back by January the 10th. Please come for it on the 11th or after.	T:	*Ichigatsu tooka-made-ni modoru hazu-desu-kara, juuichinichi-igo-ni kite-kudasai.*
F.S.:	Did you find the book you were looking for?	J.G.:	*Takahashi-san, hon, atta?*
M.S.:	Yes, but I was told I can't take it out.	D.G.:	*Atta-kedo, kashidashi-wa dekinai-tte.*
F.S.:	That's disappointing, isn't it?	J.G.:	*Soo. Zannen-ne.*
M.S.:	That's all right. I can read it at the library.	D.G.:	*Ii-yo. Toshokan-e kite yomeba ii-n-da-kara.*
F.S.:	That's right.	J.G.:	*Soo-ne.*
M.S.:	How about you?	D.G.:	*Kimi-no hoo-wa?*
F.S.:	Someone borrowed the book I wanted, and I was told I'll have to wait till the 11th.	J.G.:	*Hoka-no hito-ga karidashite-iru-no. Juuichinichi-made matte-kudasai-tte.*

Explanation

(In this lesson you will learn how to ask for permission to do something. You will also learn some more expressions used in familiar speech.)

これ、おねがいします。 **line 1**

Kore, onegai-shimasu.

Onegai-shimasu is used, as you learned in Lesson 7, to ask someone for help. Sometimes *kore* or *kore-o* is used before *onegai-shimasu,* with no particular difference in meaning.

図書館員(としょかんいん)：これは　かしだしは　できません。 **line 2**

Toshokan'in: Kore-wa kashidashi-wa dekimasen.

toshokan'in	librarian (*toshokan* 'library', *in* 'member')
kashidashi	lending service
dekimasen	is not possible (dict. *dekiru*)

ここで　読むのは　かまいませんが。　**lines 2-3**

Koko-de yomu-no-wa kamaimasen-ga.

koko-de yomu-no reading it here

kamaimasen it's all right; I don't mind (dict. *kamau*)

そとへ　もちだしては　いけないんですね。　**line 4**

Soto-e mochidashite-wa ikenai-n-desu-ne.

soto-e out; out of the building

mochidashite-wa ikenai I shouldn't take it out (*lit.* it won't do if I take it out) (dict. *mochidasu*)

'...-*te-wa ikenai*' is used to show prohibition.

ex. *Amari okane-o tsukatte-wa ikemasen.* (You shouldn't spend too much money.)

'... *n-desu-ne*' is used to make sure what is said; it roughly corresponds to 'you mean?' in English.

ex. A: *Shigoto-ga taihen-desu-kara ...* (The work is hard so...)

B: *Yameru-n-desu-ne.* (So you mean you're quitting, right?)

あの、こちらは　もちだしても　いいですか。　**line 6**

Ano, kochira-wa mochidashite-mo ii-desu-ka.

ano =*anoo* (cf. Lesson 12)

mochidashite-mo ii-desu-ka may I take it out? (dict. *mochidasu*)

'...*te-mo ii-desu-ka*' is an expression used to ask for permission to do something.

ex. *Kono denwa-o tsukatte-mo ii-desu-ka.* (May I use this phone?)

Haitte-mo ii-desu-ka. (May I come in?)

'...*te-mo ii-desu*' is used to give permission.

ex. *Ee, haitte-mo ii-desu-yo.* (Yes, you may come in.)

Kamaimasen is sometimes used in place of *ii-desu.*

ex. A: *Haitte-mo kamaimasen-ka.* (May I come in?)

B. *Ee, kamaimasen-yo.* (Yes, you may.)

期間は　何日ぐらいですか。 **line 8**

Kikan-wa nannichi-gurai-desu-ka.

kikan period

nannichi (-gurai) (about) how many days

二週間以内です。 **line 9**

Nishuukan-inai-desu.

nishuukan-inai within two weeks

しらべてみますから。 **line 11**

Shirabete-mimasu-kara.

shirabete-mimasu I'll check and see (dict. *shiraberu* and *miru*)

'*. . . te-miru*' means 'I will . . . and see what will happen.'

ex. *Itte-mimashoo.* (Let's go and see.)

Tabete-mimashita-ga, oishiku arimasen-deshita. (I tasted it and found it to be untasty.)

その　本は　ほかの　人が　かりだしています。 **lines 12-13**

Sono hon-wa hoka-no hito-ga karidashite-imasu.

hoka-no hito someone else

karidashite-imasu has borrowed and taken it out (dict. *karidasu*)

The word order here can be changed to form the sentence, *Hoka-no hito-ga sono hon-o karidashite-imasu.* Both sentences describe the same fact, but the speaker's attitude is different. When his concern is the book in question, not the person who borrowed it, the speaker starts the sentence with *Sono hon-wa.*

ex. *Watashi-wa kono hon-o kaimashita.* (—emphasis on explaining what I did)

Kono hon-wa watashi-ga kaimashita. (—emphasis on explaining how the book came to be mine)

いつ　もどりますか。 **line 14**

Itsu modorimasu-ka.

itsu when

modorimasu-ka will it be returned? (dict. *modoru*)

一月十日までに　もどる　はずですから、　十一日以後に　来てください。

Ichigatsu tooka-made-ni modoru hazu-desu-kara, juuichinichi-igo-ni kite-kudasai. **lines 15-16**

ichigatsu tooka-made-ni	by January 10th
modoru hazu-desu	it's expected to be returned
juuichinichi-igo-ni	on the 11th or after

The dictionary form plus *hazu* means 'it is expected, since it's arranged that way, or since it's agreed on.'

ex. *Tsugi-no basu-wa moo kuru hazu-desu.* (The next bus should soon be here.)

Sonna-ni takaku nai hazu-desu. (It shouldn't be that expensive.)

(The conversation in lines 17 through 24 is between good friends, a male and female student.)

高橋さん、本、あった？ **line 17**

Takahashi-san, hon, atta?

Takahashi-san	personal name (name of the male student)
atta?	did you find it? (dict. *aru*)

あったけど、かしだしは　できないって。 **line 18**

Atta-kedo, kashidashi-wa dekinai-tte.

'... *tte*' is the contraction of ... *to itta*, 'he said ...' This is often used in familiar speech.

そう。ざんねんね。 **line 19**

Soo. Zannen-ne.

Men say *zannen-da-ne* instead of *zannen-ne*.

ex. m.: *Ii (o)tenki-da-ne.* f.: *Ii otenki-ne.*
Genki-da-yo. *Genki-yo.*

いいよ。図書館へ　来て　読めば　いいんだから。 **line 20**

Ii-yo. Toshokan-e kite yomeba ii-n-da-kara.

toshokan	library
kite yomeba ii	reading here will do (*lit.* if I come and read, it's fine.)

Ii-yo is used by men. Women usually say *ii-wa (yo)*

ex. m.: *Muzukashii.* f.: *Muzukashii-wa.*
Takai-ne. *Takai-wane.*
(O)kane-ga nai-yo. *Okane-ga nai-wa (yo)*

Yomeba is derived from *yomu.* The form ending in *-eba* (See Note) shows condition. *Yomeba ii* literally means 'if I read it, it's fine.' The actual meaning is 'all I have to do is read.'

ex. *Benkyoo-sureba ii-n-desu.* (All you have to do is study.)
Kono kusuri-o nomeba ii-n-desu. (All you have to do — in order to get well — is take this medicine.)

そうね。 **line 21**

Soo-ne.

Men say *Soo-da-ne.*

きみの ほうは？ **line 22**

Kimi-no hoo-wa ?

Kimi, 'you' is used by men in addressing people of their own age or younger.

ほかの 人(ひと)が かりだしているの。 **line 23**

Hoka-no hito-ga karidashite-iru-no.

Iru-no is the contraction of *iru-no-desu*, or *iru-no-da.* Men say *iru-n-da.*

ex. m.: *Hon-ga atta-n-da.* f.: *Hon-ga atta-no.*
Konakatta-n-da. *Konakatta-no.*

十一日(いちにち)まで まってくださいって。 **lines 23-24**

Juuichinichi-made matte-kudasai-tte.

juuichinichi-made until the 11th

Note the difference between *-made*, 'until' and *-made-ni*, 'by.'

ex. *Raishuu-made machimasu.* (I'll wait until next week.)
Kayoobi-made-ni dekimasu. (It'll be ready by Tuesday.)

Note *-eba*

The *-eba* form is made by dropping the final *-u* of the verb and adding *-eba.*

taberu —— *tabereba*   *yuu*—*ieba*

nomu —— *nomeba*

kuru —— *kureba*   *motsu*—*moteba*

suru —— *sureba*   *matsu*—*mateba*

The *-eba* form of adjectives is made by dropping the final *-i* and adding *-kereba.*

takai —— *takakereba*; *muzukashii* —— *muzukashikereba*

ex. *Takakereba kaimasen.* (If it's expensive I won't buy it.)
Muzukashikereba yamemasu. (If it's difficult I'll give it up.)

Drills

I. ... *te-mo ii*, ... *te-wa ikenai*

Structure Drill Make the *-te-mo ii* form and the *-te-wa ikenai* form out of the following verbs: (See Lesson 7 for the *-te* form)

ex. *yomu* ⟶ *yonde-mo ii-desu*
⟶ *yonde-wa ikemasen*

1. *taberu* 2. *yameru* 3. *kuru* 4. *iku*
5. *denwa-o suru* 6. *matsu* 7. *tegami-o kaku*
8. *jibiki-o hiku* (look up) 9. *hon-o mochidasu* 10. *tabako-o suu* (smoke)

Usage Drill Practice the following conversation changing the underlined words.

ex. (in a library) *shinbun-o yomu, hanashi-o suru*

A: *Koko-de shinbun-o yonde-mo ii-desu-ka.*
B: *Ee, ii-desu-yo.*
A: *Hanashi-o shite-wa ikenai-n-desu-ne.*
B: *Ee, hanashi-wa komarimasu.*
A: *Hai, wakarimashita.*

1. (in a library) *tegami-o kaku, hanashi-o suru*
2. (in a classroom) *koohii-o nomu, obentoo-o taberu*
3. (in a library) *yasumu* (take a rest), *tabako-o suu*
4. (in a park) *shokuji-o suru, osake* (alcoholic beverage)*-o nomu*
5. (in a library) *tomodachi-o matsu, shokuji-o suru*

II. ... *eba ii*

Structure Drill Change the following into the *-eba* form.

ex. *uchi-e kaeru* → *Uchi-e kaereba ii-n-desu.* (All you have to do is go home.)

1. *tabako-o yameru*
2. *kusuri-o nomu* (take medicine)
3. *byooin-e iku*
4. *hayaku neru*
5. *sukoshi yasumu*
6. *denwa-o kakeru*
7. *jibiki-o hiku*
8. *takushii-de* (by taxi) *iku*
9. *chizu* (map)*-o miru*
10. *tomodachi-ni kariru* (borrow from a friend)

Usage Drill Here are several questions used for asking advice. Practice saying them alone first, then with a partner who can use answers from the Structure Drill above.

ex. Question: *Kaze-o hiita toki-wa doo sureba ii-deshoo.*
(What should I do when I've caught a cold?)
Answer: *Kusuri-o nomeba ii-n-desu.* (Structure Drill —2)

1. *Okane-ga tarinai toki-wa doo sureba ii-deshoo.*
2. *Byooki-ni natta toki-wa doo sureba ii-deshoo.*
3. *Basu-ga konai toki-wa doo sureba ii-deshoo.*
4. *Kanji-ga wakaranai toki-wa doo sureba ii-deshoo.*
5. *Tsukareta toki-wa doo sureba ii-deshoo.*
6. *Michi* (direction, how to go)*-ga wakaranai toki-wa doo sureba ii-deshoo.*
7. *Tomodachi-no uchi-e iku hima-ga nai toki-wa doo sureba ii-deshoo.*
8. *Nodo-ga itai* (have a sore throat) *toki-wa doo sureba ii-deshoo.*

III. ... *hazu*

Structure Drill Change the following by adding *hazu.*

ex. *tooka-ni modorimasu* → *Tooka-ni modoru hazu-desu.*

1. *moo kimasu*
2. *sugu kaerimasu*
3. *yoji-ni owarimasu*
4. *kyoo dekimasu*
5. *raishuu hajimarimasu*
6. *kokonoka-ni ikimasu*
7. *mikka-made-ni modorimasu*
8. *ashita tazunete-kimasu*

Usage Drill Practice the following conversation changing the underlined parts.

ex. (1)*densha* (train), (2)*kuru,* (3)*kiku*

A: (1) *Densha, mada* (2) *kimasen-ne.*

B: *Soo-desu-ne. Moo* (2) *kuru hazu-na-n-desu-ga, doo shita-n-deshoo.*

A: (3) *Kiite-mimashoo-ka.*

B: *Soo-desu-ne.* (3) *Kiite-mite-kudasai.*

1. (1)*basu,* (2)*kuru,* (3)*kiku*
2. (1)*Oota-san,* (2)*kuru,* (3)*denwa-o kakeru*
3. (1)*eega,* (2)*hajimaru,* (3)*kiku*
4. (1)*shinbun,* (2)*kuru,* (3)*denwa-o kakeru*
5. (1)*shokuji,* (2)*dekiru,* (3)*kiku*
6. (1)*kaigi* (conference), (2)*owaru,* (3)*kiku*

IV. ... *wa* ... *ga*

Structure Drill Change the following sentences by switching the word order and starting with ... *wa.*

ex. *hoka-no hito-ga sono hon-o karidashite-imasu*
⟶ *Sono hon-wa hoka-no hito-ga karidashite-imasu.*

1. *watashi-ga sono hon-o karite-imasu*
2. *hoka-no hito-ga sono shashin-o mite-imasu*
3. *dareka-ga sono tsukue-o tsukatte-imasu*

4. *watashi-ga kono shoosetsu-o kakimashita*
5. *Yamashita-san-ga kono shorui* (document)*-o shirabemashita*
6. *dareka-ga sono heya* (room)*-o tsukatte-imasu*
7. *kare-ga kono shigoto-o shimashita*
8. *dareka-ga sono osake-o nomimashita*

Usage Drill Practice the following conversation changing the underlined parts.

ex. *hon, Yoshida-san, yomu*

A: *Nanika sagashite-iru-n-desu-ka.* (Are you looking for something?)
B: *Ee, sakki koko-ni atta hon-ga nai-n-desu.*
A: *Aa, sono hon-wa Yoshida-san-ga yonde-imasu-yo.*
B: *Soo-desu-ka. Yoshida-san-wa doko-ni imasu-ka.*
A: *Tonari-no heya-da-to omoimasu.*

1. *shinbun, Suzuki-san, yomu*
2. *shashin, Michiko-san, miru*
3. *taipu* (typewriter), *Takahashi-san, tsukau*
4. *shorui, Suzuki-san-tachi, shiraberu*
5. *osake, minna, nomu*

Pronunciation Practice

Practice saying the following, paying careful attention to the accent.

A. 1．あいうえお、あいうえお　2．がぎぐげご、がぎぐげご
3．ざじずぜぞ、ざじずぜぞ　4．だじずでど、だじずでど
5．ばびぶべぼ、ばびぶべぼ　6．ぱぴぷぺぽ、ぱぴぷぺぽ

B. 1．しょうせつですか、しょうせつ
2．しんぶんですか、しんぶん
3．かしだしですか、かしだし

4. はつおん (pronunciation) ですか、はつおん

5. けいさつ (police) ですか、けいさつ

C. Say the words and phrases in B with a falling intonation.

ex. しょうせつですか。しょうせつ。

Reading Comprehension

Read the following.

大学(だいがく)の図書館(としょかん)にはいろいろな規則(きそく)(1)がある。かしだしの期間(きかん)は二週間以内(にしゅうかんいない)で*、字引(じびき)とあたらしい雑誌(ざっし)はかしだしができない。へやのなかではたばこをすってはいけない。また、大(おお)きなこえ(2)で話(はなし)をしてはいけない。

このあいだ、わたしはつかれていたので、本(ほん)を読(よ)みながらねていた。すると(3)図書館員(としょかんいん)が来(き)て、おこした(4)ので、わたしは「ねるのもいけないんですか」ときいた。図書館員(としょかんいん)は「ねるのはかまいませんが、しずかにねてください」といった。

(1) regulations (2) voice (3) then (4) woke me up

* *de* (. . . and . . .)

When two sentences are combined into one, and the first sentence ends in *-desu*, the *-desu* is replaced by *-de*.

ex. *Kore-wa hon-**desu**. Are-wa zasshi-desu.*

→*Kore-wa hon-**de**, are-wa zasshi-desu.* (This is a book, and that is a magazine.)

*Kikan-wa nishuukan-**desu**. Zasshi-no kashidashi-wa dekimasen.*

→*Kikan-wa nishuukan-**de**, zasshi-no kashidashi-wa dekimasen.*

Writing Practice

Practice writing the following *hiragana*.

か (*ka*) う カ が

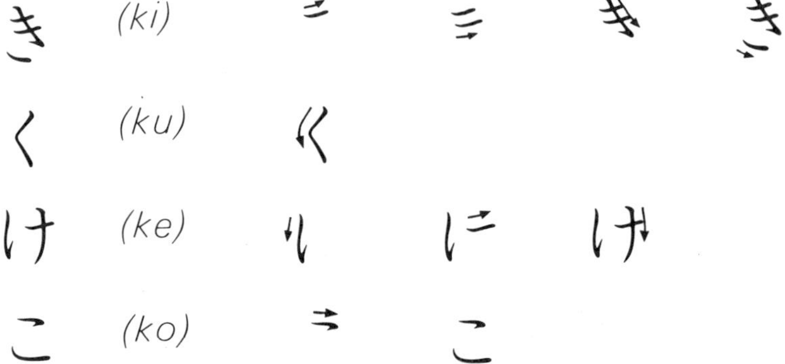

Aural Comprehension

Listen to the conversations on the tape and answer the following questions.

(A) 1. *Byookino otoko-no-hito-wa donna shitsumon* (question)*-o shimashita-ka.*

2. *Onna-no isha* (doctor)*-wa donna koto-o shite-mo ii-to iimashita-ka.*

(B) 1. *Dare-ga shinbun'ya* (newspaper shop)*-ni denwa-o kakeyoo-to iimashita-ka.*

2. *Naze* (why) *soo itta-no-desu-ka.*

3. *Denwa-bangoo-wa doko-ni arimashita-ka.*

(C) 1. *Otoko-no gakusee-wa kurasu* (class)*-ga omoshirokatta-to iimashita-ka.*

2. *Onna-no gakusee-wa doko-e issho-ni ikoo-to iimashita-ka.*

3. *Otoko-no gakusee-wa dooshite issho-ni ikanai-no-desu-ka.*

Supplementary Pronunciation Practice (1)

Listen to the tape and practice saying the following words and phrases, being especially careful of the difference between a. and b.

1. a. *obaasan* (old woman)
   b. *obasan* (woman)
2. a. *senshuu* (last week)
   b. *senshu* (champion)
3. a. *Nyuuyooku* (New York)
   b. *nyuuyoku* (taking a bath)
4. a. *iimasu* (I say)
   b. *imasu* (I am)
5. a. *itai* (have a pain)
   b. *iitai* (want to say)
6. a. *misoo* (likely to see)
   b. *miso* (*miso*)
7. a. *kookoo* (highschool)
   b. *kooko* (pickles)
8. a. *ookisoo-desu* (it looks big)
   b. *ookii-soo-desu* (I heard it's big)
9. a. *taitee imasu* (I'm usually here)
   b. *taite-imasu* (I'm cooking)
10. a. *kiite-mimashoo* (I'll ask and see)
    b. *kite-mimashoo* (I'll come and see)
11. a. *shitte-imasu* (I know)
    b. *shite-imasu* (I'm doing it)
12. a. *kitte-kudasai* (please cut it)
    b. *kite-kudasai* (please come)
13. a. *kono koto* (this thing)
    b. *kono kooto* (this coat)
14. a. *kyaku-desu* (he's a visitor)
    b. *kiyaku-desu* (it's an agreement)
15. a. *kyoo-desu* (it's today)
    b. *kiyoo-desu* (he's skillful)
16. a. *byooin-e* (to the hospital)
    b. *biyooin-e* (to the beauty parlor)
17. a. *ichiman-en* (10,000 yen)
    b. *ichimannen* (10,000 years)
18. a. *Nihon-e* (to Japan)
    b. *Nihon-ne* (it's Japan, isn't it?)
19. a. *hon-o sukoshi yomimashita* (I read a few books)
    b. *honno sukoshi yomimashita* (I read a very little of it)
20. a. *Yamaguchi-san* (Mr. Yamaguchi)
    b. *Yamauchi-san* (Mr. Yamauchi)

第十五課　日本人形を　ほしがって　います

Dialogue

(On the street, Miss Morita happens to see Johnson.)

森田：　ジョンソンさんじゃ　ありませんか。

ジョンソン：　あ、森田さん、こんにちは。

森田：　こんにちは。お買物ですか。

ジョンソン：　ええ。来月の　四日は　いもうとの　誕生日なので、おくりものを　買いたいと　おもって…

森田：　買う　ものは　きまっているんですか。

ジョンソン：　ええ、日本人形を　買う　つもりです。いもうとが　ほしがっていましたから。

森田：　ああ、それは　いいですね。

ジョンソン：　でも、じつは　ぼく、人形の　ことが　よく　わからないんで、こまっているんです。

森田：　そうですか。じゃ、わたしの　知っている　店が　ありますから、そこへ　ご案内しましょうか。

ジョンソン：　でも、それじゃ…

森田：　いいんですよ。わたしは　人形を　見るのが　だいすきで、よく　見に　いくんですから。

ジョンソン：　そうですか。じゃ、すみませんが、つれていってください。

森田：　いもうとさんは　おいくつですか。

ジョンソン：　こんど　十八に　なります。

森田：　日本へ　いらっしゃった　ことが　ありますか。

ジョンソン：　ないんです。とても　来たがっていますが。

Dialogue Lesson 15

Dai-juugoka

SHE WANTS A JAPANESE DOLL *NIHON-NINGYOO-O HOSHIGATTE-IMASU*

Morita: Hello, it's you, Mr. Johnson!	*Morita: Jonson-san-ja arimasen-ka.*
Johnson: Oh, Miss Morita. Good afternoon.	*Jonson: A, Morita-san, konnichiwa.*
M: Good afternoon. Are you shopping?	*M: Konnichiwa. O-kaimono-desu-ka.*
J: Yes. The fourth of next month is my sister's birthday, so I want to buy something for her.	*J: Ee. Raigetsu-no yokka-wa imooto-no tanjoobi-na-node, okurimono-o kaitai-to omotte....*
M: Have you decided on what to buy?	*M: Kau mono-wa kimatte-iru-n-desu-ka.*
J: Yes, I'll buy a Japanese doll, because she wanted one.	*J: Ee, nihon-ningyoo-o kau tsumori-desu. Imooto-ga hoshigatte-imashita-kara.*
M: That's a good idea.	*M: Aa, sore-wa ii-desu-ne.*
J: But, actually, I know very little about dolls and I'm not sure if I can pick up one.	*J: Demo, jitsu-wa boku, ningyoo-no koto-ga yoku wakaranai-n-de, komatte-iru-n-desu.*
M: Really? Then shall I take you to a store I know?	*M: Soo-desu-ka. Ja, watashi-no shitte-iru mise-ga arimasu-kara, soko-e go-annai-shimashoo-ka.*
J: That would be asking too much.	*J: Demo, sore-ja....*
M: No, not at all. I love to look at dolls anyway, and I often go there.	*M: Ii-n-desu-yo. Watashi-wa ningyoo-o miru-no-ga daisuki-de, yoku mi-ni iku-n-desu-kara.*
J: Do you? I hate to trouble you, but will you take me there?	*J: Soo-desu-ka. Ja, sumimasen-ga, tsurete-itte-kudasai.*
M: How old is your sister?	*M: Imooto-san-wa o-ikutsu-desu-ka.*
J: She's going to be 18.	*J: Kondo juuhachi-ni narimasu.*
M: Has she been to Japan?	*M: Nihon-e irasshatta-koto-ga arimasu-ka.*
J: No. She wants to come very much, though.	*J: Nai-n-desu. Totemo kitagatte-imasu-ga.*

Explanation

(In this lesson you will learn how to express desire and intention.)

こんにちは。お買物(かいもの)ですか。 **line 3**

Konnichiwa. O-kaimono-desu-ka.

Konnichiwa.	Hello; Good afternoon. (See Lesson 4)
o-kaimono-desu-ka	are you shopping?

See Lesson 8 for use of *o-* plus noun plus *-desu* in place of a verb. (ex. *O-dekake-desu-ka.*)

ええ。来月(らいげつ)の 四日(よっか)は いもうとの 誕生日(たんじょうび)なので、おくりものを

Ee. Raigetsu-no yokka-wa imooto-no tanjoobi-na-node, okurimono-o

買(か)いたいと おもって…… **lines 4-5**

kaitai-to omotte . . .

raigetsu	next month
yokka	the fourth day of the month
imooto	younger sister
tanjoobi	birthday
okurimono	present
. . . o kaitai-to omou	I want to buy . . . (dict. *kau*)

Tanjoobi-na-node means 'because it is her birthday.' When *-node* is added to *-da*, the plain form of *-desu, -da* changes into *-na*.

ex. *Ashita shiken-na-node isogashii.* (I'm busy since I have an examination tomorrow.)

Tai added to the verb base expresses the speaker's wish to do something. (The verb base used is the same one to which *-masu* is added.)

ex. *Mizu-o nomitai-to omoimasu.* (I want to drink some water.)
Ashita osoku kitai-n-desu-ga, ii-deshoo-ka. (I'd like to come late tomorrow. Would it be all right?)

After *kaitai-to omotte,* a phrase meaning 'I came to this shopping area' is left out. When the meaning is obvious a phrase that would otherwise complete the sentence is often omitted.

買う　ものは　きまっているんですか。 **line 6**

Kau mono-wa kimatte-iru-n-desu-ka.

kimatte-iru-n-desu-ka have you decided? (dict. *kimaru*)

Kimatte-iru literally means 'It has been (or it is) decided.'

ええ、日本人形を　買う　つもりです。 **line 7**

Ee, nihon-ningyoo-o kau tsumori-desu.

nihon-ningyoo Japanese doll in kimono

. . . o kau tsumori-desu I intend to buy . . .

Tsumori is used to show one's intention. It is added to the dictionary form of verbs.

ex. *Rainen kuni-e kaeru tsumori-desu.* (I intend to go home next year.)

It is similar to *yotee* you learned in Lesson 13; the difference is that *yotee* can be used to refer to anyone, while *tsumori* is usually used by the speaker to refer to his own intention. *Tsumori* resembles the *-yoo* or *-oo* form (ex. *ikoo-to omoimasu*) in that both are used by the speaker to refer to himself; however, the *-yoo* or *-oo* form is used to talk about more immediate intentions or actions.

ex. *Kare-wa gogo shichiji-ni deru yotee-desu.* (He's scheduled to start at seven P.M.)

(*Watashi-wa*) *gogo shichiji-ni deru tsumori-desu.* (I intend to start at seven P.M.)

Deyoo-to shita toki denwa-ga kimashita. (When I was about to leave, there was a telephone call.)

いもうとが　ほしがっていましたから。 **lines 7-8**

Imooto-ga hoshigatte-imashita-kara.

(*. . . o*) *hoshigatte-imashita* she wanted to have (. . .) (dict. *hoshigaru*)

The verb *hoshigaru* is derived from the adjective *hoshii. Hoshii* is used by the speaker to talk about his own desires; *hoshigaru* is used by the speaker to refer to a third person's desires.

ex. (*Watashi-wa*) *mizu-ga hoshii-desu.* (I want some water.)

Michiko-san-wa mizu-o hoshigatte-imasu. (Michiko wants some water.)

Hoshii follows *-ga* while *hoshigaru* follows *-o.*

Garu is used with other adjectives, too:

ex. A: *Samui-desu-nee.* (It's cold, isn't it?)

B: *Ee. Kodomo-tachi-mo samugatte-imasu.* (Yes, the children say they're cold, too.)

Garu verbs cannot be used to talk about the desires of respected persons. It sounds strange to say *Sensee-ga samugatte-imasu*, since use of the word *sensee* shows respect and the *-garu* verb doesn't.

でも、じつは ぼく、人形(にんぎょう)の ことが よく わからないんで、こまっている んです。 **lines 10-11**

Demo, jitsu-wa boku, ningyoo-no koto-ga yoku wakaranai-nde, komatte-iru-n-desu.

...no koto-ga wakaranai	I don't know about...
wakaranai-nde	=*wakaranai-node*
komatte-iru-n-desu	I'm at a loss (dict. *komaru*)

じゃ、わたしの 知(し)っている 店(みせ)が ありますから、そこへ ご案内(あんない)しましょうか。 **lines 12-13**

Ja, watashi-no shitte-iru mise-ga arimasu-kara, soko-e go-annai-shimashoo-ka.

go-annai-shimashoo-ka	shall I take you there? (dict. *annai-suru*)

Annai-suru means 'to take someone' or 'to guide someone' to a certain place. The prefix *go-* plus verb *suru* is used to make the humble form; other examples are *go-chisoo-suru* 'to treat someone to a meal,' and *go-shookai-suru* 'to introduce someone.'

でも、それじゃ… **line 14**

Demo, sore-ja...

Sore-ja is a contraction of *sore-dewa*, an expression used to show hesitation. Alone, it means 'if that is the case.' Here, the speaker uses it to mean 'if that is the case I would be causing you trouble.'

わたしは　人形(にんぎょう)を　見(み)るのが　だいすきで、よく　見(み)に　いくんですから。
Watashi-wa ningyoo-o miru-no-ga daisuki-de, yoku mi-ni iku-n-desu-kara.

lines 15-16

. . . ga daisuki-de I like to . . . very much, and
yoku often

'*. . . ga suki-desu*' means 'to like . . .'; *dai-* is used for emphasis.

ex. *Watashi-wa eega-o miru-no-ga suki-desu.* (I like to see movies.)

You can also say: *Watashi-wa eega-ga suki-desu.* (I like movies.)

じゃ、すみませんが、つれていってください。 **lines 17-18**
Ja, sumimasen-ga, tsurete-itte-kudasai.

tsurete-itte-kudasai please take me (dict. *tsureru*)

Tsurete-iku means 'to take someone along.'

ex. *Kinoo otooto-o kooen-e tsurete-ikimashita.* (I took my little brother to the park yesterday.)

いもうとさんは　おいくつですか。 **line 19**
Imooto-san-wa o-ikutsu-desu-ka.

imooto-san your sister
o-ikutsu-desu-ka how old is she?

こんど　十八(じゅうはち)に　なります。 **line 20**
Kondo juuhachi-ni narimasu.

kondo this time (*here*, this coming birthday)

日本(にほん)へ　いらっしゃった　ことが　ありますか。 **line 21**
Nihon-e irasshatta koto-ga arimasu-ka.

irasshatta koto-ga arimasu-ka has she ever been to Japan? (dict. *irassharu*)

Irassharu is used in place of *iku, kuru,* and *iru* when speaking about the actions (or existence) of a respected person.

ex. *Kinoo-wa doko-e irasshaimashita-ka.* (Where did you go yesterday?)

Ashita mata koko-e irasshaimasu-ka. (Are you coming here tomorrow, too?)

Imooto-san-wa ima doko-ni irasshaimasu-ka. (Where is your sister now?)

The plain past form of a verb plus *koto-ga aru* is used to show past experience.

ex. *Mae-ni kono uta-o kiita koto-ga arimasu.* (I have heard this song before.)

とても 来たがっていますが。 **line 22**

Totemo kitagatte-imasu-ga.

totemo very much
kitagatte-imasu she wants to come (from *kitai*)

While *kitai* is used with the first person, *kitagatte-iru* is used with the third person. Thus:

ex. *Watashi-wa nihongo-o (-ga)* hanashitai-desu.* (I want to speak Japanese.)

Imooto-wa nihongo-o hanashitagatte-imasu. (My sister wants to speak Japanese.)

(*With *-tai*, either *nihongo-o* or *nihongo-ga* can be used.)

Drills

I. ... *tai*

Structure Drill Change the following as shown in the example.

ex. *hayaku kaerimasu* ⟶ *Hayaku kaeritai-to omoimasu.*

1. *ningyoo-o kaimasu*
2. *kuni-e kaerimasu*
3. *kaisha-o yamemasu*
4. *eega-o mimasu*
5. *okurimono-o kaimasu*
6. *hon-o karimasu*
7. *tomodachi-to hanashimasu*
8. *ongaku* (music)*-o kikimasu*

Usage Drill Practice the following conversation changing the underlined parts. A asks B out to various places and B declines with a different reason in each case.

ex. *ongakukai* (concert)*-ni, shigoto-ga aru*

A: *Kore-kara* *ongakukai-ni* *iku-n-desu-ga, ... san-mo doo-desu-ka.*

B: *Watashi-mo ikitai-n-desu-ga, jitsu-wa* *shigoto-ga atte...*

A: *Soo-desu-ka. Zannen-desu-ne. Ja, kono-tsugi.* (next time)

B: *Ee, kono-tsugi tsurete-itte-kudasai.*

1. *eega-ni, shigoto-ga aru*
2. *eega-o mi-ni, yooji-ga aru*
3. *asobi-ni, isogashii*
4. *ocha-o nomi-ni, kyuu-ni yooji-ga dekiru*
5. *hanami* (flower-viewing, usually cherry-blossoms)*-ni, benkyoo-ga aru*

II. ... *tai* & .. *tagaru*

Structure Drill Practice the following table, comparing the two forms.

mitai-desu	*mitagatte-imasu*
kaitai-desu	*kaitagatte-imasu*
tabetai-desu	*tabetagatte-imasu*
kaeritai-desu	*kaeritagatte-imasu*
naritai-desu	*naritagatte-imasu*
yomitai-desu	*yomitagatte-imasu*

Usage Drill The following is a conversation for three people, showing the use for the *-tai* and *-tagaru* forms. Practice it changing the underlined parts.

ex. *ningyoo-o kau*

A: *Ningyoo-o kaitai-to omoimasu.*

B: *Soo-desu-ka.* (B walks over to C.)

C: *... san-wa nani-o shitagatte-imasu-ka.*

B: *Ningyoo-o kaitagatte-imasu.*

1. *eega-o miru*
2. *sakana* (fish)*-o taberu*
3. *shigoto-o suru*
4. *osake-o nomu*
5. *manga* (comic books)*-o yomu*
6. *Nihon-e iku*
7. *tomodachi-to hanasu*

III. . . . *ga hoshii* & . . . *o hoshigaru*

Structure Drill Change the following as shown in the example.

ex. *ningyoo-ga hoshii-desu*
→ *Imooto-wa ningyoo-o hoshigatte-imasu.*

1. *tomodachi-ga hoshii-desu*
2. *hima-ga hoshii-desu*
3. *okane-ga hoshii-desu*
4. *okurimono-ga hoshii-desu*
5. *ongakukai-no kippu-ga hoshii-desu*
6. *tegami-ga hoshii-desu*

Usage Drill Practice the following conversation with three people. Since it is fairly long, first practice Part 1, then Part 2, and then the two parts combined.

ex. *jikan, kenkyuu* (research; study) *-shitai koto*

Part 1 A: *. . . san-wa ima nani-ga hoshii-to omoimasu-ka.*
B: *Jikan-ga hoshii-desu-ne. Kenkyuu-shitai koto-ga takusan arimasu-kara.*

. . . .

Part 2 C: *. . . san-wa nani-o hoshigatte-imasu-ka.*
A: *Jikan-o hoshigatte-imasu.*
C: *Dooshite-deshoo.* (I wonder why)
A: *Kenkyuu-shitai koto-ga takusan aru-kara-deshoo.*
(probably it's because. . .)

1. *okane, kaitai mono*
2. *hima, shitai koto*
3. *jikan, mitai mono*
4. *tomodachi, hanashitai koto*
5. *shizukana heya, yomitai hon*
6. *jidoosha* (car), *ikitai tokoro*
7. *hima-to okane, ikitai tokoro*
8. *terebi, mitai bangumi* (program)

IV. . . . *ta koto-ga aru*

Structure Drill Change the following using the *-ta koto-ga aru* form.

ex. *Chuugoku-e ikimashita*→*Chuugoku-e itta koto-ga arimasu.*

1. *kono hon-o yomimashita*
2. *doitsugo* (German)*-o benkyoo-shimashita*
3. *shoosetsu-o kakimashita*
4. *terebi-ni demashita* (was on TV)
5. *byooin-ni hairimashita*
6. *arubaito-o shimashita*
7. *tsuri-ni ikimashita*
8. *shiryoo-o atsumemashita*

Usage Drill Practice the following conversation changing the underlined parts.

ex. *kono hon-o yomu, muzukashii*

A: *Kono hon-o yonda koto-ga arimasu-ka.*

B: *Arimasu. Kookoo-no toki-ni yomimashita.*

A: *Doo-deshita-ka.*

B. *Muzukashikatta-desu.*

A: *Moo ichido yomitai-to omoimasu-ka.*

B: *Iie, moo yomitaku-wa arimasen.*

1. *arubaito-o suru, taihen*
2. *doitsugo-o benkyoo-suru, taihen*
3. *byooin-ni hairu, taihen*
4. *terebi-ni deru, taihen muzukashii*
5. *shoosetsu-o kaku, muzukashii*

Reading Comprehension

森田よし子の日記

十月十日、道(1)でジョンソンさんにあった。人形を買いたいというので、わたしの知っている店へ案内した。航空便(2)でおくりたい(3)というので、ちいさい(4)人形を買った。とてもかわいい(5)人形で*、わたしもほしくなった。

(1) street (2) airmail (3) he wants to send, dict. *okuru* (4) small (5) cute

* *de*

(See Lesson 14, Reading Comprehension)

De replaces *-da* and *-datta*, too.

ex. *Kyoo-wa mikka-**da**. Ashita-wa yokka-da.*

⟶*Kyoo-wa mikka-**de**, ashita-wa yokka-da.* (Today's the third, and tomorrow is the fourth.)

*Kawaii ningyoo-**datta**. Watashi-mo hoshiku natta.*
⟶*Kawaii ningyoo-**de**, watashi-mo hoshiku natta.*

Pronunciation Practice

Practice saying the following, paying careful attention to the accent.

A. 1. あいうえお、あいうえお　2. かきくけこ、かきくけこ
3. さしすせそ、さしすせそ　4. たちつてと、たちつてと
5. なにぬねの、なにぬねの　6. はひふへほ、はひふへほ
7. まみむめも、まみむめも　8. やいゆえよ、やいゆえよ
9. らりるれろ、らりるれろ　10. わいうえお、わいうえお

B. 1. あさですか　2. あめですか　3. よるですか
4. えきですか　5. ごごですか　6. きょうですか

C. Add すみません to the phrases in B and say them with a rising intonation.
ex. すみません、あさですか。

Writing Practice

Practice writing the following *hiragana*.

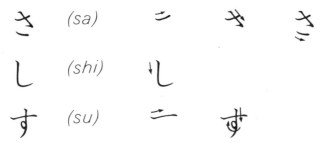

さ (sa)
し (shi)
す (su)

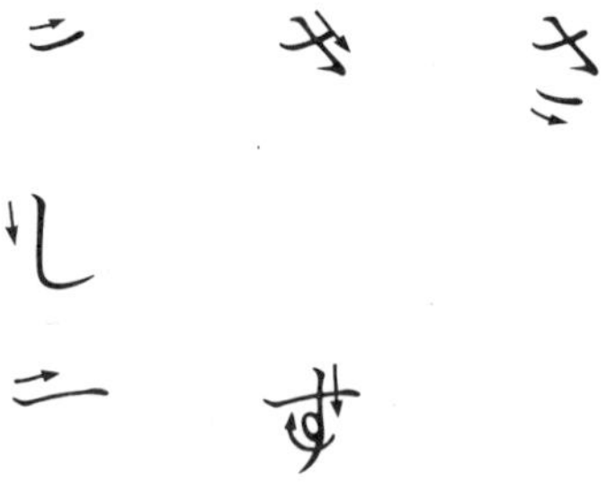

Aural Comprehension

Listen to the conversations on the tape and answer the following questions.

(A) 1. *Otoko-no-hito-wa onna-no-hito-to issho-ni doko-ni ikita-gatte-imasu-ka.*

2. *Onna-no-hito-wa iku-to iimashita-ka.*

3. *Dooshite-desu-ka.*

4. *Onna-no-hito-wa hontoo-ni* (really) *ikitasoo-desu-ka.*

(B) 1. *Otoko-no-hito-wa Yooroppa* (Europe)*-e shigoto-ni iku-n-desu-ka, asobi-ni iku-n-desu-ka.*

2. *Onna-no-hito-wa shigoto-ga omoshiroi-to omotte-imasu-ka.*

(C) 1. *Onna-no-hito-wa terebi-ni deta koto-ga arimasu-ka.*

2. *Terebi-wa doo-deshita-ka.*

3. *Onna-no-hito-wa mata terebi-ni detagatte-imasu-ka.*

第十六課(だいじゅうろっか)　火事(かじ)が　あったそうです

Dialogue

(Ishida talks to Nakamura, a young girl working for the same company.)

石田(いしだ)：　ゆうべは　たいへんでしたね。近所(きんじょ)で　火事(かじ)が　あったそうですね。

中村(なかむら)：　ええ。夜中(よなか)の　三時(さんじ)ごろでしたから、びっくりしました。

石田(いしだ)：　おたくは　だいじょうぶでしたか。

中村(なかむら)：　ええ、おかげさまで。

石田(いしだ)：　すぐ　近(ちか)くでしたか。

中村(なかむら)：　道(みち)の　むこうがわでした。消防自動車(しょうぼうじどうしゃ)の　来(く)るのが　はやかったので、こちらがわには　うつりませんでした。

石田(いしだ)：　そうですか。でも、こわかったでしょう。

中村(なかむら)：　ええ。家(いえ)が　三軒(さんげん)も　やけてしまいました。数千万円(すうせんまんえん)の　被害(ひがい)だそうです。

石田(いしだ)：　原因(げんいん)は　何(なん)だったんですか。

中村(なかむら)：　電気(でんき)ストーブ(すとーぶ)を　つけたまま　ねてしまったんだそうです。

石田(いしだ)：　あぶないですね。

(Ishida comes home and tells his wife about the fire.)

夫(おっと)：　中村(なかむら)さんの　近所(きんじょ)で　ゆうべ　火事(かじ)が　あったそうだよ。

妻(つま)：　そう。中村(なかむら)さんの　ところは　だいじょうぶだったの。

夫(おっと)：　うん。道(みち)の　むこうがわだったし、わりあい　はやく消防自動車(しょうぼうじどうしゃ)が　来(き)たんだって。

妻(つま)：　こわいわね。原因(げんいん)は　もう　わかったの。

夫(おっと)：　電気(でんき)ストーブ(すとーぶ)を　つけたまま　ねてしまったんだそうだよ。

妻(つま)：　あぶないわね。

Dialogue

Lesson 16

A FIRE BROKE OUT, I HEAR

Ishida: You must have had a terrible night. I heard a fire broke out in your neighborhood.

Nakamura: Yes, it was about three o'clock in the morning, so we were shocked.

I : Was your house all right?

N: Yes, thank God.

I : Was it very close to your home?

N: It was across the road. The fire engine arrived very quickly, so the fire didn't spread to our side.

I : Is that right? But it was frightening, I imagine.

N: Yes, very. As many as three houses were burnt down, and the damage amounts to several tens of millions of yen.

I : I wonder what caused the fire.

N: They say someone went to bed with the electric heater on.

Dai-juurokka

KAJI-GA ATTA-SOO-DESU

Ishida: Yuube-wa ▲taihen-deshita-ne. Kinjo-de ▲kaji-ga atta-soo-desu-ne.

Nakamura: Ee. Yonaka-no ▲sanji-goro-deshita-kara, bikkuri-shimashita.

I : ▲Otaku-wa daijoobu-deshita-ka.

N: Ee, okagesama-de.

I : ▲Sugu chikaku-deshita-ka.

N: Michi-no ▲mukoogawa-deshita. Shooboo-jidoosha-no kuru-noga ▲hayakatta-node, kochira-gawa-niwa ▲utsurimasen-deshita.

I Soo-desu-ka. Demo, kowakatta-deshoo.

N: Ee. Ie-ga ▲sangen-mo yakete-shimaimashita. ▲Suusenman-en-no higai-da-soo-desu.

I : ▲Gen'in-wa nan-datta-n-desu-ka.

N: ▲Denki-stoobu-o tsuketa-mama nete-shimatta-n-da-soo-desu.

I : That was a dangerous thing to do.	*I : Abunai-desu-ne.*
Husband: I heard that a fire broke out in Miss Nakamura's neighborhood last night.	*Otto: Nakamura-san-no kinjo-de yuube ▲kaji-ga atta-soo-da-yo.*
Wife: Really? Was her home all right?	*Tsuma: Soo. ▲Nakamura-san-no tokoro-wa daijoobu-datta-no.*
H: Yes. She said that the fire was across the road and the fire engine came pretty quickly.	*O: Un. Michi-no ▲mukoogawa-datta-shi, ▲wariai hayaku shooboo-jidoo-sha-ga kita-n-datte.*
W: How frightening. Did they find out the cause yet?	*T: Kowai-wane. ▲Gen'in-wa moo wakatta-no.*
H: She said that someone went to bed with the electric heater on.	*O: ▲Denki-sutoobu-o tsuketa-mama nete-shimatta-n-da-soo-da-yo.*
W: How dangerous.	*T: Abunai-wane.*

Explanation

(In this lesson you will learn how to convey something you have heard. You will also learn what changes a conversation between two acquaintances undergoes when the same topic is discussed between man and wife.)

ゆうべは たいへんでしたね。近所(きんじょ)で 火事(かじ)が あったそうですね。 **lines 1-2**

Yuube-wa taihen-deshita-ne. Kinjo-de kaji-ga atta-soo-desu-ne.

yuube	last night
kinjo	(your) neighborhood
kaji-ga atta	a fire broke out (dict. *aru*)
. . . soo-desu	I heard; they say

'...*soo-desu*' is used to report something one has heard; it usually follows a verb or adjective in the plain form.

ex. *Kimura-san-wa konai-soo-desu.* (I heard Mr. Kimura is not coming.)

Hokkaidoo-wa samui-soo-desu. (They say it's cold up in Hokkaido.)

ええ。夜中(よなか)の　三時(さんじ)ごろでしたから、びっくりしました。 **lines 3-4**

Ee. Yonaka-no sanji-goro-deshita-kara, bikkuri-shimashita.

yonaka	midnight; in the depth of night
bikkuri-shimashita	I was surprised

ええ、おかげさまで。 **line 6**

Ee, okagesama-de.

Okage-de or *Okagesama-de* is used to reply to inquiry about health or well-being. It literally means 'thanks to everything that has helped me.'

ex. A: *O-shigoto-wa doo-desu-ka.* (How's your business?)
B: *Okagesama-de.* (Thank you. It's going fairly well.)

すぐ　近(ちか)くでしたか。 **line 7**

Sugu chikaku-deshita-ka.

sugu chikaku	very close

Sugu here means 'right' as shown in the following example.

ex. *Ginkoo-wa sugu mukoogawa-desu.* (The bank is right across the street.)

道(みち)の　むこうがわでした。 **line 8**

Michi-no mukoogawa-deshita.

michi	the road
michi-no mukoogawa	across the road

消防自動車(しょうぼうじどうしゃ)の　来(く)るのが　はやかったので、こちらがわには

Shooboo-jidoosha-no kuru-no-ga hayakatta-node, kochiragawa-niwa

うつりませんでした。 **lines 8-9**

utsurimasen-deshita.

shooboo-jidoosha	fire engine
kochiragawa	this side
utsurimasen-deshita	it didn't come across (dict. *utsuru*)

でも、こわかったでしょう。 **line 10**

Demo, kowakatta-deshoo.

kowakatta-deshoo	it must have been frightening (dict. *kowai*)

家が 三軒も やけてしまいました。 **line 11**

Ie-ga sangen-mo yakete-shimaimashita.

ie	house
sangen	three houses; three buildings
sangen-mo	as many as three
yakete-shimaimashita	burnt down (dict. *yakeru*)

Ken is used to count houses and most buildings. (It's not used to count skyscrapers or similar buildings.) They are counted in the following way:

ikken, niken, sangen, yonken, goken, rokken, nanaken (or *shichiken*), *hakken, kyuuken, jikken*

(Larger numbers are counted using the set we learned for giving prices.)

Mo in *sangen-mo* is used to show that the speaker feels it's a large number.

ex. A: *Kanji-o ikutsu shitte-imasu-ka.* (How many kanji do you know?)

B: *Nisen-gurai shitte-iru-to omoimasu.* (I think I know about 2,000)

A: *Nisen-mo shitte-iru-n-desu-ka.* (You know as many as 2,000!)

Shimaimashita (dict. *shimau*) in *yakete-shimaimashita* is used to emphasize that the action is completely done.

ex. *Osake-wa watashi-ga nonde-shimaimashita.* (I drank up the wine.)

数千万円の 被害だそうです。 **lines 11-12**

Suusenman-en-no higai-da-soo-desu.

suusenman-en	several tens of millions of yen
higai	damage; loss

Suu- in *suusenman-en* stands for 'several.'

ex. *Gakusee-ga suunin tatte-imasu.* (Several students are standing.)

Kono tera-wa suuhyaku-nen-mae-ni dekimashita. (This temple was built several hundred years ago.)

Study the following large numbers:

10,000 —*ichiman*; 100,000 —*juuman*; 1,000,000 —*hyakuman*; 10,000,000 —(*is*)*senman*; 100,000,000 —*ichioku*; 1,000,000,000 — *juuoku*; 10,000,000,000 —*hyakuoku*; 100,000,000,000 —*sen'oku*; 1,000,000,000,000 —*itchoo*

原因(げんいん)は　何(なん)だったんですか。 **line 13**

Gen'in-wa nan-datta-n-desu-ka.

gen'in cause

電気(でんき)ストーブ(すとーぶ)を　つけたまま　ねてしまったんだそうです。 **lines 14-15**

Denki-sutoobu-o tsuketa-mama nete-shimatta-n-da-soo-desu.

denki-sutoobu electric heater
...o tsuketa-mama with ... on (dict. *tsukeru*)
nete-shimatta went to sleep (dict. *neru*)

Japanese have borrowed the English word 'stove' but usually use it to refer to room heaters rather than to cooking stoves.

The *-ta* form plus *-mama* as in *tsuketa-mama* means 'as it is,' or 'without doing anything about it.' *Tsuketa-mama neta* means the person who used the heater did not turn it off before going to bed.

ex. *To-o aketa-mama dekakemashita.* (I went out leaving the door open.)
Megane-o kaketa-mama nemashita. (I went to sleep with my glasses on.)

あぶないですね。 **line 16**

Abunai-desu-ne.

abunai dangerous

(The conversation in lines 17—24 is typical in style of conversation between married couples.)

中村(なかむら)さんの　ところは　だいじょうぶだったの。 **line 18**

Nakamura-san-no tokoro-wa daijoobu-datta-no.

tokoro place

No in *daijoobu-datta-no* is a contracted form of *-no-desu-ka,* and is mostly used by women.

道の　むこうがわだったし、わりあい　はやく　消防自動車が
Michi-no mukoogawa-datta-shi, wariai hayaku shooboo-jidoosha-ga
来たんだって。 **lines 19-20**
kita-n-datte.

wariai comparatively
kita-n-da-tte she says it came

Shi in *mukoogawa-datta-shi* means 'and.' It is used to connect two or more phrases that are used to explain the same fact.

ex. *Ame-ga furu-shi, samukute, iya-desu-ne.* (It's raining and cold. Unpleasant, isn't it?)
Kimura-san-wa atama-mo ii-shi, shinsetsu-desu. (Mr. Kimura is intelligent and kind.)

'...*tte*,' as you learned in Lesson 14, is used to transmit information in familiar speech.

ex. *Nete-shimatta-n-da-tte.* (I heard they went to sleep.)

Suusenman-en-no higai-datta-n-da-tte. (They say the loss was several tens of millions of yen.)

line 21
あぶないわね。
Abunai-wane.

Abunai-wane is a female form; men say *abunai-ne.*

Drills

I. …*soo-desu*

Structure Drill Change the following using the ... *soo-desu* form.

ex. *kaji-ga arimashita* →*Kaji-ga atta-soo-desu.*
kowakatta-desu →*Kowakatta-soo-desu.*
sanji-goro-deshita →*Sanji-goro-datta-soo-desu.*

1. *ie-ga sangen-mo yakemashita*
2. *sutoobu-o tsuketa-mama nemashita*
3. *kochiragawa-ni utsurimasen-deshita*
4. *abunakatta-desu*
5. *kowakatta-desu*
6. *daijoobu-deshita*
7. *sugu chikaku-deshita*
8. *suusenman-en-no higai-deshita*
9. *shooboo-jidoosha-no kuru-no-ga hayakatta-desu*
10. *bikkuri-shimashita.*

II. ... *te-shimau*

Structure Drill Change the following using the *-te-shimau* form.

ex. *yakemashita* → *Yakete-shimaimashita.*

1. *nomimashita*
2. *nemashita*
3. *tsukaimashita*
4. *kakimashita*
5. *owarimashita*
6. *kaerimashita*
7. *yomimashita*
8. *yamemashita*

Usage Drill Answer the questions as shown in the example.

ex. Question: *Osake-wa doo shita-n-desu-ka. Nonda-n-desu-ka.*

Answer: *Ee, moo nonde-shimaimashita.*

1. *Michiko-san-wa doo shita-n-desu-ka. Neta-n-desu-ka.*
2. *Okane-wa doo shita-n-desu-ka. Tsukatta-n-desu-ka.*
3. *Tegami-wa doo shita-n-desu-ka. Kaita-n-desu-ka.*
4. *Ongakukai-wa doo shita-n-desu-ka. Owatta-n-desu-ka.*
5. *Yamashita-san-wa doo shita-n-desu-ka. Kaetta-n-desu-ka.*
6. *Kesa-no shinbun-wa doo shita-n-desu-ka. Yonda-n-desu-ka.*
7. *Kaisha-wa doo shita-n-desu-ka. Yameta-n-desu-ka.* (Did you quit the company?)
8. *Ano ie-wa doo shita-n-desu-ka. Yaketa-n-desu-ka.*

III. ... *mo (sangen-mo)*

Structure Drill Change the following using *-mo.*

ex. *ie-ga sangen yaketa* → *Ie-ga sangen-mo yaketa-n-desu.*

1. *higai-ga suusenman-en atta*
2. *kaji-ga nijikan tsuzuita* (continued, dict. *tsuzuku*)
3. *hito-ga futari shinda* (died, dict. *shinu*)
4. *shinbun-kisha* (newspaper reporter)*-ga sannin kita*
5. *higai-ga ichioku-en atta*
6. *ie-ga yonken yaketa*
7. *shooboo-jidoosha-ga godai* (*-dai* is used in counting cars and machines) *kita*

Usage Drill Practice the following conversation changing the underlined parts.

ex. *ie-ga sangen-mo yaketa*

A: *Kinoo-wa taihen-deshita.*
B: *Doo shita-n-desu-ka.*
A: *Kinjo-de kaji-ga atta-n-desu.*
B: *Soo-desu-ka.*
A: *Ie-ga sangen-mo yaketa-n-desu.*
B: *Soo-desu-ka. Taihen-deshita-nee.*

1. *higai-ga ichioku-en-mo atta*
2. *hito-ga futari-mo shinda*
3. *kaji-ga nijikan-mo tsuzuita*
4. *ie-ga yonken-mo yaketa*
5. *shinbun-kisha-ga sannin-mo kita*
6. *shooboo-jidoosha-ga godai-mo kita*

IV. ... *ta-mama*

Structure Drill Change the following using the *-ta-mama* form.

ex. *sutoobu-o tsukeru, neru→Sutoobu-o tsuketa-mama nemashita.*

1. *mado-o akeru, neru*
2. *mado-o akeru, dekakeru*
3. *to-o shimeru* (close), *sutoobu-o tsukau*
4. *megane-o kakeru, neru*
5. *megane-o kakeru, ofuro-ni hairu* (take a bath)
6. *dentoo* (light)*-o tsukeru, neru*
7. *to-o akeru, kaeru*
8. *tokee-o tsukeru, ofuro-ni hairu*

Usage Drill Practice the following conversation changing the underlined parts.

ex. *sutoobu-o tsukeru*

A: *Doo shita-n-desu-ka. Nanika komatta koto-ga dekita-n-desu-ka.*

B: *Ee, jitsu-wa sutoobu-o tsuketa-mama kite-shimatta-n-desu.*

A: *Sore-wa abunai-desu-ne. Uchi-e kaetta hoo-ga ii-deshoo.*

B: *Demo mata koko-e kuru-made sanjippun-mo kakarimasu.* (it takes, dict. *kakaru*)

A: *Kamaimasen. Kissaten-de ocha-o nominagara matte-imasu-kara.*

1. *to-o akeru* 2. *mado-o akeru* 3. *gasu* (gas)*-o tsukeru*
4. *sutoobu-o tsukeru* 5. *airon* (iron)*-o tsukeru*

Pronunciation Practice

Practice saying the following, paying careful attention to the accent.

A. 1．あいうえお、あいうえお 2．がぎぐげご、がぎぐげご
3．ざじずぜぞ、ざじずぜぞ 4．だじずでど、だじずでど
5．ばびぶべぼ、ばびぶべぼ 6．ぱぴぷぺぽ、ぱぴぷぺぽ

B. 1. だれですか　2. どこですか　3. どうですか
4. どれですか　5. いつですか　6. なんですか
7. どちらですか　8. いくらですか　9. いくつですか
10. なんじですか

C. Add すみませんが to the phrases in B and say them with a falling intonation.

ex. すみませんが、だれですか。

Reading Comprehension

Read the following.

山下(やました)の日記(にっき)

十月五日(じゅうがつ いつか)　きのうジョンソン(じょんそん)さんのアパート(あぱーと)(1)へともだちがたずねてきて、とまった(2)。アレック・スミス(あれっく・すみす)という人(ひと)でおなじ(3)大学(だいがく)だそうだ。まだ日本(にほん)のことをよく知(し)らないので、いろいろてつだう(4)つもりだと、ジョンソンさんはいった。あしたは外国人登録(がいこくじんとうろく)(5)にいっしょにいくそうだ。

(1) apartment　(2) stayed overnight, dict. *tomaru*　(3) same　(4) help　(5) alien registration

Writing Practice

Practice writing the following *hiragana.*

た (ta)

ち (chi)

つ (tsu)

て (te)

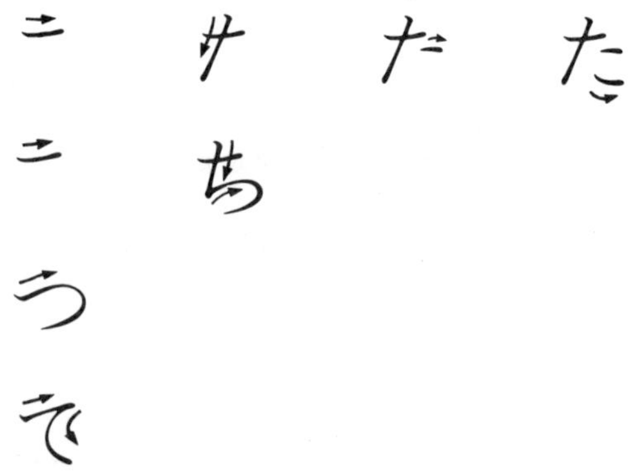

と　*(to)*　゛　ど

Aural Comprehension

Listen to the conversations on the tape and answer the following questions.

(A) 1. *Onna-no-hito-wa kanji-o yomu-no-ga suki-desu-ka, kaku-no-ga suki-desu-ka.*

2. *Otoko-no-hito-wa nisen-wa ooi* (many)*-to omotte-imasu-ka.*

3. *Onna-no-hito-wa nisen-de tariru-to omotte-imasu-ka.*

(B) 1. *Onna-no-hito-wa hajime okotte-imashita* (was angry)*-ka.*

2. *Dooshite-desu-ka.*

3. *Onna-no-hito-wa owari-niwa* (towards the end of the conversation) *moo okotte-imasen-ne. Naze-deshoo.*

(C) 1. *Shinbun-ni omoshiroi kiji* (article)*-ga arimashita-ka.*

2. *Sono kaji-no toki byookino* (sick) *obaasan-wa daijoobu-de shita-ka.*

第十七課(だいじゅうななか)　買(か)えません

Dialogue

ジョンソン(じょんそん)：　あの　自動車(じどうしゃ)は　山下(やました)さんのですか。

山下(やました)：　いいえ。あんな　いい　車(くるま)、とても　買(か)えませんよ。まえに　小(ちい)さいのを　もっていたんですが、おととしの　くれに　売(う)ってしまいました。

ジョンソン(じょんそん)：　もう　一度(いちど)　買(か)う　つもりですか。

山下(やました)：　そうですね。ほしいと　おもいますが、なかなか　もてませんね。

ジョンソン(じょんそん)：　ガソリン代(がそりんだい)が　高(たか)いですからね。

山下(やました)：ええ。そのほかに　駐車料金(ちゅうしゃりょうきん)や　税金(ぜいきん)など、とても　はらえません。

山下(やました)：　でも、どこかへ　ドライブ(どらいぶ)に　いきたいですね。

ジョンソン(じょんそん)：　かりられるでしょう。

山下(やました)：　レンタ・カー(れんた・かー)ですか。そうですね。きいてみましょうか。

ジョンソン(じょんそん)：　わたしも　料金(りょうきん)を　半分(はんぶん)　はらいますから、どこかへ　いきませんか。

山下(やました)：　そうですね。じゃ、こんどの　日曜(にちよう)は　どうですか。

ジョンソン(じょんそん)：　こんどの　日曜(にちよう)は　あさ　用(よう)が　あって、　はやく　でられないんです。

山下(やました)：　じゃ、あまり　遠(とお)くへは　いけませんね。そのつぎにしましょうか。

ジョンソン(じょんそん)：　ええ。それなら　はやく　でて　おそく　かえれると　おもいます。

Dialogue

Lesson 17 **I CAN'T BUY IT**	*Dai-juunanaka* ***KAEMASEN***
Johnson: Is that car yours, Mr. Yamashita?	*Jonson: Ano jidoosha-wa ▲Yamashita-san-no-desu-ka.*
Yamashita: Oh, no. I could never afford to buy such a fine car. I owned a small one before, but I ended up selling it at the end of the year before last.	*Yamashita: Iie. ▲Anna ii kuruma, ▲totemo kaemasen-yo. Mae-ni ▲chiisai-no-o motte-ita-n-desu-ga, ototoshi-no kure-ni ▲utte-shimaimashita.*
J: Are you going to buy another one?	*J: ▲Moo ichido kau tsumori-desu-ka.*
Y: Well, I wish I could, but it's so hard to keep a car.	*Y: Soo-desu-ne. ▲Hoshii-to omoimasu-ga, nakanaka ▲motemasen-ne.*
J: Fuel costs so much, right?	*J: ▲Gasorin-dai-ga takai-desu-kara-ne.*
Y: Yes, and in addition to that I can't afford to pay parking fees and automobile taxes.	*Y: Ee. Sono-hoka-ni ▲chuusha-ryookin-ya ▲zeekin-nado, ▲totemo haraemasen.*
Y: But it still would be nice to go for a leisurely drive.	*Y: Demo, dokoka-e ▲doraibu-ni ikitai-desu-ne.*
J: We could rent a car, couldn't we? (*lit.* We can borrow a car.)	*J: Karirareru-deshoo.*
Y: You mean rent-a-car service? That's right. Shall we ask and find out?	*Y: Renta-kaa-desu-ka. Soo-desu-ne. Kiite-mimashoo-ka.*
J: Let me pay half the cost. Why don't we go somewhere together?	*J: Watashi-mo ▲ryookin-o hanbun haraimasu-kara, dokoka-e ▲ikimasen-ka.*
Y: All right. What about next Sunday?	*Y: Soo-desu-ne. Ja, ▲kondo-no nichiyoo-wa doo-desu-ka.*
J: I've got something to take care of next Sunday morning, so I won't be able to leave early.	*J: Kondo-no nichiyoo-wa asa ▲yoo-ga atte, hayaku ▲derarenai-n-desu.*

Y:	Then we couldn't go too far. Shall we make it the Sunday after next?	Y:	*Ja, amari tooku-ewa ikemasen-ne. Sono-tsugi-ni shimashoo-ka.*
J:	Fine. Then we can have a good long day driving. (*lit.* I can leave home early and go home late.)	J:	*Ee. Sore-nara hayaku dete osoku kaereru-to omoimasu.*

Explanation

(In this lesson you will learn how to use a form called the potential form; it is used to express the idea of 'can do . . .' or 'can't do . . .')

あの　自動車(じどうしゃ)は　山下(やました)さんのですか。 **line 1**

Ano jidoosha-wa Yamashita-san-no-desu-ka.

jidoosha	automobile; car (cf. *shooboo-jidoosha*, Lesson 16)
Yamashita-san-no	Mr. Yamashita's

No in *Yamashita-san-no* stands for *-no mono.* (cf. Lesson 11)

ex. *Kore-wa anata-no-desu-ka.* (Is this yours?)
Iie, watashi-no-ja arimasen. (No, it isn't mine.)

いいえ。あんな　いい　車(くるま)、とても　買(か)えませんよ。 **line 2**

Iie. Anna ii kuruma, totemo kaemasen-yo.

kuruma	car; vehicle
anna ii kuruma	such a fine car (*anna*—cf. Lesson 5)
totemo	(not) by any means
kaemasen	I can't buy it (dict. *kau*)

Kaemasu and *kaemasen* are polite potential forms, affirmative and negative. See Note for the construction of the potential form.

まえに　小(ち)さいのを　もっていたんですが、おととしの　くれに　売(う)って しまいました。 **lines 3-4**

Mae-ni chiisai-no-o motte-ita-n-desu-ga, ototoshi-no kure-ni utte-shimai-mashita.

mae-ni	before

chiisai-no a small one
ototoshi the year before last
kure the end of the year
utte-shimaimashita I sold it off; I ended up selling (dict. *uru*)

No in *chiisai-no* stands for 'one.' (cf. Lesson 11)

line 5

もう　一度(いちど)　買(か)う　つもりですか。

Moo ichido kau tsumori-desu-ka.

moo ichido once more; again

Tsumori can be used to refer to the intention of one's equals and inferiors, but not to that of one's superiors.

lines 6-7

ほしいと　おもいますが、なかなか　もてませんね。

Hoshii-to omoimasu-ga, nakanaka motemasen-ne.

nakanaka (not) easily
motemasen I can't keep it (dict. *motsu*)

The adverb *nakanaka* is used to show that difficulty is involved.

ex. *Watashi-no nihongo-wa nakanaka joozu-ni narimasen.*
(My Japanese is slow to improve.)

line 8

ガソリン代(がそりんだい)が　高(たか)いですからね。

Gasorin-dai-ga takai-desu-kara-ne.

gasorin-dai expense for gasoline

Dai stands for 'expense' or 'charge.'

ex. *basu-dai* (bus fare); *hon-dai* (money spent on books); *furo-dai* (public bath fare)

ええ。そのほかに　駐車料金(ちゅうしゃりょうきん)や　税金(ぜいきん)など、とても　はらえません。

Ee. Sono-hoka-ni chuusha-ryookin-ya zeekin-nado, totemo haraemasen.

lines 9-10

sono-hoka-ni besides that
chuusha-ryookin parking charge
. . .ya . . .and the like
zeekin tax
. . .nado . . .and others
haraemasen I can't pay (dict. *harau*)

Both *-to* and *-ya* are used between nouns, but *-ya* implies that the speaker has mentioned only a few out of the complete set, while *-to* is used when the speaker has mentioned everything.

ex. *Yamashita-san-to Tanaka-san-ga kimashita.* (Mr. Yamashita and Mr. Tanaka came.)

Yamashita-san-ya Tanaka-san-ga kimashita. (Mr. Yamashita, Mr. Tanaka and others came.)

Nado is similar in meaning to *-ya*, but it is used after nouns.

ex. *Tsukue-no ue-ni hon-ya enpitsu-nado* (*-ga*)* *arimasu.*

(There are books, pencils and other things on the desk.)

(* *-ga* can be left out.)

Haraemasen is the polite negative potential form derived from *harau*, 'to pay.'

でも、どこかへ ドライブ(どらいぶ)に いきたいですね。 **line 11**

Demo, dokoka-e doraibu-ni ikitai-desu-ne.

doraibu-ni ikitai — we want to go driving (dict. *iku*)

かりられるでしょう。 **line 12**

Karirareru-deshoo.

karirareru — we can rent one (dict. *kariru*)

Kariru is used to express both 'renting' and 'borrowing.'

レンタ・カー(れんた・かー)ですか。 **line 13**

Renta-kaa-desu-ka.

renta-kaa — rent-a-car service

わたしも 料金(りょうきん)を 半分(はんぶん) はらいますから、どこかへ いきませんか。

Watashi-mo ryookin-o hanbun haraimasu-kara, dokoka-e ikimasen-ka.

lines 15-16

ryookin — charge; fare

hanbun — one half

Ryookin is used either by itself or in compounds like:

ex. *denwa-ryookin* (telephone fare)

takushii-ryookin (taxi fare)

Dai and *ryookin* can be used interchangeably in some cases.

ex. *basu-dai, basu-ryookin; denwa-dai, denwa-ryookin*

Ryookin sounds more official or technical.

こんどの　日曜(にちよう)は　あさ　用(よう)が　あって、はやく　でられないんです。

Kondo-no nichiyoo-wa asa yoo-ga atte, hayaku derarenai-n-desu.

lines 18-19

yoo	=*yooji* (Lesson 13)
derarenai	I can't leave home (dict. *deru*)

じゃ、あまり　遠(とお)くへは　いけませんね。 **line 20**

Ja, amari tooku-ewa ikemasen-ne.

tooku-e	far
ikemasen	we can't go (dict. *iku*)

Wa in *tooku-ewa* is used to show contrast; here it is used to contrast 'far' with 'near' which is understood.

Ikemasen is the polite negative potential form derived from *iku.*

そのつぎに　しましょうか。 **lines 20-21**

Sono-tsugi-ni shimashoo-ka.

sono-tsugi	the next; *here,* Sunday after next
...ni shimashoo-ka	shall we make it...?

ええ。それなら　はやく　でて　おそく　かえれると　おもいます。

Ee. Sore-nara hayaku dete osoku kaereru-to omoimasu. **lines 22-23**

sore-nara	in that case; if that is the case; then
kaereru	I can go home (dict. *kaeru*)

Kaereru is the plain potential form derived from *kaeru.*

Note　The potential form

The plain potential form is constructed in the following way:
Group 1 verbs (*-u* verbs): replace the final *-u* by *-eru*, (*-tsu* by *-teru*).

*ka**u** —ka**eru**; kik**u** —kik**eru**; hara**u** —hara**eru**; mo**tsu**— mo**teru***

Group 2 verbs (*-ru* verbs): replace the final *-ru* by *-rareru.*

*mi**ru** —mi**rareru**; yame**ru** —yame**rareru***

The potential form of *kuru* is *korareru*, and that of *yuu* is *ieru.*
The verb *suru* does not have a corresponding potential form. In place

of it, the verb *dekiru* is used.

The *-masu* form of the potential is made by replacing the final *-ru* of both group 1 and group 2 potential forms by *-masu*.

ex. *kau* *kaeru* *kaemasu* *kaemasen*
miru *mirareru* *miraremasu* *miraremasen*

In their potential forms, all verbs are conjugated as group 2 verbs.

ex. *kau* (group 1) —*kaeru* (group 2) —*kaenai*
iku (group 1) —*ikeru* (group 2) —*ikenai*
miru (group 2) —*mirareru* (group 2) —*mirarenai*
kuru (irregular) —*korareru* (group 2) —*korarenai*

The particle *-o* which indicates the object of an action becomes *-ga* when followed by a potential verb.

ex. *Chuugokugo-**o** hanashimasu.* (I speak Chinese.)
*Chuugokugo-**ga** hanasemasu.* (I can speak Chinese.)

Drills

I. The potential form

Structure Drill Practice saying the following table.

iku	*ikeru*	*ikenai*
harau	*haraeru*	*haraenai*
hanasu	*hanaseru*	*hanasenai*
noru (ride)	*noreru*	*norenai*
kaku	*kakeru*	*kakenai*
utau (sing)	*utaeru*	*utaenai*
yaru	*yareru*	*yarenai*
nomu	*nomeru*	*nomenai*
utsu (strike)	*uteru*	*utenai*
tsukau	*tsukaeru*	*tsukaenai*
kariru	*karirareru*	*karirarenai*
miru	*mirareru*	*mirarenai*
okiru	*okirareru*	*okirarenai*

Usage Drill Practice the following conversation changing the underlined parts:

ex. *kuruma-o kau, yasui-no-ga nai*

A: *Kuruma-o kau tsumori-desu-ka.*

B: *Ee, kaitai-to omou-n-desu-ga, nakanaka kaemasen.*

A: *Dooshite kaenai-n-desu-ka.*

B: *Yasui-no-ga nai-n-desu.*

1. *ie-o kariru, yasui-no-ga nai*
2. *ie-o kau, ii-no-ga nai*
3. *doraibu-ni iku, hima-ga nai*
4. *zeekin-o harau, okane-ga nai*
5. *eega-o miru, isogashii*
6. *asa hayaku okiru, tsukarete-iru*
7. *nihongo-o hanasu, hazukashii* (embarrassed)
8. *uma* (horse)*-ni noru* (ride), *kowai*

II. *-ga* with potential verbs

Structure Drill Change the following as shown in the example.

ex. *piano-o hikimasu* (I play the piano.)
→*Piano-ga hikemasu.*

1. *furansugo-o hanashimasu*
2. *kanji-o kakimasu*
3. *uta* (song)*-o utaimasu* (sing)
4. *tenisu* (tennis)*-o yarimasu*
5. *doitsugo-o hanashimasu*
6. *osake-o nomimasu*
7. *zeekin-o haraimasu*
8. *taipu-o uchimasu* (I type.)
9. *keesanki* (computer)*-o tsukaimasu*
10. *jibiki-o hikimasu*

Usage Drill Practice the following conversation changing the underlined parts.

ex. *piano-o hiku*

A: *...san, piano-ga hikemasu-ka.*

B: *Ee, sukoshi-wa hikeru-to omoimasu. Amari yoku-wa hikemasen-ga.*

A: *Ii-desu-ne. Watashi-wa zenzen* (not at all) *hikenai-n-desu.*

B: *Sukoshi yatte-mimasen-ka. Tetsudaimasu-yo.* (I'll help you.)

1. *furansugo-o hanasu*
2. *kanji-o kaku*
3. *uta-o utau*
4. *keesanki-o tsukau*
5. *taipu-o utsu* (type)

III. ··· *ya*

Structure Drill Make sentences using the given words and *-ya* as shown in the example.

A) ex. *hon, zasshi* (magazine)*-o yomu* → *Hon-ya zasshi-o yomimasu.*
hon, zasshi-ga yomeru → *Hon-ya zasshi-ga yomemasu.*

1. *eego, furansugo-o hanasu*
2. *eego, furansugo-ga hanaseru*
3. *yakyuu, suiee-o suru*
4. *yakyuu, suiee-ga dekiru*
5. *kuruma, kamera-o kau*
6. *kuruma, kamera-ga kaeru*
7. *hon, zasshi-o kariru*
8. *hon, zasshi-ga karirareru*

B) ex. *tokee, kamera, hoshii* → *Tokee-ya kamera-ga hoshii-desu.*

1. *ningyoo, rekoodo, hoshii*
2. *ningyoo, hana* (flowers)*, suki*
3. *ocha, koohii, daisuki*
4. *yakyuu, suiee, joozu* (good at)
5. *asobu-no, nomu-no, suki*
6. *hataraku* (work)*-no, benkyoo-suru-no, suki*
7. *hataraku-no, benkyoo-suru-no, kirai* (dislike)

IV. ··· *nara*

Structure Drill Make sentences using the given words and *...nara* and *...wa*, as shown in the example.

A) ex. *chiisai, ookii* → *Chiisai-no-nara ii-desu-ga, ookii-no-wa dame-desu.*

1. *atarashii, furui*
2. *watashi, hoka-no hito*
3. *kyoo, ashita*
4. *kochira, achira*
5. *Nihon, gaikoku* (foreign country)
6. *joobuna* (strong)*, yowai* (weak)

B) ex. *dekiru, dekinai* → *Ashita-nara dekimasu-ga, kyoo-wa dekimasen.*

1. *haraeru, haraenai*
2. *korareru, korarenai*
3. *karirareru, karirarenai*
4. *hayaku korareru, hayaku korarenai*
5. *ii, dame*
6. *daijoobu, dame*
7. *ikeru, ikenai*

Usage Drill Practice the following conversation changing the underlined parts.

ex. *kuruma-o kau, chiisai-no, ookii-no*

A: *Kuruma-o kau-n-desu-ka.*

B: *Soo-desu-ne. Chiisai-no-nara kaemasu-ga, ookii-no-wa . . . . .*

A: *Kaemasen-ka.*

B: *Ee, kaenai-daroo-to omoimasu.*

1. *kuruma-o kau, furui-no, atarashii-no*
2. *ie-o kau, yasui-no, takai-no*
3. *jidoosha-o kau, nihon-no, gaikoku-no*
4. *doraibu-ni iku, chikaku, tooku*
5. *kono okashi-o taberu, hanbun, zenbu* (all)

Pronunciation Practice

Practice saying the following, paying careful attention to the accent.

A. 1. あいうえ、あいうえお　　2. かきくけ、かきくけこ

3. さしすせ、さしすせそ　　4. たちつて、たちつてと

5. なにぬね、なにぬねの　　6. はひふへ、はひふへほ

7. まみむめ、まみむめも　　8. やいゆえ、やいゆえよ

9. らりるれ、らりるれろ　　10. わいうえ、わいうえお

B. 1. やすみ、はるやすみ (spring vacation)

2. がくせい、じょしがくせい

3. にんぎょう、にほんにんぎょう

4. ろんぶん、はかせろんぶん (dissertation)

5. かいわ (conversation), えいかいわ (English conversation)

C. Add しつれいですが……のことでしょうか to the words in B and say them with a rising intonation.

ex. しつれいですが、はるやすみのことでしょうか。

Reading Comprehension

Read the following.

東京(とうきょう)の電車(でんしゃ)はとてもこんでいる。たいていせき(1)がなくて、すわれない(2)。こんでいて、のれない(3)ときもある。でも電車(でんしゃ)のなかで本(ほん)を読(よ)んでいる人(ひと)もいる。ぼくはとても読(よ)めない。また(4)、たったまま(5)ねむっている(6)人(ひと)もいる。どうしてねむれるのだろう。ぼくもねむりたいが、なかなかねむれない。——ジョンソンの感想(7)(かんそう)

(1) seat (2) can't sit down, dict. *suwaru,* Lesson 10 (3) can't get in, dict. *noru* (4) also (5) as they're standing (6) sleeping, dict. *nemuru* (7) impression

Writing Practice

Practice writing the following *hiragana*

な (na)

に (ni)

ぬ (nu)

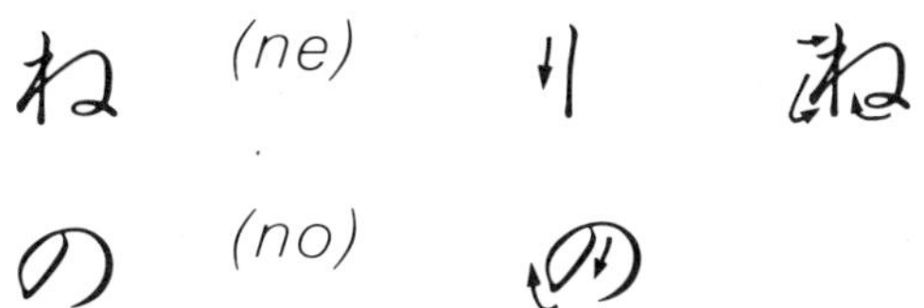

Aural Comprehension

Listen to the conversations on the tape and answer the following questions.

A) 1. *Futari-wa dochira-mo* (both) *kuruma-o motte-imasu-ka.*
2. *Futari-no kazoku* (family)*-wa doo chigaimasu-ka* (how are they different).
3. *Furui kuruma-o motte-iru hito-wa atarashii kuruma-o motte-iru hito-ni tsuite doo omotte-imasu-ka.*

(B) 1. *Kono futari-wa atarashii kuruma-o kau tsumori-desu-ka.*
2. *Kazuo-wa ikutsu-gurai-deshoo.*
3. *Futari-wa koofuku* (happy) *soo-desu-ka.*

C) 1. *Onna-no-hito-wa kore-kara piano-o hikimasu-ka.*
2. *Otoko-no-hito-wa nani-o shimasu-ka.*
3. *Donna uta-ni shimasu-ka.*

第十八課(だいじゅうはっか)　まどが　あいています

Dialogue

(A husband comes home.)

夫(おっと)：　ただいま。

妻(つま)：　おかえりなさい。

夫(おっと)：　ああ、つかれた。

妻(つま)：　おふろが　わいているけど。

夫(おっと)：　あとで　はいろう。ストーブ(すとーぶ)は　ついている？

妻(つま)：　ええ、つけてあるわ。

夫(おっと)：　今晩(こんばん)　川上(かわかみ)さんが　来(く)るそうだよ。

妻(つま)：　そう。ひさしぶりね。

夫(おっと)：　さけは　ある？

妻(つま)：　ええ。ビール(びーる)が　ひやしてあるけど、おさけの　ほうが　いいでしょうね。

夫(おっと)：　うん、あの人(ひと)には　さけの　ほうが　よさそうだよ。なにか　さかなは　ある？

妻(つま)：　ええ。おさしみが　二人前(ににんまえ)　買(か)ってあるわ。

夫(おっと)：　それは　いい。

(The visitor comes in.)

客(きゃく)：　さむいですね。

主人(しゅじん)：　もう　冬(ふゆ)ですね。

客(きゃく)：　まどが　すこし　あいていますよ。しめましょうか。

主人(しゅじん)：　あ、しめないでください。いま　ストーブ(すとーぶ)を　つけたところですから。

客(きゃく)：　あ、そうですか。じゃ、しばらく　あけておきましょうか。…いい　ストーブ(すとーぶ)ですね。石油(せきゆ)ストーブ(すとーぶ)ですね。

主人(しゅじん)：　ええ。これは　たおれると　自然(しぜん)に　きえるそうです。

客(きゃく)：　それなら　安全(あんぜん)ですね。わたしも　こういうのを　ひと-
つ　買(か)いましょう。

Dialogue

Lesson 18 **THE WINDOW IS OPEN**	*Dai-juuhakka* ***MADO-GA AITE-IMASU***
Husband: Hi, I'm home.	*Otto: Tadaima.*
Wife: Hi, dear.	*Tsuma: Okaeri-nasai.*
H: Gee, I'm tired.	*O: Aa, tsukareta.*
W: The bath is ready.	*T: ▲O-furo-ga waite-iru-kedo.*
H: I'll take it later. Is the heater on?	*O: ▲Ato-de hairoo. ▲Sutoobu-wa tsuite-iru?*
W: Yes, I've turned it on.	*T: Ee, tsukete-aru-wa.*
H: Mr. Kawakami said he's coming over tonight.	*O: Konban ▲Kawakami-san-ga kuru-soo-da-yo.*
W: Really? It's been a long time.	*T: Soo. Hisashiburi-ne.*
H: Do we have some liquor?	*O. ▲Sake-wa aru?*
W: Yes, there's some beer chilled, but he may prefer *sake*.	*T: Ee, ▲biiru-ga hiyashite-aru-kedo, ▲osake-no hoo-ga ii-deshoo-ne.*
H: Yes, he'll probably prefer *sake*. Do we have something to eat?	*O: Un, ▲ano-hito-niwa sake-no hoo-ga yosasoo-da-yo. Nanika ▲saka-na-wa aru?*
W: Yes, I've bought two servings of *sashimi*.	*T: Ee. ▲O-sashimi-ga ninin-mae katte-aru-wa.*
H: Good.	*O: ▲Sore-wa ii.*
Visitor: It's so cold.	*Kyaku: Samui-desu-ne.*
Host: It's winter already.	*Shujin: Moo ▲fuyu-desu-ne.*
V: The window is open a little. Shall I close it?	*K: ▲Mado-ga sukoshi aite-imasu-yo. Shimemashoo-ka.*
H: No, please don't. I've just turned the heater on.	*S: A, shimenaide-kudasai. Ima ▲sutoobu-o tsuketa tokoro-desu-kara.*

V : Is that right? Then I should leave it open for a while. ......You have a nice heater here. Is it a kerosene stove?

K: *A, soo-desu-ka. Ja, shibaraku akete-okimashoo-ka. ......Ii sutoobu-desu-ne. Sekiyu-sutoobu-desu-ne.*

H : Yes. I understand that the fire automatically goes out if the heater falls over.

S: *Ee. Kore-wa taoreru-to shizen-ni kieru-soo-desu.*

V : Then it's quite safe, isn't it? I'll buy one of this kind.

K: *Sore-nara anzen-desu-ne. Watashi-mo koo-yuu-no-o hitotsu kaimashoo.*

Explanation

(In this lesson you will learn two new verb usages, *-te-aru* and *-te-oku*. The former is used to express a state resulting from an action, the latter to express 'do something for later use.')

(The first conversation is typical of the style of speech used by young married couples.)

ただいま。 **line 1**

Tadaima.

Tadaima is a contraction of the more polite form *Tadaima kaeri-mashita,* meaning 'I have just come back.' This is a greeting said by a person who has come home.

おかえりなさい。 **line 2**

Okaeri-nasai.

This is an expression used to welcome someone home. A more polite way of saying the same thing is *Okaeri-nasaimase*.

おふろが　わいているけど。 **line 4**

O-furo-ga waite-iru-kedo.

o-furo, furo	bath
o-furo-ga waite-iru	the bath is ready (dict. *waku*)

Waku is an intransitive verb which means 'to heat.' An intransitive verb plus *-te-iru* is used to show the state of something; thus, *o-furo-ga* *waite-iru* means 'the bath is heated.' Japanese style baths are heated from underneath the tub, usually by gas, until the water is very hot.

The transitive verb corresponding to *waku* is *wakasu,* 'someone heats something.'

ex. *O-furo-ga waite-imasu.* (The bath is heated.)
Okusan-ga o-furo-o wakashite-imasu. (His wife is preparing the bath. *lit.* 'heating' the bath)

Kedo in ......*iru-kedo* is used to avoid sounding abrupt or too decisive. Japanese often end sentences with *-kedo* or *-ga,* especially when asking the listener's wishes. The meaning behind *O-furo-ga waite-iru-kedo* is 'The bath is ready. Would you like to take it?'

あとで はいろう。ストーブは ついている？ **line 5**

Ato-de hairoo. Sutoobu-wa tsuite-iru?

ato-de	later
hairoo	I'll take the bath. (*lit.* I'll enter) (dict. *hairu*)
tsuite-iru?	is it turned on? (dict. *tsuku*)

Tsuite-iru shows the state of the heater, 'turned on.' *Tsukeru* means 'to turn on' and *tsuku* means 'to be turned on.'

ex. *Sutoobu-ga tsuite-imasu.* (The heater is on.)
Okusan-ga sutoobu-o tsukete-imasu. (His wife is turning the heater on.)

The antonyms corresponding to *tsuku* and *tsukeru* are *kieru* and *kesu.*

ex. *Dentoo-ga kiete-imasu.* (The light is out.)
Kare-ga dentoo-o keshite-imasu. (He's turning the light off.)

ええ、つけてあるわ。 **line 6**

Ee, tsukete-aru-wa.

A transitive verb plus *-te-aru* shows that a thing is in a certain state as the result of someone's action. Both *tsuite-iru* and *tsukete-aru* mean 'it is on' but the *-te-aru* form places emphasis on the action rather than the state.

ex. *Sutoobu-ga tsuite-iru.* (The heater's on.)
Sutoobu-ga tsukete-aru. (The heater's on —because someone turned it on.)

そう。ひさしぶりね。 **line 8**

Soo. Hisashiburi-ne.

hisashiburi it's been a long time

さけは ある？ **line 9**

Sake-wa aru?

sake *here,* liquor

Sake here means liquor in general, including beer, whisky, and Japanese rice wine.

ええ、ビールが ひやしてあるけど、おさけの ほうが いいでしょうね。

Ee, biiru-ga hiyashite-aru-kedo, osake-no hoo-ga ii-deshoo-ne.

lines 10-11

biiru beer

hiyashite-aru it's been chilled (dict. *hiyasu*)

o-sake *here,* Japanese rice wine; *sake*

Hiyasu is a transitive verb; its corresponding intransitive verb is *hieru.*

ex. *Biiru-ga hiete-imasu.* (The beer is chilled.)

Biiru-ga hiyashite-arimasu. (The beer is chilled because someone put it in the refrigerator.)

うん、あの人には さけの ほうが よさそうだよ。 **line 12**

Un, ano-hito-niwa sake-no hoo-ga yosasoo-da-yo.

yosasoo is probably better (dict. *ii, yoi*)

なにか さかなは ある？ **lines 12-13**

Nanika sakana-wa aru?

sakana *here,* accompanyment of *sake;* something to eat while drinking

ええ。おさしみが 二人前 買ってあるわ。 **line 14**

Ee. O-sashimi-ga ninin-mae katte-aru-wa.

o-sashimi sliced fish (served raw)

ninin-mae two servings

Kau is a transitive verb; it has no corresponding intransitive verb.

(The second conversation is a polite conversation between two acquaintances.)

もう 冬ですね。 **line 17**

Moo fuyu-desu-ne.

fuyu winter

The names of the four seasons are: *haru*(spring), *natsu*(summer), *aki*(autumn) and *fuyu*(winter).

まどが　すこし　あいていますよ。しめましょうか。 **line 18**

Mado-ga sukoshi aite-imasu-yo. Shimemashoo-ka.

aite-imasu — it is open (dict. *aku*)
shimemashoo-ka — shall I close it? (dict. *shimeru*)

Aku is an intransitive verb; its corresponding transitive verb is *akeru.*

ex. *Mado-ga aite-imasu.* (The window is open.)
Mado-ga akete-arimasu. (Someone has opened the window.)

The antonyms corresponding to *aku* and *akeru* are *shimaru* and *shimeru.*

ex. *To-ga shimatte-imasu.* (The door is closed.)
To-ga shimete-arimasu. (Someone has closed the door.)

あ、しめないでください。いま　ストーブを　つけた　ところですから。

A, shimenaide-kudasai. Ima sutoobu-o tsuketa tokoro-desu-kara. **lines 19-20**

shimenaide-kudasai — please don't close it (dict. *shimeru*)
tsuketa tokoro — I have just turned it on (dict. *tsukeru*)

'……*naide-kudasai*' is the negative form of *-te-kudasai* (cf. Lesson 7.)

ex. *Tabete-kudasai.* (Please eat it.)
Tabenaide-kudasai. (Please don't eat it.)
Kite-kudasai. (Please come.)
Konaide-kudasai. (Please don't come.)

The plain past form of verbs plus *tokoro* means the action has just been completed.

ex. *Ima shigoto-ga owatta tokoro-desu.* (The work has just been finished.)

じゃ、しばらく　あけておきましょうか。 **lines 21-22**

Ja, shibaraku akete-okimashoo-ka.

shibaraku — for a while
akete-okimashoo — I'll leave it open (dict. *akeru*)

The *-te-oku* form is used to indicate that an action is done for future use, or that it is done by way of preparation. Here the speaker is going to leave the window open so that the air will circulate.

ex. *Denwa-o kakete-okimashita.* (I called him ahead of time— to check if he was home, to see if he was ready, to remind him to meet me, etc.)

Wakai toki-ni asonde-oita hoo-ga ii. (You had better enjoy yourself while you're young. ——This implies that one should enjoy himself before he gets too old to.)

石油ストーブですね。(せきゆすとーぶ) **line 22**

Sekiyu-sutoobu-desu-ne.

sekiyu-sutoobu	kerosene stove

これは　たおれると　自然に(しぜん)　きえるそうです。 **line 23**

Kore-wa taoreru-to shizen-ni kieru-soo-desu.

taoreru-to	when it falls down (dict. *taoreru*)
shizen-ni	by itself; automatically
kieru	go out; extinguish

The particle *-to* in *taoreru-to* is used to show condition.

ex. *Ame-ga furu-to michi-ga waruku narimasu.* (The road becomes bad when it rains.)

Haru-ga kuru-to iroirona hana-ga sakimasu. (When spring comes various flowers bloom.)

それなら　安全(あんぜん)ですね。わたしも　こういうのを　ひとつ　買(か)いましょう。

Sore-nara anzen-desu-ne. Watashi-mo koo-yuu-no-o hitotsu kaimashoo.

lines 24-25

anzen	safe (*-na* adj.)
koo-yuu	this kind of
koo-yuu-no	one like this
hitotsu	one (counter, see Lesson 7)

Drills

I. .. *te-iru* & ... *te-aru*

Structure Drill Memorize the following sets of expressions by saying them aloud.

aite-imasu	*akete-arimasu*
shimatte-imasu	*shimete-arimasu*
tsuite-imasu	*tsukete-arimasu*
kiete-imasu	*keshite-arimasu*
hiete-imasu	*hiyashite-arimasu*
haitte-imasu (it's put in)	*irete-arimasu*
kimatte-imasu (it's decided)	*kimete-arimasu*
dete-imasu (it's out)	*dashite-arimasu* (someone has put it out)
taorete-imasu	*taoshite-arimasu*
waite-imasu	*wakashite-arimasu*

Usage Drill 1 Look at the pictures and answer the questions.

ex. Q: *Kono mado-wa aite-imasu-ka, shimatte-imasu-ka.*
A: *Aite-imasu.*

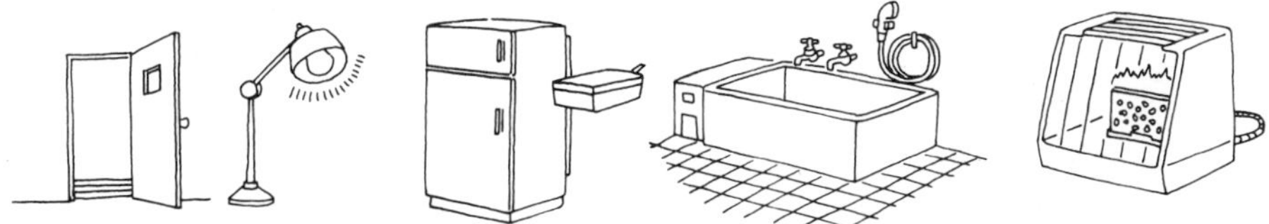

Q: *Kono to-wa aite-imasu-ka, shimatte-imasu-ka.*

Q: *Kono dentoo-wa tsuite-imasu-ka, kiete-imasu-ka.*

Q: *Kono bataa*(butter)*-wa reezooko*(refrigerator)*-ni haitte-imasu-ka, soto-ni dete-imasu-ka.*

Q: *Kono ofuro-wa mizu-ga irete-arimasu-ka, irete-arimasen-ka.*

Q: *Kono sutoobu-wa tsukete-arimasu-ka, keshite-arimasu-ka.*

Usage Drill 2 Practice the following conversation changing the underlined parts.

ex. *mado-ga aku, akeru, shimeru*

A: *Mado-ga aite-imasu-ne.*

B: *Soo-desu-ne. Dare-ga aketa-n-deshoo.*

A: *Wakarimasen-ne.*

B: *Shimemashoo-ka.*

A: *Iie, aite-iru hoo-ga ii-deshoo.*

1. *mado-ga shimaru, shimeru, akeru*
2. *dentoo-ga tsuku, tsukeru, kesu*
3. *sutoobu-ga kieru, kesu, tsukeru*
4. *bataa-ga deru, dasu, ireru*

II. . . . *te-oku*

Structure Drill Change the following into the *-te-oku* form.

ex. *biiru-o hiyashimasu* ⟶ *Biiru-o hiyashite-okimasu.*

1. *sutoobu-o tsukemasu*
2. *mado-o akemasu*
3. *osashimi-o kaimasu*
4. *kaimono-o shimasu*
5. *denwa-o kakemasu*
6. *nedan*(price)*-o shirabemasu*
7. *ofuro-o wakashimasu*
8. *sooji*(cleaning)*-o shimasu*

Usage Drill Practice the following conversation changing the underlined parts.

ex. *okyaku-ga kuru, biiru-o hiyasu*

A: *Kyoo-wa isogashisoo-desu-ne.* (You look busy today.)

B: *Ee, okyaku-ga kuru-n-desu.*

A: *Sono shitaku*(preparation)*-o shite-iru-n-desu-ne.*

B: *Ee, biiru-o hiyashite-okoo-to omotte-imasu.*

1. *okyaku-ga kuru, osashimi-o kau*
2. *shujin-ga kaette-kuru, ofuro-o wakasu*
3. *okyaku-ga kuru, sooji-o suru*

4. *ashita doraibu-ni iku, kuruma-o shiraberu*
5. *okyaku-ga kuru, okashi-ya osakana-o kau*

III. ... *naide kudasai*

Structure Drill Practice saying aloud the following table.

tsukatte-kudasai *tsukawanaide-kudasai*
nonde-kudasai *nomanaide-kudasai*
kakete-kudasai *kakenaide-kudasai*
tabete-kudasai *tabenaide-kudasai*
tsukete-kudasai *tsukenaide-kudasai*
kaite-kudasai *kakanaide-kudasai*
shitaku-o shite-kudasai *shitaku-o shinaide-kudasai*

Usage Drill Practice the following conversation changing the underlined parts.

ex. *denwa-o tsukau*

A (from across the room): *Kono denwa-o tsukatte-mo ii-desu-ka.*

B: *A, sono denwa-wa tsukawanaide-kudasai. Kotchi-no-o tsukatte-kudasai.*

A (walks over to B): *Hai. Kore-desu-ne.*

B: *Ee, soo-desu.*

1. *ocha-o nomu*
2. *tsukue-o tsukau*
3. *isu-ni kakeru*
4 *pan*(bread)*-o taberu*
5. *taoru*(towel)*-o tsukau*
6. *kami*(paper)*-ni kaku*

IV. (v)+*to*

Structure Drill Make sentences using the given words.

ex. *fuyu, samui*⟶*Fuyu-ni naru-to samuku narimasu.*

1. *haru, atatakai*(warm)
2. *natsu, atsui*(hot)
3. *yoru, samui*
4. *yoru, kurai*
5. *hiru*(daytime)*, atatakai*
6. *hiru, atsui*

Pronunciation Practice

Practice saying the following, paying careful attention to the accent.

A. 1. あいうえ、 あいうえお　2. がぎぐげ、がぎぐげご
3. ざじずぜ、 ざじずぜぞ　4. だじずで、だじずでど
5. ばびぶべ、 ばびぶべぼ　6. ぱぴぷぺ、ぱぴぷぺぽ

B. 1. やすみ、なつやすみ　2. やすみ、ふゆやすみ
3. じだい (age), だいがくじだい (college days)
4. きょういく (education), だいがくきょういく
5. きょういく、こうとうきょういく (higher education)

C. Add しつれいですが……のことでしょうか to the words in B and say them with a falling intonation.

ex. しつれいですが、なつやすみの　ことでしょうか。

Reading Comprehension

Read the following.

山下(やました)の日記(にっき)

十二月十三日(じゅうにがつじゅうさんにち)　午後(ごご)、ジョンソンさんのアパート(あぱーと)へあそびにいった。電燈(でんとう)(1)がついていたが、ジョンソンさんはいなかった。戸(と)(2)がすこしあけてあったので、なかへはいってみた。ストーブ(すとーぶ)がついていて、お湯(ゆ)がわいていた(3)。やかん(4)のなかには水(みず)があまりはいっていなかったので、すこしいれておいた。5分(ごふん)ぐらいしてから(5)、ジョンソンさんがかえってきた。ストーブ(すとーぶ)をつけたままそとへでるのはあぶないとおもった。

(1) light (2) door (3) some water was boiling (4) kettle (5) after about 5 minutes passed

Writing Practice

Practice writing the following *hiragana*.

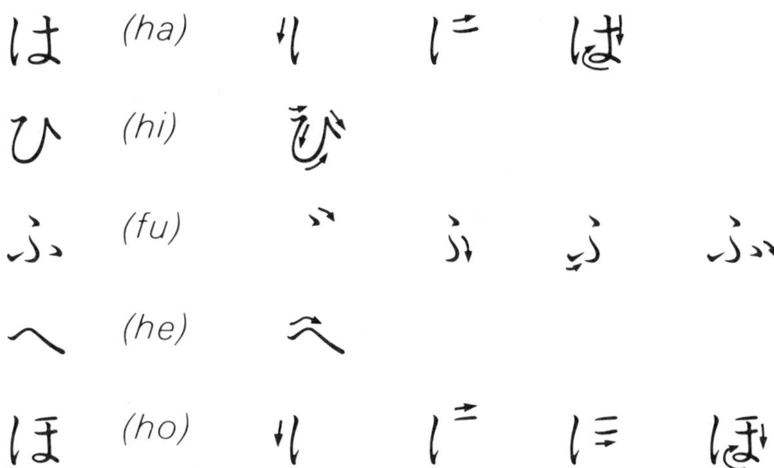

Aural Comprehension

Listen to the conversations on the tape and answer the following questions.

(A) 1. *Kinjo-no hito-wa Satoo-san-wa doko-ni iru-to omotte-imasu-ka.*
2. *Futari-wa keesatsu*(police)*-ni denwa-suru mae-ni nani-o suru tsumori-desu-ka.*

(B) 1. *Satoo-san-no heya-wa kurai-desu-ka.*
2. *Satoo-san-wa itsu kuni-kara kaette-kita-no-desu-ka.*
3. *Naze kaette-kita-n-desu-ka.*

C) 1. *Gakusee-tachi-wa shiken-no benkyoo-o shita-deshoo-ka.*
2. *Sensee-wa shiken-ni tsuite moo gakusee-ni hanashimashita-ka.*
3. *Kono shiken-dewa jibiki-o hiite-mo ii-no-desu-ka.*

Quiz (Lesson 13 – Lesson 18)

I. Choose the correct word or phrase.

1. A: *Densha,* {*mada* / *made*} *kimasen-ne.*

   B: *Ee, osoi-desu-ne. Moo kuru* {*hazu* / *tsumori*} *-na-n-desu-ga.*

   A: *Eki-no hito-ni kiite-mimashoo-ka.*

   B: *Sumimasen.* {*Onegai-shimasu.* / *Soo shimasu.*}

2. A: *Ashita-wa doo-desu-ka.*

   B: *Ashita-nara itsudemo* {*koraremasu.* / *koraremasen.*}

3. A: *Bataa-wa reezooko-*{*ni* / *o*} *iremashoo-ka.*

   B: *Ee. Demo soko-ni* {*irete* / *irenaide*} *-kudasai.*

   Soko-niwa hoka-no mono-o iremasu-kara.

4. A: *Sono hon, muzukashii-desu-ka.*

   B: *Ee, muzukashikute, nakanaka* {*yomemasen.* / *yomemasu.*}

5. Kawakami: *Kore-kara ongakukai-ni iku-n-desu-ga, Ishida-san-mo doo-desu-ka.*

   Ishida: *Soo-desu-ne. Watashi-mo* {*ikitai* / *ikitagaru*} *-n-desu-ga, kyoo-wa yooji-ga atte......*

   Kawakami: *Zannen-desu-ne.*

   Ishida: *Sumimasen. Kono-tsugi* {*tsurete-itte* / *mochidashite*} *-kudasai.*

6. A: *Kono zasshi, isshuukan-gurai* {*karite-mo* / *karite-wa*} *ii-desu-ka.*

   B: *Ee, kamaimasen-yo.*

7. A: *Sono hon-wa* { *dareka* / *dare* } *-ga karidashite-imasu.*

B: *Soo-desu-ka. Itsu modorimasu-ka.*

8. A: *Imooto-san-wa doko-ni irasshaimasu-ka.*

B: *Imooto-wa ima Amerika-ni* { *imasu.* / *irasshaimasu.* }

9. A: *Kaze-o hiite komatte-imasu.*

B: *Kono kusuri-o* { *nomeba* / *nonde-mo* } *sugu yoku narimasu-yo.*

10. A: *Gogo nani-o suru tsumori-desu-ka.*

B: *Eega-o* { *miru-daroo* / *miyoo* } *-to omotte-imasu.*

II. Put into Japanese.

1. Let's go together.
2. I can't pay.
3. The heater is turned off.
4. Have you ever been to China?
5. I hear he's writing a novel.
6. I owned a small one before.
7. I like baseball very much.
8. May I smoke?
9. Please shut the door.
10. Please leave the window open.
11. My sister wants a Japanese doll.
12. This restaurant looks expensive.
13. As many as three houses were burnt down.
14. What about next Sunday?
15. I can't go too far.

第十九課(だいじゅうきゅうか)　ご兄弟(きょうだい)は　いらっしゃいますか

Dialogue

(Johnson meets Michiko's mother.)

みちこ：　ジョンソンさん、母(はは)です。 1
母(はは)：　はじめまして。よく　いらっしゃいました。
ジョンソン：　どうぞ　よろしく。 3
母(はは)：　みちこが　いつも　おせわに　なっております。
ジョンソン：　いいえ、こちらこそ。 5
母(はは)：　どうぞ　おかけに　なってください。
ジョンソン：　はい。 7

母(はは)：　お父(とう)さんや　お母(かあ)さんは　お元気(げんき)ですか。
ジョンソン：　はい、おかげさまで。 9
母(はは)：　ジョンソンさんは　ご兄弟(きょうだい)は　いらっしゃいますか。
ジョンソン：　あねと　いもうとが　ひとりずつ　います。あ- 11
ねは　去年(きょねん)　結婚(けっこん)しました。
母(はは)：　そうですか。いもうとさんは? 13
ジョンソン：　いもうとは　大学(だいがく)の　寮(りょう)に　はいっています。
母(はは)：　そうですか。 15
ジョンソン：　ええ。ですから、いま　うちに　いるのは　両(りょう)-
親(しん)だけです。 17
母(はは)：　じゃ、おさびしいでしょうね。
ジョンソン：　ええ。いつか　日本(にほん)へ　来(き)たいと　言(い)っていま- 19
す。

母(はは)： そうですか。ジョンソン(じょんそん)さんが こちらに いらっしゃ- 21
る うちに、一度(いちど) おいでに なると いいですね。

Dialogue

Lesson 19 **DO YOU HAVE ANY BROTHERS AND SISTERS?**	*Dai-juukyuuka* *GO-KYOODAI-WA IRASSHAIMASU-KA*
Michiko: Mr. Johnson, this is Mother.	*Michiko: Jonson-san, haha-desu.*
Mother: I'm glad to meet you, Mr. Johnson.	*Haha: Hajimemashite. ▲Yoku irasshaimashita.*
Johnson: How do you do?	*Jonson: ▲Doozo yoroshiku.*
Mo: You've been very kind to Michiko.	*H: ▲Michiko-ga itsumo o-sewa-ni natte-orimasu.*
J: Oh, no. Just the opposite.	*J: Iie, kochira-koso.*
Mo: Please sit down.	*H: ▲Doozo o-kake-ni natte-kudasai.*
J: Thank you.	*J: Hai.*
Mo: How are your father and mother?	*H: Otoosan-ya okaasan-wa ▲o-genki-desu-ka.*
J: They're fine, thank you.	*J: Hai, okagesama-de.*
Mo: Do you have any brothers and sisters?	*H: Jonson-san-wa ▲go-kyoodai-wa irasshaimasu-ka.*
J: I have two sisters, one older and one younger. The older sister was married last year.	*J: Ane-to imooto-ga ▲hitori-zutsu imasu. Ane-wa kyonen ▲kekkon-shimashita.*
Mo: Oh, is that right? What about your younger sister?	*H: Soo-desu-ka. Imooto-san-wa?*
J: She lives in her university's dormitory.	*J: Imooto-wa ▲daigaku-no ryoo-ni haitte-imasu.*
Mo: Does she?	*H: Soo-desu-ka.*
J: So my parents live alone in our house.	*J: Ee. Desu-kara, ima uchi-ni iru-no-wa ▲ryooshin-dake-desu.*

Mo: They must be lonely.	*H: Ja, o-sabishii-deshoo-ne.*
J: Yes. They say they'd like to come to Japan some time.	*J: Ee. Itsuka ▲Nihon-e kitai-to itte-imasu.*
Mo: Do they? I hope they'll come while you're here.	*H: Soo-desu-ka. Jonson-san-ga ▲kochira-ni irassharu uchi-ni, ichido ▲oide-ni naru-to ii-desu-ne.*

Explanation

(In this lesson you will learn some polite expressions used to refer to others and some family terms.)

はじめまして。よく　いらっしゃいました。 **line 2**

Hajimemashite. Yoku irasshaimashita.

yoku irasshaimashita I'm glad you could come (dict. *irassharu → irasshaimasu*, irreg.)

The verb *irassharu* is a polite word meaning 'to be,' 'to come,' and 'to go.' Which one of the three meanings is expressed can be decided by the context. (cf. Lesson 15)

Yoku irasshaimashita which literally means 'You've come well,' is used as a greeting when receiving a visitor.

みちこが　いつも　おせわに　なっております。 **line 4**

Michiko-ga itsumo o-sewa-ni natte-orimasu.

itsumo	always
o-sewa-ni natte-orimasu	you are kind to her (*lit.* she's been taken care of by you)
orimasu	=*imasu* (dict. *oru*) (humble)

Sewa in *osewa* by itself means 'care,' and *sewa-ni naru* means 'to be taken care of.' *Osewa-ni natte-orimasu* (or *-imasu*) is used to greet a friend or associate of a member of one's own family, regardless of the literal meaning.

Orimasu is derived from *oru* which is the humble equivalent of *iru*. *Oru* is used when speaking about oneself or one's family members.

ex. *Otooto-wa ginkoo-ni tsutomete-orimasu.* (My brother works at a bank.)

いいえ、こちらこそ。 **line 5**

Iie, kochira-koso.

kochira-koso I should be the one to say so

Koso is added to nouns and pronouns to show emphasis.

ex. 1. A: *Shitsuree-shimashita.* (Pardon me.)

B: *Iie, kochira-koso.* (Pardon *me.*)

ex. 2. A: *Tsukareta-deshoo.* (You must be tired.)

B: *Yamashita-san-koso tsukareta-deshoo.* (*You* must be tired, Mr. Yamashita.)

どうぞ　おかけに　なってください。 **line 6**

Doozo o-kake-ni natte-kudasai.

o-kake-ni natte-kudasai please take a seat (dict. *kakeru*)

The verb *kakeru* here means 'to sit down.' The form *o-* plus the stem of the verb (for example, *kake* of *kakeru*) plus *-ni naru* is commonly used to show respect.

ex. *dekakeru—Sensee-wa o-dekake-ni narimashita.* (The professor went out.)

yomu—Kono hon-o o-yomi-ni narimasu-ka. (Are you going to read this book?)

O . . . ni natte-kudasai is more polite than the ···*te-kudasai* form.

ex. *Doozo tsukatte-kudasai.* (Please use it.)

Doozo o-tsukai-ni natte-kudasai. (Please use it.— more polite)

Ni natte is sometimes left out.

ex. *O-kake-ni natte-kudasai —O-kake-kudasai.*

O-tsukai-ni natte-kudasai —O-tsukai-kudasai.

お父(とう)さんや　お母(かあ)さんは　お元気(げんき)ですか。 **line 8**

Otoosan-ya okaasan-wa o-genki-desu-ka.

otoosan (your) father

okaasan (your) mother

ジョンソンさんは ご兄弟は いらっしゃいますか。 **line 10**

Jonson-san-wa go-kyoodai-wa irasshaimasu-ka.

go-kyoodai (your) brothers (and sisters)

Kyoodai in its narrow sense means just 'brothers,' but it also has the wider meaning of 'brothers and sisters' as it does here.

A few nouns take the polite prefix *go-* instead of *o-* For example, *go-shujin* (your husband), *go-hon* (your book), *go-benkyoo* (your study), etc.

Irassharu here is a polite equivalent of *iru,* 'to be.'; .... *ga iru* means 'to have...'

ex. *Kodomo-ga imasu.* (I have children.)

あねと いもうとが ひとりずつ います。 **line 11**

Ane-to imooto-ga hitori-zutsu imasu.

ane my elder sister

hitori-zutsu one each (for *hitori*, see Lesson 11, Note)

Zutsu is added to nouns and means 'each,' 'respectively.'

ex. *Minna-ga hyaku-en-zutsu dashimashita.* (They contributed one hundred yen each.)

あねは 去年 結婚しました。 **lines 11-12**

Ane-wa kyonen kekkon-shimashita.

kyonen last year

kekkon-shimashita she married

いもうとは 大学の 寮に はいっています。 **line 14**

Imooto-wa daigaku-no ryoo-ni haitte-imasu.

ryoo dormitory

... *ni haitte-imasu* she's in ... (dict. *hairu,* Lesson 10)

ですから、いま うちに いるのは 両親だけです。 **lines 16-17**

Desu-kara, ima uchi-ni iru-no-wa ryooshin-dake-desu.

desu-kara so; therefore

uchi-ni iru-no ones that stay home

... *dake* only ...

Dake is used in the following way:

ex. 1. A: *Hoka-no hito-mo ikimasu-ka.* (Are other people going, too?)

B: *Iie, watashi-dake-desu.* (No, just me.)

2. *Sonna-ni harawanakute-mo ii-n-desu. Sen-en-dake haratte-kudasai.* (You don't have to pay that much. Pay just 1,000 yen, please.)

じゃ、おさびしいでしょうね。 **line 18**

Ja, o-sabishii-deshoo-ne.

o-sabishii-deshoo-ne they must be lonely (from *sabishii*)

ええ。いつか　日本へ　来たいと　言っています。 **lines 19-20**

Ee. Itsuka Nihon-e kitai-to itte-imasu.

itsuka some time

kitai-to itte-imasu (they say) they want to come

The form ending in *-tai* cannot be added directly to the third person; thus you have to say either *kitai-to itte-imasu* or *kitagatte-imasu.* See Lesson 15.

ジョンソンさんが　こちらに　いらっしゃる　うちに、一度　おいでに　なると

Jonson-san-ga kochira-ni irassharu uchi-ni, ichido oide-ni naru-to

いいですね。 **lines 21-22**

ii-desu-ne.

irassharu uchi-ni while you're here (polite)

oide-ni naru they come (polite)

Uchi-ni by itself means 'within.' It is added to the dictionary form of verbs to mean 'while.'

ex. *Watashi-ga nete-iru uchi-ni tomodachi-ga kimashita.*
(A friend of mine came to visit me while I was sleeping.)

Oide-ni naru is a polite expression which means 'to be,' 'to come' and 'to go.' It is similar to the verb *irassharu* both in meaning and function. The difference between the two is that *oide-ni naru* is a little more polite than *irassharu.*

Oide-ni naru-to ii literally means 'if they come it'll be good.' The expression ... *to ii* roughly corresponds to 'I hope,' though it does not include as much expectation as the English expression.

ex. *Ashita furanai-to ii-desu-ne.* (I hope it won't rain tomorrow.)

Note **Family terms**

The following is a list of names for family members. When talking about your own family members to an outsider, use the plain terms. When talking about others' families, use the polite terms. (Plain terms can be used when talking about others' families when you do not have to show respect, but that is rather unusual.)

	plain	**polite**
(parent)	*oya*	*oyago-san*
(both parents)	*ryooshin*	*go-ryooshin*
(father)	*chichi*	*otoosan*
(mother)	*haha*	*okaasan*
(husband)	*shujin*	*go-shujin*
(wife)	*kanai*	*okusan*
	tsuma	
(older brother)	*ani*	*oniisan*
(younger brother)	*otooto*	*otooto-san*
(older sister)	*ane*	*oneesan*
(younger sister)	*imooto*	*imooto-san*

To address family members older than oneself, polite terms are used.

ex. *Otoosan, ima nanji?* (What time is it, Dad?)

For family members younger than oneself, their first names are used; *-san* or *-chan* (more familiar) may be added.

ex. *Michiko, moo dekakeyoo-yo.* (Let's go, Michiko.)
Michiko-san (or *-chan*), *moo dekakemashoo-yo.*

* * *

From this lesson on drills are given in *hiragana* (including *kanji* and *katakana*). From Lesson 19 to 24, the *romaji* equivalent is given on the right, but try to read the *hiragana* part without looking at the *romaji.*

Here are some expressions used in giving instruction.

練習(れんしゅう)しなさい	*renshuu-shinasai**	practice
かえなさい	*kaenasai**	change
例(れい)	*ree*	example
例(れい)に　ならって	*ree-ni naratte*	as shown in the example
質問(しつもん)	*shitsumon*	question
質問(しつもん)に　こたえなさい	*shitsumon-ni kotaenasai**	answer the question
下線(かせん)の	*kasen-no*	underlined
会話(かいわ)	*kaiwa*	conversation
形(かたち)の　練習(れんしゅう)	*katachi-no renshuu*	structure drill
使(つか)いかたの　練習(れんしゅう)	*tsukaikata-no renshuu*	usage drill

* Verbs ending in *-nasai* indicate command.

練習(れんしゅう)　(Drills)

I.　いらっしゃる

形(かたち)の練習(れんしゅう)

（Ａ）「いる」を「いらっしゃる」にかえなさい。

例(れい)：おにいさんは　いますか
──→おにいさんは　いらっしゃいますか。

1．おねえさんは　どこに　いますか

2．お父(とう)さんは　つとめていますか

I.　*irassharu*

Structure Drill

(A)　Change *iru* to *irassharu.*

ex.　*oniisan-wa imasu-ka*
──→*Oniisan-wa irasshaimasu-ka.*

1.　*oneesan-wa doko-ni imasu-ka*

2.　*otoosan-wa tsutomete-imasu-ka*

3. おにいさんは　結婚(けっこん)しています-(is married) か	3. *oniisan-wa kekkon-shite-imasu-ka*
4. いま　この　新聞(しんぶん)を　読(よ)んでいますか	4. *ima kono shinbun-o yonde-imasu-ka*
5. 寮(りょう)に　はいっていますか	5. *ryoo-ni haitte-imasu-ka*
6. どんな　お仕事(しごと)を　していますか	6. *donna oshigoto-o shite-imasu-ka*
7. 結婚(けっこん)しているそうです	7. *kekkon-shite-iru-soo-desu*
8. 会社(かいしゃ)に　つとめているそうです	8. *kaisha-ni tsutomete-iru-soo-desu*

(B)「行(い)く」「来(く)る」を「いらっしゃる」に　かえなさい

(B) Change *iku* and *kuru* to *irasshuru.*

例(れい)：どこへ　行(い)きますか →どこへ　いらっしゃいますか。	ex *doko-e ikimasu-ka* →*Doko-e irasshaimasu-ka.*
1. きょう　行(い)きますか	1. *kyoo ikimasu-ka*
2. いつ　ここへ　来(き)ますか	2. *itsu koko-e kimasu-ka*
3. 日本(にほん)へ　来(き)た　ことが　ありますか	3. *Nihon-e kita koto-ga arimasu-ka*
4. 映画(えいが)を　見(み)に　行(い)きました	4. *eega-o mi-ni ikimashita*
5. 旅行(りょこう)(trip)に　行(い)ったそうです	5. *ryokoo-ni itta-soo-desu*
6. きょうは　会社(かいしゃ)へ　行(い)かないそうです	6. *kyoo-wa kaisha-e ikanai-soo-desu*
7. 野球(やきゅう)を　見(み)に　行(い)きませんか	7. *yakyuu-o mi-ni ikimasen-ka*
8. 何時(なんじ)に　行(い)けば　いいんですか	8. *nanji-ni ikeba ii-n-desu-ka*

II. お…に　なる

II. *o . . . ni naru*

形の練習(かたち れんしゅう)

Structure Drill

(A)「お…に　なる」に　かえなさい。

(A) Change the following using the *o . . . ni naru* form.

例：やめる—おやめに　なる
　読(よ)む—お読(よ)みに　なる

ex. *yameru —o-yame-ni naru*
yomu —o-yomi-ni naru

1. まつ	2. たつ	1. *matsu*	2. *tatsu*
3. すわる	4. 書(か)く	3. *suwaru*	4. *kaku*
5. やる	6. きめる	5. *yaru*	6. *kimeru*
7. できる	8. わかる	7. *dekiru*	8. *wakaru*
9. 買(か)う	10. ひく	9. *kau*	10. *hiku*
11. きく	12. はなす	11. *kiku*	12. *hanasu*
13. はいる	14. かえる	13. *hairu*	14. *kaeru*
15. あう	16. はらう	15. *au*	16. *harau*
17. のむ	18. はいる	17. *nomu*	18. *hairu*
19. かける	20. 使(つか)う	19. *kakeru*	20. *tsukau*

(B) 形(かたち)の練習(れんしゅう)(A)のことばを「お…に　なった」に　かえなさい。

(B) Change the phrases in Structure Drill (A) into the *o . . . ni natta* form.

例(れい)：やめる—おやめに　なった
　読(よ)む—お読(よ)みに　なった

ex. *yameru —o-yame-ni natta*
yomu —o-yomi-ni natta

(C) 形(かたち)の練習(れんしゅう)(A)のことばを「お…に　ならない」に　かえなさい。

(C) (Change the phrases in Structure Drill (A) into the negative.)

例(れい)：やめる—おやめに　ならない
　読(よ)む—お読(よ)みに　ならない

ex. *yameru—o-yame-ni naranai*
yomu—o-yomi-ni naranai

使(つか)いかたの練習(れんしゅう)

Usage Drill

下線(かせん)の (underlined) ことばを かえて、つぎの (following) 会話(かいわ)を 練習(れんしゅう)しなさい。

Practice the following conversation changing the underlined words.

例(れい)：お金(かね)を はらう

ex. *okane-o harau*

A：いま すぐ お金(かね)を はらいましょうか。

B：いいえ、あとで おはらいに なっても かまいません。

A：そうですか。じゃ、そう します。何時(なんじ)ごろまでに はらえば いいですか。

B：五時(ごじ)ごろまでに おはらいください。

A: *Ima sugu okane-o haraimashoo-ka.*

B: *Iie, ato-de o-harai-ni natte-mo kamaimasen.*

A: *Soo-desu-ka. Ja, soo shimasu. Nanji-goro-made-ni haraeba ii-desu-ka.*

B: *Goji-goro-made-ni o-harai-kudasai.*

1. 切符(きっぷ)を 買(か)う
2. 予定(よてい)を きめる
3. くすり (medicine) を のむ
4. 電話(でんわ)を かける
5. てがみを 書(か)く

1. *kippu-o kau*
2. *yotee-o kimeru*
3. *kusuri-o nomu*
4. *denwa-o kakeru*
5. *tegami-o kaku*

III. Family terms

III. Family terms

形(かたち)の練習(れんしゅう)

Structure Drill

Note の family terms を おぼえなさい (memorize).

Memorize the family terms in the Note.

使いかたの練習 (つか れんしゅう)　Usage Drill

下線の　ことばを　かえて、つぎの　電話の　会話を　練習しなさい。

Practice the following conversation on the phone, changing the underlined words.

例：お父さん、お母さん、母

ex. *otoosan, okaasan, haha*

A：お父さんは　いらっしゃいますか。

A: *Otoosan-wa irasshaimasu-ka.*

B：いま、おりません。ちょっと　でかけました。

B: *Ima orimasen. Chotto dekakemashita.*

A：いつ　おかえりに　なりますか。

A: *Itsu o-kaeri-ni narimasu-ka.*

B：三時ごろ　かえると　おもいます。

B: *Sanji-goro kaeru-to omoimasu.*

A：お母さんは？

A: *Okaasan-wa?*

B：母は　おります。よびましょうか (shall I call her)。

B: *Haha-wa orimasu. Yobimashoo-ka.*

A：はい、おねがいします。

A: *Hai, onegai-shimasu.*

1. おにいさん、おねえさん、あね　— *oniisan, oneesan, ane*
2. お母さん、おくさん、家内　— *okaasan, okusan, kanai*
3. お父さん、ご主人、主人　— *otoosan, go-shujin, shujin*
4. ご主人、お父さん、父　— *go-shujin, otoosan, chichi*
5. おとうとさん、おにいさん、あに　— *otooto-san, oniisan, ani*
6. おくさん、お母さん、母　— *okusan, okaasan, haha*

Before starting practice, try to make sure that you understand the relation between the speaker B and his family members he refers to.

発音練習 (Pronunciation Practice)

「ん」に　気を　つけて (paying attention)　練習しなさい。

A．1．あの　あんの　あんお　あんおん

2．いの　いんの　いんお　いんおん

3．えの　えんの　えんお　えんおん

4．おの　おんの　おんお　おんおん

5．あね　あんね　あんえ　あんえん

6．いね　いんね　いんえ　いんえん

B．1．しんぶんを　2．ちゃわん(cup)を　3．ほんを　4．かばんを

5．かんわじてん (Chinese-Jap. dictionary) を

6．えいわじてん (Eng.-Jap. dict.) を

C．下線の　ところに (in the underlined parts) Bの　ことばを　入れて練習しなさい。

例：ちょっと　まってください。しんぶんを　とってきます (I'll go and bring) から。

読む練習 (Reading Comprehension)

In the Reading Comprehensions from this lesson on, *furigana* are not given for the kanji which appear in the lesson.

つぎの　文 (passage, sentences) を　読みなさい (read)。

わたしの家族(1)

わたしの家族は五人家族である*。父はある(2)銀行につとめている。母は毎日家族のせわでいそがしい。おとうとはいま高校で勉強している。ラジオやテレビをなおす(3)のがだいすきで、技師(4)になりたいと言っている。いもうとは医者(5)になりたがっているが、まだこどもなので、あとでかわる(6)かもしれない。

(1) family　(2) certain　(3) repair　(4) engineer　(5) doctor　(6) change

*…*de aru* means *"desu"*; it is used mainly in writing.

書く練習 (Writing Practice)

つぎの　ひらがなを　練習しなさい。

ま　(ma)

み　(mi)

む　(mu)

め　(me)

も　(mo)

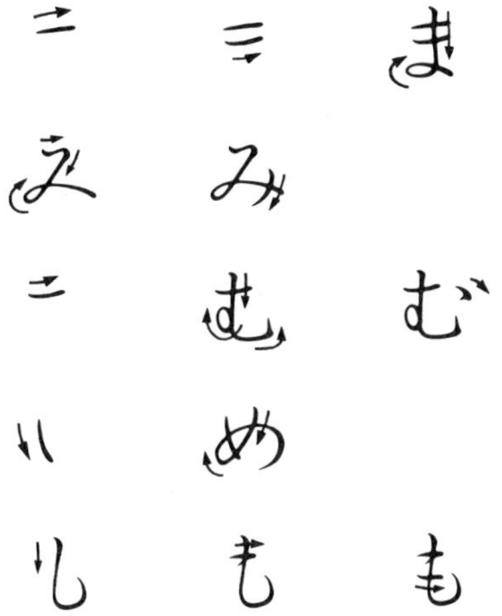

聞く練習 (Aural Comprehension)

テープ(tape)の　会話を　聞いて　質問に　こたえなさい。

1. 山本先生は　だれの　先生ですか。
2. 山本先生が　来た　とき　戸は　あいていましたか、しまっていましたか。
3. 山本先生は　へやへ　あがりましたか。
4. 山本先生は　どんな　用事で　来たのですか。
5. 女の人の　主人は　いそがしそうですか。
6. 山本先生は　このつぎ　いつ　来ると　言いましたか。

第二十課(だいにじっか)　父(ちち)が　くれたんです

Dialogue

山下(やました)：　いい　時計(とけい)ですね。どこで　買(か)ったんですか。

ジョンソン(じょんそん)：　これは　買(か)ったんじゃ　ないんです。去年(きょねん)の　誕生日(たんじょうび)の　おいわいに　父(ちち)が　くれたんです。

山下(やました)：　そうですか。あ、誕生日(たんじょうび)と　いえば、あさっては　おとうとの　誕生日(たんじょうび)だから、なにか　やらなくちゃ…すっかり　わすれていました。

ジョンソン(じょんそん)：　ところで、今晩(こんばん)　音楽会(おんがくかい)の　切符(きっぷ)が　あるんですが、どうですか。

山下(やました)：　そうですねえ…こういう　音楽(おんがく)は　どうもねえ…加藤(かとう)さんに　あげたら　どうですか。クラシック(くらしっく)が　すきだそうだから。

(Johnson offers to give the ticket to Miss Kato.)

加藤(かとう)：　そうですか。ジョンソン(じょんそん)さんは　行(い)かないんですか。

ジョンソン(じょんそん)：　ええ。国(くに)から　きゅうに　いもうとが　来(く)るので、空港(くうこう)へ　むかえに　行(い)くんです。ですから、どうぞ　かわりに　行(い)ってください。

加藤(かとう)：　でも、ただで　いただいては　もうしわけ　ないから、お金(かね)を　うけとってください。

ジョンソン(じょんそん)：　いいえ。いらなく　なった　ものを　あげるんですから、お金(かね)なんか　もらう　わけには　いきませんよ。

加藤(かとう)：　そうですか。じゃ、遠慮(えんりょ)なく　いただきます。どうも　ありがとう。

Dialogue

Lesson 20	*Dai-nijikka*
MY FATHER GAVE IT TO ME	***CHICHI-GA KURETA-N-DESU***
Yamashita: That's a nice watch you have. Where did you buy it?	*Yamashita: Ii tokee-desu-ne. Doko-de katta-n-desu-ka.*
Johnson: I didn't buy it. My father gave it to me for my birthday last year.	*Jonson: Kore-wa katta-n-ja nai-n-desu. Kyonen-no tanjoobi-no oiwai-ni chichi-ga kureta-n-desu.*
Y: Is that right? Speaking of birthdays, the day after tomorrow is my brother's birthday and I have to get something for him. I had completely forgotten it.	*Y: Soo-desu-ka. A, tanjoobi-to ieba, asatte-wa otooto-no tanjoobi-da-kara, nanika yaranakucha... Sukkari wasurete-imashita.*
J: By the way, I have a ticket for a concert this evening. Would you like to go?	*J: Tokoro-de, konban ongakukai-no kippu-ga aru-n-desu-ga, doo-desu-ka.*
Y: Well, that sounds good, but this kind of music is not my cup of tea. How about giving it to Miss Kato? I understand she likes classical music.	*Y: Soo-desu-nee... Koo-yuu ongaku-wa doomo-nee... Katoo-san-ni agetara doo-desu-ka. Kurashikku-ga suki-da-soo-da-kara.*
Katoo: So you're not going, Mr. Johnson?	*Katoo: Soo-desu-ka. Jonson-san-wa ikanai-n-desu-ka.*
J: No. My sister's suddenly coming to Japan and I have to go to the airport to meet her. So I'd like you to go.	*J: Ee. Kuni-kara kyuu-ni imooto-ga kuru-node, kuukoo-e mukae-ni iku-n-desu. Desu-kara, doozo kawari-ni itte-kudasai.*
K: But I can't take it for nothing. Please let me pay for it.	*K: Demo, tada-de itadaite-wa mooshiwake nai-kara, okane-o uketotte-kudasai.*
J: No. I'm giving you something I don't need. It won't do to	*J: Iie. Iranaku natta mono-o ageru-n-desu-kara, okane-nanka*

receive money from you. | ▲morau wake-niwa ikimasen-yo.
K: I see. Then I'll go ahead and accept it. Thank you very much. | K: Soo-desu-ka. Ja, ▲enryo-naku itadakimasu. Doomo ▲arigatoo.

Explanation

(In this lesson you will learn how to express some equivalents of 'give' and 'receive.' The choice of verb is determined by the relationship between the giver and the receiver.)

いい 時計(とけい)ですね。 **line 1**

Ii tokee-desu-ne.

tokee watch; clock

去年(きょねん)の 誕生日(たんじょうび)の おいわいに 父(ちち)が くれたんです。 **lines 2-3**

Kyonen-no tanjoobi-no oiwai-ni chichi-ga kureta-n-desu.

o-iwai (gift for) celebration (usu. with *o-*)
... no oiwai-ni as a gift to celebrate...
chichi (my) father (cf. Lesson 19)
(... o) kureta he gave (...) to me (dict. *kureru*)

The verb *kureru* is used when an equal or an inferior gives something to the speaker or to a member of the speaker's family.

ex. *Yamashita-san-ga tanjoobi-no oiwai-o kuremashita.* (Mr. Yamashita gave me a birthday present.)
Tanaka-san-ga otooto-ni hon-o kuremashita. (Mr. Tanaka gave my brother a book.)

When the giver is a superior, the speaker uses the verb *kudasaru* to mean 'gives (me).' (The *-masu* form of *kudasaru* is *kudasaimasu.*)

ex. *Sensee-ga kono jibiki-o kudasaimashita.* (My teacher gave me this dictionary.)

あ、誕生日(たんじょうび)と　いえば、あさっては　おとうとの　誕生日(たんじょうび)だから、なにか
A, tanjoobi-to ieba, asatte-wa otooto-no tanjoobi-da-kara, nanika

やらなくちゃ…　**lines 4-5**
yaranakucha...

...to ieba	speaking of ... (dict. *yuu*)
asatte	the day after tomorrow
(...o) yaranakucha	=*yaranakute-wa naranai;* I have to give him (...) (dict. *yaru*)

The verb *yaru* is used when the speaker gives something to an inferior.

ex. *Imooto-ni ningyoo-o yarimashita.* (I gave a doll to my younger sister.)
Mainichi inu-ni niku-o yarimasu. (I feed my dog meat every day.)

When one gives something to his superior he uses the verb *sashiageru.*

ex. *Kono-hon-o sensee-ni sashiagetai-n-desu.* (I want to give this book to my teacher.) or (I'd like you to accept this book, Professor.)

Be careful not to use the verb *ageru* instead of *sashiageru.* *Ageru* does not imply politeness.

Yaranakucha (or *yaranakute-wa*) *naranai* means 'have to give.' The plain negative form of a verb ending in *-nakute-wa* plus *naranai* or *narimasen* means 'must' or 'have to.' It literally means 'if you don't do something, it won't be all right.'

ex. *taberu — tabenakute-wa naranai* (I have to eat)
yomu — yomanakute-wa naranai (I have to read)

'*...nakucha*' is a contracted form of *-nakute-wa* and is used in familiar speech.

ex. *tabenakute-wa—tabenakucha; yomanakute-wa—yomanakucha*

In familiar speech, *naranai* or *narimasen* is often left out.

ex. *Moo osoi-kara nenakucha.* (I have to go to bed since it's late.)

すっかり　わすれていました。 **lines 5-6**

Sukkari wasurete-imashita.

sukkari completely

(... o) wasurete-imashita I had forgotten(...)(dict. *wasureru*)

ところで、今晩(こんばん)　音楽会(おんがくかい)の　切符(きっぷ)が　あるんですが、どうですか。 **lines 7-8**

Tokoro-de, konban ongakukai-no kippu-ga aru-n-desu-ga, doo-desu-ka.

ongak(u)kai concert

そうですねえ… **line 9**

Soo-desu-nee...

This *Soo-desu-nee* shows hesitation.

こういう　音楽(おんがく)は　どうもねえ… **line 9**

Koo-yuu ongaku-wa doomo-nee...

ongaku music

doomo somehow

After *doomo-nee,* some negative statement is suggested. Here Yamashita means that he doesn't like it very much.

加藤(かとう)さんに　あげたら　どうですか。 **lines 9-10**

Katoo-san-ni agetara doo-desu-ka.

... ni (... o) agetara doo-desu-ka what about giving (...) to ...? (dict. *ageru*)

The verb *ageru* is used to describe the action of giving something to an equal.

ex. *Matsumoto-kun,* kimi-ni ageru-yo* (This is for you, Matsumoto.) (*See Lesson 23 for the use of *-kun.*)

Satoo-san-ni agemashoo. (Let's give it to Mr. Sato.)

'*...tara doo-desu-ka*' is used to suggest or propose an action. It corresponds to the English expression 'how about ...ing?' or 'why don't you ...?'

The ... *tara* form is made by adding *-ra* to the plain past form of verbs; *iku—ittara; taberu—tabetara; suru—shitara; kuru—kitara.* This form is used to show condition.

ex. *Ashita Katoo-san-ga kitara kore-o agemashoo.* (Let's give this to Miss Kato if she comes tomorrow.)

クラシック(くらしっく)が　すきだそうだから。 **lines 10-11**

Kurashikku-ga suki-da-soo-da-kara.

kurashikku	classical music
ga suki-da	(she) like(s)··· (cf. *daisuki,* Lesson 15)

The use of *-da-kara* instead of *-desu-kara* here shows that Yamashita and Johnson are on familiar terms, though not enough to use *-da* all the time.

ええ。国(くに)から　きゅうに　いもうとが　来(く)るので　空港(くうこう)へ　むかえに行(い)くんです。 **lines 13-14**

Ee. Kuni-kara kyuu-ni imooto-ga kuru-node kuukoo-e mukae-ni iku-n-desu.

kuukoo	airport
(. . . o) mukae-ni iku	go to meet (...)(dict. *mukaeru*)

どうぞ　かわりに　行(い)ってください。 **lines 14-15**

Doozo kawari-ni itte-kudasai.

kawari-ni	in my place

でも、ただで　いただいては　もうしわけ　ないから　お金(かね)をうけとってください。 **lines 16-17**

Demo tada-de itadaite-wa mooshiwake nai-kara, okane-o uketotte-kudasai.

tada-de	for nothing
(. . . o) itadaite-wa	if I am given (. . .); if I receive (. . .) (dict. *itadaku*)
mooshiwake nai	I'm sorry (*lit.* I have no sufficient apology for it)
uketotte-kudasai	please accept it (dict. *uketoru*)

The verb *itadaku* is used when the speaker receives something from a superior. Here, Johnson and Kato are equals, but Kato uses *itadaku* because it is more common in women's speech than is its less polite equivalent *morau.*

いいえ。いらなく　なった　ものを　あげるんですから、お金(かね)なんか　もらう
Iie. Iranaku natta mono-o ageru-n-desu-kara, okane-nanka morau

わけには　いきませんよ。 **lines 18-19**
wake-niwa ikimasen-yo.

iranaku natta mono	something I don't need any more (dict. *iru,* 'need')
okane-nanka	such a thing as money
morau	receive; be given
... *wake-niwa ikimasen*	I can't very well ...

'...*nanka*' in *okane-nanka* is added to show the speaker's emotion, which can be contempt, surprise or disgust, among other feelings. Which of these emotions is shown can be judged by the context.

ex. *Ano-hito-nanka-to kekkon-shitaku arimasen.* (He's the last person I want to marry.)

Watashi-nanka totemo dekimasen. (I'm so poor at it.)

In the first example, *-nanka* expresses hatred or contempt; in the second, it expresses a humble attitude.

The dictionary form of a verb plus *wake-niwa ikanai* is used to say that one cannot do something because of social or emotional reasons.

ex. *Okane-ga hoshii-keredo, ano-hito-ni tanomu wake-niwa ikimasen.* (I want money, but I don't have the nerve to ask him.)

Minna-ga hataraite-iru toki-ni watashi-dake yasunde-iru wake-niwa ikimasen. (I can't very well be resting when others are working.)

じゃ、遠慮(えんりょ)なく　いただきます。 **line 20**
Ja, enryo-naku itadakimasu.

enryo-naku	without reserve; feeling free to

When offering gifts, one often says *Doozo go-enryo-naku,* meaning 'Please feel free to accept it.'

練習(れんしゅう) (Drills)

I. くれる、もらう

I. *kureru, morau*

形(かたち)の練習(れんしゅう)

つぎのAとBの文(ぶん)(sentence)は意味(いみ)(meaning)は　おなじ(same)ですが、形(かたち)が　ちがいます。{　}のなかの　ことばを　かえて　練習(れんしゅう)しなさい。

Structure Drill

The sentences in B show a different way of saying the corresponding expressions in A. Practice saying them changing the words in {　}

A. くれる

{おとうと／母(はは)／ともだち／山下(やました)さん} が（わたしに）{時計(とけい)／お金(かね)／おいわい／切符(きっぷ)} を　くれました。

B. もらう

（わたしは）{おとうと／母(はは)／ともだち／山下(やました)さん} に {時計(とけい)／お金(かね)／おいわい／切符(きっぷ)} を　もらいました。

A. *kureru*

{*Otooto* / *Haha* / *Tomodachi* / *Yamashita-san*} *-ga (watashi-ni)* {*tokee* / *okane* / *oiwai* / *kippu*} *-o kuremashita.*

B. *morau*

(Watashi-wa) {*otooto* / *haha* / *tomodachi* / *Yamashita-san*} *-ni* {*tokee* / *okane* / *oiwai* / *kippu*} *-o moraimashita.*

使いかたの練習 Usage Drill

(A) つぎの 会話の 下線の ことばを かえて 練習しなさい。

(A) Practice the following conversation changing the underlined words.

例：時計、かばん

ex. *tokee, kaban*

A：いい 時計ですね。どこで 買いましたか。
B：これは 買ったんじゃ ないんです。もらったんです。
A：だれに もらったんですか。
B：父に もらったんです。
A：この かばんも そうですか。
B：いいえ、それは 母が くれたんです。

A: *Ii tokee-desu-ne. Doko-de kaimashita-ka.*
B: *Kore-wa katta-n-ja nai-n-desu. Moratta-n-desu.*
A: *Dare-ni moratta-n-desu-ka.*
B: *Chichi-ni moratta-n-desu.*
A: *Kono kaban-mo soo-desu-ka.*
B: *Iie, sore-wa haha-ga kureta-n-desu.*

1. つくえ、本ばこ (bookcase)
2. せびろ (suit), ネクタイ (tie)
3. カメラ(camera)、ラジオ
4. ゆびわ (ring), ネックレス (necklace)
5. ぼうし (hat), くつ (shoes)
6. てぶくろ (gloves), マフラー (warm scarf)

1. *tsukue, honbako*
2. *sebiro, nekutai*
3. *kamera, rajio*
4. *yubiwa, nekkuresu*
5. *booshi, kutsu*
6. *tebukuro, mafuraa*

(B) ともだちの ものに ついて (A) の ような (like A)会話を 練習しなさい。

(B) Carry out similar conversations discussing a friend's possessions.

II. くださる、いただく

II. *kudasaru, itadaku*

形の練習

{ }の なかの ことばを かえて 練習しなさい。

Structure Drill

Practice saying the following sentences, changing the words in { }.

A. くださる

{田中先生 / 先生の おくさん / 山下さんの お父さん / 山下さん} が（わたしに）{字引 / 参考書 / ネクタイ / おかし} を くださいました。

B. いただく

（わたしは）{田中先生 / 先生の おくさん / 山下さんの お父さん / 山下さん} に {字引 / 参考書 / ネクタイ / おかし} を いただきました。

A. *kudasaru*

{*Tanaka-sensee* / *Sensee-no okusan* / *Yamashita-san-no otoosan* / *Yamashita-san*} *-ga (watashi-ni)* {*jibiki* / *sankoosho* / *nekutai* / *okashi*} *-o kudasai-mashita.*

B. *itadaku*

(Watashi-wa) {*Tanaka-sensee* / *Sensee-no okusan* / *Yamashita-san-no otoosan* / *Yamashita-san*} *-ni* {*jibiki* / *sankoosho* / *nekutai* / *okashi*} *-o itadaki-mashita.*

使(つか)いかたの練習(れんしゅう)

Usage Drill

つぎの　会話(かいわ)の　下線(かせん)の　ことばを　かえて　練習(れんしゅう)しなさい。

Practice the following conversation, changing the underlined words.

例(れい)：字引(じびき)、参考書(さんこうしょ)

ex. *jibiki, sankoosho*

A：いい　字引(じびき)ですね。どこで　買(か)いましたか。

B：これは　買(か)ったんじゃ　ないんです。いただいたんです。

A：どなた (who—polite) に。

B：田中先生(たなかせんせい)に　いただいたんです。

A：この　参考書(さんこうしょ)も　そうですか。

B：いいえ、それは　山下(やました)さんの　お父(とう)さんが　くださったんです。

A: *Ii jibiki-desu-ne. Doko-de kaimashita-ka.*

B: *Kore-wa katta-n-ja nai-n-desu. Itadaita-n-desu.*

A: *Donata*ni?*

B: *Tanaka-sensee-ni itadaita-n-desu.*

A: *Kono sankoosho-mo soo-desu-ka.*

B: *Iie, sore-wa Yamashita-san-no otoosan-ga kudasatta-n-desu.*

(**Donata* is the polite equivalent of *dare.*)

1. ナイフ(ないふ)(knife)、ペン(ぺん)
2. 写真(しゃしん)、地図(ちず) (map)
3. おさけ、ワイン(わいん) (wine)
4. はいざら (ash tray), たばこ (tobacco)
5. 切手(きって) (postage stamp), 切手(きって)
6. え (picture), え

1. *naifu, pen*
2. *shashin, chizu*
3. *osake, wain*
4. *haizara, tabako*
5. *kitte, kitte*
6. *e, e*

III. さしあげる、あげる、やる形の練習

{　}の　なかの　ことばを　かえて　練習しなさい。

III. *sashiageru, ageru, yaru*

Structure Drill

Practice the following sentences, changing the words in {　}.

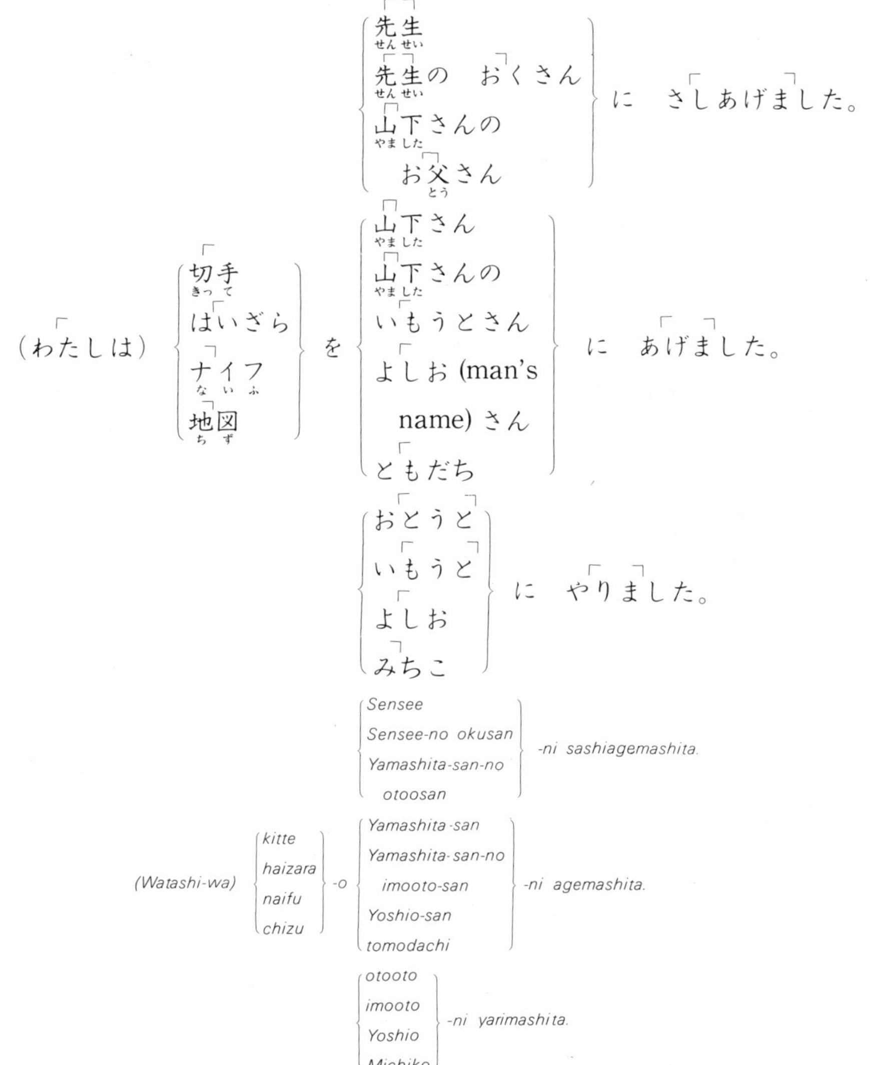

{先生 / 先生の　おくさん / 山下さんの　お父さん} に　さしあげました。

(わたしは) {切手 / はいざら / ナイフ / 地図} を {山下さん / 山下さんの　いもうとさん / よしお (man's name) さん / ともだち} に　あげました。

{おとうと / いもうと / よしお / みちこ} に　やりました。

{*Sensee* / *Sensee-no okusan* / *Yamashita-san-no otoosan*} *-ni sashiagemashita.*

(Watashi-wa) {*kitte* / *haizara* / *naifu* / *chizu*} *-o* {*Yamashita-san* / *Yamashita-san-no imooto-san* / *Yoshio-san* / *tomodachi*} *-ni agemashita.*

{*otooto* / *imooto* / *Yoshio* / *Michiko*} *-ni yarimashita.*

使(つか)いかたの練習(れんしゅう)

つぎの　会話(かいわ)の　下線(かせん)の　ことばを　かえて　練習(れんしゅう)しなさい。

例(れい)：山下(やました)さんに　あげる

A：あたらしい　カメラ(かめら)ですね。
B：ええ、このあいだ　買(か)ったんです。
A：まえのは　どう　したんですか。
B：ふるく　なったから　山下(やました)さんに　あげたんです。
A：そうですか。(jokingly) じゃ、これが　ふるく　なったら　わたしに　くださいね。
B：ええ、あげますよ。

1. おとうとに　やる
2. ともだちに　あげる
3. いもうとに　やる
4. みちこに　やる
5. 山下(やました)さんの　おとうとさんに　あげる
6. みちこさんに　あげる

Usage Drill

Practice the following conversation, changing the underlined words.

ex. *Yamashita-san-ni ageru*

A: *Atarashii kamera-desu-ne.*
B: *Ee, kono-aida katta-n-desu.*
A: *Mae-nowa doo shita-n-desu-ka.*
B: *Furuku natta-kara Yamashita-san-ni ageta-n-desu.*
A: *Soo-desu-ka. Ja, kore-ga furuku nattara watashi-ni kudasai-ne.*
B: *Ee, agemasu-yo.*

1. *otooto-ni yaru*
2. *tomodachi-ni ageru*
3. *imooto-ni yaru*
4. *Michiko-ni yaru*
5. *Yamashita-san-no otooto-san-ni ageru*
6. *Michiko-san-ni ageru*

IV. …なくちゃ　ならない

IV. ... *nakucha naranai*

形の練習

Structure Drill

つぎの　表(table)を　練習しなさい。

Practice saying the following table.

行く　行かなくては　行かなくちゃ	*iku　ikanakute-wa　ikanakucha*
食べる　食べなくては	*taberu　tabenakute-wa*
食べなくちゃ	*tabenakucha*
のむ　のまなくては	*nomu　nomanakute-wa*
のまなくちゃ	*nomanakucha*
やる　やらなくては　やらなくちゃ	*yaru yaranakute-wa yaranakucha*
あげる　あげなくては	*ageru　agenakute-wa*
あげなくちゃ	*agenakucha*
勉強する	*benkyoo-suru*
勉強しなくては	*benkyoo-shinakute-wa*
勉強しなくちゃ	*benkyoo-shinakucha*

発音練習　(Pronunciation Practice)

「ん」に　気を　つけて(paying attention)練習しなさい。

A.
1. うね　うんね　うんえ　うんえん
2. えね　えんね　えんえ　えんえん
3. おね　おんね　おんえ　おんえん
4. かに　かんに　かんい　かんいん
5. たな　たんな　たんあ　たんあん
6. しぬ　しんぬ　しんう　しんうん

B.　1. この　ちゃわんを　2. この　かばんを　3. この　しんぶんを
4. この　ほんを　5. この　かんわじてんを　6. この　えいわじてんを

C.　下線の　ところに (in the underlined part) Bの　ことばを　入れて練習しなさい。

例：ちょっと　おまちください。この　ちゃわんを　おいてきますから (I'll go and put this cup back)。

読む練習 **(Reading Comprehension)**

加藤の日記

十一月十九日　きょう、ジョンソンさんが、音楽会の切符をくれた。空港へ、いもうとさんをむかえに行くので、音楽会には行けなくなったのだそうである。ただでもらう*のはもうしわけないから、お金をあげたいと思った(1)が、ジョンソンさんは、いらないと言うので、結局(2)ただで切符をもらった。あとでお金のかわりになにかあげようと思う。

(1) I thought　(2) after all

(*When talking with Johnson she used *itadaku* since usually women prefer polite speech, but in writing women use the same language as men do.)

書く練習 **(Writing Practice)**

つぎの ひらがなを　練習しなさい。

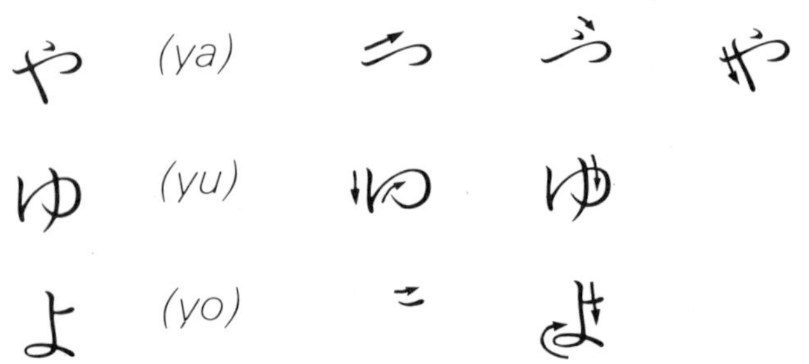

聞く練習 (Aural Comprehension)

テープ(tape)の　会話を　聞いて　質問に　こたえなさい。

1. 女の人は　これから　どこへ　行きますか。
2. むかえに　行くのですか、見おくりに (to see someone off) 行くのですか。
3. だれが　アメリカへ　行くのですか。
4. その人は　何年ぐらい　アメリカに　いる　予定ですか。
5. 女の人は　ほかに　兄弟が　いますか。
6. 女の人は　何時までに　行かなくては　なりませんか。

第二十一課(だいにじゅういっか)　見(み)ていただけませんか

Dialogue

ジョンソン：　いま　日本語(にほんご)で　手紙(てがみ)を　書(か)いているんですけど…

山下(やました)：　そうですか。

ジョンソン：　ちょっと　見(み)てもらえませんか。

山下(やました)：　ううん、わるいけど、いま　でかける　ところなんで… いそぐんですか。

ジョンソン：　ええ、まあ…

山下(やました)：　こまったな。

ジョンソン：　いいんです。だれか　ほかの　人(ひと)に　たのみますから。

山下(やました)：　じゃ、そう　してください。大家(おおや)さんの　おくさんなんか　どうですか。

(Johnson calls on Mrs. Takahashi, his landlady.)

ジョンソン：　いま　おいそがしく　ないでしょうか。

高橋(たかはし)：　いいえ、きょうは　ひまで、新聞(しんぶん)を　読(よ)んだり、テレビを　見(み)たり　していたんですよ。なにか…?

ジョンソン：　あの、じつは　いま　手紙(てがみ)を　書(か)いているんですが、ちょっと　見(み)てくださいますか。

高橋(たかはし)：　いいですよ。これですか。

ジョンソン：ええ。

高橋(たかはし)：　お礼(れい)の　手紙(てがみ)ですね。

ジョンソン：　そうです。

高橋(たかはし)：　最初(さいしょ)に　季節(きせつ)の　あいさつを　入(い)れた　ほうが　いいでしょう。「さむく　なりました」とか　「風(かぜ)が　つめたく　なりました」とか。

ジョンソン(じょんそん)：　最後(さいご)は　これで　いいでしょうか。
高橋(たかはし)：　「さようなら」の　まえに「おからだを　おだいじに」と　書(か)くと　いいですね。
ジョンソン(じょんそん)：　はい。いろいろ　教(おし)えていただいて、ありがとうございました。
高橋(たかはし)：　いいえ、どういたしまして。また　いつでも　どうぞ。

Dialogue

Lesson 21	*Dai-nijuuikka*
WOULD YOU TAKE A LOOK AT IT?	***MITE-ITADAKEMASEN-KA***
Johnson: I'm writing a letter in Japanese now.	*Jonson: Ima nihongo-de tegami-o kaite-iru-n-desu-kedo...*
Yamashita: Really?	*Yamashita: Soo-desu-ka.*
J: Will you take a look at it?	*J: Chotto mite-moraemasen-ka.*
Y: Gee, I'm sorry, but I'm going out just now. Are you in a hurry?	*Y: Uun, warui-kedo, ima dekakeru tokoro-na-nde...Isogu-n-desu-ka.*
J: Kind of.	*J: Ee, maa...*
Y: I wonder what I should do.	*Y: Komatta-na.*
J: That's all right. I'll ask someone else.	*J: Ii-n-desu. Dareka hoka-no hito-ni tanomimasu-kara.*
Y: Will you do that? How about asking the landlady?	*Y: Ja, soo shite-kudasai. Ooya-san-no okusan-nanka doo-desu-ka.*
J: Are you busy now?	*J: Ima o-isogashiku nai-deshoo-ka.*
Mrs. Takahashi: No. I don't have much to do today. I was reading the newspaper and watching TV. Can I help you?	*Takahashi: Iie, kyoo-wa hima-de, shinbun-o yondari, terebi-o mitari shite-ita-n-desu-yo. Nanika···?*

J: As a matter of fact, I'm writing a letter, and I wonder if you would correct it.	*J: Ano, jitsu-wa ima tegami-o kaite-iru-n-desu-ga, chotto mite-kudasaimasu-ka.*
T: All right. Is this the letter?	*T: Ii desu-yo. Kore-desu-ka.*
J: Yes.	*J: Ee.*
T: It's a letter of thanks, isn't it?	*T: Oree-no tegami-desu-ne.*
J: Yes.	*J: Soo-desu.*
T: You'd better say something about the season at the beginning. For instance, "It's gotten cold," or "The wind blows coldly these days," or something like that.	*T: Saisho-ni kisetsu-no aisatsu-o ireta hoo-ga ii-deshoo. "Samuku narimashita" toka, "Kaze-ga tsumetaku narimashita" toka.*
J: And is the last part all right as it is?	*J: Saigo-wa kore-de ii-deshoo-ka.*
T: Before signing off "Good-bye," it's nice to say "Take care of yourself."	*T: "Sayoonara" no mae-ni "O-karada-o o-daiji-ni" to kaku-to ii-desu-ne.*
J: I see. Thank you very much for your kind suggestions.	*J: Hai. Iroiro oshiete-itadaite, arigatoo-gozaimashita.*
T: You're welcome. Ask me any time.	*T: Iie, doo-itashimashite. Mata itsudemo doozo.*

Explanation

(A verb in its *-te* form combined with a verb of giving or receiving, learned in Lesson 20, can be used to express the actions of doing or receiving favors. You will learn several such expressions in this lesson.)

いま　日本語(にほんご)で　手紙(てがみ)を　書(か)いているんですけど…　**lines 1-2**

Ima nihongo-de tegami-o kaite-iru-n-desu-kedo...

nihongo-de	in Japanese
tegami	letter

ちょっと　見て　もらえませんか。 **line 4**

Chotto mite-moraemasen-ka.

mite-moraemasen-ka will you look at it? (dict. *morau*)

The *-te* form of a verb plus *morau* is used to describe receiving a favor from one's equal or inferior.

ex. *(Watashi-wa) Yamashita-san-ni tegami-o kaite-moraimashita.* (I had Mr. Yamashita write a letter for me.) or (Mr. Yamashita wrote a letter for me.)

Moraemasen is the negative potential form of *morau*. *Moraemasen-ka* literally means 'Can't I receive the favor?'

ううん、わるいけど、いま　でかける　ところなんで… **line 5**

Uun, warui-kedo, ima dekakeru tokoro-na-nde...

uun	well
warui-kedo	I'm sorry, but
dekakeru tokoro	I'm about to leave

Warui-kedo is more familiar than *sumimasen-kedo* (or *-ga*).

The dictionary form of a verb plus *tokoro* is used in the following way.

ex. *Matsumoto-san-ga kita toki, watashi-tachi-wa shokuji-o hajimeru tokoro-deshita.* (When Mr. Matsumoto came, we were about to start eating.)

Tokoro-na-nde is the contraction of *tokoro-na-node*. *Na* in *tokoro-na-node* is *-da*, the plain form of *-desu*, having undergone a change in sound. See Lesson 15.

After *tokoro-na-nde*, the rest of the sentence meaning 'I can't help you' is understood and therefore not mentioned.

いそぐんですか。 **line 6**

Isogu-n-desu-ka.

isogu-n-desu-ka are you in a hurry?

ええ、まあ… **line 7**

Ee, maa...

maa kind of

Maa is used to show agreement, with hesitation.

ex. A: *Takasugimasu-ka.* (Is it too expensive?)
B: *Ee. maa soo-desu-ne.* (Yes, I'm afraid it is.)

こまったな。 **line 8**

Komatta-na.

The sentence-ending particle *-na* is used when the speaker is directing the statement to himself.

だれか ほかの 人(ひと)に たのみますから。 **lines 9-10**

Dareka hoka-no hito-ni tanomimasu-kara.

ni tanomimasu I will ask... (dict. *tanomu*)

大家(おおや)さんの おくさんなんか どうですか。 **lines 11-12**

Ooya-san-no okusan-nanka doo-desu-ka.

ooya-san landlord; landlady

...*nanka doo-desu-ka* what about ..., for instance?

'...*nanka*' is used here to make a suggestion. Unlike the *-nanka* learned in Lesson 20, it is not used to impart emotion here.

いいえ、きょうは ひまで、新聞(しんぶん)を 読(よ)んだり、テレビ(てれび)を 見(み)たり

Iie, kyoo-wa hima-de, shinbun-o yondari, terebi-o mitari

していたんですよ。なにか…？ **lines 14-15**

shite-ita-n-desu-yo. Nanika...?

hima-de I don't have much to do, and

shinbun newspaper

For the use of *-de* in *hima-de,* see Reading Comprehension, Lesson 14.

Verbs ending with the *-ri* (attached to the plain past form) can be used in the following ways to show that two or more actions are representative of actions performed. Sentences in this pattern usually end in *suru.*

ex. *Okusan-wa mainichi sooji-o shitari sentaku-o shitari shimasu.* (The wife cleans and washes—and does other such things — every day.)

Gakusee-tachi-wa hon-o yondari jibiki-o hiitari shite-imasu. (Some students are reading and some are looking up words in dictionaries—and doing other such things.)

A verb ending in *-ri* can also show that one action described is representative of two or more actions.

ex. A: *Kono-goro-wa doo-desu-ka.* (How are you these days?)

B: *Genki-ni natte sanpo-o shitari shite-imasu.* (I'm better; I take walks and do other things.)

After *Nanika..., go-yoo-desu-ka* (can I help you?) or a similar phrase is left out.

あの、じつは　いま　手紙(てがみ)を　書(か)いているんですが、ちょっと　見(み)てください ますか。

Ano, jitsu-wa ima tegami-o kaite-iru-n-desu-ga, chotto mite-kudasaimasu-ka. **lines 16-17**

Mite-kudasaimasu-ka means 'Would you do me the favor of looking at it?' '*...te-kudasaru*' describes the action of one's superior doing one a favor.

ex. *Sensee-ga kaite-kudasaimashita.* (The teacher wrote it for me.)

お礼(れい)の　手紙(てがみ)ですね。 **line 20**

Oree-no tegami-desu-ne.

o-ree	thanks; gratitude (usu. with *o-*)

最初(さいしょ)に　季節(きせつ)の　あいさつを　入(い)れた　ほうが　いいでしょう。

Saisho-ni kisetsu-no aisatsu-o ireta hoo-ga ii-deshoo. **lines 22-23**

saisho	the beginning
kisetsu	seasons
aisatsu	greetings
...o ireta hoo-ga ii	you had better put in...(dict. *ireru*)

「さむく　なりました」とか　「風(かぜ)が　つめたく　なりました」とか。

"Samuku narimashita"-toka "Kaze-ga tsumetaku narimashita"-toka. **lines 23-24**

kaze	the wind

tsumetaku narimashita — it has become cold (dict. *tsumetai*)

... toka ... toka — such as ... and ...

The adjective *tsumetai* is used to refer to the coldness of things one can touch and feel, such as water, ice, hands, fingers, etc.

'*...toka*' is used when giving two or more examples.

ex. *Iroiro kaimashita, tebukuro-toka nekutai-toka.* (I bought various things, such as gloves, ties, and so on.)

Muzukashii-toka, omoshiroku nai-toka, iroiro monku-o iimashita. (He complained saying it's difficult, it's no fun, and so forth.)

The marks「　　」are used to show quoted speech.

最後(さいご)は　これで　いいでしょうか。 **line 25**

Saigo-wa kore-de ii-deshoo-ka.

saigo — the last

kore-de ii — this will do

「さようなら」の　まえに　「おからだを　おだいじに」と　書(か)くと いいですね。 **lines 26-27**

"Sayoonara"-no mae-ni "O-karada-o o-daiji-ni"-to kaku-to ii-desu-ne.

o-karada, karada — your health; your person

... o o-daiji-ni — take care of ... (*lit.* treat it carefully)

In conversation, *O-daiji-ni* is used in the same meaning as *O-karada-o o-daiji-ni.*

いろいろ　教(おし)えていただいて、ありがとうございました。 **lines 28-29**

Iroiro oshiete-itadaite, arigatoo-gozaimashita.

(... o) oshiete-itadaite — for teaching me (...) (dict. *oshieru*)

'*...te-itadaku*' means 'to receive a favor from one's superior.'

ex. *Tanaka-sensee-ni shashin-o totte-itadakimashita* (Prof. Tanaka kindly took my picture.)

Chotto kashite-itadakemasu-ka. (May I borrow it awhile? —*lit.* Could you lend it to me awhile?)

The verb *oshieru* means 'to tell how to' as well as 'to teach.'

ex. *Sumimasen-ga, eki-e iku michi-o oshiete-kudasaimasen-ka.*
(Excuse me, but could you tell me how to get to the station?)

練習(れんしゅう)　　*Renshuu*

I. …てくれる、…てもらう　　I. *...te-kureru, ...te-morau*

形(かたち)の練習(れんしゅう)　　*Katachi-no renshuu*

{ }の　なかの　ことばを　かえて　練習(れんしゅう)しなさい。

{ }*-no naka-no kotoba-o kaete renshuu-shinasai.*

A. …てくれる

{おとうと / 山下(やました)さん / 大家(おおや)さんの　おくさん / ひろし(man's name)さん} が {手紙(てがみ)を　書(か)いて / 手紙(てがみ)を　見(み)て / お金(かね)を　はらって / 教(おし)えて} くれました。

B. …てもらう

{おとうと / 山下(やました)さん / 大家(おおや)さんの　おくさん / ひろしさん} に {手紙(てがみ)を　書(か)いて / 手紙(てがみ)を　見(み)て / お金(かね)を　はらって / 教(おし)えて} もらいました。

A. *...te-kureru*

{*Otooto* / *Yamashita-san* / *Ooya-san-no okusan* / *Hiroshi-san*} *-ga* {*tegami-o kaite* / *tegami-o mite* / *okane-o haratte* / *oshiete*} *-kuremashita.*

B. *...te-morau*

Otooto / *Yamashita-san* / *Ooya-san-no okusan* / *Hiroshi-san*	*-ni*	*tegami-o kaite* / *tegami-o mite* / *okane-o haratte* / *oshiete*	*-moraimashita.*

使いかたの練習　*Tsukaikata-no renshuu*

つぎの　会話の　下線の　ことば-を　かえて　練習しなさい。

Tsugi-no kaiwa-no kasen-no kotoba-o kaete renshuu-shinasai.

例：手紙を　書く

ree : tegami-o kaku

A：この　手紙は　じぶんで (for yourself) 書いたんですか。

A: *Kono tegami-wa jibun-de kaita-n-desu-ka.*

B：いいえ、山下さんに　書いてもらったんです。

B: *Iie, Yamashita-san-ni kaite-moratta-n-desu.*

A：いつも　山下さんに　書いて-もらうんですか。

A: *Itsumo Yamashita-san-ni kaite-morau-n-desu-ka.*

B：いいえ、たいていは　いもうとが　書いてくれるんですが、この　手紙だけ　山下さんに　書いてもらったんです。

B: *Iie, taitee imooto-ga kaite-kureru-n-desu-ga, kono tegami-dake Yamashita-san-ni kaite-moratta-n-desu.*

1. 字 (character, letter) を　書く　　1. *ji-o kaku*
2. タイプを　うつ　　2. *taipu- utsu*
3. 料理 (cooked food) を　つくる (make)　　3. *ryoori-o tsukuru*
4. コーヒーを　いれる　　4. *koohii-o ireru*
5. 写真を　とる　　5. *shashin-o toru*

II. …てくださる、…ていただく　II. . . .te-kudasaru, . . .te-itadaku

形の練習　*Katachi-no renshuu*

{　}の　なかの　ことばを　かえて　練習しなさい。

{　}-no naka-no kotoba-o kaete renshuu-shinasai.

A. …てくださる

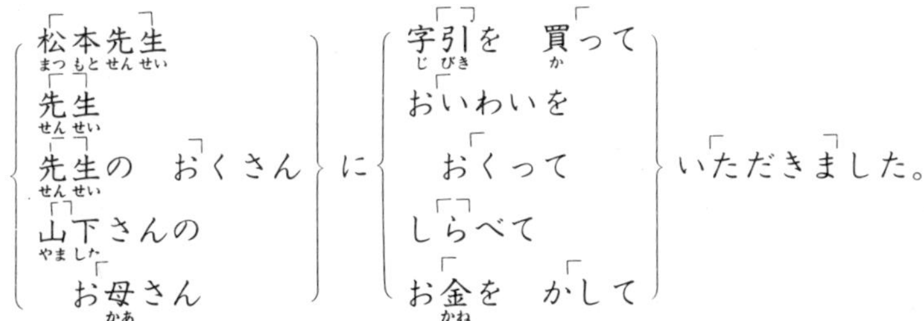

{松本先生 / 先生 / 先生の　おくさん / 山下さんの　お母さん}が{字引を　買って / おいわいを　おくって (send) / しらべて / お金を　かして (lend)}くださいました。

B. …ていただく

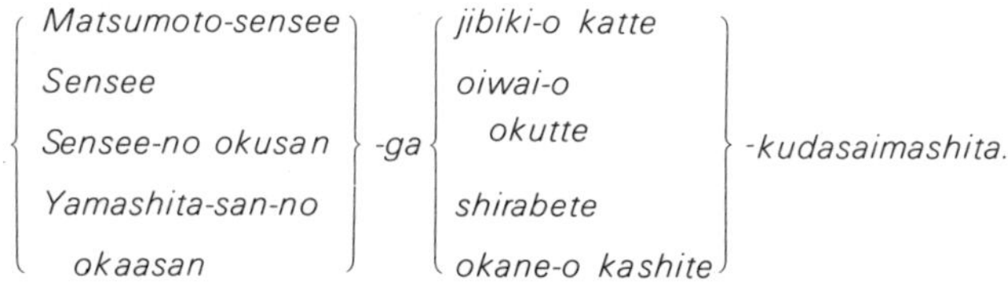

{松本先生 / 先生 / 先生の　おくさん / 山下さんの　お母さん}に{字引を　買って / おいわいを　おくって / しらべて / お金を　かして}いただきました。

A. *. . .te-kudasaru*

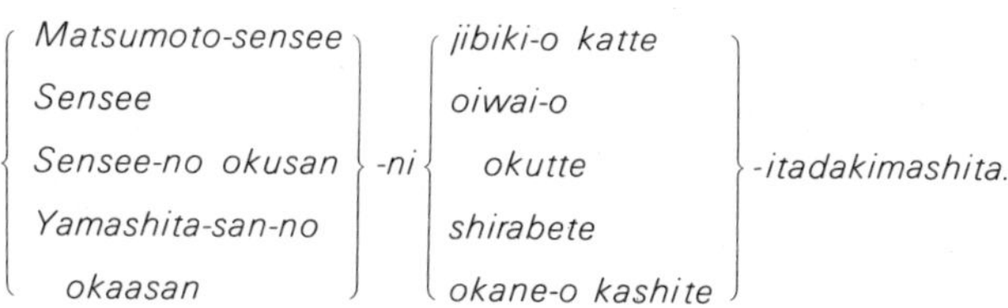

{Matsumoto-sensee / Sensee / Sensee-no okusan / Yamashita-san-no okaasan}-ga{jibiki-o katte / oiwai-o okutte / shirabete / okane-o kashite}-kudasaimashita.

B. *. . . te-itadaku*

{Matsumoto-sensee / Sensee / Sensee-no okusan / Yamashita-san-no okaasan}-ni{jibiki-o katte / oiwai-o okutte / shirabete / okane-o kashite}-itadakimashita.

使(つか)いかたの練習(れんしゅう)

つぎの　会話(かいわ)の　下線(かせん)の　ことばを　かえて　練習(れんしゅう)しなさい。

例(れい)：作文(さくぶん) (composition)、　てつだう (help)

A：この　作文(さくぶん)は　よく　できましたね。

B：じつは　てつだっていただいたのです。

A：そうですか。どなたに。

B：松本先生(まつもとせんせい)に　てつだっていただきました。

A：そうですか。ときどき　てつだっていただくんですか。

B：いいえ、今度(こんど) (this time) だけです。これからは (from now on) てつだってくださらないと　おもいます。

1. 論文(ろんぶん)、　てつだう
2. え (picture)、　てつだう
3. 翻訳(ほんやく) (translation)、　てつだう
4. 論文(ろんぶん)、　見(み)る
5. 翻訳(ほんやく)、　教(おし)える
6. え、　教(おし)える

Tsukaikata-no renshuu

Tsugi-no kaiwa-no kasen-no kotoba-o kaete renshuu-shinasai.

ree : sakubun, tetsudau

A: *Kono sakubun-wa yoku dekimashita-ne.*

B: *Jitsu-wa tetsudatte-itadaita-no-desu.*

A: *Soo-desu-ka. Donata-ni.*

B: *Matsumoto-sensee-ni tetsudatte-itadakimashita.*

A: *Soo-desu-ka. Tokidoki tetsudatte-itadaku-n-desu-ka.*

B: *Iie, kondo-dake-desu. Korekara-wa tetsudatte-kudasaranai-to omoimasu.*

1. *ronbun, tetsudau*
2. *e, tetsudau*
3. *hon'yaku, tetsudau*
4. *ronbun, miru*
5. *hon'yaku, oshieru*
6. *e, oshieru*

III. …て{もらえ / いただけ}ませんか　III. . . .te {-morae / -itadake} masen-ka

形の練習

「…てもらえませんか」を 「…て-いただけませんか」に かえなさい。

例：見てもらえませんか→見ていただけませんか。

1. なおして(correct)もらえませんか
2. てつだってもらえませんか
3. 地図を 書いてもらえませんか
4. とどけて(deliver)もらえませんか
5. おくってもらえませんか
6. 教えてもらえませんか
7. 来てもらえませんか
8. やめてもらえませんか

Katachi-no renshuu

. . . te-moraemasen-ka'-o . . . te-itadakemasen-ka'-ni kaenasai.

ree : mite-moraemasen-ka → Mite-itadakemasen-ka.

1. *naoshite-moraemasen-ka*
2. *tetsudatte-moraemasen-ka*
3. *chizu-o kaite-moraemasen-ka*
4. *todokete-moraemasen-ka*
5. *okutte-moraemasen-ka*
6. *oshiete-moraemasen-ka*
7. *kite-moraemasen-ka*
8. *yamete-moremasen-ka*

IV. …たり　…たり　IV. *. . .tari . . .tari*

形の練習

つぎの ことばを 使って 文を つくりなさい。

例：新聞を 読む、テレビを 見る

Katachi-no renshuu

Tsugi-no kotoba-o tsukatte bun-o tsukurinasai. (Make sentences using the following words.)

ree : shinbun-o yomu, terebi-o miru

→新聞(しんぶん)を　読(よ)んだり、テレビ(てれび)を　見(み)たり　しています。	→*Shinbun-o yondari, terebi-o mitari shite-imasu.*
1．お茶(ちゃ)を　のむ、おかしを　たべる	1．*ocha-o nomu, okashi-o taberu*
2．本(ほん)を　読(よ)む、字引(じびき)を　ひく	2．*hon-o yomu, jibiki-o hiku*
3．料理(りょうり)を　つくる、お茶(ちゃ)を　いれる	3．*ryoori-o tsukuru, ocha-o ireru*
4．ストーブ(すとーぶ)を　つける、おふろを　わかす	4．*sutoobu-o tsukeru, ofuro-o wakasu*
5．掃除(そうじ) (cleaning) を　する、せんたく (washing) を　する	5．*sooji-o suru, sentaku-o suru*
6．話(はなし)を　する、うたを　うたう	6．*hanashi-o suru, uta-o utau*
7．論文(ろんぶん)を　書(か)く、翻訳(ほんやく)を　する	7．*ronbun-o kaku, hon'yaku-o suru*
8．野球(やきゅう)を　やる、水泳(すいえい)を　する	8．*yakyuu-o yaru, suiee-o suru*

発音練習(はつおんれんしゅう)

「ん」に　気(き)を　つけて　練習(れんしゅう)しなさい。

A.

1．	こや	こんや	こんにゃ	こんやく	こんにゃく
2．	はや	はんや	はんにゃ	はんやく	はんにゃく
3．	かや	かんや	かんにゃ	かんやく	かんにゃく
4．	きゆ	きんゆ	きんにゅ	きんゆく	きんにゅく
5．	さよ	さんよ	さんにょ	さんよく	さんにょく

B.　1．ほんや　しんぶんを　　2．ふとん (bedding)や　ボタン(ぼたん)(button) を

3．パン(ぱん) (bread) や　うどん (noodle) を　　4．かばんや　ふとんを

5．ちゃわんや　ナプキン(なぷきん) (napkin)を　　6．しんぶんや　しゃしんを

C.　下線の　ところに　Bの　ことばを　入れて　練習しなさい。

例：きょうは　ひまだったので、ほんや　しんぶんを　買いに　行きました。

読む練習

ジョンソンの日記

12月3日　このあいだ母がセーター(1)をおくってくれた。自分(2)であんだ(3)のだそうだ。大きさもちょうど(4)いいし、とてもあたたかい(5)。日本から母になにかおくりたいけど、女のものはよくわからない。きょうみちこさんにその話をしたら、今度の日曜にいっしょにデパート(6)に行ってくれると言った。そのときなにかいいものをえらんでもらおう(7)。

(1) sweater　(2) by herself　(3) knit　(4) exactly　(5) warm　(6) department store　(7) I'll ask her to choose

書く練習

つぎの　ひらがなを　練習しなさい。

ら　(ra)

り　(ri)

る　(ru)

れ　(re)

ろ　(ro)

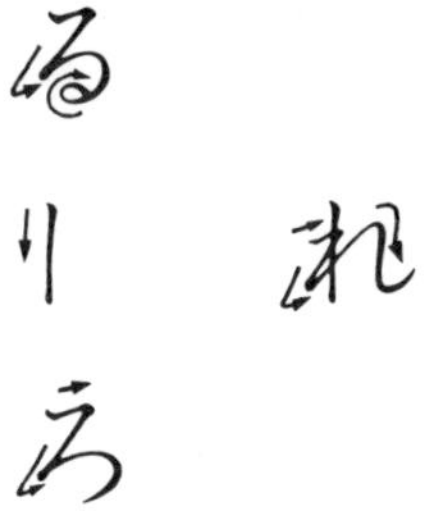

聞(き)く練習(れんしゅう)

テープ(てーぷ)の　会話(かいわ)を　聞(き)いて　つぎの　質問(しつもん)に　こたえなさい。

1. 男(おとこ)の人(ひと)は　なんの　パーティ(ぱーてぃ)に　来(き)てもらいたいと　言(い)いましたか。
2. その　大学(だいがく)の　歴史(れきし)(history)は　何年(なんねん)ぐらいですか。
3. パーティ(ぱーてぃ)では　みんなが　どんな　ことを　しますか。
4. 男(おとこ)の人(ひと)は　女(おんな)の人(ひと)を　むかえに　行(い)きますか。
5. どうして　むかえに　行(い)かなくても　いいのですか。
6. 川口(かわぐち)さんは　なぜ　大学(だいがく)の　ある　ところを　知(し)っているのですか。
7. 川口(かわぐち)さんは　女(おんな)の人(ひと)の　ともだちでしょうか、先生(せんせい)でしょうか。
8. なぜ　そう　おもいますか。

Supplementary Pronunciation Practice (2)

Listen to the tape and practice saying the following words and phrases, paying attention to nasalized sounds and voiceless sounds (cf. viii).

A. (○ indicates a nasalized sound.)

1. *higai*
2. *tegami*
3. *isogashii*
4. *agatte-kudasai*
5. *are-ga ii*
6. *kochiragawa-niwa*
7. *arigatoo-gozaimasu*
8. *soo omoimasu-ga*
9. *gakusee-ga imasu*
10. *kigyoo*
11. *sono-tsugi-ni*
12. *isogu-n-desu-ka*
13. *massugu*
14. *okagesama-de*
15. *raigetsu*
16. *ie-ga sangen-mo*
17. *nihongo-de*
18. *hachiji-goro*
19. *donna oshigoto-desu-ka*
20. *gosatsu-gurai*

B. (○ indicates a voiceless sound.)

1. *nanji-desu-ka*
2. *rokuji-desu*
3. *okimasu*
4. *okimasu-ka*
5. *hito*
6. *shitsuree-shimasu*
7. *furimashita-nee*
8. *ikimasen-deshita*
9. *yomimashita*
10. *hirokute kiree-deshita*
11. *isogashii-desu-ka*
12. *tsutsunde-kudasai*
13. *tsukemashoo*
14. *kite-kudasai*
15. *doozo yoroshiku*
16. *tsutomete-imasu*
17. *kippu*
18. *kikai*
19. *takusan*
20. *Michiko-san*
21. *sukoshi*
22. *shitte-iru*
23. *tashika-ni*
24. *kissaten*
25. *doo shita-n-desu-ka*
26. *shikata-ga nai*
27. *okusan*
28. *daisuki-desu*
29. *chikaku-deshita*
30. *Yamashita-san*

(All of the words and phrases in this practice have already appeared in this book.)

第二十二課(だいにじゅうにか)　おにもつ　お持(も)ちしましょう

Dialogue

（一） (A conversation between Mr. and Mrs. Takahashi, Johnson's landlord and landlady)

夫(おっと)：　きょう　だれか　来(き)た？

妻(つま)：　べつに　だれも…ああ、あなたが　出(で)てから　すぐ　ジョンソン(じょんそん)さんが　来(き)ました。日本語(にほんご)で　手紙(てがみ)を　書(か)いたんだけど、なおしてもらいたいと　言(い)って。

夫(おっと)：　それで、なおしてあげた？

妻(つま)：　ええ。季節(きせつ)の　あいさつの　ことばなんかを　教(おし)えてあげました。

夫(おっと)：　そう。

妻(つま)：　正夫(まさお)が　ほしがっていた　本(ほん)、　買(か)ってきてくださった？

夫(おっと)：　うん、買(か)ってきたよ。ほら。

妻(つま)：　今夜(こんや)は　もう　ねているから、あしたの　朝(あさ)　わたしてやりましょう。

（二）(A conversation between a student, Yamashita, and Professor Kawakami)

山下(やました)：　先生(せんせい)、おにもつ　おもそうですね。お持(も)ちしましょう。

川上(かわかみ)：　ありがとう。じゃ、たのみます。

山下(やました)：　あ、そこ、あぶないですよ。

川上(かわかみ)：　どうも。

山下(やました)：　先生(せんせい)、このあいだ　おかりした　本(ほん)、いつ　おかえしすれば　いいでしょうか。

川上(かわかみ)： ああ、あれは べつに いそがないから、いつでも都合(つごう)の いい とき 家(うち)へ 持(も)ってきてくれませんか。

山下(やました)： はい。

川上(かわかみ)： わたしが るすだったら、家(うち)のものに わたしてくれればいいですよ。

山下(やました)： はい。じゃ、近(ちか)いうちに 持(も)ってあがります。

川上(かわかみ)： ここで タクシー(たくしー)を ひろうから、もう けっこうですよ。どうも ありがとう。

山下(やました)： 失礼(しつれい)します。

Dialogue Lesson 22 — *Dai-nijuunika*

MAY I CARRY YOUR LUGGAGE? — *O-NIMOTSU O-MOCHI-SHIMASHOO*

I.

Husband: Did anyone come around today?

Otto: Kyoo dareka kita?

Wife: No, no one in particular... oh, Mr. Johnson came soon after you left. He said he wanted me to correct a letter he'd written in Japanese.

Tsuma: Betsu-ni daremo...aa, anata-ga dete-kara sugu Jonson-san-ga kimashita. Nihongo-de tegami-o kaita-n-da-kedo, naoshite-moraitai-to itte.

H: And did you correct it for him?

O: Sorede, naoshite-ageta?

W: Yes. I taught him about mentioning the season and things like that.

T: Ee. Kisetsu-no aisatsu-no kotoba-nanka-o oshiete-agemashita.

H: Is that so?

O: Soo.

W: Did you buy the book Masao wanted?

T: Masao-ga hoshigatte-ita hon, katte-kite-kudasatta?

H: Yes. Here.

O: Un, katte-kita-yo. Hora.

W: He's already asleep tonight, so I'll give it to him tomorrow morning.

T: Kon'ya-wa moo nete-iru-kara, ashita-no asa watashite-yarimashoo.

II.	II.
Yamashita: I see you're carrying something heavy, Professor Kawakami. May I carry it for you?	*Yamashita: Sensee, o-nimotsu omosoo-desu-ne. O-mochi-shimashoo.*
Kawakami: Thank you.	*Kawakami: Arigatoo. Ja, tanomimasu.*
Y: Be careful there.	*Y: A, soko, abunai-desu-yo.*
K: Thanks.	*K: Doomo.*
Y: When should I return the book I borrowed from you the other day?	*Y: Sensee, kono-aida o-kari-shita hon, itsu o-kaeshi-sureba ii-deshoo-ka.*
K: I won't need it any time soon. Bring it to my house whenever it suits you.	*K: Aa, are-wa betsu-ni isoganai-kara, itsudemo tsugoo-no ii toki uchi-e motte-kite-kuremasen-ka.*
Y: I will.	*Y: Hai.*
K: If I'm out, just hand it to anyone in the family.	*K: Watashi-ga rusu-dattara, uchi-no-mono-ni watashite-kurereba ii-desu-yo.*
Y: Yes. I'll bring it soon.	*Y: Hai. Ja, chikai-uchi-ni motte-agarimasu.*
K: I'll catch a taxi here. Thank you for carrying my bag.	*K: Koko-de takushii-o hirou-kara, moo kekkoo-desu-yo. Doomo arigatoo.*
Y: Good-bye.	*Y: Shitsuree-shimasu.*

Explanation

(In this lesson you will learn more expressions used for doing and receiving favors. We will also cover humble expressions used when one does something for a superior.)

べつに　だれも…　**line 2**

Betsu-ni daremo...

betsu-ni	(not) particularly

Line 2, if completed, would read *daremo kimasen-deshita.*

あなたが　出(で)てから　すぐ　ジョンソン(じょんそん)さんが　来(き)ました。　**lines 2-3**

Anata-ga dete-kara sugu Jonson-san-ga kimashita.

dete-kara	after you left (dict. *deru*)

Anata is often used by a wife to call her husband.

The *-te* form plus *-kara* is used in the following way.

ex. *Tegami-o kaite-kara dekakemasu.* (I'll go out after I write a letter.)

Tegami-o kaite-kara dekakemashita. (I went out after I wrote a letter.)

日本語(にほんご)で　手紙(てがみ)を　書(か)いたんだけど、なおしてもらいたいと　言(い)って。　**lines 3-4**

Nihongo-de tegami-o kaita-n-da-kedo, naoshite-moraitai-to itte.

naoshite-moraitai-to itte	saying that he wants me to correct it (dict. *naosu*)

'...*kedo* (=*keredo*)' in *kaita-n-da-kedo* implies that he tried writing in Japanese but he was not sure if he did well.

それで、なおしてあげた？　**line 5**

Sorede, naoshite-ageta?

sorede	and
naoshite-ageta?	did you correct it for him? (dict. *naosu*)

'...*te-ageru*' means that someone does something for his equal or for his inferior.

ええ。季節(きせつ)の　あいさつの　ことばなんかを　教(おし)えてあげました。　**lines 6-7**

Ee. Kisetsu-no aisatsu-no kotoba-nanka-o oshiete-agemashita.

kotoba	word; phrase
aisatsu-no kotoba	how to greet
... nanka-o	...and so forth
oshiete-agemashita	I showed him (dict. *oshieru*)

正夫(まさお)が　ほしがっていた　本(ほん)、買(か)ってきてくださった？ **line 9**

Masao-ga hoshigatte-ita hon, katte-kite-kudasatta?

Masao	man's name (*here,* the couple's son's name)
hoshigatte-ita	he wanted (dict. *hoshigaru,* from *hoshii* cf. Lesson 15)
katte-kite-kudasatta?	did you buy it for him?

Katte-kite-kudasatta? literally means 'did you do me the favor of buying it and bringing it home?' '…*te-kudasaru*' means that a superior does something, usually for the speaker. It can also be used when the favor is done for a member of one's family.

'…*te-kuru*' is used to emphasize coming back to the original location.

ex. (When someone knocks on the door) *Chotto mite-kimashoo.* (I'll go and see who it is.)

Sugu kaette-kimasu. (I'll be back soon.)

うん、買(か)ってきたよ。ほら。 **line 10**

Un, katte-kita-yo. Hora.

un	yes (familiar)
hora	here; look

今夜(こんや)は　もう　ねているから、あしたの　朝(あさ)　わたしてやりましょう。**lines 11-12**

Kon'ya-wa moo nete-iru-kara, ashita-no asa watashite-yarimashoo.

kon'ya	this evening (=*konban*)
watashite-yarimashoo	I'll hand it over to him (dict. *watasu*)

'…*te-yaru*' is used when someone does something for an inferior.

ex. *Kodomo-o doobutsuen-ni tsurete-itte-yarimashita.* (I took my child to the zoo.)

Men also use it in familiar speech to refer to doing a favor for an equal. (Women say … *te-ageru*)

ex. *Kore, kimi-ni kashite-yaru-yo.* (I'll lend this to you.)

先生、おにもつ　おもそうですね。お持ちしましょう。 **line 13**

Sensee, o-nimotsu omosoo-desu-ne. O-mochi-shimashoo.

o-nimotsu	what you have with you (*lit.* your luggage)
omosoo-desu-ne	it looks heavy (dict. *omoi,* 'heavy') (cf. *yosasoo,* Lesson 13)
o-mochi-shimashoo	I'll carry it for you (dict. *motsu*)

O-mochi-suru is the humble form derived from *motsu.* This form is made by adding *o-* before and *-suru* after the stem of the verb.

ex. *todokeru* (deliver) — *o-todoke-suru*

watasu — *o-watashi-suru; miseru* — *o-mise-suru*

Otaku-e o-todoke-shimashoo-ka. (Shall I deliver it to your house?)

Sensee-ni o-watashi-shimashita. (I handed it over to the teacher.)

どうも。 **line 16**

Doomo.

Doomo is the first part of *Doomo arigatoo* or *Doomo sumimasen.* It is used alone as an expression of thanks or apology.

先生、このあいだ　おかりした　本、いつ　おかえしすれば　いいでしょうか。

Sensee, kono-aida o-kari-shita hon, itsu o-kaeshi-sureba ii-deshoo-ka.

lines 17-18

o-kari-shita	I borrowed from you (humble)
o-kaeshi-suru	I return it to you (humble)
itsu . . . sureba ii-deshoo-ka	when can I . . . ?

O-kari-suru and *o-kaeshi-suru* are the humble forms of *kariru* and *kaesu,* respectively.

'…*sureba ii-deshoo-ka*'. (or, *-desu-ka*) is used with question words to ask for instruction.

ex. *Kono kanji-wa doo kakeba ii-deshoo-ka.* (How should I write this kanji?)

Nanji-ni kureba ii-deshoo-ka. (What time shall I come?)

あれは　べつに　いそがないから、いつでも　都合(つごう)の　いい　とき　家(うち)へ
Are-wa betsu-ni isoganai-kara, itsudemo tsugoo-no ii toki uchi-e
持(も)ってきてくれませんか。　**lines 19-20**
motte-kite-kuremasen-ka.

isoganai	I'm not in a hurry (dict. *isogu*)
tsugoo	convenience
tsugoo-no ii toki	when it's convenient for you
motte-kite-kuremasen-ka	won't you bring it?(dict. *motte-kuru*)

'…*te-kuremasen-ka*' is used to ask an equal or inferior to do one a favor. To ask a superior for a favor, use … *te-kudasaimasen-ka.*

わたしが　るすだったら、家(うち)のものに　わたしてくれれば　いいですよ。
Watashi-ga rusu-dattara, uchi-no-mono-ni watashite-kurereba ii-desu-yo.
lines 22-23

rusu-dattara	if I'm out; if I'm not home
uchi-no-mono	one of my family members
watashite-kurereba ii	you can hand it (*lit.* if you hand it, it's all right)

Ra added to the plain past form of a verb or adjective indicates condition, as you learned in Lesson 20 (*agetara doo-desu-ka*). In *rusu-dattara, -ra* is added to *-datta,* the plain past form of *-desu.*

ex. *Ii tenki-dattara doraibu-ni ikimashoo.* (If the weather is good, let's go driving.)

Uchi-no-mono is a humble term used to refer to members of one's own family. When speaking about a member of someone else's family, use *uchi-no-hito,* or more politely, *o-uchi-no-kata.*

じゃ、近(ちか)いうちに　持(も)ってあがります。　**line 24**
Ja, chikai-uchi-ni motte-agarimasu.

chikai-uchi-ni	some time in the near future
motte-agarimasu	I'll bring it (humble)

The verb *agaru* is used as a humble equivalent of *iku,* when it means 'to visit someone.'

ex. *Sensee-no otaku-ewa mada agatta koto-ga arimasen.* (I have never visited the Professor.)

ここで タクシー(たくしー)を ひろうから、もう けっこうですよ。 **lines 25-26**

Koko-de takushii-o hirou-kara, moo kekkoo-desu-yo.

takushii-o hirou I'll catch a taxi (*lit.* pick up a taxi)

moo kekkoo-desu thank you (*lit.* I don't need your help any more)

Moo kekkoo-desu is also used in the following way.

ex. A: *Okashi-o moo sukoshi ikaga-desu-ka.* (Please have more candy.)

B: *Hai, demo moo kekkoo-desu.* (No, thank you. I've had plenty.)

練習(れんしゅう) — *Renshuu*

I. …てあげる — I. *. . . te-ageru*

形(かたち)の練習(れんしゅう) — *Katachi-no renshuu*

{ }の なかの ことばを かえて 練習(れんしゅう)しなさい。

{ }-no naka-no kotoba-o kaete renshuu-shinasai.

A. (わたしは) { みちこさん / 山下(やました)さん / ともだち / となり(next door)の 人(ひと) } に

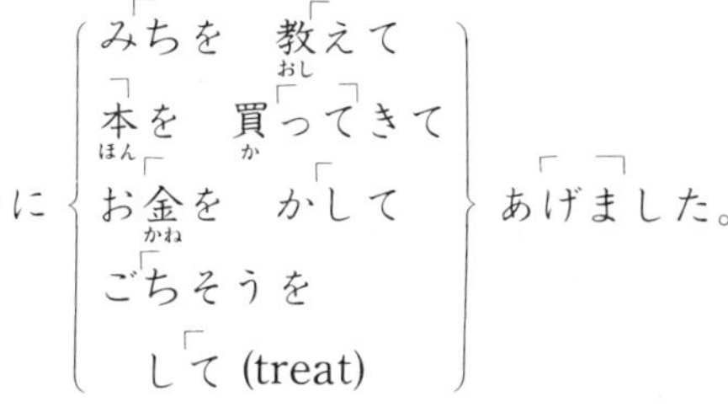

{ みちを 教(おし)えて / 本(ほん)を 買(か)ってきて / お金(かね)を かして / ごちそうを して (treat) } あげました。

A. *(Watashi-wa) { Michiko-san / Yamashita-san / tomodachi / tonari-no hito } -ni { michi-o oshiete / hon-o katte-kite / okane-o kashite / gochisoo-o shite } -agemashita.*

B.
みちこさんの 勉強(べんきょう)
山下(やました)さんの 作文(さくぶん)
ともだちの 宿題(しゅくだい) (homework)
となりの 人(ひと)の 仕事(しごと)
を てつだってあげました。

B.
Michiko-san-no benkyoo
Yamashita-san-no sakubun
Tomodachi-no shukudai
Tonari-no hito-no shigoto
-o tetsudatte-agemasnita.

C.
みちこさんの にもつを 持(も)って
山下(やました)さんの 翻訳(ほんやく)を なおして
ともだちの 宿題(しゅくだい)を 見(み)て
となりの 人(ひと)の 手紙(てがみ)を だして
あげました。

C.
Michiko-san-no nimotsu-o motte
Yamashita-san-no hon'yaku-o naoshite
Tomodachi-no shukudai-o mite
Tonari-no hito-no tegami-o dashite
-agemashita.

使(つか)いかたの練習(れんしゅう)

Tsukaikata-no renshuu

つぎの 会話(かいわ)の 下線(かせん)の ことばを かえて 練習(れんしゅう)しなさい。

Tsugi-no kaiwa-no kasen-no kotoba-o kaete renshuu-shinasai.

例(れい)：手紙(てがみ)を なおす

ree : tegami-o naosu

A：きょう だれか 来(き)ましたか。
B：高橋(たかはし)さんが 来(き)ました。手紙(てがみ)を なおしてもらいたいと 言(い)って。
A：それで なおしてあげたんですか。
B：ええ、なおしてあげました。

A: *Kyoo dareka kimashita-ka.*
B: *Takahashi-san-ga kimashita. Tegami-o naoshite-moraitai-to itte.*
A: *Sorede naoshite-ageta-n-desu-ka.*
B: *Ee, naoshite-agemashita.*

1. 作文を　なおす
2. 本を　かす
3. 英語 (English) を　教える
4. 手紙を　読む
5. 話を　聞く
6. 仕事を　てつだう

II.…てやる

形の練習

例に　ならって (as shown in the example) 練習しなさい。

例：見せる→おとうとが　見せてもらいたいと　言ったので、見せてやりました。

1. 教える　　2. なおす
3. わたす　　4. 読む
5. 持つ　　6. かす
7. かえす　　8. 買う

使いかたの練習

つぎの　会話の　下線の　ことばを　かえて　練習しなさい。

例：本を　かす

A：きょう　だれか　来ましたか。
B：ええ、おとうとが　来ました。
A：そうですか。おとうとさんが？

1. *sakubun-o naosu*
2. *hon-o kasu*
3. *eego-o oshieru*
4. *tegami-o yomu*
5. *hanashi-o kiku*
6. *shigoto-o tetsudau*

II. *. . . te-yaru*

Katachi-no renshuu

Ree-ni naratte renshuu-shinasai.

ree : miseru→Otooto-ga misete-moraitai-to itta-node, misete-yarimashita.

1. *oshieru*　　2. *naosu*
3. *watasu*　　4. *yomu*
5. *motsu*　　6. *kasu*
7. *kaesu*　　8. *kau*

Tsukaikata-no renshuu

Tsugi-no kaiwa-no kasen-no kotoba-o kaete renshuu-shinasai.

ree : hon-o kasu

A: *Kyoo dareka kimashita-ka.*
B: *Ee, otooto-ga kimashita.*
A: *Soo-desu-ka. Otooto-san-ga?*

B：ええ、本を　かしてもらいたい-と　言って。

A：それで、かしてあげたんですね。

B：ええ、かしてやりました。

1. お金を　かす
2. 仕事を　てつだう
3. 写真を　見せる
4. カメラを　なおす
5. 道を　教える
6. 手紙を　翻訳する

B: *Ee, hon-o kashite-moraitai-to itte.*

A: *Sorede, kashite-ageta-n-desu-ne.*

B: *Ee, kashite-yarimashita.*

1. *okane-o kasu*
2. *shigoto-o tetsudau*
3. *shashin-o miseru*
4. *kamera-o naosu*
5. *michi-o oshieru*
6. *tegami-o hon'yaku-suru*

III. お…する

形の練習

例に　ならって　つぎの　ことば-を　かえなさい。

例：かりました—おかりしました

1. 持ちました
2. かえしました
3. わたします
4. まちます
5. はらいましょう
6. おくりましょう
7. とどけましょうか
8. かしましょうか

III. *o. . . suru*

Katachi-no renshuu

Ree-ni naratte tsugi-no kotoba-o kaenasai.

ree : karimashita — o-kari-shi-mashita

1. *mochimashia*
2. *kaeshimashita*
3. *watashimasu*
4. *machimasu*
5. *haraimashoo*
6. *okurimashoo*
7. *todokemashoo-ka*
8. *kashimashoo-ka*

使(つか)いかたの練習(れんしゅう)

つぎの　会話(かいわ)の　下線(かせん)の　ことばを　かえて　練習(れんしゅう)しなさい。

(A)

例(れい)：ビール(びーる)、とどける

A：ビール(びーる)、どう　しましょうか。

B：そうですねえ…

A：おとどけしましょうか。

B：ええ、そう　してください。すみませんね。

A：いいえ。いつ　おとどけすれば　いいでしょう。

B：あしたの　朝(あさ)　とどけていただけますか。

A：はい。じゃ、あしたの　朝(あさ)　おとどけします。

1．かさ、かえす

2．ガソリン代(がそりんだい)、はらう

3．にもつ、おくる

4．写真(しゃしん)、とどける

5．参考書(さんこうしょ)、かえす

(B)

例(れい)：家内(かない)、おくさん

A：おたくへ　おとどけしましょうか。

Tsukaikata-no renshuu

Tsugi-no kaiwa-no kasen-no kotoba-o kaete renshuu-shinasai.

(A)

ree : biiru, todokeru

A: *Biiru, doo shimashoo-ka.*

B: *Soo-desu-nee . . .*

A: *O-todoke-shimashoo-ka.*

B: *Ee, soo shite-kudasai. Sumimasen-ne.*

A: *Iie. Itsu o-todoke-sureba ii-deshoo.*

B: *Ashita-no asa todokete-itadakemasu-ka.*

A: *Hai. Ja, ashita-no asa o-todoke-shimasu.*

1. *kasa, kaesu*

2. *gasorin-dai, harau*

3. *nimotsu, okuru*

4. *shashin, todokeru*

5. *sankoosho, kaesu*

(B)

ree : kanai, okusan

A: *Otaku-e o-todoke-shimashoo-ka.*

B：ええ、そう　してください。

A：おるすだったら、どうしましょう。

B：家内(かない)に　わたしてください。

A：はい。じゃ、おくさんに　おわたしします。

1．父(ちち)、お父(とう)さん
2．いもうと、いもうとさん
3．家(うち)のもの、お家(うち)のかた
4．兄(あに)、おにいさん
5．母(はは)、お母(かあ)さん
6．おとうと、おとうとさん
7．だれか、どなたか(someone—polite)
8．あね、おねえさん

B: *Ee, soo shite-kudasai.*

A: *O-rusu-dattara, doo shimashoo.*

B: *Kanai-ni watashite-kudasai.*

A: *Hai. Ja, okusan-ni o-watashi-shimasu.*

1．*chichi, otoosan*
2．*imooto, imooto-san*
3．*uchi-no-mono, o-uchi-no-kata*
4．*ani, oniisan*
5．*haha, okaasan*
6．*otooto, otooto-san*
7．*dareka, donataka*
8．*ane, oneesan*

IV. …だったら

IV. *. . . dattara*

形(かたち)の練習(れんしゅう)

例(れい)に　ならって　練習(れんしゅう)しなさい。

(A)

例(れい)：雨(あめ)→雨(あめ)だったら　やめましょう。

1．いい　天気(てんき)　　2．るす
3．病気(びょうき)　　4．へた (not skillful)
5．むずかしい　仕事(しごと)
6．むずかしそう

Katachi-no renshuu

Ree-ni naratte renshuu-shinasai.

(A)

ree : ame → Ame-dattara yamemashoo.

1．*ii tenki*　　2．*rusu*
3．*byooki*　　4．*heta*
5．*muzukashii shigoto*
6．*muzukashisoo*

(B)

例：ねている→ねていたら　やめましょう。

1．かれが　来る
2．雨が　ふる
3．さむく　なる
4．つかれる
5．おそく　なる
6．お金が　かかる (it costs)

(B)

ree : nete-iru → Nete-itara yamemashoo.

1．*kare-ga kuru*
2．*ame-ga furu*
3．*samuku naru*
4．*tsukareru*
5．*osoku naru*
6．*okane-ga kakaru*

(C)

例：いそがしい→いそがしかったら　やめましょう。

1．さむい
2．天気が　わるい (bad)
3．おもしろく　ない
4．じょうず (skillful) じゃ　ない
5．かれが　来ない
6．お金が　たりない

(C)

ree : isogashii → Isogashikattara yamemashoo.

1．*samui*
2．*tenki-ga warui*
3．*omoshiroku nai*
4．*joozu-ja nai*
5．*kare-ga konai*
6．*okane-ga tarinai*

使いかたの練習

つぎの　会話の　下線の　ことばを　かえて　練習しなさい。

例：雨

A：あしたは　▲雨かも　しれませんね。
B：そうですね。

Tsukaikata-no renshuu

Tsugi-no kaiwa-no kasen-no kotoba-o kaete renshuu-shinasai.

ree : ame

A: *Ashita-wa ame-kamo shiremasen-ne.*
B: *Soo-desu-ne.*

A：雨だったら　どう　しましょう。 A: *Ame-dattara doo shimashoo.*

B：雨だったら　やめましょうよ。 B: *Ame-dattara yamemashoo-yo.*

A：そうですか。ざんねんですね。 A: *Soo-desu-ka. Zannen-desu-ne.*

B：しかたが　ありませんよ。 B: *Shikata-ga arimasen-yo.*

1．雨が　ふる　2．雪 (snow)　1．*ame-ga furu*　2．*yuki*

3．るす　4．かれが　来ない　3．*rusu*　4．*kare-ga konai*

5．さむく　なる　5．*samuku naru*

6．天気が　わるい　6．*tenki-ga warui*

発音練習

「ん」に　気を　つけて　練習しなさい。

A.　1．あわ　あんわ　あんうわ　あんうんわ

2．かんち　かんし　かんちん　かんしん

3．かんつ　かんす　かんつん　かんすん

4．かんさ　かんさん　5．かんせ　かんせん

6．かんそ　かんそん

B.　1．ほんや、ほん　2．かばんや、かばん　3．パンや、パン

4．ふとんや、ふとん　5．ちゃわんや、ちゃわん　6．うどんや、うどん

C.　下線の　ところに　Bの　ことばを　入れて　練習しなさい。

例：あの、ほんやへ　行って　ほんを　買ってきてくださいませんか。

読む練習

山下の手紙　（高校のときの先生にだす手紙）

お元気でいらっしゃいますか。* おかげさまでぼくは元気で、毎日大学で勉

強しています。きょう、へやを掃除(そうじ)していたら(1)、先生の本が出(で)てきました(2)。三年(さんねん)もまえにおかりして、おかえしするのをわすれていたのです。どうもながいあいだ(3)すみませんでした。これから郵便局(ゆうびんきょく)へ行っておおくりします。おたくが近ければ(4)持ってあがるのですが… これからさむくなりますから、先生どうぞおからだをお大事(だいじ)に。

(1) when I was cleaning (2) came out (3) for a long time (4) if it is near

* '... *de irasshaimasu-ka*' is a polite equivalent of '... *desu-ka.*'

ex. *Yamada-sensee-de irasshaimasu-ka.* (Are you Prof. Yamada?)

書(か)く練習(れんしゅう)

つぎの　ひらがなを　練習(れんしゅう)しなさい。

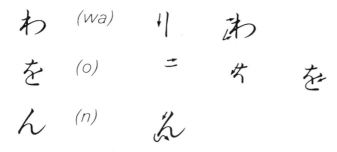

わ (wa)

を (o)

ん (n)

聞(き)く練習(れんしゅう)

テープ(てーぷ)の　会話(かいわ)を　聞(き)いて　質問(しつもん)に　こたえなさい。

（あたらしい　ことば——あずかる to keep for someone）

1. これは　だれと　だれの　会話(かいわ)ですか。
2. 男(おとこ)の人(ひと)は　斎藤(さいとう)さんの　家(うち)へ　なにを　しに　来(き)たのですか。
3. 斎藤(さいとう)さんの　主人(しゅじん)は　どんな　仕事(しごと)を　している　人(ひと)ですか。
4. 男(おとこ)の人(ひと)は　電話(でんわ)を　してから　来(き)たのですか。
5. 女(おんな)の人(ひと)は　いつまで　かさを　あずかる (keep)と　言(い)いましたか。

第二十三課（だいにじゅうさんか）　ぼくに　やらせてください

Dialogue

（一）（Conversation between Michiko and her mother)

母（はは）：　みちこさん。

みちこ：　はい。

母（はは）：　いま　勉強（べんきょう）？

みちこ：　いいえ。テレビ（てれび）を　見（み）てたの。

母（はは）：　じゃ、ちょっと　おつかいに　行（い）ってきてくれない？

みちこ：　はい。どこへ。

母（はは）：　やおやさん。ねぎを　三本（さんぼん）と　キャベツ（きゃべつ）を　ひとつ　買（か）ってきて。

みちこ：　はい。行（い）ってきます。

(Johnson comes soon after Michiko leaves.)

ジョンソン（じょんそん）：　みちこさん、まだ　学校（がっこう）ですか。

母（はは）：　いいえ。かえってきましたけど、さっき　おつかいに　行（い）かせたんです。もう　かえる　ころですから、あがって　まっててください。

ジョンソン（じょんそん）：　はい。じゃ、またせていただきます。

（二）（A section chief and a few members of his section discussing business)

課長（かちょう）：　そんな　わけで、だれかに　調査（ちょうさ）してもらいたいんだが。

鈴木（すずき）：　ぜひ　ぼくに　やらせてください。

課長（かちょう）：　でも、君（きみ）は　ほかの　仕事（しごと）が　あって　いそがしいんじゃ　ないか。

鈴木(すずき)：　いいえ、あちらは　たいした　こと　ありません。きょうじゅうに　かたづけます。

課長(かちょう)：　そうか。

鈴木(すずき)：　はい。この　仕事(しごと)には　興味(きょうみ)が　あるんです。

課長(かちょう)：　じゃ、鈴木君(すずきくん)に　やってもらおうか。だが、いま　鈴木君(すずきくん)が　やってる　仕事(しごと)の　ほうは、だれかに　てつだってもらわなければ　ならないだろう。

松本(まつもと)：　わたしで　よかったら　おてつだい　させてください。

課長(かちょう)：　じゃ、松本君(まつもとくん)、たのむよ。

Dialogue Lesson 23

LET ME DO IT, PLEASE

I.

Mother: Michiko!

Michiko: Yes, Mom.

Mo: Are you studying now?

Mi: No, I've been watching TV.

Mo: Then, will you go on an errand for me?

Mi: Yes. Where to?

Mo: To the vegetable store. Go and buy three green onion stalks and a cabbage, will you?

Mi: All right, Mom. Bye!

Johnson: Has Michiko come back from school yet?

Mo: Yes, she came home, but I had her go shopping for me a while ago. It's about time she came back. Please come in and wait.

J: Thank you. I will.

Dai-nijuusanka

BOKU-NI YARASETE KUDASAI

I.

Haha: Michiko-san.

Michiko: Hai.

H: Ima benkyoo?

M: Iie. Terebi-o mite-ta-no.

H: Ja, chotto otsukai-ni itte-kite-kurenai?

M: Hai. Doko-e.

H: Yaoya-san. Negi-o sanbon-to kyabetsu-o hitotsu katte-kite.

M: Hai. Itte-kimasu.

Jonson: Michiko-san, mada gakkoo-desu-ka.

H: Iie. Kaette-kimashita-kedo, sakki o-tsukai-ni ikaseta-n-desu. Moo kaeru koro-desu-kara, agatte matte-te-kudasai.

J: Hai. Ja, matasete-itadakimasu.

II.

Section Chief: So, I want someone to do the investigation.

Suzuki: Let me do it, by all means.

S.C.: But you're busy with other work, aren't you?

Su: No, it isn't much. I can finish it up today.

S.C.: Can you?

Su: Yes. I'm very interested in this work.

S.C.: Then I'll have you do it, Suzuki, but I think you must have someone help you with the work you're doing now.

Matsumoto: I'd like to help him, if I may.

S.C.: All right, please help him.

II.

Kachoo: Sonna wake-de, dareka-ni choosa-shite-moraitai-n-daga.

Suzuki: Zehi boku-ni yarasete-kudasai.

K: Demo, kimi-wa hoka-no shigoto-ga atte isogashii-n-ja nai-ka.

S: Iie, achira-wa taishita koto arimasen. Kyoo-juu-ni katazukemasu.

K: Soo-ka.

S: Hai. Kono shigoto-niwa kyoomi-ga aru-n-desu.

K: Ja, Suzuki-kun-ni yatte-moraoo-ka. Daga, ima Suzuki-kun-ga yatte-ru shigoto-no hoo-wa, dareka-ni tetsudatte-morawanakereba naranai-daroo.

Matsumoto: Watashi-de yokattara o-tetsudai sasete-kudasai.

K: Ja, Matsumoto-kun, tanomu-yo.

Explanation

(In this lesson you will learn how the action of having someone do something is expressed and how to ask for permission to do something.)

いいえ。テレビを　見てたの。 **line 4**

Iie. Terebi-o mite-ta-no.

Mite-ta is the contraction of *mite-ita*. The *i* sound of *iru, ite,* and *ita* is often dropped in informal speech.

ex. *Ima nani (-o) shite-ru-no.*=*Ima nani (-o) shite-iru-no.*
Koko-de matte-te-kudasai.=*Koko-de matte-ite-kudasai.*

The particle *-no* in *mite-ta-no* is used by women or children to explain a situation. You can take it as the shortened form of *-no-desu*. Here, *mite-ta-no* is pronounced with a falling intonation. When it is pronounced with a rising intonation, it means a question. Men also use *-no* to ask a question in familiar speech, but they usually do not say ... *no* to explain a situation. (cf. Lesson 14)

じゃ、ちょっと おつかいに 行(い)ってきてくれない？ **line 5**

Ja, chotto otsukai-ni itte-kite-kurenai?

o-tsukai-ni iku	go on an errand (usu. with *o-*)
itte-kite-kurenai?	won't you go for me?

Chotto is often used when asking a favor.

ex. *Chotto onegai-shimasu.* (Will you help me?—*lit.* Please do me a little favor.)

Itte-kuru means 'to go and come back.' cf. *katte-kuru*, Lesson 22.

やおやさん。ねぎを 三本(さんぼん)と キャベツ(きゃべつ)を ひとつ 買(か)ってきて。 **lines 7-8**

Yaoya-san. Negi-o sanbon-to kyabetsu-o hitotsu katte-kite.

yaoya-san	green grocer('s); vegetable store
negi	*negi;* long (green) onion
sanbon	three stalks
kyabetsu	cabbage

After *Yaoya-san*, '... *e itte-kite-kurenai?*' is left out.

Ya is a suffix which means 'a dealer,' or 'a shop.'

ex. *nikuya*—butcher('s); *sakanaya* --fishmonger('s)
kusuriya—pharmacist, pharmacy, drugstore

Hon or *-bon* is a counter used for counting long, thin objects, such as pencils, pens, needles and so on. Such objects are counted in the following way:

ippon, nihon, sanbon, yonhon, gohon, roppon, nanahon, happon, kyuuhon, jippon (the larger numbers are counted using the same set used for minutes.)

Here, the *kudasai* of *katte-kite-kudasai* is left out. This omission is often heard in familiar speech.

ex. *Chotto matte.=Chotto matte-kudasai.*

はい。行ってきます。 **line 9**

Hai. Itte-kimasu.

Itte-kimasu (or more politely, *itte-mairimasu*) is an expression said when leaving the home temporarily, for example, when going to work, school or shopping. Anyone remaining at home says *Itte-irasshai* or *Itte-rasshai* in response. (cf. *tadaima,* Lesson 18)

いいえ。かえってきましたけど、さっき　おつかいに　行かせたんです。

Iie. Kaette-kimashita-kedo, sakki o-tsukai-ni ikaseta-n-desu. **lines 11-12**

sakki	a while ago
ikaseta	I made her go (dict. *iku*)

Ikaseta is derived from *iku.* This form which can be called the causative or the *-seru, -saseru* form means 'someone makes someone do something.' Causative verbs are formed in the following way. For *-u* verbs, add *-seru* to the stem used for plain negative verbs (*-nai* form). For *-ru* verbs the causative ending is *-saseru.*

-u verbs: *iku --ikanai --ikaseru; yomu --yomanai --yomaseru*

-ru verbs: *taberu --tabenai --tabesaseru; yameru --yamenai --yamesaseru*

kuru --konai --kosaseru; suru --shinai --saseru

もう　かえる　ころですから、あがって　まっててください。 **lines 12-13**

Moo kaeru koro-desu-kara, agatte matte-te-kudasai.

kaeru koro	it's about time she came back
agatte	come in and (dict. *agaru*)

はい。じゃ、またせていただきます。 **line 14**

Hai. Ja, matasete-itadakimasu.

matasete-itadakimasu I will wait for her (humble)

This expression shows a different use of the causative form. *Mataseru* is the causative form of *matsu.* Here, the causative form plus

-te-itadaku literally means 'I am given the kindness of permitting me to do something.' The corresponding English expression might be 'with your permission I will do something' or 'since you kindly permit me, I'll go ahead and do something.'

ex. A: *Doozo o-kake-kudasai.* (Please sit down.)
B: *Hai, dewa kakesasete-itadakimasu.* (Thank you. I will.)

The causative form plus *-te-kudasai* or *-te-itadakitai-n-desu-ga* can be used to make a request.

ex. *Sumimasen-ga, kyoo-wa moo kaerasete-kudasai.* (I'm sorry, but I'd like to be excused for today.)
Kono denwa-o chotto tsukawasete-itadakitai-n-desu-ga. (I'd like to use this telephone, if you don't mind.)

そんな　わけで、だれかに　調査(ちょうさ)してもらいたいんだが。 **lines 15-16**
Sonna wake-de, dareka-ni choosa-shite-moraitai-n-da-ga.

sonna wake-de	so; that's why
choosa-shite-moraitai	I want someone to investigate (dict. *choosa-suru*)

ぜひ　ぼくに　やらせてください。 **line 17**
Zehi boku-ni yarasete-kudasai.

zehi	by all means
boku-ni yarasete-kudasai	please let me do it (dict. *yaru*)

The particle *-ni* follows a noun indicating the person who is made to do something.

ex. *Watashi-wa Yamada-kun-ni kono shigoto-o yarasemashita.* (I made Yamada do this work.)
Dare-ni katazukesasemashoo-ka. (Whom shall I have finish it?)

いいえ、あちらは　たいした　こと　ありません。 **line 20**
Iie, achira-wa taishita koto arimasen.

taishita koto(-wa) arimasen	it's not much; it's not very hard

Taishita koto(-wa) nai can be used in the following ways.

ex. A: *Kaze-desu-ka.* (You've caught cold?)

B: *Ee, demo taishita koto-wa arimasen.* (Yes, but it's nothing serious.)

Yuube kinjo-ni kaji-ga arimashita-ga, taishita koto-wa arimasen-deshita. (There was a fire in my neighborhood last night, but it wasn't a big one.)

きょうじゅうに　かたづけます。 **lines 20-21**

Kyoo-juu-ni katazukemasu.

kyoo-juu-ni	by the end of today
katazukemasu	I'll finish it up (dict. *katazukeru*)

Katazukeru is also used to mean 'to tidy up.'

ex. *Chotto o-machi-kudasai. Heya-no naka-o katazukemasu-kara.* (Please wait a moment. I'll tidy up the room.)

この　仕事(しごと)には　興味(きょうみ)が　あるんです。 **line 23**

Kono shigoto-niwa kyoomi-ga aru-n-desu.

... ni kyoomi-ga aru I am interested in ...

だが、いま　鈴木君(すずきくん)が　やってる　仕事(しごと)の　ほうは、だれかに　てつだって-

Daga, ima Suzuki-kun-ga yatte-ru shigoto-no hoo-wa dareka-ni tetsudatte-

もらわなければ　ならないだろう。 **lines 24-26**

morawanakereba naranai-daroo.

daga	but (used by men)
yatte-ru	=*yatte-iru*
... no hoo-wa	as for ....
tetsudatte-morau	have someone help you (dict. *tetsudau*)
... te-morawanakereba naranai	you have to have someone do .... for you

Kun is attached to men's names and shows intimacy. It is used by men when addressing someone the same age or younger.

'*... nakereba naranai*' literally means 'if you don't do it, it won't be good' and corresponds to the English 'must' or 'have to.' This expression is used in the same way as ... *nakute-wa* (or, *-nakucha naranai*), learned in Lesson 20, although it is slightly more formal.

ex. *Mainichi hatarakanakereba narimasen.* (I have to work every day.)
Hikooki-wa juuji-ni deru-kara, kuji-made-ni kuukoo-e ikanakereba naranai. (Since the plane takes off at 10, I have to be at the airport by 9.)

わたしで　よかったら　おてつだい　させてください。 **line 27**

Watashi-de yokattara o-tetsudai sasete-kudasai.

watashi-de yokattara if (you think) I'm good enough (dict. *ii*)
o-tetsudai sasete-kudasai please let me help him

'... *de ii*' means '... will do,' while '... *ga ii*' means '... is positively good.'

ex. Customer: *Hontoo-wa kuroi-no ga ii-n-da-kedo.* (I'd like a black one, really.)
Shopkeeper: *Sumimasen. Kyoo-wa shiroi-no-dake-desu.* (Sorry, I have only white ones today.)
Customer: *Ja, shiroi-no-de ii-desu.* (OK, a white one will do.)

Notice that Matsumoto uses *watashi* while Suzuki uses *boku.* This difference shows the difference in their ages or their relationship to the section chief, whom they are addressing.

Note **On the causative form**

The causative form when used to mean 'make someone do something,' implies that force is involved. Therefore this form is usually reserved for describing situations in which a superior has an inferior do something, for example, when a teacher has pupils do something, a parent makes his child do something, or when an elder sibling makes a younger brother or sister do something. It is also sometimes used when a man makes his wife do something.

練習（れんしゅう）

I. …せる、…させる

形（かたち）の練習（れんしゅう）

(A) つぎの 表（ひょう） (table) を 練習（れんしゅう）しなさい。

あらう (wash) ―あらわせる
つくる―つくらせる
わかす―わかさせる
見（み）る―見（み）させる
みがく (polish) ―みがかせる
すてる(throw away)―すてさせる
たべる―たべさせる
する―させる
かたづける―かたづけさせる

(B) 例（れい）に ならって かえなさい。

例（れい）：こどもが 掃除（そうじ）を します
　→こどもに 掃除（そうじ）を させます。

1. おとうとが おふろを わかします
2. いもうとが ちゃわんを あらいます
3. 家内（かない）が 朝（あさ）ごはん (breakfast) を つくります

Renshuu

I. *---seru, ---saseru*

Katachi-no renshuu

(A) *Tsugi-no hyoo-o renshuu-shinasai.*

arau — arawaseru
tsukuru—tsukuraseru
wakasu — wakasaseru
miru — misaseru
migaku — migakaseru
suteru — sutesaseru
taberu — tabesaseru
suru — saseru
katazukeru — katazukesaseru

(B) *Ree-ni naratte kaenasai.*

ree : kodomo-ga sooji-o shimasu
　→ *Kodomo-ni sooji-o sasemasu*

1. *otooto-ga ofuro-o wakashimasu*
2. *imooto-ga chawan-o araimasu*
3. *kanai-ga asagohan-o tsukurimasu*

4. こどもが くつを みがきます

4. *kodomo-ga kutsu-o migaki-masu*

5. 学生(がくせい)が まどを あけます

5. *gakusee-ga mado-o akemasu*

6. みちこが ごみ(garbage, waste)を すてます

6. *Michiko-ga gomi-o sutemasu*

7. こどもが へやを かたづけます

7. *kodomo-ga heya-o katazuke-masu*

8. こどもが 買物(かいもの)を します

8. *kodomo-ga kaimono-o shi-masu*

使(つか)いかたの練習(れんしゅう)

Tsukaikata-no renshuu

つぎの 会話(かいわ)の 下線(かせん)の ところを かえて 練習(れんしゅう)しなさい。

Tsugi-no kaiwa-no kasen-no tokoro-o kaete renshuu-shinasai.

例(れい)：おふろを わかす

ree : ofuro-o wakasu

A：おたくでは こどもさんが うちの 仕事(しごと)を てつだいますか。

B：ええ、すこし てつだわせます。

A：どんな ことを させるんですか。

B：おふろを わかさせたり、おつかいに 行(い)かせたり します。

A：そうですか。いい おこさん(＝こどもさん)ですね。

B：そんな ことは ありません。

A: *Otaku-dewa kodomo-san-ga uchi-no shigoto-o tetsudai-masu-ka.*

B: *Ee, sukoshi tetsudawasema-su.*

A: *Donna koto-o saseru-n-desu-ka.*

B: *Ofuro-o wakasasetari, otsu-kai-ni ikasetari shimasu.*

A: *Soo-desu-ka. Ii okosan-desu-ne.*

B: *Sonna koto-wa arimasen.*

▲言わないと (if I don't tell them to help)、やらないんですよ。

Iwanai-to yaranai-n-desu-yo.

1. くつを　みがく
2. 掃除を　する
3. へやを　かたづける
4. ごみを　すてる
5. ちゃわんを　あらう

1. *kutsu-o migaku*
2. *sooji-o suru*
3. *heya-o katazukeru*
4. *gomi-o suteru*
5. *chawan-o arau*

II. …(さ)せて {いたダく／もらう}

II. *. . . (sa)sete* {*-itadaku* / *-morau*}

形の練習

Katachi-no renshuu

例に　ならって　かえなさい。

例：かえる→かえらせていただきたいんですが。
かえらせてもらえますか。

Ree-ni naratte kaenasai.

ree : kaeru → Kaerasete-itadakitai-n-desu-ga.
Kaerasete moraemasu-ka.

1. 休む　2. 使う
3. しめる　4. ひく
5. 行く　6. 読む
7. しらべる　8. まつ

1. *yasumu*　2. *tsukau*
3. *shimeru*　4. *hiku*
5. *iku*　6. *yomu*
7. *shiraberu*　8. *matsu*

使いかたの練習

Tsukaikata-no renshuu

つぎの　会話の　下線の　ところを　かえて　練習しなさい。

Tsugi-no kaiwa-no kasen-no tokoro-o kaete renshuu-shinasai.

(A) 例(れい)：きょう　はやく　かえる

A(会社員(かいしゃいん))：あの、おねがいが　あるんですが。

B(課長(かちょう))：なんだね。

A：<u>きょう　はやく　かえらせていただきたいんですが。</u>くにから母(はは)が　来(き)ますので。

B：仕事(しごと)は　だいじょうぶかな。

A：はい、いそいで(in a hurry)やります。

B：じゃ、いいだろう。お母(かあ)さんを大事(だいじ)にね。

A：はい、ありがとうございます。

1. あした　休(やす)む
2. 二(に)、三日(さんにち)(two, three days)休(やす)む
3. きょう　午後(ごご)　かえる
4. 三時(さんじ)ごろ　かえる
5. 二時間(にじかん)ぐらい　でかける

(A) *ree : kyoo hayaku kaeru*

A (company employee) : *Ano, onegai-ga aru-n-desu-ga.*

B (section chief) : *Nan-da-ne.*

A: *Kyoo hayaku kaerasete-itadakitai-n-desu-ga. Kuni-kara haha-ga kimasu-node.*

B: *Shigoto-wa daijoo-bu-ka-na.*

A: *Hai, isoide yarimasu.*

B: *Ja, ii-daroo. Okaasan-o daiji-ni-ne.*

A: *Hai, arigatoo-gozaimasu.*

1. *ashita yasumu*
2. *ni-sannichi yasumu*
3. *kyoo gogo kaeru*
4. *sanji-goro kaeru*
5. *nijikan-gurai dekakeru*

(B) 例(れい)：この　電話(でんわ)、使(つか)う

A：あの、ちょっと　いいですか。

B：はい。

A：<u>この　電話(でんわ)、使(つか)わせて</u>もらえますか。

B：ええと(well)、いま　すぐですか。

(B) *ree : kono denwa, tsukau*

A: *Ano, chotto ii-desu-ka.*

B: *Hai.*

A: *Kono denwa, tsukawasete-moraemasu-ka.*

B: *Eeto, ima sugu-desu-ka.*

A：ええ、でも　すぐ　おわりますから。

B：じゃ、いいですよ。どうぞ。

A：すみません。

1. となりの　へや、使(つか)う
2. ピアノ(ぴあの)、ひく
3. この　雑誌(ざっし)、読(よ)む
4. この　書類(しょるい)、しらべる

A: *Ee, demo sugu owarimasu-kara.*

B: *Ja, ii-desu-yo. Doozo.*

A: *Sumimasen.*

1. *tonari-no heya, tsukau*
2. *piano, hiku*
3. *kono zasshi, yomu*
4. *kono shorui, shiraberu*

III. …なければ　ならない

III. *. . . nakereba naranai*

形(かたち)の練習(れんしゅう)

Katachi-no renshuu

例(れい)に　ならって　かえなさい。

Ree-ni naratte kaenasai.

例(れい)：てつだう→てつだわなければ　なりません。

ree : tetsudau →Tetsudawanakereba narimasen.

1. 行(い)く　　2. 勉強(べんきょう)する
3. 家(うち)に　いる　　4. 国(くに)へ　かえる
5. 人(ひと)に　あう
6. 会議(かいぎ)(conference)に　出(で)る(attend)
7. 手紙(てがみ)を　書(か)く　　8. 休(やす)む

1. *iku*　　2. *benkyoo-suru*
3. *uchi-ni iru*　　4. *kuni-e kaeru*
5. *hito-ni au*
6. *kaigi-ni deru*
7. *tegami-o kaku*　　8. *yasumu*

使(つか)いかたの練習(れんしゅう)

Tsukaikata-no renshuu

つぎの　会話(かいわ)の　下線(かせん)の　ところを　かえて　練習(れんしゅう)しなさい。

Tsugi-no kaiwa-no kasen-no tokoro-o kaete renshuu-shinasai.

例(れい)：病院(びょういん)に　行(い)く

ree : byooin-ni iku

A：今度 いつ 来ていただけますか。　A: *Kondo itsu kite-itadakemasu-ka.*

B：いつが いいでしょうね。　B: *Itsu-ga ii-deshoo-ne.*

A：来週の 木曜日は どうですか。　A: *Raishuu-no mokuyoobi-wa doo-desu-ka.*

B：あ、その 日は ちょっと 都合が わるいです。病院に 行かなければ なりませんから。　B: *A, sono hi-wa chotto tsugoo-ga warui-desu. Byooin-ni ikanakereba narimasen-kara.*

A：そうですか。じゃ、火曜日は？　A: *Soo-desu-ka. Ja, kayoobi-wa?*

B：火曜日なら けっこうです。　B: *Kayoobi-nara kekkoo-desu.*

1．家に いる　2．国へ かえる　1. *uchi-ni iru*　2. *kuni-e kaeru*

3．人に あう　4．会議に 出る　3. *hito-ni au*　4. *kaigi-ni deru*

5．父の 仕事を てつだう　5. *chichi-no shigoto-o tetsudau*

発音練習

「っ」に 気を つけて 練習しなさい。

A.	1．かこ (*ka-ko*)	かっこ (*ka-k-ko*)	かあこ (*ka-a-ko*)	かこお (*ka-ko-o*)	かっこお (*ka-k-ko-o*)
	2．さと	さっと	さあと	さとお	さっとお
	3．あと	あっと	ああと	あとお	あっとお
	4．かた	かった	かあた	かたあ	かったあ
	5．さち	さっち	さあち	さちい	さっちい

B.　1．きってきて　2．みてきて　3．とってきて

4．きてきて(dict. *kiru* wear)　5．あってきて　6．してきて

C.　下線の ところに Bの ことばを 入れて 練習しなさい。

例：すみませんが、持ってきていただけませんか。

読む練習

ある[(1)]企業がほしいものをつくるときは、いろいろな調査をする。ほんとうに客[(2)]のほしがるものを知る[(3)]ために[(4)]調査するのだが、人の心[(5)]を知るのはむずかしいことだ。それに[(6)]、調査をしたときほしいと思った人も、ものができたときにはもうほしくないと思うかもしれない。だから、いまのことだけでなく[(7)]将来[(8)]のことも調査しなければならない。

(1) certain (2) customer (3) know, Lesson 9 (4) in order to (5) heart
(6) besides (7) not only (8) future

書く練習

つぎの　ひらがなを　練習しなさい。

1. が *(ga)* か が が
2. ぎ *(gi)* き ぎ ぎ
3. ぐ *(gu)* く ぐ ぐ
4. げ *(ge)* け げ げ
5. ご *(go)* こ ご ご

6. ざ *(za)* さ ざ
7. じ *(ji)* し じ
8. ず *(zu)* す ず
9. ぜ *(ze)* せ ぜ
10. ぞ *(zo)* そ ぞ

聞く練習

テープの　会話を　聞いて　つぎの　質問に　こたえなさい。

1. 男の人は　家の　なかで　主人を　まっていますか。
2. 主人は　どこへ　行ったのですか。
3. だれの　参考書を　買いに　行ったのですか。
4. こどもの　なまえ (name) は　なんと　いいますか。
5. こどもは　なんの　勉強が　すきですか。
6. ほかの　勉強は　あまり　しませんか。

第二十四課(だいにじゅうよんか)　カメラを　とられました

Dialogue

（一）

ジョンソン：　きのう　たいへんな　ことが　ありました。

山下(やました)：　どう　したんですか。

ジョンソン：　どろぼうに　はいられたんです。

山下(やました)：　なにか　とられましたか。

ジョンソン：　ええ。現金(げんきん)　五万円(ごまんえん)と　カメラを　とられました。

山下(やました)：　そうですか。　警察(けいさつ)に　とどけましたか。

ジョンソン：　ええ。すぐ　しらべに　来(き)てくれました。でも、ぬすまれた　ものは　なかなか　出(で)ないそうですね。

山下(やました)：　ええ、出(で)ないかも　しれませんね。

（二）

男子学生(だんしがくせい)：　きょうは　いやな　ことばかりだったよ。

女子学生(じょしがくせい)A：　どうして。

男子学生(だんしがくせい)：　電車(でんしゃ)の　なかでは　足(あし)を　ふまれたし、電車(でんしゃ)を　おりてからは　雨(あめ)に　ふられたし、教室(きょうしつ)では　いねむりを　して　わらわれたし…。

女子学生(じょしがくせい)A：　でも、発音(はつおん)が　いいって　先生(せんせい)が　ほめてくれたじゃ　ないの。

男子学生(だんしがくせい)：　ほめてくれたんじゃ　なくて、まえより　いいって　言(い)っただけだよ。

女子学生(じょしがくせい)A：　でも、いいわ。わたしなんか　何度(なんど)　言(い)わせられても　うまく　言(い)えないんですもの。…あら、原田(はらだ)さん、ねむそうね。

女子学生(じょしがくせい)B：　ええ。ゆうべ　となりの　あかちゃんに　なかれて、よく　ねむれなかったの。

男子学生(だんしがくせい)：　それは　たいへんだったね。　ぼくの　へやの　となりにも　あかんぼうが　いるんで、ときどき　夜中(よなか)に　おこされるんだよ。

Dialogue

Lesson 24 **I HAD MY CAMERA STOLEN**	*Dai-nijuuyonka* *KAMERA-O TORAREMASHITA*

I.

Johnson: Something terrible happened to me yesterday.

Yamashita: What happened?

J: A thief broke into my room.

Y: Did he take anything?

J: Yes, he stole 50,000 yen in cash and a camera.

Y: Is that right? Did you report it to the police?

J: Yes, I did. They came to investigate right away. But I was told it's very hard to get things back once they're stolen.

Y: Maybe so.

I.

Jonson: Kinoo ▲taihenna koto-ga arimashita.

Yamashita: ▲Doo shita-n-desu-ka.

J: ▲Doroboo-ni hairareta-n-desu.

Y: Nanika ▲toraremashita-ka.

J: Ee. Genkin ▲goman-en-to ▲kamera-o toraremashita.

Y: Soo-desu-ka. Keesatsu-ni ▲todokemashita-ka.

J: Ee. ▲Sugu shirabe-ni kite-kuremashita. Demo, nusumareta mono-wa nakanaka ▲denai-soo-desu-ne.

Y: Ee, ▲denai-kamo shiremasen-ne.

II.

Male Student: I had nothing but awful things happen to me today.

Female Student. A: What's the matter?

II.

Danshi Gakusee: Kyoo-wa ▲iyana koto-bakari-datta-yo.

Joshi Gakusee A: Dooshite.

M : Someone stepped on my foot on the train; I was caught in the rain after I got off the train; and in the classroom, I fell asleep and everybody laughed at me.	*D: Densha-no naka-dewa ▲ashi-o fumareta-shi, densha-o orite-kara-wa ▲ame-ni furareta-shi, kyooshitsu-dewa inemuri-o shi-te ▲warawareta-shi. . .*
FA: But the teacher praised your pronunciation, didn't she?	*JA: Demo,hatsuon-ga ii-tte sense-e-ga ▲homete-kureta-ja nai-no.*
M : She didn't praise me; she just said I did better than before.	*D: ▲Homete-kureta-n-ja nakute, ▲mae-yori ii-tte itta-dake-da-yo.*
FA: Still it's a good thing, isn't it? I can't pronounce well no matter how many times I'm asked to say things··· Hey, Sachiko (Miss Harada), you look sleepy.	*JA: Demo ▲ii-wa. Watashi-nanka ▲nando iwaserarete-mo umaku ienai-n-desu-mono. . .Ara, Harada-san, nemusoo-ne.*
FB: I guess so. The baby next door cried a lot and I couldn't sleep well last night.	*JB: Ee. Yuube ▲tonari-no akachan-ni nakarete, yoku ▲nemurena-katta-no.*
M : That must have been awful. The family next door to my place has a baby, too, and I'm awakened at midnight sometimes.	*D: ▲Sore-wa taihen-datta-ne. ▲Boku-no heya-no tonari-nimo akanboo-ga iru-nde, tokidoki yonaka-ni ▲okosareru-n-da-yo.*

Explanation

(In this lesson you will learn the passive form or the *-reru, -rareru* form. One use of the passive form shows that someone suffers a sequence as a result of another's action.)

きのう　たいへんな　ことが　ありました。 **line 1**

Kinoo taihenna koto-ga arimashita.

taihenna koto something terrible

どろぼうに　はいられたんです。 **line 3**

Doroboo-ni hairareta-n-desu.

doroboo thief; robber

doroboo-ni hairareta I was robbed (dict. *hairu*)

Hairareru is the passive form of *hairu,* 'to enter.' *Doroboo-ni hairareta* literally means 'I suffered from a thief entering the room.'

The passive form is made by replacing *-nai* of the plain negative form by *-reru* for *-u* verbs and by *-rareru* for *-ru* verbs.

-u verbs: *iku --ikareru; toru --torareru; matsu --matareru*

-ru verbs: *miru --mirareru; taberu --taberareru*

suru --sareru; kuru --korareru

なにか　とられましたか。 **line 4**

Nanika toraremashita-ka.

toraremashita-ka — were you robbed? (dict. *toru*)

ええ。現金(げんきん)　五万円(ごまんえん)と　カメラ(かめら)を　とられました。 **lines 5-6**

Ee. Genkin goman-en-to kamera-o toraremashita.

genkin goman-en — 50,000 yen in cash

kamera — camera

. . . o toraremashita — I had . . . stolen

Note the use of *-o* and *-ga* in the following passive sentences. When the speaker's concern is the person who suffered a consequence, the particle *-o* is used; otherwise *-ga* precedes the verb.

ex. *Watashi-wa* (*Ishida-san-wa*) *okane-o toraremashita.* (I had my money stolen.) or (Mr. Ishida had his money stolen.)

Yuumeena e-ga nusumaremashita. (A famous picture was stolen.)

警察(けいさつ)に　とどけましたか。 **line 7**

Keesatsu-ni todokemashita-ka.

keesatsu — police station

. . . ni todokemashita-ka — did you report it to. . . .? (dict. *todokeru*)

すぐ　しらべに　来(き)てくれました。 **line 8**

Sugu shirabe-ni kite-kuremashita.

shirabe-ni — to investigate (dict. *shiraberu*)

でも、ぬすまれた　ものは　なかなか　出(で)ないそうですね。 **lines 8-9**

Demo, nusumareta mono-wa nakanaka denai-soo-desu-ne.

nusumareta mono	stolen goods (dict. *nusumu*)
nakanaka denai	it's hard to find (dict. *deru,* 'to come out')

きょうは　いやな　ことばかりだったよ。 **line 11**

Kyoo-wa iyana koto-bakari-datta-yo.

iyana koto	unpleasant things
. . . bakari-datta	there was nothing but . . .

電車(でんしゃ)の　なかでは　足(あし)を　ふまれたし、電車(でんしゃ)を　おりてからは　雨(あめ)に　ふられたし、教室(きょうしつ)では　いねむりを　して　わらわれたし…。 **lines 13-15**

Densha-no naka-dewa ashi-o fumareta-shi, densha-o orite-kara-wa ame-ni furareta-shi, kyooshitsu-dewa inemuri-o shite warawareta-shi. . .

densha	train
ashi	foot ; feet; leg(s)
. . . o fumareta	someone stepped on . . . (dict. *fumu,* 'to step on')
. . . o orite-kara	after I got off . . . (dict. *oriru*)
ame-ni furareta	I was rained on (dict. *furu*)
kyooshitsu	classroom
inemuri	sleeping while sitting
warawareta	I was laughed at (dict. *warau*)
. . . shi, . . . shi	. . . and . . . and (cf. Lesson 16)

As you can see in this sentence, the passive form in Japanese is often used to indicate that the speaker suffers from someone else's action or that he experiences something unpleasant, such as being rained on.

Inanimate objects seldom become the subjects of sentences in the passive voice except in written language.

でも、発音(はつおん)が　いいって　先生(せんせい)が　ほめてくれたじゃ　ないの。 **lines 16-17**

Demo, hatsuon-ga ii-tte sensee-ga homete-kureta-ja nai-no.

hatsuon	pronunciation
ii-tte	=*ii-to* (cf. Lesson 14)
homete-kureta	he (she) praised (dict. *homeru*)
…ja nai-no	…, didn't he (she) ?

ほめてくれたんじゃ　なくて、　まえより　いいって　言(い)っただけだよ。

Homete-kureta-n-ja nakute, mae-yori ii-tte itta-dake-da-yo. **lines 18-19**

...ja nakute	it isn't ....
...dake-da	only ....(cf. Lesson 19)

わたしなんか　何度(なんど)　言(い)わせられても　うまく　言(い)えないんですもの。**lines 20-21**

Watashi-nanka nando iwaserarete-mo umaku ienai-n-desu-mono.

nando	how many times
nando iwaserarete-mo	no matter how many times I am made to say
umaku ienai	I can't say it well
...desu-mono	because ...(used by women)

Iwaserareru is the passive form of *iwaseru*, which is the causative form of *yuu*, 'to say.' The resultant verb means 'to be forced to say.' The following are examples of the causative followed by the passive.

ex. *uta-o utawaserareru*—to be made to sing songs (dict. *utau*)
benkyoo-o saserareru—to be made to study (dict. *benkyoo-suru*)

'...*serareru*' is sometimes shortened to ... *sareru*.

ex. *iwaserareru*—*iwasareru*; *utawaserareru*—*utawasareru*
ikaserareru (to be made to go)—*ikasareru*

あら、原田(はらだ)さん、ねむそうね。 **lines 21-22**

Ara, Harada-san, nemusoo-ne.

ara	interjection of surprise, used by women
nemusoo	you look sleepy (dict. *nemui*)

Students usually call fellow classmates by their last name. Female students attach *-san*, while male students attach *-kun* or use the last name alone.

ゆうべ　となりの　あかちゃんに　なかれて、よく　ねむれなかったの。**lines 23-24**

Yuube tonari-no akachan-ni nakarete, yoku nemurenakatta-no.

akachan	baby (polite)
akachan-ni nakareta	the baby cried (and I was affected) (dict. *naku*)

nemurenakatta　　I couldn't sleep (dict. *nemuru*)

In English, such verbs as 'cry,' 'die,' and 'come' are not usually used in the passive form. In Japanese, however, these verbs often occur in their passive forms.

ex. *Shiken-no mae-no hi-ni tomodachi-ni korareta.* (A friend came to see me on the day before the exam—and I couldn't study much.)

Chiisai toki-ni chichi-ni shinarete komarimashita. (My father died when I was very young and I had to live a hard life.) (dict. *shinu*, 'to die')

For the particle *-no* at the end of the sentence "... *nemurenakatta-no*" see Lesson 23.

ぼくの　へやの　となりにも　あかんぼうが　いるんで、ときどき　夜中(よなか)に
Boku-no heya-no tonari-nimo akanboo-ga iru-nde, tokidoki yonaka-ni
おこされるんだよ。　**lines 25-27**
okosareru-n-da-yo.

heya　　room; apartment
akanboo　　baby (plain)
yonaka-ni　　in the middle of the night
okosareru　　I am awakened (dict. *okosu*)

Notice that the male student uses the word *akanboo*, the plain form, while the female student uses *akachan*. However, talking to others about their baby, it is polite for members of either sex to use the word *akachan*.

練習(れんしゅう) — Renshuu

I. …れる、…られる (passive) — I. . . . *reru*, . . . *rareru*

形の練習(かたちのれんしゅう) — *Katachi-no renshuu*

(A) つぎの 表(ひょう) (table) を 練習(れんしゅう) しなさい。

(A) *Tsugi-no hyoo-o renshuu-shinasai.*

はいる	はいられる	*hairu*	*hairareru*
どろぼうに はいられる		*doroboo-ni hairareru*	
なく	なかれる	*naku*	*nakareru*
あかんぼうに なかれる		*akanboo-ni nakareru*	
わらう	わらわれる	*warau*	*warawareru*
ともだちに わらわれる		*tomodachi-ni warawareru*	
来(く)る	来(こ)られる	*kuru*	*korareru*
お客(きゃく)に 来(こ)られる		*okyaku-ni korareru*	
しぬ	しなれる	*shinu*	*shinareru*
父(ちち)に しなれる		*chichi-ni shinareru*	
ふる	ふられる	*furu*	*furareru*
雨(あめ)に ふられる		*ame-ni furareru*	
とる	とられる	*toru*	*torareru*
お金(かね)を とられる		*okane-o torareru*	
ぬすむ	ぬすまれる	*nusumu*	*nusumareru*
カメラ(かめら)を ぬすまれる		*kamera-o nusumareru*	
ふむ	ふまれる	*fumu*	*fumareru*
足(あし)を ふまれる		*ashi-o fumareru*	
のむ	のまれる	*nomu*	*nomareru*
さけを のまれる		*sake-o nomareru*	

うたう	うたわれる	utau	utawareru
うたを	うたわれる	uta-o	utawareru
する	される	suru	sareru
パーティーを	される	paatii-o	sareru

(B) ｛　｝の なかの ことばを かえて 練習しなさい。

(B) ｛　｝-no naka-no kotoba-o kaete renshuu-shinasai.

（わたしは）｛だれか／どろぼう｝に｛現金／さいふ／カメラ｝を｛ぬすまれました。／とられました。｝

(Watashi-wa) ｛dareka／doroboo｝-ni｛genkin／saifu／kamera｝-o｛nusumaremashita.／toraremashita.｝

(C) 例に ならって かえなさい。

(C) Ree-ni naratte kaenasai.

例：あかんぼうが なきました
　→あかんぼうに なかれて こまりました。

ree: akanboo-ga nakimashita
　→ Akanboo-ni nakarete komarimashita.

1. どろぼうが はいりました
2. ともだちが 来ました
3. 父が しにました
4. 母が 病気に なりました
5. おてつだいさん (maid) が やめました
6. 雨が ふりました

1. doroboo-ga hairimashita
2. tomodachi-ga kimashita
3. chichi-ga shinimashita
4. haha-ga byooki-ni narimashita
5. otetsudai-san-ga yamemashita
6. ame-ga furimashita

使いかたの練習　Tsukaikata-no renshuu

つぎの　会話の　下線の　ところを　かえて　練習しなさい。

Tsugi-no kaiwa-no kasen-no tokoro-o kaete renshuu-shinasai.

例：どろぼうに　はいられる、
　　どろぼう

ree: doroboo-ni hairareru,
doroboo

A：きのうは　たいへんだったそうーですね。
B：ええ、<u>どろぼうに　はいられて</u>、たいへんでした。
A：こまったでしょう。
B：ええ、とても　こまりました。
　<u>どろぼうは</u>　いやですね。
A：ほんとですね (It certainly is)。

A: *Kinoo-wa taihen-datta-soo-desu-ne.*
B: *Ee, <u>doroboo-ni hairarete</u> taihen-deshita.*
A: *Komatta-deshoo.*
B: *Ee, totemo komarimashita.*
<u>Doroboo-wa</u> iya-desu-ne.
A: *Honto-desu-ne.*

1. 雨に　ふられる、雨
2. こどもに　病気に　なられる、病気
3. さいふを　ぬすまれる、どろぼう
4. ともだちに　さけを　のまれる、よっぱらい (drunkard)
5. となりの　人に　けんか (quarrel) を　される、けんか

1. *ame-ni furareru, ame*
2. *kodomo-ni byooki-ni narareru, byooki*
3. *saifu-o nusumareru, doroboo*
4. *tomodachi-ni sake-o nomareru, yopparai*
5. *tonari-no hito-ni kenka-o sareru, kenka*

II. …(さ)せられる(causative +passive)

II. ... *(sa) serareru*

形の練習

Katachi-no renshu

例に　ならって　かえなさい。

Ree-ni naratte kaenasai.

例：練習を　しました
　──→練習を　させられました。
　本を　読みました
　──→本を　読ませられました。

ree: renshuu-o shimashita
→Renshuu-o saseraremashita.
hon-o yomimashita
→Hon-o yomaseraremashita.

1. 掃除を　しました
2. くすりを　のみました
3. 作文を　書きました
4. 夕飯を　つくりました
5. うたを　うたいました
6. おつかいに　行きました
7. 三十分　まちました

1. *sooji-o shimashita*
2. *kusuri-o nomimashita*
3. *sakubun-o kakimashita*
4. *yuuhan-o tsukurimashita*
5. *uta-o utaimashita*
6. *otsukai-ni ikimashita*
7. *sanjippun machimashita*

使いかたの練習

Tsukaikata-no renshuu

つぎの　会話の　下線の　ところを　かえて　練習しなさい。

Tsugi-no kaiwa-no kasen-no tokoro-o kaete renshuu-shinasai.

例：作文を　書かせられる

ree: sakubun-o kakaserareru

A：こどもの　とき　いろいろな　ことを　させられました。

A: *Kodomo-no toki iroirona koto-o saseraremashita.*

B：そうですか。たとえば(for example)どんな　ことですか。

A：本を　読ませられたり、作文を書かせられたり　しました。

B：いやだと　おもいましたか。

A：ときどき　そう　おもいましたが、その　経験(experience)がいま　やくに　たっています。

B：そうでしょうね。

B: *Soo-desu-ka. Tatoeba donna koto-desu-ka.*

A: *Hon-o yomaseraretari, sakubun-o kakaseraretari shimashita.*

B: *Iya-da-to omoimashita-ka.*

A: *Tokidoki soo omoimashita-ga, sono keeken-ga ima yaku-ni tatte-imasu.*

B: *Soo-deshoo-ne.*

1. ピアノを　練習させられる
2. うたを　うたわせられる
3. おつかいに　行かせられる
4. 掃除を　させられる
5. 手紙を　書かせられる
6. 夕飯を　つくらせられる

1. *piano-o renshuu-saserareru*
2. *uta-o utawaserareru*
3. *otsukai-ni ikaserareru*
4. *sooji-o saserareru*
5. *tegami-o kakaserareru*
6. *yuuhan-o tsukuraserareru*

III. 何度…ても

III. *nando . . . te-mo*

形の練習

Katachi-no renshuu

例に　ならって　かえなさい。

Ree-ni naratte kaenasai.

例：練習する——→何度　練習しても　うまく　できません。

言う——→何度　言っても　うまく　言えません。

ree: renshuu-suru →Nando renshuu-shite-mo umaku dekimasen.

yuu →Nando itte-mo umaku iemasen.

言わせられる→何度　言わせられても　うまく　言えません。

iwaserareru → Nando iwaserarete-mo umaku iemasen.

1. やる　2. 読む
3. 読ませられる　4. 練習する
5. やらせられる　6. 言ってみる
7. うたってみる　8. 書く

1. *yaru*　2. *yomu*
3. *yomaserareru*　4. *renshuu-suru*
5. *yaraserareru*　6. *itte-miru*
7. *utatte-miru*　8. *kaku*

使いかたの練習

Tsukaikata-no renshuu

つぎの　会話の　下線の　ところを　かえて　練習しなさい。

Tsugi-no kaiwa-no kasen-no tokoro-o kaete renshuu-shinasai.

例：言う

ree: yuu

A：もう　一度　言って　ください。
B：もう　だめです。わたしは　何度　やっても　うまく　言えません。
A：そんな　ことは　ありません。何度も (many times) 言ってみれば　きっと (surely) うまく　なります。
B：はい。じゃ、もう　一度　言ってみます。

A: *Moo ichido itte-kudasai.*
B: *Moo dame-desu. Watashi-wa nando yatte-mo umaku iemasen.*
A: *Sonna koto-wa arimasen. Nando-mo itte-mireba kitto umaku narimasu.*
B: *Hai. Ja, moo ichido itte-mimasu.*

1. 発音する　2. うたう
3. 読む　4. 書く
5. ひく　6. つくる
7. やる

1. *hatsuon-suru*　2. *utau*
3. *yomu*　4. *kaku*
5. *hiku*　6. *tsukuru*
7. *yaru*

発音練習

「っ」に　気をつけて　練習しなさい。

A．1．いし　　いっし　　いいし　　いしい　　いっしい

(i-shi)　(i-s-shi)　(i-i-shi)　(i-shi-i)　(i-s-shi-i)

2．こと　　こっと　　こおと　　ことお　　こっとお

3．かく　　かっく　　かあく　　かくう　　かっくう

4．しそ　　しっそ　　しいそ　　しそお　　しっそお

5．せと　　せっと　　せえと　　せとお　　せっとお

B．1．きてきて　　2．きいてきて

3．いってきて　　4．かってきて

5．とりかえてきて(dict. *torikaeru* 'to exchange')

C．下線の　ところに　Bの　ことばを　入れて　練習しなさい。

例：すみませんが、着てきていただけませんか。

読む練習

大学のとき、島田というともだちがいた。島田はある政党(1)にはいっていた(2)。お金がなくて夕飯をたべない日(3)もあった。けれども、下宿(4)から大学まで、いつも電車にのった。「近いのだから、あるいて(5)行けるじゃないか」とわたしが言ったら「電車のなかで機関紙(6)を読めば、となりの客(7)が見る。それで政党に興味をもたせることができるかもしれない」と言った。

(1) political party　(2) belonged　(3) day　(4) lodging house　(5) by walking
(6) bulletin, party newspaper　(7) passenger

書(か)く練習(れんしゅう)

つぎの　ひらがなを　練習(れんしゅう)しなさい。

1.	だ *(da)*	た	だ		6.	ば *(ba)*	は	ば
2.	じ *(ji)*	ち	ぢ*		7.	び *(bi)*	ひ	び
3.	ず *(zu)*	つ	づ*		8.	ぶ *(bu)*	ふ	ぶ
4.	で *(de)*	て	で		9.	べ *(be)*	へ	べ
5.	ど *(do)*	と	ど		10.	ぼ *(bo)*	ほ	ぼ

* usually replaced by じ and ず

11.	ぱ	*(pa)*	は	ぱ
12.	ぴ	*(pi)*	ひ	ぴ
13.	ぷ	*(pu)*	ふ	ぷ
14.	ぺ	*(pe)*	へ	ぺ
15.	ぽ	*(po)*	ほ	ぽ

聞(き)く練習(れんしゅう)

テープ(てーぷ)の　会話(かいわ)を　聞(き)いて　質問(しつもん)に　こたえなさい。

1. 女(おんな)の人(ひと)は　どんな　ことを　たのみましたか。
2. 男(おとこ)の人(ひと)は　すぐ　いいと　言(い)いましたか。
3. いいと　言(い)う　まえに　どんな　ことを　聞(き)きましたか。
4. 女(おんな)の人(ひと)の　お父(とう)さんは　いつごろ　しにましたか。
5. 女(おんな)の人(ひと)の　お母(かあ)さんは　その　あと　もう　一度(いちど)　結婚(けっこん)しましたか。
6. 男(おとこ)の人(ひと)は　仕事(しごと)に　ついて　どんな　ことを　言(い)いましたか。

クイズ（19課－24課）　Quiz (Lesson 19 — Lesson 24)

I. つぎは　Aと　Bの会話です。(1)と　(2)の　なかで　よい　ほうに　○を書いてください。

I. *Tsugi-wa A-to B-no kaiwa-desu.* (1)*-to* (2)*-no naka-de yoi hoo-ni* ○*-o kaite-kudasai.*

例：A：　おはようございます。
B：(1) おはようございます。
(2) さようなら。

ree: A: *Ohayoo-gozaimasu.*
B: (1) *Ohayoo-gozaimasu.*
(2) *Sayoonara.*

1．A：はじめまして。よく　いらっしゃいました。
B：(1) どうぞ　よろしく。
(2) こちらこそ。

1. A: *Hajimemashite. Yoku irasshaimashita.*
B: (1) *Doozo yoroshiku.*
(2) *Kochira-koso.*

2．A：(1) こどもが　いつも　おせわに　なっております。
(2) どうぞ　おかけください。
B：こちらこそ。

2. A: (1) *Kodomo-ga itsumo o-sewa-ni natte-orimasu.*
(2) *Doozo o-kake-kudasai.*
B: *Kochira-koso.*

3．A：(1) ご兄弟は　いらっしゃいますか。
(2) お父さんや　お母さんは　お元気　ですか。
B：はい、おかげさまで。

3. A: (1) *Go-kyoodai-wa irasshaimasu-ka.*
(2) *Otoosan-ya okaasan-wa ogenki-desu-ka.*
B: *Hai, okagesama-de.*

4．A：行ってきます。
B：(1) 行っていらっしゃい。
(2) ただいま。

4. A: *Itte-kimasu.*
B: (1) *Itte-irasshai.*
(2) *Tadaima.*

5. A：どうぞ　お読(よ)みください。
B：(1) はい、では　読(よ)ませていただきます。
(2) はい、では　読(よ)んでいただきます。

5. A: *Doozo o-yomi-kudasai.*
B: (1) *Hai, dewa yomasete-itadakimasu.*
(2) *Hai, dewa yonde-itadakimasu.*

6. A：(1) おたくの　あかんぼうは　いかがですか。
(2) おたくの　あかちゃんは　いかがですか。
B：はい、おかげさまで　大(おお)きく　なりました。

6. A: (1) *Otaku-no akanboo-wa ikaga-desu-ka.*
(2) *Otaku-no akachan-wa ikaga-desu-ka.*
B: *Hai, okagesama-de ookiku narimashita.*

7. A：(1) その　仕事(しごと)は　おわったんですか。
(2) その　仕事(しごと)は　たいへんでしょう。
B：いいえ、大(たい)したことは　ありません。

7. A: (1) *Sono shigoto-wa owatta-n-desu-ka.*
(2) *Sono shigoto-wa taihen-deshoo.*
B: *Iie, taishita koto-wa arimasen.*

8. A：おくさんは　仕事(しごと)を　していらっしゃいますか。
B：(1) はい、学校(がっこう)で　教(おし)えております。
(2) はい、学校(がっこう)で　教(おし)えていらっしゃいます。

8. A: *Okusan-wa shigoto-o shite-irasshaimasu-ka.*
B: (1) *Hai, gakkoo-de oshiete-orimasu.*
(2) *Hai, gakkoo-de oshiete-irasshaimasu.*

II. つぎの（a）、（b）、（c）の　なかに　ひとつだけ　よく　ない　ものが　あります。
それに　×を　書(か)いてください。

II. *Tsugi-no* (a), (b), (c)*-no naka-ni hitotsu-dake yoku nai mono-ga arimasu. Sore-ni* × *-o kaite-kudasai.*

1. 父(ちち)と　母(はは)は　日本(にほん)へ

(a) 来(き)たいと　言(い)っています。

(b) 来(き)たがっています。

(c) 来(き)たいです。

1. *Chichi-to haha-wa Nihon-e*

(a) *kitai-to itte-imasu.*

(b) *kitagatte-imasu.*

(c) *kitai-desu.*

2. いもうとさんは　いま　どこに

(a) おいでに　なりますか。

(b) おりますか。

(c) いらっしゃいますか。

2. *Imooto-san-wa ima doko-ni*

(a) *oide-ni narimasu-ka.*

(b) *orimasu-ka.*

(c) *irasshaimasu-ka.*

3. この　セーター(せーたー)は

(a) 母(はは)が　くれたんです。

(b) 母(はは)が　つくってくれたん-です。

(c) 母(はは)に　つくっていただい-たんです。

3. *Kono seetaa-wa*

(a) *haha-ga kureta-n-desu.*

(b) *haha-ga tsukutte-kure-ta-n-desu.*

(c) *haha-ni tsukutte-itadaita-n-desu.*

4. この　字引(じびき)は

(a) 先生(せんせい)に　いただいたので-す。

(b) 先生(せんせい)が　いただいたので-す。

(c) 先生(せんせい)が　くださったので-す。

4. *Kono jibiki-wa*

(a) *sensee-ni itadaita-no-de-su.*

(b) *sensee-ga itadaita-no-de-su.*

(c) *sensee-ga kudasatta-no-desu.*

5. 先生(せんせい)、

(a) 持(も)ってあげましょう。

(b) お持(も)ちしましょう。

(c) 持(も)たせてください。

5. *Sensee,*

(a) *motte-agemashoo.*

(b) *o-mochi-shimashoo.*

(c) *motasete-kudasai.*

6. わたしが　るすだったら、

(a) 家(うち)のものに　わたして–ください。

(b) 家(うち)のものに　わたして–くれれば　いいですよ。

(c) 家(うち)のものに　おわたし–して　ください。

6. *Watashi-ga rusu-dattara,*

(a) *uchi-no-mono-ni wata-shite-kudasai.*

(b) *uchi-no-mono-ni wata-shite-kurereba ii-desu-yo.*

(c) *uchi-no-mono-ni o-wata-shi-shite-kudasai.*

7. こどもの　とき

(a) 父(ちち)に　しなれました。

(b) 父(ちち)が　しなれました。

(c) 父(ちち)が　しにました。

7. *Kodomo-no toki*

(a) *chichi-ni shinaremashi-ta.*

(b) *chichi-ga shinaremashi-ta.*

(c) *chichi-ga shinimashita.*

8. (a) いろいろ　おしえて–くださって、

(b) いろいろ　おしえて、

(c) いろいろ　おしえて–いただいて、

どうも　ありがとうございました。

8. (a) *Iroiro oshiete-kudasatte,*

(b) *Iroiro oshiete,*

(c) *Iroiro oshiete-itadaite,*

doomo arigatoo-gozaimashita.

III. つぎの　英語(えいご)を　日本語(にほんご)に　翻(ほん)–訳(やく)して (translate) ください。

III. *Tsugi-no eego-o nihongo-ni hon'yaku-shite-kudasai.*

1. My elder sister was married last year.
2. Speaking of birthdays, the day after tomorrow is my brother's birth-day.
3. How about giving it to Miss Kato?

4. A: When should I return the book?
   B: Bring it to my house whenever it suits you.
5. Go and buy three pencils*, please. (**enpitsu*)
6. Please let me do it.
7. I'm very interested in this work.
8. I must help Mr. Yoshida.
9. They came to investigate right away.
10. I was caught in the rain after I got off the train.
11. I can't pronounce well no matter how many times I try.
12. I couldn't sleep well last night.

第二十五課(だいにじゅうごか)　不公平(ふこうへい)ですね

Dialogue

㈠ (Two office workers talking at a bus stop)

岡田(おかだ)：　きょうの　夕刊(ゆうかん)に　ボーナス(ぼーなす)の　平均額(へいきんがく)が　出(で)ていますよ。

林(はやし)：　そうですか。ちょっと　見(み)せてください。

岡田(おかだ)：　ほら、ここです。

林(はやし)：　ううん、大企業(だいきぎょう)と　中小企業(ちゅうしょうきぎょう)では　ずいぶん　差(さ)が　あるんですね。

岡田(おかだ)：　そうですね。

林(はやし)：　仕事(しごと)は　おなじなのに、ボーナス(ぼーなす)が　こんなに　ちがうのは　不公平(ふこうへい)ですね。

岡田(おかだ)：　まったくですね。

㈡ (A secretary visiting her boss in the hospital)

山崎(やまざき)：　入院(にゅういん)なさった　ことを　きのうまで　知(し)らなかったものですから、　おみまいに　あがるのが　おそく　なりまして…

渡辺(わたなべ)：　いいんだよ。たいした　ことは　ないんだから。

山崎(やまざき)：　でも、手術(しゅじゅつ)を　なさったそうで…

渡辺(わたなべ)：　手術(しゅじゅつ)と　いっても　かんたんな　ものなんだよ。

山崎(やまざき)：　そうですか。

渡辺(わたなべ)：　あと　二(に)、三日(さんにち)で　退院(たいいん)できるって　医者(いしゃ)が　言(い)ってたよ。

山崎(やまざき)：　それは　よかったですね。

渡辺(わたなべ)：　来週(らいしゅう)あたりから　仕事(しごと)に　出(で)るよ。

山崎(やまざき)：　むりを　なさらない　ほうが　いいんじゃ　ありませんか。

渡辺(わたなべ)：　だいじょうぶだよ。たいした　病気(びょうき)でも　ないのに、会社(かいしゃ)を　休(やす)んでいるのは、かえって　体(からだ)に　わるいよ。

山崎(やまざき)：　でも、どうぞ　おだいじに　なさってください。

渡辺(わたなべ)：　ありがとう。

山崎(やまざき)：　じゃ、そろそろ　失礼(しつれい)いたします。

渡辺(わたなべ)：　わざわざ　ありがとう。みんなに　よろしく。

Dialogue

Lesson 25

IT'S UNFAIR, ISN'T IT?

I.

Okada: Today's evening paper gives a figure for the average bonus.

Hayashi: Is that right? May I have a look at it?

O: It's written here.

H: Well, there's a great difference between the big enterprises and the smaller ones.

O: That's right.

H: It's unfair, isn't it, that people are given different amounts of bonus for the same work?

O: You're quite right.

II.

Yamazaki: I didn't know until yesterday that you were in the hospital. I'm sorry I didn't come to see you sooner.

Dai-nijuugoka

FUKOOHEE-DESU-NE

I.

Okada: Kyoo-no yuukan-ni ▲boonasu-no heekin-gaku-ga dete-imasu-yo.

Hayashi: Soo-desu-ka. ▲Chotto misete-kudasai.

O: Hora, koko-desu.

H: Uun, dai-kigyoo-to chuushoo-kigyoo-dewa ▲zuibun sa-ga aru-n-desu-ne.

O: Soo-desu-ne.

H: ▲Shigoto-wa onaji-na-noni, boonasu-ga konna-ni chigau-no-wa ▲fukoohee-desu-ne.

O: Mattaku-desu-ne.

II.

Yamazaki: Nyuuin-nasatta koto-o ▲kinoo-made shiranakatta-mono-desu-kara, ▲omimai-ni agaru-no-ga osoku narimashite…

Watanabe: That's all right. It's nothing serious.

Watanabe: Ii-n-da-yo. Taishita koto-wa nai-n-da-kara.

Y : But I heard you had an operation.

Y : Demo, shujutsu-o nasatta-soode....

W: It was an operation all right, but it was a very simple one.

W: Shujutsu-to itte-mo kantanna mono-na-n-da-yo.

Y : Is that so?

Y : Soo-desu-ka.

W: The doctor said I can leave the hospital in two or three more days.

W: Ato ni-sannichi-de taiin-dekiru-tte isha-ga itte-ta-yo.

Y : I'm glad to hear that.

Y : Sore-wa yokatta-desu-ne.

W: I'll start coming to the office next week or so.

W: Raishuu-atari-kara shigoto-ni deru-yo.

Y : It might be better not to overwork yourself.

Y : Muri-o nasaranai hoo-ga ii-n-ja arimasen-ka.

W: Don't worry. Being away from the office when I'm not really sick is actually bad for the health.

W: Daijoobu-da-yo. Taishita byooki-demo nai-noni, kaisha-o yasunde-iru-no-wa, kaette karada-ni warui-yo.

Y : But please take care of yourself.

Y : Demo, doozo odaiji-ni nasatte-kudasai.

W: Thanks.

W: Arigatoo.

Y : I should be leaving now.

Y : Ja, sorosoro shitsuree-itashimasu.

W: Thank you very much for coming. Say hello to everyone for me, will you?

W: Wazawaza arigatoo. Minna-ni yoroshiku.

Explanation

(In this lesson you will learn the expressions···*noni*,···*no-wa*, and···*to itte-mo*. They are used to combine long phrases and make it possible to express complicated ideas or thoughts.)

きょうの　夕刊に　ボーナスの　平均額が　出ていますよ。 **lines 1-2**

yuukan	the evening edition of a newspaper (cf. *chookan*, 'morning edition')
boonasu	bonus (a lump sum of money given to employees, usually twice a year)
heekin-gaku	average amount (*heekin*, 'average'; *gaku*, 'amount')
····*ga dete-iru*	····is printed; ····is on (dict. *deru*)

ううん、大企業と　中小企業では　ずいぶん　差が　あるんですね。

lines 5-6

dai-kigyoo	big enterprises (*dai*, 'big'; *kigyoo* 'enterprise' Lesson 13)
chuushoo-kigyoo	small and medium enterprises (*chuu*, 'middle': *shoo*, 'small')
····*to*····*dewa*	between ···· and ····; when we compare ···· and ····
sa	difference

'...*to*...*dewa*' is used to emphasize the contrast between two nouns or two pronouns.

ex. *Watashi-to Mori-san-dewa kangae-ga chigaimasu.* (Mr. Mori and I think in different ways.)

Sometimes *-de* is left out.

ex. *Kore-to are-wa nedan-ga chigaimasu.* (The price of this one is different from that one.)

仕事は　おなじなのに、ボーナスが　こんなに　ちがうのは　不公平ですね。

lines 8-9

onaji	the same
onaji-na-noni	although they're the same
chigau	are different; to be different
····*no-wa*	the fact that····is
fukoohee-desu	it's unfair

A verb followed by *-no* forms a phrase similar in function to an English····ing verb. (cf. *Arubaito-o shinagara benkyoo-suru-no-wa taihen-deshoo-ne*, Lesson 12)

'… *noni*' means 'although,' 'in spite of,' or 'even though.'

ex. *Byooki-na-noni shigoto-ni ikimashita.* (He went to work in spite of his illness.)

Wakai-noni genki-ga arimasen. (He lacks energy even though he's young.)

Shigoto-wa onaji-na-noni boonasu-ga chigau. (We are given different amounts of bonus for the same work.)

まったくですね。 **line 10**

mattaku-desu-ne I completely agree with you

入院(にゅういん)なさった　ことを　きのうまで　知(し)らなかったものですから、おみまいに あがるのが　おそく　なりまして… **lines 11-13**

nyuuin-nasatta	you were(have been) hospitalized (dict. *nasaru* → *nasaimasu*, irreg.)
····*koto*	the fact that ····
kinoo-made	until yesterday
····*mono-desu-kara*	because....
o-mimai-ni	to visit when someone's ill
o-mimai-ni agaru-no	coming to visit you when you're ill

With compound verbs such as *nyuuin-suru*, *kekkon-suru*, *nasaru* replaces *suru* to make the expression polite.

ex. *Imooto-san-ga kekkon-nasaru-soo-de*····(I heard your sister is going to get married.)

'····*mono-desu-kara*' is used to make an apology.

ex. *Osoku natte gomen-nasai. Deyoo-to shita toki denwa-ga kita-mono-desu-kara*···· (I'm sorry I'm late. There was a telephone call when I was about to leave.)

でも、手術(しゅじゅつ)を　なさったそうで… **line 15**

shujutsu	surgical operation
····*o nasatta*	you had ····(*lit.* you did)

手術(しゅじゅつ)と　いっても　かんたんな　ものなんだよ。 **line 16**

····to itte-mo although it's····; it's····all right, but

kantanna simple

'*····to itte-mo*' is followed by a statement which modifies or corrects the statement preceding it.

ex. *Byooki(da)-to itte-mo taishita koto-wa arimasen.* (He's sick all right, but it's nothing serious.)

A: *Odori-o o-narai-ni natta-n-da-soo-desu-ne.* (I heard you studied dancing.)

B. *Naratta-to itte-mo ikkagetsu-dake-desu.* (It's true that I studied it, but it was only for a month.)

あと 二、三日で 退院できるって 医者が 言ってたよ。 **lines 18-19**

ato ni-sannichi-de in a few more days(*ato* 'more') See Note.

taiin-dekiru I can leave the hospital

isha doctor(more politely, *o-isha-san*)

Ato, when followed by a number, means 'more.'

ex. Student: *Sensee, jikan-wa mada arimasu-ka.* (Do we have some more time left?)

Teacher: *Ato gofun arimasu.* (We have five minutes more to go.)

来週あたりから 仕事に 出るよ。 **line 21**

raishuu-atari around next week

Atari is similar to *-gurai* in meaning, but is used mostly with words designating time or place, and is often rhetorical.

ex. A: *Doko-de aimashoo-ka.* (Where shall we meet?)

B: *Shinjuku-atari-wa doo-desu-ka.* (What about Shinjuku?)

むりを なさらない ほうが いいんじゃ ありませんか。 **lines 22-23**

muri-o nasaranai hoo-ga (for you)not to overwork yourself (*muri-o suru* 'to overwork oneself')

ii-n-ja arimasen-ka isn't it better?

だいじょうぶだよ。たいした 病気(びょうき)でも ないのに、会社(かいしゃ)を 休(やす)んでいるのは、かえって 体(からだ)に わるいよ。 **lines 24-25**

taishita byooki-demo nai-noni	when I'm not very sick
····*o yasunde-iru-no-wa*	being absent from the office (····*o yasumu* 'to be absent from····')
taishita byooki-demo nai-noni, kaisha-o yasun-de-iru-no-wa	being absent from the office when I'm not very sick
kaette	on the contrary; against your expectation
karada-ni warui	bad for the health

でも、どうぞ おだいじに なさってください。 **line 26**

o-daiji-ni nasatte-kudasai	please take care of yourself (cf. *okarada-o odaiji-ni*, Lesson 21)

じゃ、そろそろ 失礼(しつれい)いたします。 **line 28**

sorosoro shitsuree-itashi-masu	I'll be leaving; it's about time I should be excused

Sorosoro is used in the following way, too.

ex. *Sorosoro juuji-desu-kara moo kaerimashoo.* (Let's go home since it's almost ten now.)

Itashimasu (dict. *itasu*) is used to describe the speaker's action; it shows a humble attitude, and therefore sounds more polite than *suru*.

ex. *o-todoke-shimasu—o-todoke-itashimasu* (I'll deliver it to you.)

ex. *o-mochi-shimasu—o-mochi-itashimasu.* (I'll carry it for you.)

In situations more pleasant than the one described here, a visitor will say this and the host will say something to invite him to stay longer such as "*Mada ii-deshoo.*" or "*Doozo go-yukkuri.*"

わざわざ　ありがとう。みんなに　よろしく。 **line 29**

wazawaza — taking so much trouble

minna-ni yoroshiku — give my best regards to everybody

Note *Ni-san-nichi*

Here are some expressions similar to *ni-san-nichi*:

shi-go-nichi (4, 5 days)
go-roku-nichi (5, 6 days)
ni-san-nin (2, 3 people)
shi-go-nin (4, 5 people)
go-roku-nin (5, 6 people)
ni-san-byaku-en (2, 3 hundred yen)
shi-go-sen-en (4, 5 thousand yen)
go-rokujuu-man-en (500 to 600 thousand yen)

練習

I. …のに

形の練習(かたちのれんしゅう)

例(れい)にならってかえなさい。

（A）例：練習(れんしゅう)した、できなかった→練習(れんしゅう)したのに、できませんでした。

1. 勉強(べんきょう)した、うまく　ならない
2. 待(ま)っていた、来(こ)なかった
3. 待(ま)っていた、来(き)てくれなかった
4. 大学(だいがく)を　出(で)た（graduated）、仕事(しごと)が　ない
5. 読(よ)んだ、わすれた
6. はたらかなかった、つかれた

（B）例：わかい（young）、元気(げんき)（energy）が　ない→わかいのに　元気(げんき)が　ありません。

1. ほしい、お金(かね)が　ない
2. 買(か)いたい、買(か)えない

3．やさしかった (was easy)、できなかった

4．むずかしかった、よく　できた

5．あたらしい、きれいじゃ　ない

6．高い、おいしく　ない

（C）例：病気だ、会社に　出た→病気なのに　会社に　出ました。

1．元気だ、休んでいる

2．こどもだ、元気が　ない

3．仕事が　おなじだ、ボーナスが　ちがう

4．病気だ、休まなかった

5．仕事は　たいへんだ、月給 (monthly pay) が　やすい

6．学生だ、勉強しない

使いかたの練習

つぎの会話の下線のところをかえて練習しなさい。

（A）例：試験 (exam)、勉強した

A：試験は　どうでした。

B：だめでした。

A：そうですか。

B：あんなに　勉強したのに…

A：ざんねんでしたね。

1．試験、練習した

2．成績 (grades)、勉強した

3．試合 (match, game)、練習した

4．競馬 (horse race)、研究した

（B）例：もう　わかく　ないのに　むりを　した。

A：しばらく (for some time) あいませんでしたね。

B：ええ、ちょっと　病気で　会社を　休んでいたものですから。

A：それは　いけませんね (That's too bad)。もう　いいんですか。

B：ええ、もう　だいじょうぶです。
A：むりを　したからじゃ　ありませんか。
B：ええ、もう　わかく　ないのに　むりを　したからでしょう。

1. 体が　よわい(weak)のに　むりを　した
2. かぜを　ひいたのに　むりを　した
3. つかれたのに　休まなかった
4. いそがしいのに　てつだってもらわなかった
5. かぜを　ひいたのに　くすりを　のまなかった

II.　…といっても

形の練習

例にならって文(sentence)をつくりなさい。

例：手術、かんたんな→手術と　いっても　かんたんな　ものなんです。

1. 試験、かんたんな
2. 試験、やさしい
3. 仕事、らくな (easy)
4. 会社、小さい
5. 参考書、かんたんな

使いかたの練習

つぎの会話の下線のところをかえて練習しなさい。

例：会社を　おつくりに　なる

A：さいきん　会社を　おつくりに　なったそうで…
B：ええ。
A：たいへんですね。
B：ええ。でも、会社と　いっても　かんたんな　ものなんですよ。
A：そうですか。でも、あまり　むりを　なさらないでください。
B：はい、ありがとうございます。気を　つけます。

1. 試験(しけん)を　お受(う)けに　なる (dict. 受(う)ける　to take)
2. 本(ほん)を　お出(だ)しに　なる (dict. 出(だ)す　to publish)
3. 翻訳(ほんやく)を　なさる
4. 論文(ろんぶん)を　お書(か)きに　なる

III. …と…では

形の練習

例にならって文をつくりなさい。

例：大企業(だいきぎょう)、中小企業(ちゅうしょうきぎょう)→大企業(だいきぎょう)と　中小企業(ちゅうしょうきぎょう)では　ずいぶん　ちがうんですね。

1. 日本語(にほんご)、英語(えいご)
2. 男(おとこ)の人(ひと)、女(おんな)の人(ひと)
3. 夏(なつ) (summer)、冬(ふゆ)
4. うち (inside)、そと (outside)
5. 映画(えいが)、歌舞伎(かぶき) (kabuki)
6. 朝刊(ちょうかん) (morning paper)、夕刊(ゆうかん)

IV. …のは…

形の練習

例にならって文をかえなさい。

例：はたらいているのに　お金(かね)が　たりない
　　→こんなに　はたらいているのに　お金(かね)が　たりないのは　なぜでしょう。

1. 勉強(べんきょう)しているのに　じょうずに　ならない (I don't improve)
2. 食(た)べたのに　まだ　おなかが　すいている (I'm hungry)
3. はたらいているのに　ボーナス(ぼーなす)が　すくない (of small amount)
4. 練習(れんしゅう)しているのに　うまく　言(い)えない
5. 待(ま)っているのに　手紙(てがみ)が　来(こ)ない
6. はたらいているのに　生活(せいかつ) (life) が　らくに　ならない

使いかたの練習

つぎの話(はなし) (speech) の下線のところをかえて練習しなさい。

例：ボーナス(ぼーなす)、大企業(だいきぎょう)と　中小企業(ちゅうしょうきぎょう)

きょうの　夕刊(ゆうかん)に　▲ボーナス(ぼーなす)の　ことが　出(で)ています。読(よ)んでみると、大企業(だいきぎょう)と　中小企業(ちゅうしょうきぎょう)では　▲ずいぶん　差(さ)が　ある　ことが　わかります。仕事(しごと)は　おなじなのに、ボーナス(ぼーなす)が　こんなに　ちがうのは　▲不公平(ふこうへい)だと　思(おも)います。

1. 月給(げっきゅう)(monthly pay)、大企業(だいきぎょう)と　中小企業(ちゅうしょうきぎょう)
2. 休暇(きゅうか)(vacation)、大企業(だいきぎょう)と　中小企業(ちゅうしょうきぎょう)
3. 月給(げっきゅう)、男性(だんせい)(male)と　女性(じょせい)(female)
4. 月給(げっきゅう)、わかい　人(ひと)と　としより(old people)
5. 月給(げっきゅう)、大学(だいがく)を　出(で)た　人(ひと)と　高校(こうこう)を　出(で)た　人(ひと)

発音練習

Syllable の数(かず) (number) に気(き)をつけて練習しなさい。

A.
1. びおう *(bi-o-o)*　びよう *(bi-yo-o)*　びょう *(byo-o)*　ぼう *(bo-o)*
2. みおう　みよう　みょう　もう
3. じおう　じよう　じょう　ぞう
4. りおう　りよう　りょう　ろう
5. におう　によう　にょう　のう
6. ぎおう　ぎよう　ぎょう　ごう

B.
1. びょういん、びよういん (beauty parlor)
2. じゅう (gun), じゆう (freedom)
3. にじゅうえん、じゅうきゅうえん
4. きょう、きよう (skillful)

C．下線のところにBのことばを入れて練習しなさい。

例：びょういんじゃ　なくて、びょういんですよ。

読む練習

明治時代(めいじじだい)[(1)]に石川啄木(いしかわたくぼく)という人がいた。新聞記者(しんぶんきしゃ)[(2)]をしながら歌(うた)[(3)]をつくった。彼(かれ)がつくった歌(うた)はことばがやさしくて、わかりやすい[(4)]。そのなかに「こんなにはたらいているのに生活(せいかつ)[(5)]がらくにならないのはどうしてだろう。そう思(おも)いながら自分(じぶん)の手(て)[(6)]を見(み)る」という意味(いみ)[(7)]の歌がある。

(1) Meiji Era, 1868-1912　(2) newspaper reporter　(3) poem　(4) easy to understand　(5) life　(6) hand　(7) meaning

書く練習

（A）（「ゃ」「ゅ」「ょ」を小(ちい)さく書(か)きなさい）

きゃ *(kya)*	きゅ *(kyu)*	きょ *(kyo)*
ぎゃ *(gya)*	ぎゅ *(gyu)*	ぎょ *(gyo)*
しゃ *(sha)*	しゅ *(shu)*	しょ *(sho)*
じゃ *(ja)*	じゅ *(ju)*	じょ *(jo)*
ちゃ *(cha)*	ちゅ *(chu)*	ちょ *(cho)*
にゃ *(nya)*	にゅ *(nyu)*	にょ *(nyo)*
ひゃ *(hya)*	ひゅ *(hyu)*	ひょ *(hyo)*
びゃ *(bya)*	びゅ *(byu)*	びょ *(byo)*
ぴゃ *(pya)*	ぴゅ *(pyu)*	ぴょ *(pyo)*
みゃ *(mya)*	みゅ *(myu)*	みょ *(myo)*
りゃ *(rya)*	りゅ *(ryu)*	りょ *(ryo)*

（B）「っ」before *k*, *t*, *s* sounds　（「っ」を小(ちい)さく書(か)きなさい）

(before *k*)　ゆっくり *(yukkuri)*、いっかげつ *(ikkagetsu)*

(before *t*)　きって *(kitte)*、しって *(shitte)*、まったく *(mattaku)*

(before *s*)　きっさてん *(kissaten)*、けっして (*kesshite*, never)

聞く練習

テープの会話を聞いて質問にこたえなさい。

（A） 1．女の人は、どのくらい　入院していましたか。

2．男の人は、みまいに　行きましたか。

3．女の人は、いま　会社に　出て　はたらいていますか。

4．女の人の　お医者さんは、ねている　ほうが　いいと　言いましたか。

（B） 1．男の人の　名前は、何と　いいますか。

2．男の人の　会社は、ことし (this year) は　どうでしたか。

3．その　会社では、よく　はたらいた　人が　たくさん　ボーナスを　もらいますか。

第二十六課(だいにじゅうろっか)　いくつ　あるか　知(し)りません

Dialogue

(Before a meeting starts)

ジョンソン(じょんそん)：　東京(とうきょう)の　町(まち)は　学生(がくせい)が　多(おお)いですね。

小林(こばやし)：　ええ。大学(だいがく)が　たくさん　ありますからね。

ジョンソン(じょんそん)：　いくつぐらい　あるんでしょう。

小林(こばやし)：　そうですね。東京(とうきょう)に　いくつ　あるかは　知(し)りませんが、全国(ぜんこく)で　８９０(はっぴゃくきゅうじゅう)　あるそうです。

ジョンソン(じょんそん)：　８９０(はっぴゃくきゅうじゅう)ですか。多(おお)いですね。

小林(こばやし)：　ええ、それが　かなり　東京(とうきょう)に　集中(しゅうちゅう)してるんじゃないでしょうか。

ジョンソン(じょんそん)：　そうでしょうね。その　８９０校(はっぴゃくきゅうじっこう)の　なかには　短大(たんだい)も　はいっているんでしょうか。

小林(こばやし)：　はいっていると　思(おも)いますよ。何校(なんこう)だか　わすれましたが。

ジョンソン(じょんそん)：　そんなに　大学(だいがく)が　たくさん　あるのに、入学(にゅうがく)試験(しけん)が　むずかしいのは　なぜでしょうね。

小林(こばやし)：　そうですね。入学志望者(にゅうがくしぼうしゃ)も　多(おお)いし、それが　有名(ゆうめい)な　大学(だいがく)に　集中(しゅうちゅう)するからでしょうね。

ジョンソン(じょんそん)：　有名(ゆうめい)な　大学(だいがく)が　かならずしも　いいとは　かぎらないでしょう。自分(じぶん)に　とって　適当(てきとう)か　どうかと　いう　ことの　ほうが　たいせつだと　思(おも)いますが。

小林(こばやし)：　ええ、ぼくも　そう　考(かんが)えますが、でも、一般的(いっぱんてき)にいえば、有名校(ゆうめいこう)を　出(で)ると　有利(ゆうり)だって　ことは　事実(じじつ)ですね。

ジョンソン(じょんそん)：　そうですね。人間(にんげん)の　心理(しんり)と　して、有利(ゆうり)な　ほうを　えらぶのは　自然(しぜん)でしょうね。 23

小林(こばやし)：　ところで、もう　そろそろ　時間(じかん)でしょう。大野(おおの)さんたち　おそいですね。 25

ジョンソン(じょんそん)：　そうですね。どう　したんでしょう。 27

Dialogue

Lesson 26	*Dai-nijuurokka*
I DON'T KNOW HOW MANY THERE ARE	***IKUTSU ARU-KA SHIRIMASEN***
Johnson: There are many students in Tokyo, aren't there?	*Jonson: Tookyoo-no machi-wa gakusee-ga ooi-desu-ne.*
Kobayashi: Yes, that's because there are so many universities in Tokyo.	*Kobayashi: Ee. Daigaku-ga takusan arimasu-kara-ne.*
J: How many are there?	*J: Ikutsu-gurai aru-n-deshoo.*
K: Well, I don't know how many there are in Tokyo, but I heard there are 890 universities in the whole country.	*K: Soo-desu-ne. Tookyoo-ni ikutsu aru-ka-wa shirimasen-ga, zenkoku-de happyaku-kyuujuu aru-soo-desu.*
J: 890? That's a great number, isn't it?	*J: Happyaku-kyuujuu-desu-ka. Ooi-desu-ne.*
K: Yes, and many of them are probably concentrated in Tokyo.	*K: Ee, sore-ga kanari Tookyoo-ni shuuchuu-shite-ru-n-ja nai-deshoo-ka.*
J: That's probably so. Are junior colleges included in that figure?	*J: Soo-deshoo-ne. Sono happyakukyuujikkoo-no naka-niwa tandai-mo haitte-iru-n-deshoo-ka.*
K: I think they are. I forgot how many there are, though.	*K: Haitte-iru-to omoimasu-yo. Nankoo-da-ka wasuremashita-ga.*
J: Why is it that people have to take difficult examinations in order to get into universities and colleges when there are so many of them?	*J: Sonna-ni daigaku-ga takusan aru-noni, nyuugaku-shiken-ga muzukashii-no-wa naze-deshoo-ne.*

K: Well, I think it is because the number of applicants is great, and most of them want to enter famous universities.	*K: Soo-desu-ne. ▲Nyuugaku-shiboo-sha-mo ooi-shi, sore-ga ▲yuumee-na daigaku-ni shuuchuu-suru-kara-deshoo-ne.*
J: I think famous universities are not necessarily the best ones for everyone. What is more important is whether they are good for one's needs.	*J: Yuumeena daigaku-ga ▲kanarazu-shimo ii-towa kagiranai-deshoo. Jibun-ni totte tekitoo-ka doo-ka-to yuu koto-no hoo-ga ▲taisetsu-da-to omoimasu-ga.*
K: I agree, but it's also true that, generally speaking, it's advantageous to graduate from a famous university.	*K: Ee, ▲boku-mo soo kangaemasu-ga, demo ▲ippanteki-ni ieba, yuu-meekoo-o deru-to yuuri-da-tte koto-wa ▲jijitsu-desu-ne.*
J: That's true. It's only natural for humans to choose the advantageous course in life.	*J: Soo-desu-ne. ▲Ningen-no shinri-to shite, yuurina hoo-o erabu-no-wa ▲shizen-deshoo-ne.*
K: By the way, it's about time, isn't it? Mr. Ono and others are late.	*K: Tokoro-de moo sorosoro ▲jikan-deshoo. Oono-san-tachi ▲osoi-desu-ne.*
J: Yes, they are. I wonder what happened.	*J: Soo-desu-ne. ▲Doo shita-n-deshoo.*

Explanation

(This lesson introduces several kinds of complex sentences.)

東京(とうきょう)の　町(まち)は　学生(がくせい)が　多(おお)いですね。 **line 1**

Tookyoo-no machi	streets in Tokyo
. . . ga ooi	there are many . . .

Notice how sentences in the *. . . wa . . . ga* construction are used to describe attributes of the topic.

ex. *Tookyoo-no machi-wa gakusee-ga ooi.* (Tokyo has many students.)

Michiko-wa me-ga ookii. (Michiko has large eyes.)

This same construction is used in the following way with verbs:

ex. (*Watashi-wa*) *onaka-ga sukimashita.* (I'm hungry—*lit.* I have an empty stomach.)

Ano-hito-wa nihongo-ga joozu-ni natta. (His Japanese has improved—*lit.* As for him, his Japanese has become skillful.)

東京(とうきょう)に　いくつ　あるかは　知(し)りませんが、全国(ぜんこく)で　８９０(はっぴゃくきゅうじゅう)　あるそうです。

lines 4-5

ikutsu aru-ka (*-wa*) *shirimasen*	I don't know how many there are
zenkoku-de	in the whole country (*zen* 'whole,' *koku* 'country')

Questions imbedded in sentences are relatively simple in Japanese. The word order of the 'question clause' does not change (as it does in English). If the clause begins with a question word such as *dare*, *doko*, *ikutsu*, etc. add *-ka* at the end of the clause. Remember that the verb within the clause should always be in the plain form.

ex. *Dare-ga kita-ka shirimasen.* (I don't know who came.)

Doko-ni aru-ka oshiete-kudasai. (Please tell me where it is.)

ええ、それが　かなり　東京(とうきょう)に　集中(しゅうちゅう)してるんじゃ　ないでしょうか。

lines 7-8

kanari	considerably
shuuchuu-shite-ru	they are concentrated; they are gathered

その　８９０校(はっぴゃくきゅうじっこう)の　なかには　短大(たんだい)も　はいっているんでしょうか。

lines 9-10

happyaku-kyuujikkoo	890 schools (*-koo* is the counter for schools)
tandai	junior colleges
haitte-iru	are included (dict. *hairu*)

何校(なんこう)だか　わすれましたが。

lines 11-12

nankoo-da-ka how many schools there are

When questions ending in *-desu-ka* or *-deshita-ka* are imbedded in a sentence the question word is followed by *-da-ka* or *-datta-ka.* Notice how the following questions change when they become part of a sentence.

ex. 1. *Ikura-desu-ka.* (How much is it?)
Ikura-da-ka shirimasen. (I don't know how much it is.)

ex. 2. *Dare-deshita-ka.* (Who was it?)
Dare-datta-ka wasuremashita. (I forgot who it was.)

そんなに　大学(だいがく)が　たくさん　あるのに、入学試験(にゅうがくしけん)が　むずかしいのは　なぜでしょうね。

lines 13-14

nyuugaku-shiken entrance examination
muzukashii difficult
naze why

入学志望者(にゅうがくしぼうしゃ)も　多(おお)いし、それが　有名(ゆうめい)な　大学(だいがく)に　集中(しゅうちゅう)するからでしょうね。

lines 15-16

nyuugaku-shiboosha applicants (*lit.* those who wish to enter colleges)
yuumeena famous

有名(ゆうめい)な　大学(だいがく)が　かならずしも　いいとは　かぎらないでしょう。

lines 17-18

kanarazushimo (not) always
...to(-wa) kagiranai not always ...(dict. *kagiru,* 'to limit')

Both *kanarazushimo ....nai* and *kanarazushimo ....to-wa kagiranai* mean 'not always .....'

ex. *Kane-no aru hito-wa kanarazushimo shiawase-to-wa kagiranai.*
Kane-no aru hito-wa kanarazushimo shiawase-ja nai. (The rich are not always happy.)

自分にとって適当かどうかというこ とのほうがたいせつだと思いますが。 **lines 18-19**

jibun	oneself
...ni totte	for ....
tekitoo	suitable (*na* adj.)
tekitoo-ka doo-ka	whether it is suitable or not
...to yuu koto	the fact ...; the question...
...no hoo-ga taisetsu-da	...is more important

'*...ni totte*' is used to mean 'for (an individual)' in the following sense.

ex. *Nichiyoobi-wa watashi-ni totte tsugoo-ga warui.* (Sundays are inconvenient for me.)

Kodomo-ni totte-wa muzukashii. (It's difficult for children.)

'*...ka doo-ka*' corresponds to 'whether or not.'

ex. *Ashita hareru-ka doo-ka wakarimasen.* (I don't know if the weather will be clear tomorrow or not.)

Takai-ka doo-ka-to yuu koto-wa taisetsu-ja arimasen. (It doesn't matter whether it's expensive or not.)

ぼくもそう考えますが、でも一般的にいえば、有名校を出ると有利だってことは事実ですね。 **lines 20-22**

kangaemasu	I think (dict. *kangaeru*)
ippanteki-ni ieba	generally speaking
yuumeekoo	famous schools; schools of prestige
...o deru-to	if you graduate from...
yuuri-da	advantageous
yuuri-da-tte koto	the fact that it's advantageous (=*yuuri-da-to yuu koto*)
...wa jijitsu-desu	it is true that...

Kangaeru is synonymous to *omou*; the difference is that *kangaeru* has more emphasis on intellectual aspect than does *omou*.

人間の心理として、有利なほうをえらぶのは自然でしょうね。

lines 23-24

ningen human beings
shinri psychology
ningen-no shinri-to shite as human beings; from the viewpoint of human feelings
erabu choose
shizen-deshoo is probably natural

'...*to shite*' is used in the following way.

ex. *Hito-o aisuru-no-wa ningen-to shite shizenna koto-desu.* (It's natural for human beings to love others.)

Isha-to shite-wa rippana hito-desu-ga, oya-to shite-wa dame-desu. (He's a fine doctor, but as a parent he's a failure.)

ところで、もうそろそろ時間でしょう。 **line 25**

sorosoro jikan-deshoo It's about time, isn't it? (cf. Lesson 25)

練習

I. Question word…か

形の練習

例にならってこたえなさい。

A. 例：大学はいくつありますか ──→いくつあるか知りません。

1. だれが来ますか
2. どこにありますか
3. どこへ行きましたか
4. いくらはらいましたか
5. 山下さんは何と言いましたか
6. 学生は何人いますか
7. 会議(meeting)はいつおわりーましたか
8. どうして彼はわらいましたか

B．例：短大(たんだい)は　何校(なんこう)ですか　⟶　何校(なんこう)(だ)か　わかりません。

1．それは　何曜日(なにようび)ですか　　2．会議(かいぎ)は　いつですか

3．家賃(やちん) (rent) は　いくらですか　　4．家賃(やちん)は　いくらぐらいですか

5．えんぴつは　何本(なんぼん)ですか　　6．議長(ぎちょう) (chairman) は　だれですか

C．例：火事(かじ)は　何時(なんじ)でしたか　⟶　何時(なんじ)だったか　知(し)りません。

1．家賃(やちん)は　いくらでしたか

2．会議(かいぎ)は　何時(なんじ)でしたか

3．会議(かいぎ)が　おわったのは　何時(なんじ)でしたか

4．そこに　あった　えんぴつは　何本(なんぼん)でしたか

5．火事(かじ)が　あったのは　何時(なんじ)ごろでしたか

6．おくれて (late) 来(き)たのは　だれと　だれでしたか

D．例：いくつ　あるんですか　⟶　いくつ　あるのか　知(し)りません。

1．だれが　やったんですか　　2．何人(なんにん)ぐらい　来(く)るんですか

3．どこに　あるんですか　　4．どうして　行(い)かないんですか

5．どうして　そう　なったんですか　　6．なぜ　行(い)かなかったんですか

使(つか)いかたの練習(れんしゅう)

つぎの会話(かいわ)の下線(かせん)のところをかえて練習(れんしゅう)しなさい。

例：どこへ　行(い)ったんでしょう。

A：▲和英辞典(わえいじてん) (Jap.-Eng. dictionary) が　ありませんね。

B：そうですね。

A：▲どこへ　行(い)ったんでしょう。

B：どこへ　行(い)ったのか　▲わかりませんね。しらべてみましょう。

A：▲わかったら　教(おし)えてください。

B：はい、▲そう　します。

1. どう　したんでしょう
2. どこに　あるんでしょう
3. だれが　持(も)っていったんでしょう
4. なぜ　ここに　ないんでしょう
5. いつ　なくなったんでしょう

II. …か　どうか

形の練習

例にならってこたえなさい。

（A）例：時間(じかん)が　ありますか　⟶あるか　どうか　わかりません。

1. みんな　すぐ　来(き)ますか
2. 短大(たんだい)も　はいっていますか
3. まだ　おぼえています(remember)か
4. その　ほうが　有利(ゆうり)ですか
5. それは　事実(じじつ)ですか
6. それが　一番(いちばん)(most)　安(やす)いですか

（B）例：その　ほうが　有利(ゆうり)なんですか　⟶有利(ゆうり)なのか　どうか　わかりません。

1. 短大(たんだい)も　はいっているんですか
2. 入学試験(にゅうがくしけん)は　たいへんなんですか
3. 東京(とうきょう)に　集中(しゅうちゅう)しているんですか
4. ずいぶん　ちがうんですか
5. その　大学(だいがく)は　有名(ゆうめい)なんですか
6. みんなが　そう　思(おも)うのですか

使いかたの練習

つぎの会話の下線のところをかえて練習しなさい。

例：小林(こばやし)さん、来(く)る

A：小林(こばやし)さんは　▲来(き)ますか。

B：さあ、▲来(こ)ないかも　しれません。

A：きいてみましたか。

B：まだです。

A：じゃ　あした　▲きいてみてください。

B：はい、来(く)るか　どうか　▲たしかめて (dict. *tashikameru,* to make sure) みます。

1. 小林さん、お金を　持っている　　2. 大野さん、きのう　来た
3. あの人、日本語が　話せる　　4. お金、百万円で　たりる

III. …と　いう　ことは　…です

形の練習

{　　}のなかのことばをかえて練習しなさい。

（A）{有名校を　出る／お金を　持っている／かお (face) が　きれいだ／ともだちが　多い}と　有利だと　いう　ことは　事実です。

（B）人間の　心理と　して{有利な　ほうを　えらぶ／やさしい　ほうを　とる／安い　ほうを　買う／らくな　仕事を　したがる}と　いう　ことは　自然です。

使いかたの練習

つぎの話(speech)の下線のところをかえて練習しなさい。

例：有利な

人間の　心理と　して　▲ふたつの　道(way)が　あれば、有利な　ほうを　えらぶのは　▲自然です。　しかし (but)、人間は　ときどき　したく　ない　ことも　しなければ　ならないと　いう　ことは　▲事実です。ですから、▲こどもの　ときから、したく　ない　ことも　すると　いう　訓練(training)をして　おく　ことが　▲たいせつだと　思います。

1. やさしい　2. らくな (easy)　3. すきな　4. やりやすい (easy to do)

発音練習

A.

1.	ちおう(chi-o-o)	ちよう(chi-yo-o)	ちょう(cho-o)	ちょっと(cho-t-to)
2.	しおう	しよう	しょう	しょっと
3.	ひおう	ひよう	ひょう	ひょっと
4.	きおう	きよう	きょう	きょっと
5.	ちう(chi-u)	ちゆ (chi-yu)	ちゅう(chu-u)	ちゅっと(chu-t-to)
6.	しう	しゆ	しゅう	しゅっと
7.	ひう	ひゆ	ひゅう	ひゅっと
8.	きう	きゆ	きゅう	きゅっと

B.
1. せん　ひゃく　ごじゅうきゅうねん（1159年）、せん　ひゃく　ろくじゅうきゅうねん
2. せん　にひゃく　ごじゅうきゅうねん　　　、せん　にひゃく　ろくじゅうきゅうねん
3. せん　さんびゃく　ごじゅうきゅうねん　　　、せん　さんびゃく　ろくじゅうきゅうねん
4. せん　よんひゃく　ごじゅうきゅうねん　　　、せん　よんひゃく　ろくじゅうきゅうねん

C. 下線のところにBのことばを入れて練習しなさい。

例：せん　ひゃく　ごじゅうきゅうねんじゃ　なくて、せん　ひゃく　ろくじゅうきゅうねんでしょう。

読む練習

入学試験をどうかえる(1)かということは、大きな*問題(2)である。この問題についてはいろいろな考えかた(3)がある。ひとつは大学と大学の差があってはいけないという考えかたである。また、大学の数(4)がたりないという考えかたもある。しかし、それよりもたいせつなことは、どうすれば社会(5)にとってほんとうに役に立つ人間を教育する(6)ことができるかということであろう**。

(1) change (2) problem (3) way of thinking (4) number (5) society (6) educate

* ＝大きい；*ookina* and *chiisana* (small) are used only before nouns and pronouns.

** ＝でしょう; it is used in written language.

書く練習

つぎのことばや文(ぶん)をひらがなで書(か)きなさい。

1．*okaasan* 2．*obaasan* 3．*Aa, wakarimashita.*
4．*oishii* 5．*sabishii* 6．*muzukashii*
7．*yuube* 8．*yuuhan* 9．*tabako-o suu*
10．*gakusee* 11．*see-ga takai* 12．*keesatsu*
13．*doozo* 14．*kinoo* 15．*doroboo*
16．*Kono hen-ga yosasoo-desu-ne.*

（1. おかあさん 2. おばあさん 3. ああ、わかりました。
4. おいしい 5. さびしい 6. むずかしい
7. ゆうべ 8. ゆうはん 9. たばこを すう
10. がくせい 11. せいが たかい 12. けいさつ
13. どうぞ 14. きのう 15. どろぼう
16. この へんが よさそうですね。）

聞く練習

テープ(てーぷ)の話(はなし)を聞(き)いて、質問(しつもん)にこたえなさい。

1．一番(いちばん) たいせつなのは、どんな 人間(にんげん)に こどもを 教育(きょういく)する (educate) ことですか。

2．人間(にんげん)の 心理(しんり)と して やさしい ほうと むずかしい ほうと どちら を えらびますか。

3．人間(にんげん)は いつも すきな ことだけ している ことが できますか。

4．こういう 教育(きょういく)は いつ はじめる (start)のが 適当(てきとう)ですか。

第二十七課　のれなく　なっちゃう

Dialogue

（一）（A conversation between two acquaintances）

ジョンソン：　おすまいは　どちらですか。

大野：　郊外の　公団住宅です。

ジョンソン：　公団住宅なら、安くて　いいですね。

大野：　そうでも　ありません。それに　会社から　遠いので、通勤に　時間が　かかります。

ジョンソン：　どのくらい　かかるんですか。

大野：　片道　二時間も　かかるんですから、たまりませんよ。

ジョンソン：　それは　たいへんですね。

大野：　都心に　うつりたいと　思うんですが、都心の　家は　高すぎて、いくら　はたらいても　買えませんね。

（二）（A conversation between a customer and a taxi driver）

客：　運転手さん、上野駅まで　行きたいんだけど、10分ぐらいで　行くだろうかね。

運転手：　そうですね。道が　こんでいなけりゃ、10分で　行きますが、こんでると、20分ぐらい　かかりますよ。

客：　こまったな。20分以上　かかると、特急に　のれなく　なっちゃうんだよ。

運転手：　まあ、いそいでみましょう。でも、保証は　できませんよ。

客：　しかたが　ない。たのむよ。

(The customer gets in the car. The car starts.)

運転手(うんてんしゅ)： お客(きゃく)さん、あの　かどを　まがっても　いいですか。少(すこ)し　遠(とお)まわりに　なるんですが、すいていそうだから、その　ほうが　かえって　早(はや)いだろうと　思(おも)いますが。

客(きゃく)： ああ、いいよ。

Dialogue

Lesson 27

I'LL MISS THE TRAIN!

I.

Johnson: Where do you live?

Ono: In public-funded housing in the suburbs.

J: Then it's inexpensive, isn't it?

O: Not really. Besides, it's far from the office, and I have to spend a lot of time commuting.

J: How long does it take?

O: It takes as much as two hours one way. It's more than I can stand.

J: That's awful.

O: I'd like to move to the center of the city, but the houses are so expensive I can't buy one no matter how hard I work.

II.

Customer: Driver, I want to go to Ueno Station. Can you take me there in 10 minutes or so?

Driver: Well, I can get you there

Dai-nijuunanaka

NORENAKU NATCHAU

I.

Jonson: O-sumai-wa ▲dochira-desu-ka.

Oono: Koogai-no ▲koodan-juu-taku-desu.

J: Koodan-juutaku-nara,▲yasukute ii-desu-ne.

O: ▲Soo-demo arimasen. Sore-ni ▲kaisha-kara tooi-node,▲tsuukin-ni jikan-ga kakarimasu.

J: ▲Dono-kurai kakaru-n-desu-ka.

O: Katamichi nijikan-mo kakaru-n-desu-kara, tamarimasen-yo.

J: ▲Sore-wa taihen-desu-ne.

O: ▲Toshin-ni utsuritai-to omou-n-desu-ga, toshin-no ie-wa▲taka-sugite, ikura hataraite-mo▲kae-masen-ne.

II.

Kyaku: Untenshu-san, ▲Ueno-eki-made ikitai-n-da-kedo, jip-pun-gurai-de▲iku-daroo-kane.

Untenshu: Soo-desu-ne.

	English		Japanese
	in 10 minutes if the traffic isn't heavy, but if it is, it'll take about 20 minutes.		*Michi-ga ▲konde-inakerya, ▲jippun-de ikimasu-ga, konde-ru-to, ▲nijippun-gurai kakarimasu-yo.*
C:	That's too bad. If it takes more than 20 minutes, I'll miss the special express.	*K:*	*Komatta-na. ▲Nijippun-ijoo kakaru-to, tokkyuu-ni ▲norenaku natchau-n-da-yo*
D:	All right. I'll try to hurry, but I can't promise you to be in time.	*U:*	*Maa, isoide-mimashoo. Demo, ▲hoshoo-wa dekimasen-yo.*
C:	I understand. Thanks. (Please do your best.)	*K:*	*Shikata-ga nai. Tanomu-yo.*
D:	Can I turn at that corner? It'll be going somewhat out of the way, but the traffic seems easier that way, and it'll be faster in the long run.	*U:*	*Okyaku-san, ▲ano kado-o magatte-mo ii-desu-ka. Sukoshi ▲toomawari-ni naru-n-desu-ga, suite-isoo-da-kara, sono hoo-ga kaette ▲hayai-daroo-to omoimasu-ga.*
C:	All right.	*K:*	*Aa, ii-yo.*

Explanation

(In this lesson you will learn the expressions *-sugiru* which means 'too ...,' *ikura ...te-mo* which means 'no matter how much I may...,' and contracted forms for *-nakereba* and *-te-shimau*.)

おすまいは　どちらですか。 **line 1**

o-sumai — your residence

郊外(こうがい)の　公団住宅(こうだんじゅうたく)です。 **line 2**

koogai — the suburbs

koodan-juutaku — public-funded housing (*koodan* 'public cooperation,' *juutaku* 'housing')

公団住宅(こうだんじゅうたく)なら、安(やす)くて　いいですね。 **line 3**

koodan-juutaku-nara (*lit.* if it's public-funded housing)

'... *nara*' is used to mean 'if.' See *sore-nara*, Lesson 17.

ex. A: *Kondo-no nichiyoobi-ni shimashoo-ka.* (Shall we make it this Sunday?)

B: *Kondo-no nichiyoo-nara* (or, *Sore-nara*) *daijoobu-desu.* (Next Sunday will be all right with me.) or (That will be all right with me.)

そうでも　ありません。 **line 4**

'... *demo arimasen*' sounds more reserved than *-ja arimasen.*

ex. A: *Ikitaku nai-n-desu-ka.* (You don't want to go?)

B: *Soo-demo arimasen-ga, doomo...* (It's not quite that, but...)

それに　会社(かいしゃ)から　遠(とお)いので、通勤(つうきん)に　時間(じかん)が　かかります。 **lines 4-5**

sore-ni	besides
tooi	far (opp. *chikai*)
tsuukin-ni	for going to work
...ga kakarimasu	it takes...; it requires ...(dict. *kakaru*)

片道(かたみち)　二時間(にじかん)も　かかるんですから、たまりませんよ。 **line 7**

katamichi	one way
nijikan-mo	as much as two hours (cf. *sangen-mo*, Lesson 16)
tamarimasen	I can't stand it (dict. *tamaru*, usually used in the negative)

都心(としん)に　うつりたいと　思(おも)うんですが、都心(としん)の　家(いえ)は　高(たか)すぎて、いくら　はたらいても　買(か)えませんね。 **lines 9-10**

toshin	the central part of the city
utsuritai-to omou	I want to move (dict. *utsuru*, Lesson16)
takasugite	they're too expensive and... (dict. *takasugiru*)
ikura hataraite-mo	no matter how hard I work

'...*sugiru*' in *takasugite* is added to the stem of adjectives and verbs to indicate excessive degree.

adj: *takai —taka-sugiru* (too expensive; too high)
muzukashii —muzukashi-sugiru (too difficult)

verbs: *taberu —tabe-sugiru* (to eat too much)
benkyoo-suru —benkyoo-shi-sugiru (to study too hard)

ex. *Hataraki-sugite byooki-ni narimashita.* (He overworked himself and became ill.)
Kono jibiki-wa furu-sugite yaku-ni tachimasen. (This dictionary is too old to be useful.)

Ikura ... te-mo is used in the following way.

ex. *Ikura tabete-mo futoranai.* (I don't gain weight no matter how much I eat.)
Okane-wa takusan aru-n-desu-kara ikura tsukatte-mo kamaimasen-yo. (I have a lot of money so you can spend any amount.)

運転手(うんてんしゅ)さん、上野駅(うえのえき)まで　行(い)きたいんだけど、10分(じっぷん)ぐらいで　行(い)くだろうかね。

lines 11-12

untenshu	driver (*unten* 'driving', *shu* 'person')
untenshu-san	(term used to address a driver; see Note)
Ueno-eki	Ueno Station (one of the largest stations in Tokyo)
jippun-gurai-de	in about ten minutes

... *daroo-kane*' is a familiar expression used mostly by men.

道(みち)が　こんでいなけりゃ、10分(じっぷん)で　行(い)きますが、こんでると、20分(にじっぷん)ぐらいかかりますよ。

lines 13-14

konde-inakerya	if it isn't crowded
konde-ru-to	if it's crowded

'... *eba*' becomes ...*ya* in its contracted form; *ireba* becomes *irya*, and *inakereba* becomes *inakerya*.

Thus:	*yomu*	*yameba —yomya*	*yamanakereba —yomanakerya*
	taberu	*tabereba —taberya*	*tabenakereba —tabenakerya*
	suru	*sureba —surya*	*shinakereba —shinakerya*
	kuru	*kureba —kurya*	*konakereba —konakerya*

Consequently, the *-nakereba naranai* form (must, have to), when contracted, becomes *-nakerya naranai.*

ex. *Uchi-ga tooi-node hayaku denakerya narimasen.* (Since I live far away, I have to leave home early.)

20分以上(にじっぷんいじょう) かかると、特急(とっきゅう)に のれなく なっちゃうんだよ。 **lines 15-16**

nijippun-ijoo	twenty minutes or more
tokkyuu	special express
. . . ni norenaku natchau	I'll miss . . . (*lit.* I'll be unable to ride . . .) (dict. *noru*)

'. . . *chau*' as in *natchau* is the contraction of *-te-shimau*, which indicates completion of an action or implies that the action is undesirable. (Lesson 16)

ex. *Moo tabete-shimaimashita.—Moo tabechaimashita.* (I have eaten it.)

Gakkoo-ni okurete-shimatta.—Gakkoo-ni okurechatta. (I ended up being late for school.)

まあ、いそいでみましょう。でも、保証(ほしょう)は できませんよ。 **lines 17-18**

maa	well
isoide-mimashoo	I'll try to hurry (dict. *isogu*)
hoshoo	guarantee

お客(きゃく)さん、あの かどを まがっても いいですか。 **line 20**

okyaku-san	(term used to address a customer, see Note)
kado	corner
magatte-mo ii-desu-ka	may I turn? (dict. *magaru*)
. . . o magaru	turn at . . .

少し　遠まわりに　なるんですが、すいていそうだから、その　ほうが　かえって　早いだろうと　思いますが。 **lines 21-22**

toomawari	detour
suite-isoo-da	it looks like it's not crowded

Note　Addressing with ***-san***

To address someone in a service occupation, you can call them by the occupation title plus *-san*. This is a use of *-san* different from its function as an equivalent of Mr., Mrs., or Miss. Some common terms of address using *-san* are: *sakanaya-san*, *nikuya-san*, *yuubin'ya-san* (mailman), *shinbun'ya-san* (newspaper boy) and *denkiya-san* (electric appliance salesman or repairman). A driver is called an *untenshu-san*, and a train conductor a *shashoo-san*. Addressing someone by their occupation title without adding *-san*, although sometimes heard, should be avoided as it is considered impolite.

練習

I.　いくら…ても

形の練習

例にならって質問にこたえなさい。

（A）例：いそげば　特急に　のれるでしょうか。

→さあ、いくら　いそいでも　のれないと　思いますよ。

1．はたらけば　家が　買えるでしょうか。
2．たのめば　仕事を　してくれるでしょうか。
3．お金を　はらえば　てつだってくれるでしょうか。
4．くすりを　のめば　なおるでしょうか。
5．待っていれば　この　雨は　やむ (stop) でしょうか。(やまない)
6．読んでみれば　意味 (meaning) が　わかるでしょうか。

(B) 例：古ければ　着ませんか (dict. 着る wear)。
　　→いいえ、いくら　古くても　着るつもりです。

1. 高ければ　買いませんか。
2. 遠ければ　行きませんか。
3. むずかしければ　読みませんか。
4. おもければ　持っていきませんか (dict. 持っていく take)。
5. おいしく　なければ　食べませんか。
6. 天気が　わるければ　歩きませんか (dict. 歩く walk)。

(C) 例：遠い　ところなら　やめますか。
　　→いいえ、いくら　遠い　ところでも　かまいません。

1. うるさい (noisy)　ところなら　やめますか。
2. むずかしい　本なら　やめますか。
3. たいへんな　仕事なら　やめますか。
4. おもしろく　ない　映画なら　やめますか。
5. 使いにくい (not easy to use) 字引なら　やめますか。
6. 読みにくい　論文なら　やめますか。

Note：「どんなに…ても」も　おなじです。(A) から (C) までを「どんなに…ても」の形を使って練習しなさい。

使いかたの練習

つぎの 会話の下線のことばをかえて練習しなさい。

(A) 例：字引を　ひく

A：どう　したんですか。
B：ここが　わからないんです。
A：もう　字引を　ひきましたか。
B：ええ。でも　いくら　字引を　ひいても　わからないんです。

1. しらべてみる　　2. 参考書(さんこうしょ)を　見(み)る　　3. ともだちに　きく

4. 教(おし)えてもらう　　5. 説明(せつめい)して (explain) もらう

（B）例：だれかに　たのむ

A：たいへんでしょう、この　仕事(しごと)は。 (—with sympathy)

B：ええ、つかれますね。

A：だれかに　たのんだら　どうですか。

B：ええ、たのみたいと　思(おも)いますがね。

A：たのめないんですか。

B：ええ、いくら　たのみたくても　いまは　たのめないんです。

1. ちょっと　休(やす)む　　2. だれかに　やってもらう

3. だれかに　てつだってもらう　　4. だれかに　かわって (take place)-もらう

5. 休暇(きゅうか) (vacation) を　とる

（C）例：わかる、松本(まつもと)さん

A：これは　むずかしいですね。

B：ええ、わたしには　どうも　わかりませんね。

A：松本(まつもと)さんなら　わかるでしょうか。

B：さあ、いくら　松本(まつもと)さんでも　これは　わからないかも　しれませんよ。

1. できる、松本(まつもと)さん　　2. わかる、お医者(いしゃ)さん

3. なおせる (can fix)、電気屋(でんきや)さん　　4. つくれる、大工(だいく) (carpenter) さん

5. わかる、専門家(せんもんか) (specialist)

II. そうでも　ありません。それに…

使いかたの練習

つぎの会話の下線のことばをかえて練習しなさい。

例：通勤(つうきん)に　時間(じかん)が　かかります

A：おすまいは　どちらですか。

B：郊外の　公団住宅です。

A：公団住宅なら　安くて　いいですね。

B：そうでも　ありません。それに　都心から　遠いので、通勤に　時間が　かかります。

1. 通学 (going to school) に　時間が　かかります
2. 買物が　不便 (inconvenient) です
3. 交通費 (transportation expenses) が　かかります
4. かえり (returning home) が　おそく　なります
5. いろいろ　不便な　ことが　あります

III. …から、たまりません

使いかたの練習

つぎの会話の下線のことばをかえて練習しなさい。

例：へや代 (room rent)、三万円

A：へや代が　ずいぶん　かかります。

B：どのくらい　かかるんですか。

A：一か月(a month)に　三万円も　かかるんですから、たまりませんよ。

B：それは　たいへんですね。

1. 本代 (money spent on books)、一万円
2. 交通費、二万円
3. バス代、八千円
4. 電話料金、五千円
5. ガソリン代、二万円

発音練習

〔d〕の音 (sound) と〔r〕の音のちがい (difference) に気をつけて練習しなさい。

A. 1. らりるれろ　　2. だじずでど
3. らりるれろ　　4. だじずでど
5. らりるれろ　　6. だじずでど
7. りるれろら　　8. じずでどだ
9. りるれろら　　10. じずでどだ
11. りるれろら　　12. じずでどだ

B. 1. らいしん、だいしん　　2. らいどう、だいどう
3. らんどり、だんどり　　4. れんきゅう、でんきゅう
5. ろうがん、どうがん　　6. ろだい、どだい　　(° nasalized)

C. 下線のところにBのことばを入(い)れて練習しなさい。

1. ▲らいしんと 言(い)っても ▲だいしんと 言(い)っても、▲たいした ちがいは ないでしょうか。

読む練習

住宅の不足(ふそく)(1)は大(おお)きな問題(もんだい)(2)である。なぜこんなに住宅がたりないのか、その理由(りゆう)(3)は、かんたんである。大きな都市(とし)(4)に会社や工場(こうじょう)(5)がたくさんできて、人口(じんこう)(6)が集中(しゅうちゅう)した。しかし、人の住(す)む(7)ところはあまりない。だから人々(ひとびと)(8)は郊外にうつらなければならなくなった。郊外の住宅から会社まで片道二時間以上もかかって通勤する人もたくさんいる。

(1) shortage　(2) problem　(3) reason　(4) city　(5) factory　(6) population
(7) live in　(8) people

書く練習

つぎのことばや文(ぶん) (sentence) をひらがなで書(か)きなさい。

1. *asatte*　　2. *zutto*　　3. *sukkari*
4. *shitte-iru*　　5. *irassharu*　　6. *komatte-iru*
7. *naratta*　　8. *wakatta*　　9. *itta*

10. *yokatta* 11. *oishikatta* 12. *takakatta*

13. *rippana* 14. *rippa-da* 15. *genki-datta*

16. *Otera-ga rippa-datta-node, bikkuri-shimashita.*

(1. あさって 2. ずっと 3. すっかり
4. しっている 5. いらっしゃる 6. こまっている
7. ならった 8. わかった 9. いった
10. よかった 11. おいしかった 12. たかかった
13. りっぱな 14. りっぱだ 15. げんきだった
16. おてらが りっぱだったので、びっくりしました。)

聞く練習

テープの会話を聞いて質問にこたえなさい。

1. 二人は いま 何の 相談 (discussion, talk) を していますか。
2. 松本さんは 外国 (foreign country) へ 行った ことが ありますか。
3. この 仕事には どんな 人が 適当ですか。
4. 松本さんの かわりに だれに たのむ ことに きめました (dict. *kimeru*, to decide) か。
5. その人に ついて、男の人と 女の人と どちらの ほうが 熱心 (enthusiastic) ですか。

第二十八課　人気が　あるらしいです

Dialogue

(Johnson and Ito are staying at an inn, and have come out to see a festival in the neighborhood.)

ジョンソン：　あ、おみこしですね。ぼくは　はじめてです。

伊藤：　そうですか。

ジョンソン：　かつぐ　人が　ずいぶん　おおぜい　いますね。

伊藤：　ええ、そうですね。数年まえまでは　かつぎ手が　たりなかったそうですがね。

ジョンソン：　どうして　かわったんでしょう。

伊藤：　古い　ものを　見なおすと　いう　傾向が　つよく　なってきたからでしょうね。

ジョンソン：　いろいろな　店が　出ていますね。あ、植木も　売っていますよ。あれ　いいですね。いくらぐらいでしょう。

伊藤：　さあ、このごろの　ことだから、千円は　するでしょうね。

ジョンソン：　あれは　何の　お面ですか。

伊藤：　何とか　いう　漫画の　主人公ですよ。

ジョンソン：　スーパーマンの　ような　ものでしょうか。

伊藤：　ええ。ああいうのが　こどもには　人気が　あるらしいんですよ。

ジョンソン：　あれは　何でしょう。

伊藤：　なにかの　みせものですね。

ジョンソン(じょんそん)：　人(ひと)が　おおぜい　あつまってる　ところを　みると、きっと　おもしろいんですよ。ぼくたちも　はいってみましょうか。

伊藤(いとう)：　そうですね。でも、もう　時間(じかん)が　あまり　ないようですよ。あの　番組(ばんぐみ)を　見(み)る　ためには　もう　かえらなきゃ……

ジョンソン(じょんそん)：　あれが　はじまるのは　何時(なんじ)でしたか。

伊藤(いとう)：　五時(ごじ)です。

ジョンソン(じょんそん)：　じゃ、もう　二十分(にじっぷん)しか　ありませんね。かえりましょう。

Dialogue

Lesson 28	*Dai-nijuuhakka*
IT SEEMS TO BE POPULAR	***NINKI-GA ARU-RASHII-DESU***
Johnson: There goes an *omikoshi!* This is the first time I've ever seen one.	*Jonson: A, omikoshi-desu-ne. Boku-wa ▲hajimete-desu.*
Ito: Is it?	*Itoo: Soo-desu-ka.*
J: There sure are a lot of people carrying it.	*J: Katsugu hito-ga ▲zuibun oozee imasu-ne.*
I: Yes. I understand there weren't enough people to carry them until a few years ago.	*I: Ee, soo-desu-ne. Suunen-mae-made-wa katsugite-ga ▲tarinakatta-soo-desu-gane.*
J: I wonder what's happened.	*J: ▲Dooshite kawatta-n-deshoo.*
I: Perhaps it's because people have become interested in looking at old things in a new light.	*I: ▲Furui mono-o minaosu-to yuu keekoo-ga tsuyoku natte-kita-kara-deshoo-ne.*
J: There are lots of stalls put up. Some are even selling plants. That one over there is nice. I wonder how much it costs.	*J: ▲Iroirona mise-ga dete-imasu-ne. A, ▲ueki-mo utte-imasu-yo. Are ▲ii-desu-ne. Ikura-gurai-deshoo.*

I: Well, the way things are nowadays, it probably costs at least a thousand yen.	*I: Saa, ▲kono-goro-no koto-da-kara, ▲sen-en-wa suru-deshoo-ne.*
J: What kind of mask is that over there?	*J: Are-wa▲nan-no omen-desu-ka.*
I: That's the mask of some sort of comic strip character.	*I: Nan-to-ka yuu▲manga-no shujin-koo-desu-yo.*
J: A character like a superman?	*J: ▲Suupaaman-no yoona mono-deshoo-ka.*
I: Yes, that kind of hero seems to be popular among children.	*I: Ee. ▲Aa-yuu-no-ga kodomo-niwa ninki-ga aru-rashii-n-desu-yo.*
J: What's that?	*J: ▲Are-wa nan-deshoo.*
I: A show of something or other.	*I: Nanika-no▲misemono-desu-ne.*
J: It must be something interesting since there's a big crowd. Let's go in and see.	*J: ▲Hito-ga oozee atsumatte-ru tokoro-o miru-to, kitto▲omoshiroi-n-desu-yo. Bokutachi-mo▲haitte-mimashoo-ka.*
I: All right, but I'm afraid we don't have much time. We have to head back to see that TV program.	*I: Soo-desu-ne. Demo, moo jikan-ga▲amari nai-yoo-desu-yo. ▲Ano bangumi-o miru tame-niwa moo kaeranakya . . . .*
J: What time does it start?	*J: Are-ga hajimaru-no-wa ▲nanji-deshita-ka.*
I: At five.	*I: Goji-desu.*
J: Then we have only twenty minutes left. Let's go back.	*J: Ja, moo▲nijippun-shika arimasen-ne. Kaerimashoo.*

Explanation

(In this lesson you will learn the following expressions: . . .*rashii*, 'it seems'; . . .*yoo-na*, 'looks like'; . . .*tokoro-o miru-to* 'judging from . . .' and . . .*shika* . . .*nai* 'only. . .')

あ、おみこしですね。ぼくは　はじめてです。 **line 1**

o-mikoshi	portable shrine (a miniature shrine carried on men's shoulders at festivals) (usu. with *o-*)
hajimete	for the first time

かつぐ　人(ひと)が　ずいぶん　おおぜい　いますね。 **line 3**

katsugu	carry on one's shoulder(s)
oozee	many (people)

数年(すうねん)まえまでは　かつぎ手(て)が　たりなかったそうですがね。 **lines 4-5**

suunen-mae-made-wa	until a few years ago
katsugite	= *katsugu hito*

Te means 'hand' and is used to refer to a performer of an action in such compounds as: *hanashite* (speaker); *kikite* (listener); *hataraki-te* (man who supports his family by working).

どうして　かわったんでしょう。 **line 6**

(...ga) kawatta	(it) has changed (dict. *kawaru*) (cf. *...o kaeru*)

古(ふる)い　ものを　見(み)なおすと　いう　傾向(けいこう)が　つよく　なってきたからでしょうね。 **lines 7-8**

...o minaosu	see something in a new light; think better of ...
....to yuu keekoo	tendency that ....
tsuyoku natte-kita	has become stronger (dict. *tsuyoi* 'strong')

'*...te-kuru*' is used in the following way:

ex. *Samuku natte-kimashita-ne.* (It has become cold, hasn't it?)
Daibu joozu-ni natte-kimashita. (He has improved a great deal.)

あ、植木(うえき)も　売(う)っていますよ。 **lines 9-10**

ueki	plants

さあ、このごろの　ことだから、千円(せんえん)は　するでしょうね。 **lines 11-12**

saa	well; I don't know but
kono-goro-no koto-da-kara	since things are as they are now
sen-en-wa suru	it costs (at least) 1,000 yen

'*... no koto-da-kara*' is used in the following examples:

ex. *Ano-hito-no koto-da-kara yamenai-deshoo.* (Since he is such a person, he won't give it up.)

Hiroi Tookyoo-no koto-da-kara, shiranai tokoro-mo takusan arimasu. (Since Tokyo is a big city, there are many places I don't know.)

'*... wa*' in *sen-en-wa suru* means 'at least.'

ex. A: *Dono-kurai renshuu-shinakerya narimasen-ka.* (How long do I have to practice it?) (*kurai=gurai*)

B: *Soo-desu-ne. Sankagetsu-wa renshuu-shinakerya dame-desu-ne.* (Well, you have to practice it for at least three months.)

あれは　何(なん)の　お面(めん)ですか。 **line 13**

o-men	mask

何(なん)とか　いう　漫画(まんが)の　主人公(しゅじんこう)ですよ。 **line 14**

nan-to-ka yuu	I forgot what it's called
manga	comic; cartoon
shujinkoo	hero; main character

スーパーマン(すーぱーまん)の　ような　ものでしょうか。 **line 15**

suupaaman	superman
... no yoona mono	something like ...

'*... no yoona*' is used before nouns and pronouns.

ex. *joyuu-no yoona onna-no-hito* (a woman who is like an actress); *taki* (waterfall)*-no yoona ame* (pouring rain)

Before adjectives and verbs *yoo-ni* is used.

ex. *joyuu-no yoo-ni kiree-na onna-no-hito* (a woman beautiful like an actress); *taki-no yoo-ni furu ame* (rain falling like a waterfall)

At the end of sentence, *-yoo-desu* is used to mean 'it seems.' (See lines 23-24)

ex. *O-matsuri-ga aru-yoo-desu.* (It seems they're having a festival.)

ええ。ああいうのが こどもには 人気(にんき)が あるらしいんですよ。**lines 16-17**

aa-yuu-no — that kind of thing (cf. *koo-yuu-no,* Lesson 18)

kodomo — child; children

...ni ninki-ga aru — be popular among... (*lit.* there is popularity in...)

... rashii-desu — it seems...

'*...rashii-desu*' is similar in meaning to *-yoo-desu*; the difference is that *-rashii-desu* is used when the speaker has reliable grounds for his judgment, while *-yoo-desu* can be used when the speaker does not have good basis for his judgment.

'*...no yoona*' and *...rashii* are used differently:

ex. *onna-no yoona hito* (a man who looks like a woman)
onna-rashii hito (a womanly woman)
joyuu-no yoona hito (a woman who looks like an actress but is not really an actress)
joyuu-rashii hito (a woman who actually is an actress and who has every characteristic one would expect in an actress)

なにかの みせものですね。 **line 19**

misemono — a show (usually of unusual, mysterious nature)

人(ひと)が おおぜい あつまってる ところを みると、きっと おもしろいん-ですよ。 **lines 20-21**

...ga atsumatte-ru — =*...ga atsumatte-iru* (have gathered)

(dict. *atsumaru*) (cf. . . .*o atsumeru*, Lesson 13)

. . .tokoro-o miru-to	judging from that . . .
kitto omoshiroi-n-desu	it must be interesting

あの 番組を 見る ために は もう かえらなきゃ… **lines 24-25**

bangumi	(TV or radio) program
miru tame-niwa	in order to see
kaeranakya . . .	=*kaeranakereba. . .* (we have to go back)

Tame is added to the dictionary form of verbs to indicate purpose.

ex. *Joozu-ni hanasu tame-ni renshuu-shite-imasu.* (We're practicing so that we can speak well.)

Ikiru tame-ni taberu. (We eat to live.)

It is also added to expressions consisting of a noun+*no*.

ex. *Sono kikai-wa nan-no tame-ni kau-n-desu-ka.* (What are you going to buy that machine for?)

Otoko-wa tsuma-to kodomo-no tame-ni hataraku. (A man works for his wife and children.)

The contraction *-kerya* for *-kereba* was introduced in Lesson 27; *-kereba* has another contracted form, *-kya*. This form is slightly more popular, especially among young people.

ex.			
iku	*ikanakereba*	*ikanakerya*	*ikanakya*
taberu	*tabenakereba*	*tabenakerya*	*tabenakya*
suru	*shinakereba*	*shinakerya*	*shinakya*
kuru	*konakereba*	*konakerya*	*konakya*

ex. *Moo dekakenakya ma-ni awanai.* (I won't be in time unless I leave now.)

Kusuri-o nomanakya dame-desu-yo. (You have to take some medicine.)

Sometimes the part following *-nakya* is left out when the meaning is clear, as in lines 24-25.

ex. *Moo dekakenakya.* (I have to start now.)

Kusuri-o nomanakya. (You have to take some medicine.)

あれが　はじまるのは　何時(なんじ)でしたか。 **line 26**

The past form is sometimes used when trying to recall something, as it is in this sentence.

ex. *Anoo, shitsuree-desu-ga donata-deshita-ka.* (Excuse me, but I've forgotten who you are.)

じゃ、もう　二十分(にじっぷん)しか　ありませんね。 **line 28**

'*...shika ...nai*' is used when the speaker feels that the amount referred to is small. It's the opposite of *...mo* (*aru*), explained in Lessons 16 and 27.

ex. A: *Ikutsu-gurai kanji-o shitte-imasu-ka.* (How many kanji do you know?)

B: *Nihyaku-gurai-shika shirimasen.* (I know only two hundred.)

B's answer can be

B: *Nihyaku-mo shitte-imasu.* (I know as many as two hundred.)

練習

I.　…ようです

形の練習

例にならって練習しなさい。

（A）例：人気(にんき)が　あります。→人気(にんき)が　あるようです。

1．かつぎ手(て)が　おおぜい　います。　2．こまっています。

3．植木(うえき)も　売(う)っています。　4．千円(せんえん)は　します。

5．時間(じかん)が　あまり　ありません。　6．九時(くじ)から　はじまります。

（B）例：なにかの　みせものです。→なにかの　みせものの　ようです。

1．漫画(まんが)の　主人公(しゅじんこう)です。　2．主人公(しゅじんこう)の　お面(めん)です。

3．あれは　おみこしです。　4．おもしろい　番組(ばんぐみ)です。

5．田中(たなか)さんは　はじめてです。　6．有名(ゆうめい)な　大学(だいがく)です。

（C）例：スーパーマン、もの→スーパーマンの　ような　ものです。

1．漫画、もの
2．おまつり (festival)、もの
3．女優 (actress)、人
4．大臣 (minister)、人
5．みせもの、もの
6．劇場 (theater)、ところ

（D）例：おまつり、にぎやか　→おまつりの　ように　にぎやかです。

1．こども、元気
2．漫画、おもしろい
3．スーパーマン、つよい
4．女優、きれい
5．公園、ひろい
6．お寺、しずか

使いかたの練習

下線のところに適当なことばを入れて話をしなさい。

きょうは ▲わたしの　国の　おまつりに　ついて　すこし　話したいと思います。

わたしの　国の　おまつりも　日本の　おまつりの　ように ▲にぎやかです*。日本の ▲おみこし(1)の　ような　ものも　あります。店も ▲たくさん　出て、▲植木(2)の　ような　ものや ▲お面(2)の　ような　ものを　売ります。

（*If opposite, say…おまつりは　日本の　おまつりの　ように　にぎやかじゃありません。）

（1）みせもの、おどり (dance)、しばい (play)

（2）人形、おもちゃ (toy)、道具 (tool)

II.　…しか（…）ない

形の練習

例にならってかえなさい。

（A）例：時間が　二十分　あります。→二十分しか　ありません。

1. 人(ひと)が　十人(じゅうにん)　います。
2. 人(ひと)が　五人(ごにん)　来(き)ます。
3. お金(かね)を　百円(ひゃくえん)　持(も)っています。
4. 本(ほん)を　一ページ(いちぺーじ)(page) 読(よ)みます。
5. 店(みせ)が　二軒(にけん)　あります。
6. 日本語(にほんご)は　すこし　話(はな)せます。

（B）例(れい)：人(ひと)が　五人(ごにん)　来(き)ました。→人(ひと)が　五人(ごにん)しか　来(き)ませんでした。

1. おまつりを　一度(いちど)　見(み)ました。
2. 日本語(にほんご)を　一年(いちねん)　勉強(べんきょう)しました。
3. これは　千円(せんえん)　しました。
4. 人(ひと)が　すこし　あつまりました。
5. 植木(うえき)が　三本(さんぼん)　ありました。
6. お金(かね)を　千円(せんえん)　もらいました。

使いかたの練習

つぎの質問(しつもん)に「…しか（…）ない」の形を使ってこたえなさい。

例(れい)：あの　へやに　人(ひと)が　▲何人(なんにん)ぐらい　いますか。
　　——→▲ひとりしか　いません。

1. この　本(ほん)を　何ページ(なんぺーじ) (how many pages) 読(よ)みましたか。
2. いま　お金(かね)を　いくら　持(も)っていますか。
3. 日本語(にほんご)の　ことばを　いくつぐらい　知(し)っていますか。
4. 日本語(にほんご)を　何(なん)か月(げつ)ぐらい　勉強(べんきょう)しましたか。
5. 日本人(にほんじん)の　ともだちは　何人(なんにん)ぐらい　いますか。
6. きのう　何時間(なんじかん)ぐらい　ねむりましたか。
7. きょう　何回(なんかい) (how many times) 食事(しょくじ) (meal) を　しましたか。

Note： おなじ練習を「…も」を使ってしなさい。 (The answers could be humorous.)

III. …ために

形の練習

例にならって文(ぶん)をつくりなさい。

（A）例：日本語(にほんご)を　勉強(べんきょう)する　→日本語(にほんご)を　勉強(べんきょう)する　ために　ここへ　来(き)-
ました。

1. おまつりを　見る　　2. ともだちに　会う

3. 大学に　はいる　　4. 植木を　買う

5. 仕事を　さがす (look for)　　6. 試験を　受ける (take)

（B）例：日本語の　勉強→日本語の　勉強の　ために　来ました。

1. 仕事　　2. 調査　　3. 研究 (research)

4. 会社の　仕事　　5. 会議　　6. 見物 (sightseeing)

（C）例：こども→こどもの　ために　はたらいています。

1. 両親　　2. 家族 (family)　　3. つま (wife)

4. 会社　　5. 母　　6. 国

IV. …ところを　みると

形の練習

例にならって文をつくりなさい。

例：人が　おおぜい　あつまっている

→人が　おおぜい　あつまっている　ところを　みると、きっと　おもしろいんですよ。

1. みんなが　読んでいる　　2. みんなが　わらっている

3. よく　売れている (selling)　　4. 買う　人が　多い

5. おおぜいの　人が　読んでいる　　6. あんなに　人が　あつまっている

使いかたの練習

つぎの会話の下線のところをかえて練習しなさい。

例：おもしろい　ものを　売っている

A：あれ、何でしょうね。

B：人が ▲おおぜい　あつまっていますね。

A：あんなに　あつまっている　ところを　みると、なにか　あるんですよ。

B：おもしろい　ものを　売(う)っているのかも　しれませんね。

A：行(い)ってみましょうか。

B：ええ、そう　しましょう。

1．やすい　ものを　売(う)っている
2．おもしろい　みせものを　やっている
3．有名(ゆうめい)な　人(ひと)が　来(き)た
4．だれかが　けんかを　している

V．…なきゃ

形の練習

例にならって練習しなさい。

例：行(い)く→行(い)かなければ、行(い)かなきゃ

1．たべる　2．読(よ)む　3．買(か)う　4．する

5．かえる　6．やめる　7．来(く)る　8．来(き)てもらう

VI．…てくる

使いかたの練習

つぎの会話の下線のところをかえて練習しなさい。

例：さむく　なる、冬(ふゆ)

A：さむく　なってきましたね。

B：ええ、もう　すぐ　冬(ふゆ)ですね。

A：そろそろ　冬(ふゆ)の　準備(じゅんび)(preparation)を　しなきゃ　なりませんね。

B：そうですね。いろいろ　冬(ふゆ)の　ものを　買(か)わなきゃ…

1．さむく　なる、クリスマス(Christmas)
2．あたたかく(warm)なる、春(はる)
3．あつく　なる、夏(なつ)
4．すずしく(cool)なる、秋(あき)
5．さむく　なる、お正月(しょうがつ)(New Year's Day)
6．出発(しゅっぱつ)(departure)が　近(ちか)づく(draw near)、旅行(りょこう)(trip)

発音練習

A．ひとつひとつの (each) 音を、はっきり (clearly) 発音してください。

1．さしすせそ　　2．さしすせそ

3．させしす　　4．せそさそ

5．しゃせししゅ　　6．せしょしゃしょ

B．1．しゃしん　2．れんしゅう　3．ししゅう

4．へんしゅう　5．ふうしゅう　6．さいしゅう

7．しっそ、ちっそ　8．してき、ちてき　9．しほう、ちほう

10．しゅうしょく、ちゅうしょく　11．しゅうしゅう、しゅうちゅう

12．しゃしょう、しゃちょう

C．Bの 7 ～12のことばを入れて練習しなさい。

例：しっそと　言ったんじゃ　ありません。ちっそと　言ったんです。

読む練習

このごろ、体の不自由な(1)人をだいじにするという傾向がつよくなってきた。けさの新聞によると(2)、多くの企業がこういう人たちをやとう(3)ようになってきた(4)そうである。これはたいへんよいことだ。目(5)の見えない(6)人、耳(7)のきこえない(8)人などを、とくべつの(9)人のように考えて自分と関係(10)がないように思うことはやめなければならない。

(1) handicapped　(2) according to ～　(3) employ　(4) come to ～, Lesson 30
(5) eye　(6) cannot see, dict. 見える　(7) ear　(8) cannot hear, dict. きこえる
(9) special　(10) relation

*dict. 見える。 **dict. きこえる。

書く練習

ひらがなで書きなさい。

1．*kaisha*　　2．*chawan*　　3．*kyaku*

4. *kyuu-ni*　5. *nyuugaku*　6. *shuuchuu*
7. *kyoo*　8. *joozu*　9. *toshokan*
10. *hon-o yomu*　11. *gohan-o taberu*
12. *gakkoo-e iku*　13. *uchi-e kaeru*
14. *Ja, moo uchi-e kaerimashoo.*

(1. かいしゃ　2. ちゃわん　3. きゃく
4. きゅうに　5. にゅうがく　6. しゅうちゅう
7. きょう　8. じょうず　9. としょかん
10. ほんを　よむ　11. ごはんを　たべる　12. がっこうへ　いく
13. うちへ　かえる　14. じゃ、もう　うちへ　かえりましょう。)

かたかなを読む練習

つぎのかたかなを読みなさい。

1. コーヒー　2. スポーツ　3. リボン
4. ホテル　5. アルバイト　6. ビール
7. ドライブ　8. ストーブ　9. ボーナス
10. キャベツ　11. クラシック　12. レンタ・カー

(1. *koohii*　2. *supootsu*　3. *ribon*
4. *hoteru*　5. *arubaito*　6. *biiru*
7. *doraibu*　8. *sutoobu*　9. *boonasu*
10. *kyabetsu*　11. *kurashikku*　12. *renta-kaa*)

聞く練習

テープの話を聞いて質問にこたえなさい。

1. この人(ひと)は　いつ　日本(にほん)へ　来(き)たのですか。
2. 日本(にほん)に　一(いっ)か月(げつ)しか　いなかったのですか。
3. 来月(らいげつ)　国(くに)へ　かえるのは　何(なん)の　ためですか。
4. なぜ　国(くに)へ　かえるのが　ざんねんなのですか。

第二十九課(だいにじゅうきゅうか)　おめでとうございます

Dialogue

(Yoshio, Michiko's brother, has found a job. The family invites Johnson over to celebrate.)

ジョンソン：　おめでとうございます。

良夫(よしお)：　ありがとうございます。

ジョンソン：　どんな　会社(かいしゃ)ですか。

良夫(よしお)：　造船会社(ぞうせんがいしゃ)、つまり　船(ふね)を　つくる　会社(かいしゃ)です。

ジョンソン：　いいですね。

良夫(よしお)：　ぼくには　むいていそうです。

ジョンソン：　朝(あさ)は　何時(なんじ)に　出勤(しゅっきん)ですか。

良夫(よしお)：　九時(くじ)って　ことに　なってますが、新入社員(しんにゅうしゃいん)は　十五分(じゅうごふん)ぐらい　早(はや)く　来(く)る　ように　言(い)われてます。

みちこ：　じゃ、六時(ろくじ)ごろ　おきなくちゃ。にいさんは　朝(あさ)ねぼうだから、おきられるか　どうか　心配(しんぱい)だわ。

良夫(よしお)：　だいじょうぶさ。みちこが　まだ　ねてる　うちに　出(で)ていくよ。

ジョンソン：　はりきっていますね。でも、はりきりすぎて　体(からだ)を　こわさない　ように　してください。

良夫(よしお)：　ご心配(しんぱい)なく。わかいんですから、少(すこ)しぐらい　むりを　したって　平気(へいき)ですよ。

母(はは)：　ジョンソンさん、もう　少(すこ)し　ビール、いかが。それとも、ウイスキーでも　持(も)ってきましょうか。きょうは　おいわいなんですから、たくさん　のんでください。

ジョンソン：　はい。でも、もう　ビールは　やめて、ごはんを　いただく　ことに　します。

母(はは)：　そうですか。じゃ、そう　しましょうか。 23

みちこ：　ええ。いま　ごはんと　おみそしる、持(も)ってくるわ。

Dialogue

Lesson 29	*Dai-nijuukyuuka*
CONGRATULATIONS!	***OMEDETOO-GOZAIMASU***
Johnson: Congratulations, Yoshio!	*Jonson: Omedetoo-gozaimasu.*
Yoshio: Thank you.	*Yoshio: Arigatoo-gozaimasu.*
J: What type of company are you going to work for?	*J: Donna kaisha-desu-ka.*
Y: A shipbuilding company.	*Y: Zoosen-gaisha, tsumari fune-o tsukuru kaisha-desu.*
J: That's good!	*J: Ii-desu-ne.*
Y: It seems to be the kind of work I'm best suited to.	*Y: Boku-niwa muite-isoo-desu.*
J: What time do you have to be there in the morning?	*J: Asa-wa nanji-ni shukkin-desu-ka.*
Y: Nine is the starting time, but the new employees are supposed to be there about fifteen minutes ahead of time.	*Y: Kuji-tte koto-ni natte-masu-ga, shinnyuu-shain-wa juugofun-gurai hayaku kuru yoo-ni iwarete-masu.*
Michiko: Then you have to get up at about six. Since you're a late riser, I'm worried that you may not be able to get up in time.	*Michiko: Ja, rokuji-goro okinaku-cha. Niisan-wa asaneboo-da-kara, okirareru-ka doo-ka shinpai-da-wa.*
Y: Don't worry. I'll get up and be out before you get up.	*Y: Daijoobu-sa. Michiko-ga mada nete-ru uchi-ni dete-iku-yo.*
J: You're certainly enthusiastic about your job, Yoshio. But please try not to overwork yourself and damage your health.	*J: Harikitte-imasu-ne. Demo, harikirisugite karada-o kowasanai yoo-ni shite-kudasai.*
Y: Don't worry. I'm young. Overworking a little bit won't hurt me. in the least.	*Y: Goshinpai-naku. Wakai-n-desu-kara, sukoshi-gurai muri-o shitatte heeki-desu-yo.*

Mother: Mr. Johnson, have some more beer, please. Would you rather have some whiskey? We're celebrating today, so please drink your fill.

J: Thank you, but I think I'll stop drinking and start on my meal.

Mo: Yes, let's do that.

Mi: All right. I'll bring the rice and *misoshiru.*

Haha: Jonson-san, moo sukoshi bi-iru ikaga. Soretomo, uisukii-demo motte-kimashoo-ka. Kyoo-wa oi-wai-na-n-desu-kara, takusan non-de-kudasai.

J: Hai. Demo, moo biiru-wa yamete, gohan-o itadaku koto-ni shimasu.

H: Soo-desu-ka. Ja, soo shimashoo-ka.

M: Ee. Ima gohan-to omisoshiru, mo-tte-kuru-wa.

Explanation

(In this lesson you will learn the following expressions; ····*yoo-ni yuu*, 'to tell someone to ····'; ····*koto-ni suru*, 'to decide on ····ing'; and ····*koto-ni naru*, 'to be decided.')

おめでとうございます。 **line 1**

omedetoo-gozaimasu congratulations

Omedetoo or *Omedetoo-gozaimasu*(more polite) is used either by itself as it is used here, or with a word preceding it as in the following examples.

ex. *Shinnen omedetoo-gozaimasu.* (Happy New Year!)
Akemashite omedetoo-gozaimasu. (Happy New Year!)
O-tanjoobi omedetoo-gozaimasu. (Happy birthday!)

造船会社(ぞうせんがいしゃ)、つまり 船(ふね)を つくる 会社(かいしゃ)です。 **line 4**

zoosen-gaisha shipbuilding company (*zoosen* 'shipbuilding')

tsumari namely; in other words

fune ship; boat

····*o tsukuru* make ····

ぼくには　むいていそうです。 **line 6**

....ni muite-isoo it looks like it suits....(dict. *muku* 'to suit')

朝は　何時に　出勤ですか。 **line 7**

shukkin going to office

九時って　ことに　なってますが、新入社員は　十五分ぐらい　早く来る　ように　言われてます。 **lines 8-9**

....tte koto =...*to yuu koto* (the fact that....)
....koto-ni natte-iru it has been decided that....
kuji-tte koto-ni natte-masu we're supposed to come at nine (*lit.* it's been decided that the time is 9)
hayaku kuru yoo-ni iwarete-masu we have been told to come early

'*....koto-ni natte-iru*' means 'it has been decided.' (cf. *....koto-ni suru*)

ex. A: *Oshoogatsu-niwa nani-o shimasu-ka.* (What do you do to celebrate New Year's Day?)

B: *Otoso-o nomu koto-ni natte-imasu.* (We have a custom of having *otoso*—special drink for New Year's Day.)

'*....yoo-ni yuu*' is used in conveying someone's command. The verb preceding *yoo-ni* takes the dictionary form.

ex. *Katoo-sensee-ga kono tegami-o dasu yoo-ni osshaimashita**. (Prof. Kato told me to mail this letter.) (*said—polite, dict. *ossharu*→*osshaimasu*, irreg.)

O-isha-san-ni ni-sannichi yasumu yoo-ni iwaremashita. (I was told by the doctor to take a rest for a couple of days.)

じゃ、六時ごろ　おきなくちゃ。 **line 10**

okinakucha =*okinakute-wa (naranai)*

'*....nakute-wa*' means 'if you do not....' The expression....*nakute-wa naranai* means 'must, have to,' just as....*nakereba naranai* does.

ex. *dekakenakute-wa naranai=dekakenakereba naranai*
yomanakute-wa narimasen=yomanakereba narimasen

The expression ····*nakute-wa* is very often used in its contracted form, ····*nakucha.*

ex. *dekakenakute-wa=dekakenakucha*
yomanakute-wa=yomanakucha (cf. Lesson 20)

にいさんは 朝(あさ)ねぼうだから、おきられるか どうか 心配(しんぱい)だわ。

lines 10-11

niisan	older brother
asa-neboo	late riser
okirareru-ka doo-ka	whether he (you) can get up or not
shinpai-da-wa	I'm worried (*wa* is a feminine ending.)

Niisan can mean 'someone's older brother' or can be used as it is here by Michiko, to address one's own older brother.

だいじょうぶさ。 みちこが まだ ねてる うちに 出(で)ていくよ。

lines 12-13

Sa in *daijoobu-sa* is used to give emphasis to the statement. It is similar to *-yo*, but a little lighter; it is used mostly by men.

mada	still
nete-ru uchi-ni	while you're sleeping; before you wake up (dict. *neru*)
dete-iku	I'll go out

'····*uchi-ni*' is used to mean 'before some change takes place.' (cf. ····*Nihon-ni irassharu uchi-ni*····, Lesson 19)

ex. *Akarui uchi-ni kaerimashoo.* (Let's go home while it is light.)
Kuraku naranai uchi-ni kaerimashoo. (Let's go home before it becomes dark.)

はりきっていますね。でも、はりきりすぎて 体(からだ)を こわさない ように してください。

lines 14-15

harikitte-imasu-ne	you're in high spirits; you're anxious to work (dict. *harikiru*)

harikirisugite being overanxious (dict. *harikirisugiru*)

karada-o kowasanai yoo-ni shite-kudasai please try not to ruin your health (dict. *kowasu* 'to damage')

'....*yoo-ni suru*' means 'to endeavor to do something.'

ex. *Asa hayaku okiru yoo-ni shite-kudasai.* (Please try to get up early in the morning.)

Kuraku naranai uchi-ni kaeru yoo-ni shimashoo. (Let's try to go home before it becomes dark.)

It is different from ....*te-miru*, which is used when one tries something and sees the result; *yoo-ni suru* is used when efforts to overcome difficulty are involved.

'....*nai yoo-ni suru*' means 'try not to....'

ex. *Karada-ga yowai-node muri-o shinai yoo-ni shite-imasu.* (I try not to overwork myself because I'm not very healthy.)

ご心配(しんぱい)なく。 **line 16**

go-shinpai-naku don't worry

Here are some other idiomatic phrases with *naku*.

go-enryo-naku (don't be reserved)

o-kamai-naku (don't bother)

わかいんですから、少(すこ)しぐらい　むりを　したって　平気(へいき)ですよ。 **lines 16-17**

wakai young

sukoshi-gurai a little bit

muri-o shitatte even if I overwork myself

shitatte =*shite-mo*

heeki all right; doesn't matter (*-na* adj.)

'...*tatte*' is more colloquial than ...*te-mo*.

ex. *Ikura kangaetatte wakaranai.* (I don't understand no matter how hard I try to figure it out.)

Ima-kara ittatte ma-ni aimasen-yo. (We won't reach there in time if we start now.)

ジョンソン(じょんそん)さん、もう　少(すこ)し　ビール(びーる)　いかが。 **line 18**

ikaga(-desu-ka) =*doo(-desu-ka)* (polite)

The use of polite word *ikaga* here, instead of *doo*, and without adding *-desu-ka* is a feminine usage.

ex. *Kono-goro o-genki?* (How are you these days?)

それとも、ウイスキーでも　持ってきましょうか。 **lines 18-19**

soretomo	or; rather than that
uisukii-demo	whiskey or something like that
... *(o)motte-kimashoo-ka*	shall I bring ...? (dict. *motte-kuru;* here, *-o* is replaced with *-demo*)

'... *demo*' in *uisukii-demo* means '... or something like that'; it is used to soften the sentence, especially in suggesting something.

ex. *Ocha-demo nomimashoo-ka.* (Shall we have some tea?)

はい。でも、もう　ビールは　やめて、ごはんを　いただく　ことに　します。

lines 21-22

gohan	meal; cooked rice
····*o itadaku koto-ni shimasu.*	I'll have ···(*lit.* I decide on having ····)

'···*koto-ni suru*' is used when one decides on something.

ex. *Kuni-e kaeru koto-ni shimashita.* (I've decided to return to my country.)

ええ。いま　ごはんと　おみそしる、持ってくるわ。 **line 24**

gohan-to o-misoshiru	cooked rice and *miso* soup

When alcoholic drinks are served as part of meal, usually the beverages are served with the main dishes. Rice and *miso* or clear soup are served only after one is through drinking.

練習

I. …ことに　なっている

形の練習

例にならって練習しなさい。

（A）例：九時(くじ)に　はじまります→九時(くじ)に　はじまる　ことに　なっています。

1. 八時(はちじ)に　出勤(しゅっきん)します
2. 土曜(どよう)と　日曜(にちよう)は　休(やす)みます
3. 十五日(じゅうごにち)に　お金(かね)を　はらいます
4. 一日(いちにち)おきに (every other day) 行(い)きます
5. 日曜(にちよう)には　朝(あさ)ねぼうを　します
6. お正月(しょうがつ)には　おいわいを　します

（B）例：出勤(しゅっきん)は　九時(くじ)→出勤(しゅっきん)は　九時(くじ)って　ことに　なってます。

1. 仕事(しごと)は　毎日(まいにち)
2. 九時(くじ)に　出勤(しゅっきん)
3. 土曜(どよう)と　日曜(にちよう)は　休(やす)み
4. お金(かね)を　はらうのは　十五日(じゅうごにち)
5. お茶(ちゃ)は　十時(じゅうじ)
6. 日曜日(にちようび)は　朝(あさ)ねぼう

II. …ことに　する

形の練習

例にならって練習しなさい。

例：日本語(にほんご)を　ならいます (learn)→日本語(にほんご)を　ならう　ことに　しました。

1. 造船会社(ぞうせんがいしゃ)に　はいります
2. 十五分(じゅうごふん)　早(はや)く　出勤(しゅっきん)します
3. 朝(あさ)、六時(ろくじ)に　おきます
4. ごはんを　いただきます
5. ビール(びーる)を　やめます
6. 国(くに)へ　かえります

I, II の使いかたの練習

つぎの会話の下線のところをかえて練習しなさい。

例：夏休(なつやす)み、国(くに)へ　かえる

A：夏休(なつやす)みは　いつから　はじまりますか。
B：十日(とおか)から　はじまる　ことに　なっています。
A：どんな　ことを　する　つもりですか、夏休(なつやす)みには。
B：国(くに)へ　かえる　ことに　しました。

1. 夏休(なつやす)み、旅行(りょこう)を　する
2. 冬休(ふゆやす)み、ここに　いる
3. 春休(はるやす)み、国(くに)へ　かえる
4. 休(やす)み、アルバイト(あるばいと)を　する

III. …ように　言(い)う

形の練習

例にならって練習しなさい。

（A）例：朝(あさ)　早(はや)く　おきます　→朝(あさ)　早(はや)く　おきる　ように　言(い)われました。

1. 夜(よる)　早(はや)く　ねます
2. たばこを　やめます
3. 毎週(まいしゅう)(every week)手紙(てがみ)を　出(だ)します
4. へやの　かぎを　かけます(lock)
5. いそいで　やります
6. 九時(くじ)に　出勤(しゅっきん)します

（B）例：むりを　しません　→むりを　しない　ように　しています。

1. おさけを　あまり　のみません
2. たばこを　あまり　すいません
3. はりきりすぎません
4. 体(からだ)を　こわしません
5. 心配(しんぱい)を　しません
6. 人(ひと)に　お金(かね)を　かりません

使いかたの練習

つぎの話の下線のところをかえて練習しなさい。

例：朝(あさ)　早(はや)く　おきる

わたしが　国(くに)を　出(で)る　時(とき)、母(はは)は　心配(しんぱい)して、いろいろな　ことを　言(い)いました。むりを　しない　ようにとか、朝(あさ)　早(はや)く　おきる　ようにとか…ですから　わたしは　母(はは)に　言(い)われたとおり*、朝(あさ)　早(はや)く　おきるようにしています。（* as I was told)

1. 夜早く　ねる
2. おさけを　あまり　のまない
3. はりきりすぎない
4. 人に　お金を　かりない
5. 毎週　手紙を　出す

IV. …たって

形の練習

例にならって練習しなさい。

例：むりを　しても　だいじょうぶです　→むりを　したって　だいじょうぶです。

1. 字引を　ひいても　わかりません。
2. くすりを　のんでも　なおりません。(dict. *naoru* get well)
3. 練習しても　うまく　なりません。
4. どんなに　はたらいても　お金が　たりません。
5. タクシーで　行っても　のれません。
6. ねても　なおりません。

使いかたの練習

つぎの会話の下線のところをかえて練習しなさい。

例：くすりを　のむ、なおる

A：くすりを　のんでみたら　どうですか。
B：くすりを　のんだって　なおりませんよ。
A：そうですか。くすりを　のめば　なおるかも　しれないと　思いますが…
B：そうですか。
A：のんでみなきゃ、なおるか　どうか　わからないでしょう。
B：そうですね。じゃ、のんでみましょう。

1. 字引(じびき)を　ひく、わかる　　2. 早(はや)く　ねる、なおる.
3. タクシー(たくしー)で　行(い)く、のれる　　4. もっと　練習(れんしゅう)する、うまく　なる
5. もう　一度(いちど)　たのむ、やってくれる

発音練習

か゚き゚く゚け゚こ゚は　鼻音化(びおんか)した(nasalized)　音(おと)をあらわします(show)。

A. 1. が　ぎ　ぐ　げ　ご、　か゚　き゚　く゚　け゚　こ゚

2. が　ぎ　ぐ　げ　ご、　か゚　き゚　く゚　け゚　こ゚

3. が　ぎ　ぐ　げ　ご、　か゚　き゚　く゚　け゚　こ゚

4. が　ぎ　ぐ　げ　ご、　か゚　き゚　く゚　け゚　こ゚

5. が　ぎ　ぐ　げ　ご、　か゚　き゚　く゚　け゚　こ゚

6. が　ぎ　ぐ　げ　ご、　か゚　き゚　く゚　け゚　こ゚

B. 1. かか゚み(mirror)　2. かこ゚(basket)　3. かき゚(key)

C. 下線のところにBのことばを入れて練習しなさい。

例：すみませんが゚　かか゚みを　かしてください。すぐ゚　かえしますから(I'll return it)。

読む練習

人間(にんげん)は、自分(じぶん)にむいている仕事をしている時がもっとも(1)しあわせ(2)である。自分のすきな仕事ならはりきってやれるし、はりきっている時は、少しぐらいむりをしても体をこわさずに(3)*つづける(4)ことができる。朝、出勤のために電車(でんしゃ)にのる会社員(かいしゃいん)(5)のなかで、何パーセント(なんぱーせんと)(6)の人が自分にむいた仕事をしているだろうか。

(1) most　(2) happy　(3) without ruining one's health　(4) continue
(5) company employee　(6) how many percent

* ＝…ないで(without... ing) 例：字引(じびき)を使(つか)わずに読(よ)みます(I read without using dictionaries)。

書く練習

つぎの文をひらがなで書きなさい。

1. *Nan-to yuu hito-desu-ka.*
2. *Moo daijoobu-desu-yo.*
3. *Otooto-ga itsumo osewa-ni natte-orimasu.*
4. *Ofuro-ni hairoo-to shita toki, denwa-ga kakatte-kimashita.*

（1．なんと　いう　ひとですか。　　2．もう　だいじょうぶですよ。
3．おとうとが　いつも　おせわに　なっております。
4．おふろに　はいろうと　した　とき　でんわが　かかってきました。）

かたかなを　読む練習

1．カメラ	2．テレビ	3．ペン	4．ネクタイ
5．ミルク	6．テニス	7．ナイフ	8．ケーキ
9．チーズ	10．ロケット	11．マッチ	12．ソックス
13．テープ	14．チョコレート	15．ニュース	16．シャツ
17．メニュー	18．ノートブック	19．コップ	20．カセットレコーダー
21．フォーク	22．ビルディング	23．カヌー	24．バイオリン

1．*kamera*　2．*terebi*　3．*pen*
4．*nekutai*　5．*miruku* (milk)　6．*tenisu* (tennis)
7．*naifu* (knife)　8．*keeki* (cake)　9．*chiizu* (cheese)
10．*roketto* (rocket)　11．*matchi* (match)　12．*sokkusu* (socks)
13．*teepu* (tape)　14．*chokoreeto* (chocolate)　15．*nyuusu* (news)
16．*shatsu* (shirt)　17．*menyuu* (menu)
18．*nootobukku* (notebook)　19．*koppu* (glass)
20．*kasetto rekoodaa* (cassette recorder)　21．*fooku* (fork)
22．*biruding* (building)　23．*kanuu* (canoe)　24．*baiorin* (violin)

聞く練習

テープの話を聞いてつぎの質問にこたえなさい。

1．この人(ひと)は　いま　病気(びょうき)で　ねていますか。
2．なぜ　夜(よる)　あそびに　出(で)かけない　ことに　しているのですか。
3．きのうは　なぜ　ビール(びーる)を　のみましたか。
4．きょうは　あたまが　いたいので、どう　しなければ　なりませんか。

第三十課（だいさんじっか）　ごちそうさま

Dialogue

(Continued from Lesson 29. Johnson is invited by the Saitos to celebrate Yoshio's new job.)

ジョンソン（じょんそん）：　ごちそうさま。

母（はは）：　あら、もう　おわりですか。ごはんの　おかわりは?

ジョンソン（じょんそん）：　もう　十分（じゅうぶん）　いただきました。

みちこ：　じゃ、お茶（ちゃ）に　しましょう。

ジョンソン（じょんそん）：　おさしみも　てんぷらも　たいへん　おいしかったです。日本料理（にほんりょうり）は　いいですね。

良夫（よしお）：　そうですね。でも、日本料理（にほんりょうり）と　いっても、材料（ざいりょう）は　ほとんど　輸入品（ゆにゅうひん）なんですよ。

ジョンソン（じょんそん）：　そうですか。

良夫（よしお）：　ええ。この　エビ（えび）は　南米（なんべい）あたりから　来（き）た　ものだし、マグロ（まぐろ）は　アフリカ（あふりか）からでしょうね。

母（はは）：　このごろは　海（うみ）が　よごれてしまって、近海（きんかい）では　あまり　おさかなが　とれないんですってね。

ジョンソン（じょんそん）：　ざんねんですね。

みちこ：　海（うみ）ばかりじゃ　なくて、陸（りく）の　ほうだって、公害（こうがい）が　ひどいんですもの。いやに　なっちゃうわ。

ジョンソン（じょんそん）：　でも、このごろは　日本（にほん）でも　公害（こうがい）を　なくそうと　いう　運動（うんどう）が　さかんに　なってきたんじゃ　ないでしょうか。

良夫（よしお）：　ええ、そうですね。公害（こうがい）は　けっして　いい　ことじゃ　ないけど、でも　公害（こうがい）の　おかげで、日本人（にほんじん）も　社会（しゃかい）に　たいして　もっと　関心（かんしん）を　持（も）つ　ように　なってきたんじ-

ゃ ないかと 思いますね。

ジョンソン： なるほどね。

良夫： おい、みちこ、まだ つけものが のこってるぞ。

みちこ： もう おなかが いっぱいで、食べられや しないわ。

母： さあ、お茶が はいりましたよ。どうぞ。

Dialogue

Lesson 30	*Dai-sanjikka*
THANK YOU FOR THE MEAL	***GOCHISOOSAMA***
Johnson: It was a delicious meal, thank you very much.	*Jonson: Gochisoosama.*
Mother: Oh, are you through already? How about another helping of rice?	*Haha: Ara, ▲moo owari-desu-ka. ▲Gohan-no okawari-wa?*
J: No, thank you. I've had plenty.	*J: Moo ▲juubun itadakimashita.*
Michiko: Let's have some tea, then.	*Michiko: Ja, ▲ocha-ni shimashoo.*
J: Both the *sashimi* and *tempura* were very good. Japanese cuisine is wonderful.	*J: Osashimi-mo tenpura-mo taihen oishikatta-desu. Nihon-ryoori-wa ▲ii-desu-ne.*
Yoshio: That's true, but even though it's called Japanese cuisine, actually most of the foodstuffs are imported.	*Yoshio: Soo-desu-ne. Demo, ▲nihon-ryoori-to ittemo, zairyoo-wa ▲hotondo yunyuuhin-na-n-desu-yo.*
J: Really?	*J: Soo-desu-ka.*
Y: Yes. The shrimp is probably from somewhere in South America, and the tuna is very likely from Africa.	*Y: Eee. Kono ebi-wa ▲Nanbee-atari-kara kita mono-da-shi, maguro-wa ▲Afurika-kara-deshoo-ne.*
Mo: With the sea polluted these days they can't catch much fish near the coast, I hear.	*H: Kono-goro-wa ▲umi-ga yogorete-shimatte, kinkai-dewa amari o-sakana-ga ▲torenai-n-desu-tte-ne.*

J : That's too bad.	*J : Zannen-desu-ne.*
Mi : Pollution is bad not only in the sea but also on land, too. It's really discouraging.	*M : Umi-bakari-ja nakute, riku-no hoo-datte, koogai-ga hidoi-n-desu-mono. Iya-ni natchau-wa.*
J : But these days campaigns for getting rid of pollution are becoming more popular in Japan, too, aren't they?	*J : Demo, kono-goro-wa Nihon--demo koogai-o nakusoo-to yuu undoo-ga sakan-ni natte-kita-n-ja nai-deshoo-ka.*
Y : Yes, they are. I think pollution is not a blessing by any means, but it has helped Japanese develop their concern for society.	*Y : Ee, soo-desu-ne. Koogai-wa kesshite ii koto-ja nai-kedo, demo koogai-no okage-de, nihonjin-mo shakai-ni taishite motto kanshin-o motsu yoo-ni natte-kita-n-ja nai-ka-to omoi-masu-ne.*
J : I see.	*J : Naruhodo-ne.*
Y : Hey, Michiko. You haven't eaten your pickles yet.	*Y : Oi, Michiko, mada tsukemono-ga nokotte-ru-zo.*
Mi : I'm so full. I can't eat any more.	*M : Moo onaka-ga ippai-de, tabe-rare-ya shinai-wa.*
Mo : The tea is ready, everybody.	*H : Saa, ocha-ga hairimashita-yo. Doozo.*

Explanation

(In this lesson you will learn the expressions ...*ja nai-deshoo-ka* and ...*ja nai-ka-to omoimasu* used when stating opinions, together with several useful idiomatic expressions.)

ごちそうさま。 **line 1**

Gochisoosama is said at the end of a meal and *Itadakimasu* is an expression used at the beginning of a meal. These greetings are expressions of thanks for everything (and to everyone) that has made the meal possible. They are used in the home as well as when treated to a meal by someone else. In the latter case, one usually uses them as expressions of thanks to the host.

あら、もう　おわりですか。ごはんの　おかわりは？ **line 2**

owari	the end; it's over
okawari	another helping

もう　十分（じゅうぶん）　いただきました。 **line 3**

juubun	plenty (*lit.* sufficient)

This is a set expression corresponding to 'No, thank you. I've had plenty.'

じゃ、お茶（ちゃ）に　しましょう。 **line 4**

ocha-ni shimashoo	Let's have tea (*lit.* let's decide on having tea)

'*... ni suru*' is used in the following ways:

ex. *Gohan-ni shimashoo.* (Let's eat.)
Kore-de owari-ni shiyoo. (Let's call it a day.)
Osake-ni shimasu-ka, biiru-ni shimasu-ka. (Would you like sake or beer?)

おさしみも　てんぷらも　たいへん　おいしかったです。日本料理（にほんりょうり）は　いいーですね。 **lines 5-6**

tenpura	*tempura*.
nihon-ryoori	Japanese cuisine (*ryoori* 'cooking')

でも、日本料理（にほんりょうり）と　いっても、材料（ざいりょう）は　ほとんど　輸入品（ゆにゅうひん）なんですよ。 **lines 7-8**

zairyoo	material; foodstuff
hotondo	almost all
yunyuuhin	imported good (opp. *yushutsuhin*)

この　エビ(えび)は　南米(なんべい)あたりから　来(き)た　ものだし、マグロ(まぐろ)は　アフリカ(あふりか)からでしょうね。 **lines 10-11**

ebi	shrimp; prawn
Nanbee	South America
...atari	around...(cf. *raishuu-atari*, Lesson 25)
maguro	tuna
Afurika	Africa

このごろは　海(うみ)が　よごれてしまって、近海(きんかい)では　あまり　おさかながとれないんですってね。 **lines 12-13**

umi	the sea
yogorete-shimatte	has been polluted (dict. *yogoreru*, 'to become dirty')
kinkai	near the coast
torenai	can't be caught (dict. *toru*)
... n-desu-tte	I understand ... (used usu. by women)

'*... desu-tte*' is a contraction of *-desu-to* and stands for *-desu-to kikimashita* (I heard) or *-desu-to iimashita* (someone said). This contraction is used mostly by women in polite speech; in familiar conversation both men and women use *-da-tte* instead.

ex. A: *Kare, itsu kaesu-tte itta?* (When did he say he will return it?)

B: *Toobun kaesenai-n-da-tte* (He said he can't return it for the time being.)

海(うみ)ばかりじゃ　なくて、陸(りく)の　ほうだって、公害(こうがい)が　ひどいんですもの。いやーになっちゃうわ。 **lines 15-16**

umi-bakari-ja nakute	not only the sea
riku-no hoo-datte	the land also
... datte	=...*mo*
koogai	pollution (*lit.* public nuisance)
hidoi	very bad; serious
iya-ni natchau	I get disgusted (*natchau*= *natte-shimau*)

'...*bakari-ja naku (te)* ...*mo* (or *datte*)' corresponds to 'not only .. but also...'

ex. *Kono-goro-wa onna-no-hito-bakari-ja nakute otoko-no-hito-mo oshare-ni narimashita-ne.* (Nowadays not only women but also men try hard to look stylish.)

Nihon-bakari-ja nakute hoka- no kuni-mo soo-desu. (Not only Japan but also other countries are that way.)

Sometimes *-dake* is used instead of *-bakari.*

Kono-goro-wa onna-no hito-dake-ja nakute otoko-no-hito-mo oshare-ni narimashita-ne.

'... *datte*' is used in place of *-mo* in familiar speech.

でも、このごろは　日本(にほん)でも　公害(こうがい)を　なくそうと　いう　運動(うんどう)が　さかんに なってきたんじゃ　ないでしょうか。 **lines 17-19**

...*o nakusoo-to yuu undoo*	campaign to eliminate...(dict. *nakusu*)
sakan-ni natte-kita	it has become popular
...*n-ja nai-deshoo-ka*	isn't it...?; don't you think...?

'...*n-ja nai-deshoo-ka*' is often added to one's statement and used to solicit agreement in a reserved manner.

ex. *Nihongo-wa wariai yasashii-n-ja nai-deshoo-ka.* (Japanese is comparatively easy, don't you think?)

Moo yameta hoo-ga ii-n-ja nai-deshoo-ka. (Isn't it better to stop now?)

公害(こうがい)は　けっして　いい　ことじゃ　ないけど、でも　公害(こうがい)の　おかげで、日本人(にほんじん)も　社会(しゃかい)に　たいして　もっと　関心(かんしん)を　持(も)つ　ように　なってきたんじゃ　ないかと　思(おも)いますね。 **lines 20-23**

kesshite	(not) by any means
koogai-no okage-de	thanks to pollution
nihonjin	Japanese (people)
shakai	society
...*ni taishite*	to...; towards...; against...
kanshin	concern; interest
...*o motsu yoo-ni naru*	come to have...

Jin is added to the names of countries and indicates the people.

ex. *Amerika* (America) —*amerikajin* ;
Igirisu (England) —*igirisujin* ;
Furansu —*furansujin* ; *Chuugoku* —*chuugokujin* ;
Roshia —*roshiajin*

'...*ni taishite*' is used as in the following examples.

ex. *Minna-ga kare-ni taishite hantai-shita.* (Everybody opposed him.)
Kanojo-wa dare-ni taishite-mo shinsetsu-desu. (She's kind to everybody.)

'...*ni taisuru*' is used as in the following examples.

ex. *Kare-ni taisuru hantai-ga tsuyoku natte-kita.* (People have come to oppose him more strongly.)

A verb in the present form plus *yoo-ni naru* means 'come to ...'

ex. *Nihongo-ga sukoshi wakaru yoo-ni narimashita.* (Now I understand Japanese a little bit.)
Zuibun joozu-ni hanaseru yoo-ni narimashita-ne. (You can speak very well !)

'...*n-ja nai-ka-to omoimasu*' is similar to ...*n-ja nai-deshoo-ka*, but sounds somewhat more formal.

なるほどね。 **line 24**

naruhodo (*-ne*)	I see

おい、みちこ、まだ　つけものが　のこってるぞ。 **line 25**

oi	hey (used by men)
tsukemono	pickles
...*ga nokotte-ru-zo*	...is (are) left (dict. *nokoru*)

Zo in *nokotte-ru-zo* is used to emphasize the statement. It is similar to *-yo*, but it is used only by men and only in familiar speech.

もう　おなかが　いっぱいで、食べられや　しないわ。 **lines 26-27**

onaka	stomach
onaka-ga ippai	I'm full (opp. *onaka-ga suite-iru*)
taberare-ya shinai	I can't eat

The stem of a verb plus *-wa* or *-ya* and *shinai* is emphatic.

iku —iki-wa (*iki-ya*) *shinai* ; *suru —shi-wa* (*shi-ya*) *shinai*

kuru —ki-wa (*ki-ya*) *shinai* ; *ikeru —ike-wa* (*ike-ya*) *shinai*

ex. *Anna muzukashii koogi, wakari-ya shinai.* (I could never understand such a difficult lecture as that.)

さあ、お茶(ちゃ)が　はいりましたよ。 **line 28**

saa — come; come on (used to invite someone to do something; different from *saa* in Lesson 28)

ocha-ga hairimashita — tea is served (dict. *hairu*; cf. *ocha-o ireru,* Lesson 7)

練習

I.　…ばかりじゃ　なく(て)　…も（＝だって）

形の練習

例にならって練習しなさい。

（A）例：海(うみ)も　陸(りく)も　公害(こうがい)が　ひどい　→海(うみ)ばかりじゃ　なくて、陸(りく)も　公害(こうがい)が　ひどいんです。

1．さしみも　てんぷらも　食(た)べる

2．マグロ(まぐろ)も　エビ(えび)も　輸入(ゆにゅう)する

3．日本人(にほんじん)にも　外国人(がいこくじん) (foreigner)-にも　人気(にんき)が　ある

4．新聞(しんぶん)も　雑誌(ざっし)も　読(よ)んだ

5．発音(はつおん)も　文法(ぶんぽう) (grammar)　も　ちがう

6．肉(にく)も　野菜(やさい)(vegetable)も　食(た)べ-なきゃ　いけない

（B）例：本(ほん)を　読(よ)む、テープ(てーぷ)を　聞(き)く→本(ほん)を　読(よ)むばかりじゃ　なくて、テープ(てーぷ)も　聞(き)きます。

1. 輸入(ゆにゅう)を　する、輸出(ゆしゅつ) (export) を　する

2. 勉強(べんきょう)を　する、スポーツ(すぽーつ)を　する

3. たばこを　やめる、おさけを　へらす (decrease)

4. たばこを　すう、おさけを　のむ

5. 風(かぜ)が　ふく (blow)、雨(あめ)が　ふる

6. ひまが　ある、お金(かね)を　持(も)っている

（C）例：安(やす)い、おいしい→安(やす)いばかりじゃ　なくて、おいしいんです。
かんたんだ、便利(べんり)だ (convenient)→かんたんなばかりじゃ　なくて、便利(べんり)なんです

1. 高(たか)い、おいしく　ない

2. 安(やす)い、サービス(さーびす) (service) が　いい

3. あたらしい、きれいだ

4. 便利(べんり)だ、きれいだ

5. きれいだ、安(やす)い

6. 必要(ひつよう)だ (necessary)、たいせつだ

使いかたの練習

つぎの会話の下線のところをかえて練習しなさい。

例：おいしく　ない

A：こんど　できた　食堂(しょくどう)は　どうですか。行(い)ってみましたか。

B：ええ、先週(せんしゅう)　行(い)ってみましたけど、どうもねえ。

A：おいしく　ないんですか。

B：ええ、おいしく　ないばかりじゃ　なくて、高(たか)いんですよ。

A：そうですか。ざんねんですね。

1. あじ (taste) が　わるい

2. サービス(さーびす)が　わるい

3. さかなが　古(ふる)い

4. 料理(りょうり)が　おそい

II. …(の) おかげで

形の練習

例にならって練習しなさい。

例：先生→先生の　おかげで　日本語が　じょうずに　なってきました。
勉強した→勉強した　おかげで　日本語が　じょうずに　なってきました。

1. 松本先生　　2. みなさん　　3. テープを　聞いた
4. 先生が　教えてくださった　　5. 先生に　教えていただいた
6. 毎日　よく　練習した

III. …(よ)うと　いう

形の練習

例にならって練習しなさい。

例：公害を　なくす→公害を　なくそうと　いう　運動が　さかんに　なってきました。

1. 古い　ものを　見なおす　　2. 不公平を　なくす
3. 入学試験を　かえる　　4. 外国の　ことを　勉強する
5. 外国人の　考えかた (way of thinking) を　勉強する　　6. 外国の　ことに　もっと　関心を　もつ

IV. …んじゃ　ないでしょうか
…んじゃ　ないかと　思います

形の練習

III.「…(よ)うと　いう」の文に「…んじゃ　ないでしょうか」と「…んじゃ　ないかと　思います」をつけて練習しなさい。

例：公害を　なくす→公害を　なくそうと　いう　運動が　さかんに　なってきたんじゃ　ないでしょうか。

→公害を　なくそうと　いう　運動が　さかんに　なってきたんじゃ　ないかと　思います。

使いかたの練習

つぎの話の下線のところをかえて練習しなさい。

例：六か月、日本人の　考えかた

わたしは　日本語の　勉強を　はじめてから　▲<u>六か月</u>に　なります。日本語と　わたしの　国の　ことばは　▲発音ばかりじゃ　なく、▲文法も　ずいぶん　ちがいますから、日本語を　勉強するのは　▲なかなか　たいへんです。でも、▲日本語を　勉強した　おかげで、<u>日本人の</u>　<u>考えかた</u>が　▲少し　わかるように　なってきたんじゃ　ないかと　思います。これからも　▲勉強を　つづけていこう (I'll continue) と　思っています。

1. 一年、日本の　こと
2. 十か月ぐらい、日本人の　気もち (feelings)
3. 一年ちかく (nearly 1 year)、日本の　社会
4. 一年半、日本人の　性格 (character)

発音練習

◦の音 (sound) は　母音 (vowel) が　無声 (voiceless) になります。

A.
1. かき　かきか　きかき　きかきか
2. かく　かくか　くかく　くかくか
3. さし　さしさ　しさし　しさしさ

4. さす　さすさ　すさす　すさすさ
5. しき　すく　ちき　つく
6. ひき　ふく　ぴし　ぷす
7. ます　ます　まし　まし　ました
8. です　です　でし　でし　でした

B. 1. しかく　2. ちかく　3. きかく　4. ひかく　5. ふかく
6. ししょく　7. ちこく　8. きしゅく　9. きかく　10 ひかく

C. Bの1(いち)～5(ご)には「でした」を、6(ろく)～10(じゅう)には「しました」をつけて 練習しなさい。

例： 1. しかく→しかくです。　6. ししょく→ししょくしました。

読む練習

日本料理のなかで外国人に人気があるのは、てんぷら、すし、すきやきなどである。こういう料理は、日本料理といっても材料は輸入品が多い。さかなは近海のものよりも南米やアフリカなど、遠(とお)い外国[(1)]から来たもののほうが多い。一方(いっぽう)[(2)]日本人、とくにわかい人には西洋(せいよう)[(3)]料理や中国(ちゅうごく)[(4)]料理のほうが人気があるのではないかと思われる[(5)]。

(1) foreign country (2) on the other hand (3) Western (4) Chinese (5) it seems

字(じ) (character) を読む練習

つぎのことばを読みなさい。

1. アメリカ　2. イギリス　3. フランス
4. ドイツ　5. カナダ　6. オーストラリア
7. ニュージーランド　8. ソビエト　9. ヨーロッパ

10．アジア　11．ニューヨーク　12．ワシントン

13．パリ　14．ソニー　15．トヨタ

16．ナジョナル　17．ジャパン　タイムズ　18．ソ連(れん)

19．スペイン語　20．日本人とユダヤ人　21．フォークで食べる

22．アメリカ英語(えいご)の発音

1．*Amerika*　2．*Igirisu*　3．*Furansu*　4．*Doitsu*
5．*Kanada* (Canada)　6．*Oosutoraria* (Australia)
7．*Nyuujiirando* (New Zealand)　8．*Sobieto* (Soviet)
9．*Yooroppa* (Europe)　10．*Ajia* (Asia)
11．*Nyuuyooku* (New York)　12．*Washinton* (Washington)
13．*Pari* (Paris)　14．*Sonii* (Sony)　15．*Toyota* (Toyota)
16．*Nashonaru* (National)　17．*Japan Taimuzu* (Japan Times)
18．*Soren* (USSR)　19．*supeingo* (Spanish)
20．*nihonjin-to yudayajin* (Jew)　21．*fooku-de taberu*
22．*amerika-eego-no hatsuon*

聞く練習

テープの話を聞いて質問にこたえなさい。

1．海外旅行(かいがいりょこう)と　外国旅行(がいこくりょこう)は　おなじ　意味(いみ) (meaning) ですか。

2．わかい　人(ひと)と　としより (old people) では、どちらが　多(おお)く　海外旅行(かいがいりょこう)をしますか。

3．外国(がいこく)の　なかで　行(い)く　人(ひと)が　多(おお)いのは　東南(とうなん)アジア(あじあ) (Southeast Asia)と　どこですか。

4．この人(ひと)は　外国旅行(がいこくりょこう)を　やめて　日本(にほん)の　なかだけ　旅行(りょこう)した　ほうがいいと　言(い)っていますか。

5．何(なん)の　ために　日本(にほん)の　なかを　旅行(りょこう)する　ことが　たいせつなのですか。

クイズ(くいず)　（２５課—３０課）(にじゅうごか—さんじっか)

I.　つぎは　AとBの会話(かいわ)です。　(1)　と　(2)　のなかでよいほうに
　○を書(か)いてください。

例：A：おはようございます。

　　B：⑴ おはようございます。（○）
　　　 (2)　さようなら。

1．A：おめでとうございます。
　　B：(1)　ありがとうございます。
　　　 (2)　ご心配(しんぱい)なく。

2．A：これで　失礼(しつれい)します。
　　B：(1)　みなさんに　よろしく。
　　　 (2)　おかえりなさい。

3．A：あと　二(に)、三日(さんにち)で　退院(たいいん)できるそうです。
　　B：(1)　それは　ざんねんですね。
　　　 (2)　それは　よかったですね。

4．A：片道(かたみち)　二時間(にじかん)も　かかるんです。
　　B：(1)　それなら　早(はや)くて　いいですね。
　　　 (2)　それは　たいへんですね。

5．A：むりを　なさらない　ほうが　いいんじゃ　ありませんか。
　　B：(1)　だいじょうぶですよ、わかいんですから。
　　　 (2)　どうぞ　おだいじに。

II.　つぎのa. b. のなかのただしい (correct) ほうに○を書(か)いてください。

a. も b.も どちらもただしいときは、両方(りょうほう) (both) に○を書(か)いてください。

例1：{ a. あした / ⓑ きのう } ここへ　来(き)ました。　例2：{ ⓐ お茶(ちゃ) / ⓑ コーヒー(こーひー) } をのみました。

1. 待(ま)っていたのに { a. 来(き)ました。 / b. 来(き)ませんでした。 }

2. 有名校(ゆうめいこう) { a. を / b. に } 出(で)ると　有利(ゆうり)です。

3. でも、もう　時間(じかん)が　ない { a. よう / b. らしい } ですよ。

4. もう { a. かえらなきゃ / b. かえらなければ } 間(ま)に　合(あ)いません。

5. この　町(まち)は　おまつりの { a. ように / b. ような } にぎやかです。

6. 学校(がっこう)へ　行(い)く { a. はず / b. ため } には　お金(かね)が　いります。

7. あの人(ひと)は　男(おとこ)だけれど { a. 女(おんな)らしい / b. 女(おんな)の　ような } 人(ひと)です。

8. あれは { a. 何(なん)とかいう / b. 何(なに)かという } 漫画(まんが)の　主人公(しゅじんこう)の　お面(めん)です。

9. 仕事(しごと)が　はじまるまで　もう　二十分(にじっぷん)しか　ありませんから、

{ a. すぐ　かえりましょう。 / b. まだ　かえらなくても　いいです。 }

10. ずいぶん　いい　植木(うえき)ですから { a. 千円(せんえん)は　する / b. 千円(せんえん)は　しない } でしょう。

11. 手術（しゅじゅつ）と　いっても {a. かんたんな / b. たいへんな} ものなんですから、心配（しんぱい）しないでください。

12. あんなに　はたらいた {a. のに / b. けれども} お金（かね）を　少（すこ）ししか　くれなかった。

13. 大企業（だいきぎょう）と　中小企業（ちゅうしょうきぎょう） {a. には / b. では} ボーナス（ぼーなす）が　ずいぶん　ちがいます。

14. ずいぶん　さがしましたが、どこへ {a. 行（い）ったのか / b. 行（い）ってしまったのか} わかりません。

15. 人（ひと）が　おおぜい　あつまってる　ところを　みると、きっと {a. おもしろい / b. おもしろく　ない} んですよ。

16. 短大（たんだい）は {a. いくつ / b. 何校（なんこう）} あるのか　知（し）りません。

17. 人間（にんげん）の　心理（しんり）と　して　安（やす）い　ほうを {a. えらぶ / b. 買（か）いたがる} のは　自然（しぜん）です。

18. 一年（いちねん）しか　練習（れんしゅう）しなかったのですから、まだ　じょうずには {a. 話（はな）せます。 / b. 話（はな）せません。}

19. 安（やす）い　植木（うえき） {a. が / b. を} 売（う）っていますね。

20. 体(からだ)を　こわさない { a. ように / b. ようと } してください。

21. 公団住宅(こうだんじゅうたく) { a. なら / b. でも } 安(やす)くて　いいですね。

22. 都心(としん)の　家(いえ)は　高(たか)すぎて　いくら　はたらいても { a. 買(か)えません。 / b. 買(か)えます。 }

23. 少(すこ)しぐらい　むりを { a. したって / b. しても } だいじょうぶです。

24. こどもが { a. ねている　うちに / b. おきる　まえに } 出(で)ていきます。

25. 道(みち)が　こんでいなけりゃ { a. 10分(じっぷん)で / b. 20分(にじっぷん)で } 行(い)きますが、こんでると { a. 10分(じっぷん) / b. 20分(にじっぷん) } ぐらい　かかります。

26. もう　おなかが　いっぱいで { a. 食(た)べられません。 / b. 食(た)べられや　しません。 }

27. { a. 海(うみ)ばかりじゃ　なくて　陸(りく)の　ほうも / b. 海(うみ)も　陸(りく)も } 公害(こうがい)が　ひどく　なりました。

28. 近海(きんかい)では　あまり　さかなが　とれない { a. そうですね。 / b. んですってね。 }

29. なぜ { a. 行(い)かなかったの / b. 行(い)かなかったのか } 知(し)りません。

30. もう　おそいから { a. かえらなくちゃ。 / b. かえらなくちゃ　なりません。 }

III. つぎの英語を日本語に翻訳してください。

1. Can I turn at that corner?
2. By the way, it's about time, isn't it?
3. It must be something interesting.
4. Then you have to get up at about six.
5. Both the *sashimi* and *tempura* were very good.
6. Even though it's called Japanese cuisine, actually most of the foodstuffs are imported.
7. I didn't know until yesterday that you were in the hospital.
8. It's also true that it's advantageous to graduate from a famous university.

ANSWERS TO QUIZZES

(Lesson 1 — Lesson 6)

I. 1. *Tsukue-desu.* 2. *Isu-desu.* 3. *Tokee-desu.* 4. *Yuubinkyoku-desu.* 5. *Jibiki-desu.* 6. *Suiee-desu.* 7. *Yakyuu-desu.* 8. *Eki-desu.*

II. 1. *Sen gohyaku-en.* 2. *Happyaku-en.* 3. *Nanasen nihyaku-en.* 4. *Gogatsu tsuitachi.* 5. *Ichigatsu mikka.* 6. *Kuji sanjippun* or *kuji-han.* 7. *Juuji nijippun.* 8. *Sanji juugofun.* 9. *Gogo shichiji sanjippun* (or *-han*). 10. *Gozen juuichiji-gojuugofun* or *juuniji gofun-mae.*

III. 1. *dare* 2. *nan* 3. *doko* 4. *doko* 5. *doo* 6. *nanji* 7. *ikura* 8. *nanji*

IV. 1. *arimasu* 2. *nomimashita* 3. *imasu* 4. *furimashita* 5. *ikimashita* 6. *imashita* 7. *mimashita* 8. *yomimashita* 9. *aimashita*

V. 1—c; 2—a; 3—d; 4—e; 5—b

VI. 1. *Ima nanji-desu-ka.* 2. *Kore-wa ikura-desu-ka.* 3. *Kore-mo gosen-en-desu-ka.* 4. *Kore-wa mado-desu-ka, to-desu-ka.* 5. *Hoteru-wa hirokute kiree-deshita.* 6. *Ano shiroi tatemono-wa byooin-desu.* 7. *Senshuu-wa isogashiku(wa) arimasen-deshita.* or *Senshuu-wa hima-deshita.* 8. *Maiasa rokuji-han-ni okimasu.* 9. *Donna hon-o yomimashita-ka.* 10. *Supootsu-wa shimasen*(or *yarimasen)-deshita-ka.*

(Lesson 7 — Lesson 12)

I. 1. *Yonin imasu.* 2. *Hai, suwatte-imasu.* 3. *Denwa-o kakete-imasu.* 4. *Ocha-o irete-imasu.* 5. *Otoko-no-hito-no hoo-ga futotte-imasu.* 6. *Asonde-imasu.*

II. 1. *mittsu* 2. *nijuunin-gurai* 3. *Doredemo* 4. *donna* 5. *tsukatte-kudasai*

III. 1. *...goro nemashita.* 2. *Hai* or *Iie.* 3. *...o shimasu.* 4. *Hai* or *Iie.* 5. *Hai* or *Iie.* 6. *Hon, pen, okane, tokee,* etc. 7. *...no hoo-ga ookii-desu.* 8. *...en-gurai motte-imasu.* 9. *Hai* or *Iie.* 10. *Hai* or *Iie.*

IV. 1—d; 2—e; 3—f; 4—b; 5—a; 6—g; 7—c

V. 1. *Doozo okamai-naku.* 2. *Komakai okane-o motte-imasu-ka.* 3. *Denwa-bangoo-o shitte-imasu-ka.* 4. *Senshuu ryooshin-ga tazunete-kimashita.* 5. *Dewa, shikata-ga arimasen-ne.* 6. *Michiko-san-wa kyoo konai-kamo shiremasen.* 7. *Ano kissaten-de nanika nomimashoo.* 8. *Koko-wa konde-imasu. Yameta hoo-ga ii-to omoimasu.* (or, *Hairanai hoo-ga ii-to omoimasu.*)

(Lesson 13 — Lesson 18)

I. 1. *mada; hazu; Onegai-shimasu.* 2. *koraremasu* 3. *ni; irenaide* 4. *yomema-*

sen 5. *ikitai, tsurete-itte* 6. *karite-mo* 7. *dareka* 8. *imasu* 9. *nomeba* 10. *mi-yoo*

II. 1. *Issho-ni ikimashoo.* 2. *(Watashi-wa) haraemasen.* 3. *Sutoobu-ga kiete-imasu.* 4. *Chuugoku-e itta* (or *irasshatta*) *koto-ga arimasu-ka.* 5. *Shoosetsu-o kaite-iru-soo-desu.* 6. *Mae-ni chiisai-no-o motte-imashita.* 7. *Watashi-wa ya-kyuu-ga daisuki-desu.* 8. *Tabako-o sutte-mo ii-desu-ka.* 9. *To-o shimete-kuda-sai.* 10. *Mado-o akete-oite-kudasai.* 11. *Imooto-wa nihon-ningyoo-o hoshigat-te-imasu.* 12. *Kono shokudoo-wa takasoo-desu.* 13. *Ie-ga sangen-mo yakete-shimaimashita.* 14. *Kondo-no nichiyoo-wa doo-desu-ka.* 15. *Amari tooku-ewa ikemasen.*

(Lesson 19 — Lesson 24)

I. 1. (1) 2. (1) 3. (2) 4. (1) 5. (1) 6. (2) 7. (2) 8. (1)

II. ×—1. (c) 2. (b) 3. (c) 4. (b) 5. (a) 6. (c) 7. (b) 8. (b)

III. 1. あねは　去年　結婚しました。　2. 誕生日と　いえば、あさっては　おとうとの　誕生日です。　3. 加藤さんに　あげたら　どうですか。　4. A：あの　本は　いつ　かえせば(or おかえしすれば) いいでしょう(か)。 B：いつでも　都合の　いい　とき　うちへ　持ってきてください。　5. えんぴつを　三本　買ってきてください。　6. わたし(or ぼく)に　やらせてください。　7. この　仕事に(は)　とても(or たいへん)　興味が　あります。　8. 吉田さんを　てつだわなければ　(or てつだわなくちゃ)　なりません。　9. すぐ　しらべに　来ました(or 来てくれました)。　10. 電車を　おりてから　雨に　ふられました。　11. 何度　やって(or やってみて)も　うまく　発音できません(or 言えません)。　12. ゆうべは　よく　ねむれませんでした。

(1. *Ane-wa kyonen kekkon-shimashita.* 2. *Tanjoobi-to ieba, asatte-wa otooto-no tan-joobi-desu.* 3. *Katoo-san-ni agetara doo-desu-ka.* 4. A: *Ano hon-wa itsu kaeseba* (or *o-kaeshi-sureba*) *ii-deshoo(ka).* B: *Itsudemo tsugoo-no ii toki uchi-e motte-kite-kuda-sai.* 5. *Enpitsu-o sanbon katte-kite-kudasai.* 6. *Watashi* (or *Boku*)*-ni yarasete-kudasai.* 7. *Kono shigoto-ni(wa) totemo* (or *taihen*) *kyoomi-ga arimasu.* 8. *Yoshida-san-o tetsu-dawanakereba* (or *tetsudawanakucha*) *narimasen.* 9. *Sugu shirabe-ni kimashita* (or *kite-kuremashita*). 10. *Densha-o orite-kara ame-ni furaremashita.* 11. *Nando yatte* (or *yatte-mite*)*-mo umaku hatsuon-dekimasen* (or *iemasen*). 12. *Yuube-wa yoku nemuremasen-deshita.*)

(Lesson 25 — Lesson 30)

I. 1. (1) 2. (1) 3. (2) 4. (2) 5. (1)

II. 1. b 2. a 3. a, b 4. a, b 5. a 6. b 7. b 8. a 9. a 10. a 11. a 12. a, b 13. b 14. a, b 15. a 16. a, b 17. a, b 18. b 19. b 20. a 21. a 22. a 23. a, b 24. a, b 25. a, b 26. a, b 27. a, b 28. a, b 29. b 30. a, b

III. 1. あの　かどを　まがっても　いいですか。　2. ところで、もう　そろそろ　時間ですね。　3. きっと　おもしろいんですよ。　4. じゃ、六時ごろ　おきなければ (or おきなきゃ、おきなくちゃ)　(なりません)。 5. さしみも　てんぷらも　とても　おいしかったです。　6. 日本料理と　いっても、じつは　材料は　ほとんど　輸入品なんです。　7. 入院なさった　ことを　きのうまで　知りませんでした。　8. 有名な　大学を　出ると　有利だって　ことも　事実です。

ANSWERS TO AURAL COMPREHENSION

Lesson 1

(A) *Goji-desu.* (It's 5 o'clock.) (B) *Rokuji-desu.* (It's 6.) (C) *Sanji-han-desu.* (It's half past 3.)

Lesson 2

(A) 1. *Kyuusen-en.* (She pays 9,000 yen.) 2. *Akai-desu.* (It's red.)

(B) *Hassen gohyaku-en* (He pays 8,500 yen.)

(C) 1. *Roppyaku-en.* (She pays 600 yen.) 2. *Nairon-desu.* (They're nylon.)

Lesson 3

(A) 1. *Byooin.* (She's looking for a hospital.) 2. *Ginkoo-no tonari-ni arimasu.* (It's next to the bank.)

(B) 1. *Kissaten-no mae.* (He's standing in front of the coffee shop.) 2. *Tanaka-san-no goshujin-desu.* (He's Mr. Tanaka.)

(C) 1. *Shokudoo.* (He's looking for a restaurant.) 2. *Yuubinkyoku-no soba-ni arimasu.* (It's near the post office.) 3. *Shiroi-desu.* (It's white.)

Lesson 4

(A) 1. *Hachiji-han-desu.* (It's half past 8.) 2. *Juuniji-ni nemasu.* (He goes to bed at 12.) 3. *Terebi-o mimasu.* (He watches TV.)

(B) 1. *Ginkoo-e ikimasu.* (She's going to the bank.) 2. *Juuji-han-desu.* (It's half past 10.)

(C) 1. *Kin'yoobi-desu.* (It's Friday.) 2. *Eega-o mimasu.* (They're going to the movies.) 3. *Yoji-ni eki-no mae-de.* (They're going to meet in front of the station at 4.)

Lesson 5

(A) 1. *Eega-o mimashita.* (She saw a movie.) 2. *Hai.* (Yes.) 3. *Iie, dekakemasen-deshita.* (No, he didn't go out.)

(B) 1. *Hai, yomimashita.* (Yes, he has.) 2. *Iie, yomimasen.* (No, he's not going to read it.)

(C) 1. *Iroiro kaimashita.* (She bought various things.) 2. *Isshuukan-ni ichido-gurai ikimasu.* (She goes to the department store about once a week.) 3. *Ichinen-ni ichido ikimasu.* (He goes there once a year.)

Lesson 6

(A) *Iie, shizuka-ja arimasen.* (No, it isn't quiet.) 2. *Gakusee-ga futari imasu.* (Two students live.) 3. *Hai.* (Yes.) 4. *Hanashi-o shimasu.* (They talk.)

(B) 1. *Hoteru-no shokudoo-de aimashita.* (She met Yoshiko at the restaurant in a hotel.) 2. *Iie, jikan-ga arimasen-deshita.* (No, she didn't have much time.)

(C) 1. *Iie, hima-desu.* (No, it isn't.) 2. *Iie.* (No.)

Lesson 7

(A) 1. *Meron-o kaimasu.* (He buys a melon.) 2. *Nisen-en.* (He pays 2,000 yen.) 3. *Mikan.* (She suggests that he buy tangerines.)

(B) 1. *Iie, imasen.* (No.) 2. *Iie.* (No.)

(C) 1. *Okusan.* (The wife does.) 2. *Hai.* (Yes.)

Lesson 8

(A) 1. *Toshokan-ni tsutomete-imasu.* (He works at a library.) 2. *Hai.* (Yes.) 3. *Iie.* (No.)

(B) 1. *Hai.* (Yes.) 2. *Ashita denwa-o shimasu.* (He's going to call tomorrow.)

(C) 1. *Juugonen-desu.* (It has been 15 years.) 2. *Dokoka-e ikimasu.* (They're going to go somewhere.) 3. *Kissaten-e ikimasu.* (They're going to a coffee shop.)

Lesson 9

(A) 1. *Ima hanashite-iru hito-no namae*(name)*-desu.*(She wants to know the name of the person talking now.) 2. *Daigaku-no keezai-no sensee-desu.* (He teaches economics at a university.) 3. *Gojuu-gurai-desu.* (He's about 50.)

(B) 1. *Nijippun machimashita.* (They've been waiting for 20 minutes.) *Hai, kikimashita.* (Yes, they did.) 3. *Hai.* (Yes.)

(C) 1. *Shigoto-ga arimasen.* (He's out of work.) 2. *Moo yonjuu-da-kara-desu.* (Because he's already 40.)

Lesson 10

(A) 1. *Hai.* (Yes.) 2. *Amari kimasen.* (He doesn't come very often.) 3. *Hai.* (Yes.)

(B) 1. *Iie, imasen-deshita.* (No, he wasn't.) 2. *Kyooto-kara kaetta-to iimashita.* (He said that he had returned from Kyoto.)

(C) 1. *Hai.* (Yes.) 2. *Kaban-no soba-ni okimashita.* (She put it by the bag.)

3. *Iroirona hito-ga kimasu-kara, kaban-no naka-ga ii-to omoimashita.* (He thought that he had better put the money in the bag because all kinds of people come into the room.)

Lesson 11

(A) 1. *Iie.* (No.) 2. *Konde-iru-kara-desu.* (Because it is crowded.) 3. *Hoka-o sagashimasu.* (They're going to try to find another coffee shop.)

(B) 1. *Takai hoo-o kaimasu.* (She decides on the more expensive one.) 2. *Iie.* (No.)

Lesson 12

(A) 1. *Atama-ga itakatta-no-desu.* (He had a headache.) 2. *Hai.* (Yes.) 3. *Iie.* (No.)

(B) 1. *Hai.* (Yes.) 2. *Iie.* (No.)

(C)&(D) D*-no hoo-desu.* (He seems to be hen-pecked in D.)

Lesson 13

(A) 1. *Kaisha-o deyoo-to shita toki Yamada-san-kara denwa-ga atta-kara-desu.* (Because Mr. Yamada called when he was about to leave his office.) 2. *Shigoto-ga hayaku owatta-node, ato-de kuru-to iimashita.* (He said that he would come because he had finished his work early.) 3. *Omoshiroi* (or *nigiyakana*) *hito-deshoo.* (He must be an interesting —or merry—person.)

(B) 1. *Ichijikan-han arimasu.* (They have one hour and a half.) 2. *Nanika tabemasu.* (They're going to eat something.)

(C) 1. *Hajime-no mise-wa takasoo-deshita. Tsugi-no mise-wa konde-imashita.* (The first one looked expensive; the second one was crowded.) 2. *Takai hoo-no mise-ni shimashita.* (They decided on the more expensive one.) 2. *Jikan-ga nakattakara-desu.* (Because they didn't have much time.)

Lesson 14

(A) 1. *Tabako-to osake-ni tsuite kikimashita.* (He asked about smoking and drinking.) 2. *Osake-o sukoshi nonde-mo ii-to iimashita.* (She said that he may drink a little.)

(B) 1. *Shujin-ga iimashita.* (The husband did.) 2. *Okusan-ga isogashisoo-datta-kara-desu.* (Because his wife seemed busy.) 3. *Denwa-no soba-ni arimashita.* (He found it by the telephone.)

(C) 1. *Iie.* (No.) 2. *Eega-ni ikoo-to iimashita.* (She asked him to go to the movies with her.) 3. *Arubaito-ga aru-kara-desu.* (Because he has to work.)

Lesson 15

(A) 1. *Tsuri-ni ikitagatte-imasu.* (He wants to go fishing with her.) 2. *Iie.* (No.) 3. *Hoka-ni yooji-ga aru-kara-desu.* (Because she has something else to do. 4. *Iie.* (No.)

(B) 1. *Shigoto-ni iku-n-desu.* (He's going there on business.) 2. *Iie.* (No.)

(C) 1. *Hai.* (Yes.) 2. *Taihen-deshita.* (It was tough.) 3. *Iie.* (No.)

Lesson 16

(A) 1. *Yomu-no-mo kaku-no-mo (dochira-mo) suki-desu.* (She likes both.) 2. *Hai.* (Yes.) 3. *Iie.* (No.)

(B) 1. *Hai.* (Yes.) 2. *Otoko-no hito-ga osoku natta-kara-desu.* (Because the man was late.) 3. *Osoku natta gen'in-ga wakatta-kara-deshoo.* (Probably because she now understands why he was late.)

(C) 1. *Iie, betsu-ni.* (Not in particular.) 2. *Iie.* (No.)

Lesson 17

(A) 1. *Hai.* (Yes.) 2. A-*wa kodomo-ga arimasu.* B-*wa arimasen.* (A has children; B doesn't.) 3. B-*wa raku-da-to omoimasu.* (He envies B.)

(B) 1. *Iie.* (No.) 2. *Juuhachi-gurai-deshoo.* (He should be about 18.) 3. *Hai.* (Yes.)

(C) 1. *Hai.* (Yes.) 2. *Uta-o utaimasu.* (He's going to sing.) 3. *Yasashii uta-ni shimasu.* (They decide on easy songs.)

Lesson 18

(A) 1. *Kuni-ni iru-to omotte-imasu.* (They think that he's in his home town.) 2. *Shirabete-mimasu.* (They're going to check.)

(B) 1. *Iie, dentoo-ga tsuite-imasu.* (No, the lights are on.) 2. *Yuube osoku kaerimashita.* (He returned late last night.) 3. *Kyuu-ni yoo-ga dekita-kara-desu.* (Because some urgent business came up.)

(C) 1. *Iie.* (No.) 2. *Hai.* (Yes, she did.) 3. *Iie.* (No.)

Lesson 19

1. こどもの 先生(せんせい)です。 2. しまっていました。 3. いいえ、あがりませんでした。 4. PTA(ぴーていえい)の 仕事(しごと)の 話(はなし)で 来(き)たのです。 5. はい、いそがしそうです。 6. こんどの 日曜(にちよう)に 来(く)ると 言(い)いました。

(1. *Kodomo-no sensee-desu.* 2. *Shimatte-imashita.* 3. *Iie, agarimasen-deshita.* 4. PTA-*no shigoto-no hanashi-de kita-no-desu.* 5. *Hai, isogashisoo-desu.* 6. *Kondo-no nichiyoo-ni kuru-to iimashita.*)

Lesson 20

1. 空港へ 行きます。 2. 見おくりに 行くのです。 3. 女の人の にいさんが 行くのです。 4. 2年ぐらい いる 予定です。 5. はい、おとうとが います。 6. 6時までに 行かなくては なりません。

(1. *Kuukoo-e ikimasu.* 2. *Miokuri-ni iku-no-desu.* 3. *Onna-no-hito-no niisan-ga iku-no-desu.* 4. *Ninen-gurai iru yotee-desu.* 5. *Hai, otooto-ga imasu.* 6. *rokuji-made-ni ika-nakute-wa narimasen.*)

Lesson 21

1. 大学の おいわいの パーティーに 来てもらいたいと 言いました。 2. 90年ぐらいです。 3. 音楽を やったり、ダンスを したり します。 4. いいえ。 5. 川口さんに おしえてもらいますから。 6. まえに 行った ことが あるからです。 7. ともだちでしょう。 8. あまり ていねいな(polite) ことばを 使いませんから。(「おしえて<u>もらう</u>」とか「<u>行った</u> ことが ある」とか、言いましたから。)

(1. *Daigaku-no oiwai-no paatii-ni kite-moraitai-to iimashita.* 2. *Kyuujuunen-gurai-desu.* 3. *Ongaku-o yattari, dansu-o shitari shimasu.* 4. *Iie.* 5. *Kawaguchi-san-ni oshiete-moraimasu-kara.* 6. *Mae-ni itta koto-ga aru kara-desu.* 7. *Tomodachi-deshoo.* 8. *Amari teeneena kotoba-o tsukaimasen-kara.* (*``Oshiete-<u>morau</u>''-toka ``<u>itta</u> koto-ga aru''-toka iimashita-kara.*)

Lesson 22

1. 木村と いう 学生と、斎藤さんの となりの おくさんの 会話です。 2. かさを かえしに 来たのです。 3. 大学の 先生です。4. いいえ。 5. 斎藤さんが かえるまで あずかると 言いました。

(1. *Kimura-to yuu gakusee-to, Saitoo-san-no tonari-no okusan-no kaiwa-desu.* 2. *Kasa-o kaeshi-ni kita-no-desu.* 3. *Daigaku-no sensee-desu.* 4. *Iie.* 5. *Saitoo-san-ga kaeru-made azukaru-to iimashita.*)

Lesson 23

1. はい。 2. 近所の 本屋へ 行ったのです。 3. こどもの 参考書を 買いに 行ったのです。 4. 「まさお」と いいます。 5. 英語なんか(が) すきです。 6. ええ、しません。

(1. *Hai.* 2. *Kinjo-no hon'ya-e itta-no-desu.* 3. *Kodomo-no sankoosho-o kai-ni itta-no-desu.* 4. *``Masao''-to iimasu.* 5. *Eego-nanka(-ga) suki-desu.* 6. *Ee, shimasen.*)

Lesson 24

1. あした 休ませてもらいたいと たのみました。 2. いいえ、きゅうに 休まれては こまると 言いました。 3. どうして 休みたいのか 聞きました。 4. 15年まえに しにました。 5. いいえ。 6. 北沢さんに たのめば いいと 言いました。

(1. *Ashita yasumasete-moraitai-to tanomimashita.* 2. *Iie, kyuu-ni yasumarete-wa komaru-to iimashita.* 3. *Dooshite yasumitai-no-ka kikimashita.* 4. *Juugonen-mae-ni shinimashita.* 5. *Iie.* 6. *Kitazawa-san-ni tanomeba ii-to iimashita.*)

Lesson 25

(A) 1. 2週間ぐらい 入院していました。 2. いいえ。 3. いいえ、うちの なかの 仕事を したり、買いものに 出たり しています。 4. いいえ、たいした 病気でも ないのに、一日中 ねているのは、かえって よく ないと 言いました。

(B) 1. 福田と いいます。 2. ボーナスが 去年より たくさん 出ました。 3. いいえ、よく はたらいた 人も あまり はたらかない 人も おなじです。

Lesson 26

1. したく ない ことも する ことが できる 人間に 教育する ことです。 2. やさしい ほうを えらびます。 3. いいえ、すきな ことだけ している わけには いきません。 4. 小さい ときから はじめるのが 適当です。

Lesson 27

1. だれかに 仕事を たのむ 相談を しています。 2. いいえ、ありません。 3. 外国で 仕事を した ことの ある 人が 適当です。 4. 小林さんに たのむ ことに きめました。 5. 男の人の ほうが 熱心です。

Lesson 28

1. 去年の 夏に 来ました。 2. いいえ、一年間 いました。 3. 仕事の ためです。 4. 日本の ことが 少し わかってきたからです。

Lesson 29

1. いいえ。 2. 夜 おそく ねると、朝 なかなか おきられないからです。 3. ともだちの 結婚の おいわいの ために のみました。 4. 早く かえって ねなければなりません。

Lesson 30

1. そうです。 2. わかい 人の ほうが 多いです。 3. ヨーロッパです。 4. いいえ。外国ばかりじゃ なくて、日本の なかも 旅行した ほうが いいと 言っているのです。 5. 日本を 見なおす ためです。

INDEX TO WORDS AND PHRASES

∗The number following each entry refers to the page where it first appears with its English equivalent; italics indicate that the word appears in a dialogue.
∗Verbs and adjectives are given in their dictionary forms except in special cases. Whether a verb is a *-u* verb or *-ru* verb is indicated in parentheses; with adjectives, (*-i*) indicates *-i* adjectives and (*-na*) *-na* adjectives.

A

B

C

D

E

F

G

H

I

J

K

M

N

O

T

U

W

Y

Supplementary index to verbs

Contractions

-dewa → -ja (sore-dewa → sore-ja)
-eba → ya (ireba → irya)
iru; ita; ite → ru; ta; te(mite-iru → mite-ru; mite-ita → mite-ta; matte-ite-kudasai → matte-te-kudasai)
-kereba → kya (shinakereda → shinakya)
-no → -n (iku-no-desu → iku-n-desu; iku-node → iku-nde)
-te-shimau → chau (natte-shimau → natchau)
-to itta → tte(matte-kudasai-to itta → matte-kudasai-tte)
-to yuu → tte (yuuri-da-to yuu koto → yuuri-da-tte koto)